International Migration of Children for a Better Life

International Migration of Children for a Better Life

Human Rights, State Power, and Nations' Duties

JAMES G. DWYER

Arthur B. Hanson Professor of Law, William & Mary Law School, Williamsburg, VA, USA

OXFORD
UNIVERSITY PRESS

OXFORD
UNIVERSITY PRESS

Oxford University Press is a department of the University of Oxford.
It furthers the University's objective of excellence in research, scholarship,
and education by publishing worldwide. Oxford is a registered trade mark of
Oxford University Press in the UK and in certain other countries.

Published in the United States of America by Oxford University Press
198 Madison Avenue, New York, NY 10016, United States of America.

Library of Congress Cataloging-in-Publication Data
Names: Dwyer, James G., author.
Title: International migration of children for a better life : human rights, state power, and nations' duties / James G. Dwyer.
Description: New York : Oxford University Press, 2025. |
Includes bibliographical references and index.
Identifiers: LCCN 2024058404 (print) | LCCN 2024058405 (ebook) |
ISBN 9780197752302 (hardback) | ISBN 9780197752333 (online) |
ISBN 9780197752326 (updf) | ISBN 9780197752319 (epub)
Subjects: LCSH: Immigrant children—Legal status, laws, etc. |
Refugee children—Legal status, laws, etc. | Unaccompanied immigrant
children—Legal status, laws, etc. | Emigration and immigration law. |
Children (International law) | Children's rights. | International law and human rights. |
Freedom of movement (International law)
Classification: LCC K3275 .D89 2025 (print) | LCC K3275 (ebook) |
DDC 341.4/86083—dc23/eng/20241205
LC record available at https://lccn.loc.gov/2024058404
LC ebook record available at https://lccn.loc.gov/2024058405

DOI: 10.1093/9780197752333.001.0001

Printed by Marquis Book Printing, Canada

Note to Readers

This publication is designed to provide accurate and authoritative information in regard to the subject matter covered. It is based upon sources believed to be accurate and reliable and is intended to be current as of the time it was written. It is sold with the understanding that the publisher is not engaged in rendering legal, accounting, or other professional services. If legal advice or other expert assistance is required, the services of a competent professional person should be sought. Also, to confirm that the information has not been affected or changed by recent developments, traditional legal research techniques should be used, including checking primary sources where appropriate.

(Based on the Declaration of Principles jointly adopted by a Committee of the American Bar Association and a Committee of Publishers and Associations.)

To my immigrant wife, Katya, and our immigrant son, Stepan

Contents

Acknowledgments

I am grateful for helpful feedback received on various parts of the book from Layla Abi-Falah, Paulo Barrozo, Elizabeth Bartholet, Jacqueline Bhabha, Michael Blake, Linda Cleary, Evan Criddle, Ryan Hanlon, Peter Spiro, Jonathan Todres, Timothy Zick, and my students at William & Mary.

I am also grateful for financial support for travel and research-focused summers that I received from The Cabell Foundation, Joseph J. Plumeri, William & Mary Reves Center for International Studies, William & Mary Law School Dean A. Benjamin Spencer, and the William & Mary Law School Foundation.

Abbreviations

CDP	Categorical Domestic Preference
CEDAW	Convention on the Elimination of All Forms of Discrimination against Women
CIL	customary international law
CRC	UN Children's Rights Convention
CRComm	UN Children's Rights Committee
CRPD	Convention on the Rights of Persons with Disabilities
IA	international adoption
ICCPR	International Covenant on Civil and Political Rights
ICESCR	International Covenant on Economic, Social and Cultural Rights
ICJ	International Court of Justice
IHL	international humanitarian law
IMF	International Monetary Fund
IO	international organization
OHCHR	Office of the UN High Commissioner for Human Rights
UDHR	Universal Declaration of Human Rights
UN	United Nations
UNHCR	United Nations High Commissioner for Refugees
UNHRC	United Nations Human Rights Committee
WTO	World Trade Organization

Introduction

In much of the earth's territory, children are prey. In much of the earth's territory, parental abandonment is an act of love. In much of the earth's territory, a person's fate is decided before reaching adulthood, if they do. The fate of so many girls is to be used for rape and reproduction, of so many boys to kill or be killed, of so many children to die of starvation or bombing. We who live in a very different part of the world, with far greater social order and resources, cannot fathom the reality children in some other parts of the world face daily.

It is called "the accident of birth." Humans' fate is largely determined by morally arbitrary facts, circumstances that have nothing to do with deservingness—in particular, who their birth parents are and where their parents happen to live. The locations where most begin life are tragically dangerous, disease-ridden, oppressive, and/or impoverished. Try to imagine the fate of a child born today in the Democratic Republic of the Congo, long wracked with violent internal conflict. Over seven million people in the DRC are internally displaced as of 2024. How does one move one's family hundreds of miles and survive with no vehicle or money? Half of all children in the DRC, displaced or not, suffer from chronic malnutrition. Thousands—many not even ten years of age—are forced into military service, while others work in brutal, dangerous conditions in mines.

Or imagine a young child in El Salvador, site of the highest murder rate in the world in 2024, where pervasive gangs forcibly recruit boys as members and girls for commercial sex, the child poverty rate is over 50 percent in rural areas, and over forty percent of children do not attend school.[1] In Syria, half the total population was displaced because of brutal conflict between a repressive government and multiple factions competing to overthrow it, and an earthquake in 2022 left 1.5 million of those who remained homeless with little hope for rebuilding in the foreseeable future. In Ukraine and Gaza, bombs fell daily in 2024. Slaughter on the ground occurs routinely in Myanmar, Sudan, Haiti, and other countries, amidst pervasive chaos that makes healthy development impossible for most children.

Aggregate global figures for various forms of life-diminishing harms to children are difficult to fathom. Five million die before age five each year, three million of them by starvation. Eight million live in state institutions, likely subject

[1] *See* Susan Bibler Coutin, "Roots of Juvenile Migration from El Salvador," *in* JACQUELINE BHABHA ET AL. EDS., RESEARCH HANDBOOK ON CHILD MIGRATION 113–25 (2010).

International Migration of Children for a Better Life. James G. Dwyer, Oxford University Press.
 DOI: 10.1093/9780197752333.001.0001

to routine maltreatment. Over a million will be sold as slaves this year. Over one hundred million live on the streets in urban areas. Two hundred fifty million females now living were married before age fifteen.

Could migration be the best solution for many of these children? A boy approaches his twelfth birthday in Guatemala knowing that if he stays in his family's home, he will soon face a choice between joining the drug-trafficking gang that dominates the local area or being killed by them. He has had no schooling but is fit for manual labor. His parents gather all the money they can to pay "coyotes" to escort him on the treacherous journey to the United States, where he could live with a cousin that preceded him.[2] The money is enough for plane fare to Des Moines or Richmond fifty times over, but the U.S. government will not allow him to arrive that way.

Parents in Kyrgyzstan anonymously abandoned a baby girl at an orphanage, knowing there was little domestic interest in adoption. After three years in an institution, she died from a medical condition easily treatable in Western Europe or North America, where she could also have joined a family and been cared for by loving parents rather than indifferent staff. But Kyrgyzstan had shut down its international adoption program in 2008, foreclosing that option for her.[3]

A girl is growing up in Yemen, immersed in a culture that denies females education, bodily integrity, and basic liberties, in a country where civil war and terrorism have caused widespread destruction, disease, and danger. Her parents plan to try to sell her into an unregistered marriage to a wealthy middle-aged man when she enters adolescence, or earlier, hoping the money received will keep them from dying of malnutrition-related causes. Failing that, they will sell her to sex traffickers. If they wait too long, she will likely be kidnapped by traffickers and the parents will get no money. Even better for the family would be her escape to Western Europe, where she might be placed with a family, attend school, and eventually be able to work and send money to her parents. But even if she were older, she could not travel alone in this orthodox Muslim country, with militias monitoring all roads, and her family has no money for her transportation, let alone for her and an escort. UNICEF tries to get food, safe water, and medical care to children inside Yemen, but helping children relocate to another country is not on its list of strategies for saving them from early death, even though its director has observed that "Yemen has become a living hell for children." Perhaps this is because militant Islamic forces would not permit removal of any children. But in Gaza, too, where there might be no resistance to evacuating children (with parental permission), to spare them from bombing

[2] *See* Sonia Nazario, Enrique's Journey: The Story of a Boy's Dangerous Odyssey to Reunite with His Mother (2006).

[3] *See* Rebecca J. Compton, Adoption Beyond Borders (2016). The Kyrgyz Republic is now open for IA, with comparatively modest restrictions.

and starvation and crippling disease, the sole approach of UNICEF and other humanitarian organizations is to try to keep children alive within a living hell.[4]

Twins are born in the famine-struck Tigray region of Ethiopia to a woman suffering from severe malnutrition and living in an encampment that international aid does not reach because of government obstruction and theft, malaria sweeping through the encampment unchecked and untreated, their father recently killed by the Ethiopian military because he had social ties to someone in a rebel militia group. Wealthy nations are not willing to welcome and facilitate the transport of the many millions of adults in dire circumstances like these, but many would accept young children, perhaps by mass evacuation but certainly via one-at-a-time foster care or adoption placements.

If these children could speak to us, what would they say about which life path they would choose among all those potentially available to them? Who, might they say, owes them any obligation to try to spare them from their current fate, given the history of behavior by the governments of their native country and by modern Western states? What power should international law accord their home state to control their destiny—that is, whether they are able to migrate to a better life?

Life in the world's most inhospitable places can contain nurturing relationships and joyful experiences, but for most children it entails painful hardships, persistent fear, premature death of loved ones, and high risk of their own early death. There is little or no prospect of their developing their inherent talents and abilities or realizing the kinds of fulfillment similarly constituted children in other parts of the world enjoy. Even the best parents cannot compensate for the suffering and threats such environments present, and many millions of children have parents suffering from conditions that undermine their ability to care and protect. Or they have no parents at all.

But this is no accident. It is the result of deliberate choices, at multiple levels of government, about the laws that govern children's lives, including international legal norms that dictate, or acquiesce to claims regarding, the powers, rights, and liberties nations have with respect to persons generally or more specifically with respect to children. Those norms could be different, in ways that would facilitate children's escape from places of danger and deep deprivation to more hospitable environments—preferably with their families, of course, but by themselves if that is not possible.

Normative theorizing about state power over persons has predominantly presupposed autonomous adults as the individuals whose corresponding liabilities, vulnerabilities, duties, and rights are at issue. Political theorists rarely

[4] *See* Mark Landler, "Nowhere to Go: How Gaza Became a Mass Death Trap," N.Y. TIMES, Oct. 7, 2024.

consider whether a different analysis is needed for the third of the human population that is non-autonomous. Failure to lay a theoretical foundation for ascription of human rights to children has, Paulo Barrozo observes, resulted in reasoning about their situation in a consequentialist manner, in which children are seen as instruments of or threats to the state, rather than from a deontological perspective that asks what duties states and international organizations owe to each child.[5] Some theorists and policy experts have observed that migration policy, specifically, suffers from lack of concerted attention to the question whether children's situation differs from that of adults, practically and/or normatively. This book directly addresses that question, answers it affirmatively, and concludes that the international law regime that now plays an integral role in consigning many millions of children to tragic lives—particularly its rules regarding citizenship, state sovereignty, emigration, and immigration—is ripe for fundamental reimagining.

This book takes as given continued extreme disparity globally in material conditions for living. It looks at this reality from the standpoint of a child whom fate has situated in one of the world's most inhospitable places. Those places change over time, but typically improvement in any given place takes many years, even decades—too long to enable a child born today in one of them to have a decent life. So instead of the usual focus among theorists, legal actors, and advocacy organizations on how to improve conditions in such places, this book asks: Why must that child remain there? Why should any government or institution—whether in the child's native country or in any other country or in the international community—have the power to prevent the child from relocating transnationally if the practical ability to do so exists, or could exist if barriers were eliminated, and if that would greatly improve the child's situation, perhaps save his or her life? And why, conversely, does no government have a duty affirmatively to facilitate such child's migration to a safer, healthier place? Is the answer to such questions different than it would be for similar questions as to adults living in those same places? Does the answer depend on whether a child has parents living and, if so, whether the child is in their custody? Or on the possibility—substantial or slight—of improved circumstances by a domestic rather than international relocation?

The reality is that developed countries and their people are generally more welcoming of children than of adults coming from outside. They could collectively welcome millions more children, many of whom have relatives already living in those countries. Not all arms are open to all "alien children." But we should also step back from the concept of "alien" and ask: Why is any child

[5] Paulo Barrozo, *Finding Home in the World: A Deontological Theory of the Right to Be Adopted*, 55 N.Y.L. Sch. L. Rev. 701 (2010–2011).

viewed anywhere as foreign, as belonging to another place, bearing the brand of some other nation? Can we imagine a global legal regime in which children are not legally affiliated with any state, but rather are "free agents" with respect to nationality, owed duties of care by all nations despite not belonging in a possessory sense to any, while also under the direct protection of international organizations? A regime in which humane international laws determine children's country of residence and constrain that country's rules for establishing parentage and guiding children's upbringing, based solely on evidence-based judgments of their welfare interests? In which nations and their political subunits have prescribed duties toward children but no entitlements—just as, analogously, I might have duties but no rights as to a baby I find in my back yard? If we can imagine this, we should ask: Do children have a moral right to this alternative global legal regime? Does respect for them as persons require this?

This is the first book to bring the disciplines of law and philosophy together to examine such child-focused theoretical questions in international law and foreign policy and to create a normative framework for establishing: what moral rights children possess, at the time of their birth or later, to avoid or move away from the world's most unlivable places, or to migrate in order to join a family, or to receive transnational assistance; what powers states may properly exert over children who have not meaningfully consented to imposition of any citizenship and who arguably owe no debt to any nation; and what duties nations and the international legal community owe to those children—positive duties to assist and protect as well as negative duties not to support any state's harmful confinement or exclusion of children. The best answers to those questions might have disruptive implications for the global order and for philosophical analysis of international justice.

As a practical matter, there are several ways by which children can migrate away from desperate circumstances. Some are familiar, and some are frightening: Refugees cross land and sea to arrive at the border of another nation and request temporary shelter or permanent relocation. Thousands of "unaccompanied minors," mostly older children, arrive at America's southern border every day or at the shores of Mediterranean countries, after treacherous journeys, as do many younger children brought by parents. Each year thousands of young children who are unparented and living in orphanages in their home country exit one at a time to join families in another country, and hundreds of thousands more could do so if their country of birth did not block this path to a better life. Many children migrate with their mother to a faraway nation where she will marry a man who is a citizen there. Some move with one parent who is running away from the other parent.

Much less common have been mass evacuations from crisis situations. Some instances are profoundly troubling—for example, Russia's removal of children from Ukraine in 2022. But there have also been well-intentioned and well-regarded instances, such as the evacuation of children from lands threatened by the Nazis in the years leading up to World War II—the *Kindertransport* to the United Kingdom and elsewhere. In between, in time and purity of intentions, have been several other instances of urgently removing large groups of children from dire circumstances. One of the most well-known, Operation Babylift at the end of America's Vietnam War, entailed removal of thousands from orphanages and streets in South Vietnam before the massive North Vietnamese offensive in 1975—seen at the time as a commendable act of mercy, later criticized by some as presumptuous and overreaching. This book will mostly concern itself with normative arguments in favor or against particular means of migration out of horrible circumstances as a theoretical matter, including whether children's departure could ever constitute an injustice to anyone else. The analysis will naturally suppose that any implementation of conclusions should be mindful of past mistakes and aim to minimize unintended adverse consequences in the relocation process.

A primary real-world obstacle to migration for many children is the longstanding and fundamental international law principle of state sovereignty over domestic matters ("internal sovereignty"), which gives nations plenary control over persons within their territory and movement across their borders, and a right against interference by other states' individually or collectively ("external sovereignty"). Many nations exercise that power to prevent people from leaving, and nearly all limit entry. Several legal developments in recent decades have eroded sovereignty—in particular, ascendance of human rights, refugee law, and the concept of international "Responsibility to Protect" (R2P). Acute crises have also forced some rethinking of basic assumptions about global governance. The clearest example, perhaps, is the decision by Russia—a nuclear power that is also among the five veto-wielding permanent members of the Security Council—to initiate a war of aggression in Europe. This book will present normative challenges to assumptions about state entitlement to control individuals' lives—in particular, children's.

At the same time, a migration solution to a child's predicament arguably challenges sovereignty and other established principles far less, and demands less of international institutions, than do some alternative measures, particularly those aimed at transforming local conditions by coercion or even occupation. The later chapters of this book will consider, though, whether nations sometimes have a duty and privilege to act in the territory of a state that resists humanitarian assistance or blocks emigration, for the sake of sparing children from great harm.

To anticipate some skeptical responses: hellish circumstances in some parts of the world, one might object, can be traced causally to past interstate injustices. Colonialism destroyed native governing structures, imposed territorial boundaries inconsistent with people's understanding of their community and nation, and set the stage for corrupt and oppressive postcolonial regimes. Competing global powers have used less developed nations to serve strategic aims, supporting tyrants and fomenting civil war with little regard for the impact on local populations, economies, and political systems. So how can we who belong to an oppressor nation now condemn practices or conditions in victim countries? Further, developed nations bear greatest responsibility historically for the climate change now manifest in natural disasters and alterations to weather patterns and landscapes that undermine traditional ways of life. Removing children from a nation struggling to overcome such crippling forces might appear to add insult to those various injuries, a fresh injustice. Some might view, for example, Americans' adoption of children from Central America as of a piece with Russia's seizure and relocation of children from Ukraine; a powerful nation intrudes and destroys, then cites the destruction as warrant for removing children.

The normative question whether an historical explanation for current conditions matters to any individual's right to leave one place and move to another, or to any government's powers over or obligations toward persons, is one that arises also in the domestic sphere in some countries. In the United States, for example, child protection systems today disproportionately remove children from parents who are members of historically subordinated groups, because of parental incapacity that can plausibly be traced to centuries of systemic injustice. Comparing international and domestic situations and the intuitions people have about right and wrong in each is an analytical strategy I will often use in this book. So, too, will be comparing intuitions about adults and the rights we demand for ourselves to intuitions about children and their rights. One would be hard pressed to find any political theorist who concludes from historic domestic injustices that adults do not have a right to get out of a relationship with a member of an historically subordinated group who is abusing them, and whose violent inclination can be traced to a lifetime of unjust adversity, because this would pile additional suffering on that which the abuser has already experienced throughout life. Or who concludes from historical international injustices that adults do not have a right to emigrate out of a now-dysfunctional victim nation if given the opportunity to leave and to immigrate into an oppressor nation where they can enjoy a profoundly better life. Should children ever be in a worse position than adults, in terms of having opportunity to escape bad circumstances? Should they, to the contrary, sometimes be in a better position than adults?

Another skeptical reaction is that any international-law solution to a perceived large-scale problem is a pipe dream. It is not an aim of this book to convince anyone that a global government protective of children is a realistic possibility in the foreseeable future. This is a work of moral and political theory whose core aim is to clarify normative issues regarding the rights of children and the duties and permissions of nations. Theory is valuable, even crucial, in advance of practical realizability. By providing some sense of what an ideal regime looks like, it can alter conversations among legal actors as they inch toward creation of new institutions and norms, generating acceptance of some normative positions while cutting the intellectual or rhetorical legs out from under others. This can influence decisions in the real world.

I would note my agreement, though, with those who respond to the international law pessimists by contending that international law differs from domestic law, in terms of efficacy and promise for realizing justice, not categorically but in degree. No domestic legal system is entirely successful at detecting, adjudicating, punishing, or deterring illegalities and injustices. Both domestic legal systems and the international legal regime rely on a myriad of formal and informal penalties and rewards to alter behavior of both individuals and state actors. Critics plausibly maintain that the challenge cultural difference poses for legislating, enforcing, and adjudicating is greater at the global level than it is internally for most nations, perhaps all.[6] But governments of many individual nations must deal with quite substantial internal cultural and ideological diversity, in part because of international migration, and global cultural difference appears to diminish every year with ever-increasing interaction and intermixing.

It is important to be reminded how current institutions fall short of hopes that motivated their creation, but one should also be mindful that the history of international law—like histories of domestic legal systems within nations across the globe—has been marked by a succession of developments previously thought impossible. This has included creation of global authorities in the twentieth century, not just the UN but also innumerable other international organizations (IOs)—public (World Trade Organization, human rights offices and committees, etc.) and private (nongovernmental organizations)—that constrain state behavior internally and externally. Also, that some international institutions and norms have been quite effective at times. Further, that some international norms and the practices and institutions enacting them are relatively nascent, still on a steep learning curve.

Rigorous normative theorizing is necessary to assess confidently whether the actual or anticipated real-world impact of new developments is positive or negative. One example is the so-called "subsidiarity" norm that certain IOs have forced upon the international child welfare world, under which local solutions

[6] Eric Posner persuasively makes this and other points explaining the relative inefficacy of international law. *See* Eric A. Posner, The Twilight of Human Rights Law (2014); Eric A. Posner, The Perils of Global Legalism (2009). He might be faulted, though, for failing to acknowledge how evolution of societies in an increasingly integrated world might create new possibilities, and for failing to acknowledge how many now-well-functioning nations have had to overcome similar obstacles.

to adversities for children are declared categorically preferable to ones that entail emigration. This norm has intuitive appeal for many people, and it has been quite impactful. UNICEF, which is a significant source of financial assistance to developing countries, invoked it in past decades to justify a very effective campaign of coercing those countries into shutting down their international adoption (IA) programs. But is that good for children? Theorizing can inform an objective assessment of whether the subsidiarity norm and this practical consequence of it are in fact defensible, by establishing what UNICEF and individual nations should have to prove to support their policies concerning IA, against charges that they are violating children's human rights to family life and to leave any country. (Must they show positive outcomes for children, or do states have a sovereign right that suffices as justification regardless of child welfare impact? What even constitutes a relevant positive outcome—fewer children leaving, fewer children growing up without parents, less embarrassment for a nation's government?).

By way of foundation for the normative theorizing in this book: I will be considering individuals' moral rights against governments, which is another way of asking what legal rights individuals *ought* to have. Those rights can be positive or negative, which in the context of rights-theory refers to the type of duties on the part of others that a right entails. Having a positive right means some other entity, which could be a government or a private individual, owes one an affirmative duty to provide some benefit, to take some action. Having a negative right, in contrast, means others owe one a duty to refrain from doing certain adverse things.[7] For example, people generally view a right to receive education and economic support from government as a positive right, and as weaker or more difficult to establish, than negative rights such as those against arbitrary arrest or taking of property. As will be seen, that distinction often collapses, but it sometimes adds conceptual clarity.

Substantively, the ethical premises of the book will principally be deontological, consistent with the prevailing approach to reasoning about human rights more broadly, emphasizing governments' duties toward persons in light of their inherent dignity, experience as human beings, and basic needs. Few today would deny that children are "persons" commanding moral respect, arguably equal to the respect autonomous adults are due.[8] Yet their lack of voice and political

[7] The view that a right necessarily also contains a power to waive or enforce the correlative duty, which might preclude ascription of rights to any non-autonomous persons, has little support among legal philosophers today and has never had strong theoretical or empirical foundation. *See* James G. Dwyer, *Clarifying Questions About the Nature of Rights*, 12 Jurisprudence 47 (2021).

[8] I have previously offered an argument for viewing children as occupying a moral status superior to that of adults, which I hoped would at least undermine any lingering tendency to think of children as occupying an inferior moral status. *See* James G. Dwyer, Moral Status and Human Life: The Case for Children's Superiority (2011). That book also explains that the term "person," though often used to connote the individuals who matter morally, has no inherent meaning.

power makes it unlikely that the existing international legal regime, even though including a nearly universally ratified international treaty called the Children's Rights Convention, embodies that respect.

Some schematizing will be useful to framing the book. It assumes at least the following phenomena pose serious threats to children's basic welfare: violence in proximity to or directed at children, whether stemming from war, state oppression of its own people, local gang activity, unchecked individual violent crime, or domestic abuse; starvation and dehydration stemming from famine and drought or from government denial of access to food and water; living unparented in an institution or unhoused because of parental death or incapacity; natural disasters that threaten safety and prevent access to basic necessities; perilous conditions during migration; and lack of opportunity for education and employment. Some threats to well-being exist more for some subgroups of children—marked by ethnicity, religion, or gender—than for others. Possible avenues of relocation to be considered include unsupported individual migration (voluntary or forced) with or without an accompanying adult, international adoption, and state-supported mass evacuation. Legal rules facilitating or inhibiting movement include citizenship; requirements for exiting a country, such as documentation and individualized government approval; requirements for entry to another country, principally immigration laws; laws of war; refugee treaties; treaties establishing negative and positive human rights; and the law of humanitarian intervention.

The basic structure of the book is this: it has three parts, containing three chapters each. The first part expounds on children's individual human rights, especially the right to emigrate. The second addresses the normative position of a child's country of birth and of the international legal order in terms of the powers they should have in relation to the child—in particular, power to impose citizenship and the liabilities that attend it. The third part examines the duties and permissions to assist that international bodies and nations other than a home state have with respect to children and the duty of a child's home state not to obstruct assistance from such outside sources.

Within Part I, the first chapter is ground clearing. Scholars and legal actors in the international law realm uniformly frame discussion of children's rights in terms of the UN Convention on the Rights of the Child, and readers might expect this book's analysis to work within that Convention's framework or at least treat its provisions as presumptively authoritative. Chapter 1 explains why it will instead focus on the universal human rights treaties in expounding the existing legal rights of children. Relatedly, the book will eschew the tendency in philosophical writing about various aspects of children's lives toward sui generis treatment of them. It will instead begin analysis of moral rights at each step with general principles that theorists have developed in adult-centered contexts and explore whether and how application of those principles might differ as between autonomous adults and children because of differences in their characteristics or circumstances.

Much of the next five chapters concerns emigration, children's exit from their country of birth, which seems the most difficult component of international migration for many children. Many countries, for various reasons, do not want children leaving and so currently block their exit. Migration entails two elemental rights—a right to leave one place and a right to enter another. Though in practice one typically needs both to relocate, the two are conceptually distinct. We can, for purpose of theorizing, imagine someone trying to exit to the open seas, and ask whether they have a right to leave without considering whether they also have a right to enter some other country. This focuses attention on children's normative position relative to their home state. Later chapters address a child's normative position relative to other countries, including their right to immigrate, and to international legal bodies.

So Chapter 2 analyzes in a general way the right to emigrate, phrased in human rights treaties as the "right to leave any country." It explores the right's normative foundation, which for autonomous adults is in part the moral right to autonomous choice of membership in a political community and society, and for all persons includes moral rights regarding fundamental aspects of well-being such as satisfaction of basic physical needs, cognitive development, and family life, fulfillment of which might be most feasible or only possible by emigrating. Chapter 2 will suggest that the latter type of foundation is generally stronger for children than it is for adults, and that on the whole children have a more compelling moral right than adults to emigrate when trapped in horrible circumstances.

Chapter 3 addresses justifications states might offer for infringing the right of emigration. It explains why the few plausible justifications for preventing some adults from emigrating apply to a lesser extent or not at all to children. Further, supposed justifications asserted only or primarily in connection with children are either illegitimate or disingenuous and lacking in empirical support. Connection to culture and kin will receive close attention here.

Within Part II, Chapters 4 and 5 challenge international law's conferral on states of the power to claim children as theirs. Chapter 4 explains how nationality or citizenship can constitute more of a liability than a benefit, and why this is generally truer for children—in particular, when it lends legitimacy to state misuse of control over children's lives, including their ability to leave. Chapter 5 then asks when, if ever, is it morally permissible for a state to claim any persons—and, in particular, non-autonomous persons—as their subjects without consent? For adults, the answer is "rarely." For children, it is "never." Supporting this latter conclusion is speculation that children in general would be better off if they all were stateless—that is, if citizenship and nationality were reserved for adults.

This would remove that status, which is as morally arbitrary as stars on Sneetch bellies, as a basis for discriminating among children. It might also bring children into a more direct relation to international institutions, so that power over their lives becomes more diffuse, with additional checks against maltreatment. The chapter's proposal of universal child statelessness raises practical questions that I address, including how citizenship would be determined if everyone reaches adulthood as a "free agent." That in turn invites the normative question of when, if ever, a nation *must* recognize someone as its national.

An obvious alternative to doing away with nationality, for those who have not autonomously chosen it, is to alter its legal consequences. International law might constrict states power over nationals, to eliminate the possibility that being a subject of a particular state could be overall a liability. Chapter 6 develops a theory, grounded in political liberalism, of the limits of nations' power over children. Whereas Chapters 2 and 3 address limits on state power arising from individuals' right to emigrate, Chapter 6 looks to the general foundation for states having any power over any individuals. With respect to power over non-autonomous persons, it calls attention to the conceptual distinction between police power and parens patriae functions of government, then explains why the latter function, conceptualized as a fiduciary role, is the appropriate one in connection with fundamental aspects of children's private lives, such as family formation and residential location.

Part III shifts focus from home state to potential external sources of assistance for children in dire circumstances. Chapter 7 considers whether IOs, such as UN bodies, owe such children duties of protection and assistance. Duties might exist because the international community bears some responsibility for the adverse circumstances in which those children now live, or simply because they have the capacity to fulfill a vital need. The R2P norm in international law is increasingly viewed as extending beyond prevention of interstate aggression to also encompass humanitarian response to crisis from any cause. Chapter 7 suggests that what might be called "intervention to relocate" has stronger support in morality and international law than "intervention to transform," as a response to crises, and that this will often be the most effective intervention for children. Chapter 8 asks similar questions about nations other than a child's home country, and it adds liberalized immigration as a means of fulfilling any duty those nations owe. It rehearses some of the arguments for and against more open borders that political theorists have advanced, which generally have only autonomous adults in mind, and it asks whether these arguments are stronger or weaker as applied to children.

The final chapter inquires into the permissibility of gratuitous humanitarian intervention in a nation even against the will of that nation's governing authority, by another nation or international organizations. Even if the conclusions of Chapters 7 and 8 were that no international body or individual state has any *obligation* to assist or protect children within another state's territory, would it nevertheless be *permissible* for them to do so, without violating that other state's sovereignty properly understood—including by the dramatic means of mass evacuation? This brings the analysis back around to the question of state sovereignty and its meaning today, now focused on a state's power to exclude outside sources of assistance to people on its territory. Once again, the analysis considers whether a different position is warranted regarding children.

Here the international/domestic comparison casts a new light on old questions. Many nations or political subunits have dedicated child protection agencies with removal powers, and they have substantive laws on the basis of which adjudicative bodies can declare that some people have committed child maltreatment and are unfit to have custody of children. Should there be a global child-protection agency with comparable removal powers in cases of "national child maltreatment" or "national unfitness for custody of children"? And declarations of some nations as unfit for childrearing? Even if no international agency exists, may other nations sometimes take matters into their own hands, as private individuals and organizations in the United States did regarding parental maltreatment before state and local governments created child protection agencies? Further, if nations also fail to act, might private individuals and organizations take matters into *their* own hands, attempting to save children however best they can from a dire fate, as American missionaries did in Haiti after the devastating 2010 earthquake? Such questions tend to produce a viscerally negative reaction in those who see such situations through an adult-centered or culture-protective lens, but might a child-centered perspective require being more open-minded about such possibilities, and thinking about how to regulate such action rather than prohibiting it?

As should be clear from these chapter descriptions, this book is more ideal theory than real-world law and policy analysis, but this allows for more tantalizing questions and provocative answers, so I hope you will enjoy the adventure. I believe there is great value in imagining a radically different approach, legal regime, and normative framework for addressing the tragic reality of millions of children living in horrific circumstances. Doing so can clarify the end toward which current incremental reforms should aim or reveal the wisdom of shifting efforts from one immediate objective to another. For example, recognizing that ascription of citizenship could make some children worse off might lead some actors in international law creation and enforcement to step back from the push to eliminate statelessness and focus all that effort instead on eliminating discrimination based on citizenship. And it might lead theorists to focus more on the question of whether it is sometimes illegitimate for a state to claim a person as its subject, to get at the root problem of nations abusing the power over children that international law now confers upon them. The book's conclusions will be predominantly of a substantive normative nature, then, and they will have dramatic real-world implications.

1
Eschewing Special Rights

1.1 Introduction

The dominant approach to reasoning about children's rights under international law is to identify relevant provisions of the UN Children's Rights Convention (CRC) and deliberate about their meaning and implications, looking to the UN Children's Rights Committee (CRComm) for guidance. When the CRC was promulgated in 1989, the child advocacy world hailed it as a great step forward in respecting children's personhood and protecting their well-being throughout the world. Child rights advocates continue to celebrate it; 2019 saw numerous thirtieth anniversary events. An onlooker might even form the impression that children had no rights at all under international law prior to the CRC. But that is patently false; general human rights law has always applied to children as well as to adults. In fact, this chapter explains how the CRC set back the cause of improving children's position under international law and concludes that theorists and legal scholars should shake themselves free of the CRC's spell and think instead in terms of how general human rights laws apply to non-autonomous persons, including children in connection with their migration away from intolerable conditions.

The focus on the CRC reflects what I term "the special-rights fallacy." People generally suppose that enacting a special charter of rights for a particular group is necessarily and unqualifiedly advantageous for them. I therefore begin by showing why this supposition is false, as illustrated by the CRC and by dispensing with the CRC framework for purposes of this book.

1.2 The Pitfalls of Special Rights

When any law is passed pronouncing rights for a particular group of people, one might think this must mark an improvement of their position. If a rule-making body goes to the trouble of declaring that Group A has a right not to be treated in a certain way, then it must be the case that Group A has suffered from being treated that way, has had no negative right against such treatment, but now will receive that right and be better off. Or if Group A will now have a positive right to a benefit of a particular kind, its members must have lacked that benefit in the

International Migration of Children for a Better Life. James G. Dwyer, Oxford University Press. © Oxford University Press 2025.
DOI: 10.1093/9780197752333.003.0001

past and now will get it. International rights covenants for particular groups have proliferated since the 1970s, including the 1979 Convention on the Elimination of All Forms of Discrimination against Women (CEDAW), the CRC in 1989, the 1990 Convention on the Protection of the Rights of All Migrant Workers and Members of Their Families, and the 2006 Convention on the Rights of Persons with Disabilities (CRPD). These emerged subsequent to and despite entry into force of universal human rights instruments—the 1949 Universal Declaration of Human Rights (UDHR),[1] the 1967 International Covenant on Civil and Political Rights (ICCPR),[2] and the 1967 International Covenant on Economic, Social and Cultural Rights (ICESCR).[3] The implication is that the universal-rights declarations were inadequate in some respects, not fully protecting the just claims of certain people—in particular, members of historically subordinated groups. To receive proper respect and protection, any such group must have its own charter of rights.

And so it was that in 1979, the idea emerged that children should have their own charter, and ten years later the UN Convention on the Rights of the Child (CRC) was open for signature. The CRC's promoters recognized that limited resources and varied levels of commitment would make fulfillment of the Convention's promise slower and less complete in certain places, but they saw only upside potential to giving children their own set of rights, even after having to make numerous compromises over the course of the drafting process. They cheered when their handiwork received near-universal ratification soon after the final draft emerged. It quickly became the dominant, even sole, source of law and normative principles concerning children for international lawyers and scholars, and even for lawyers and scholars who have a solely domestic focus within nations other than the United States (the lone nonparty). Ever since, these authorities situate any child welfare issue within the CRC and rarely raise their gaze to look beyond it.[4]

[1] Universal Declaration of Human Rights, G.A. Res. 217 (III) A, U.N. Doc. A/RES/217(III) (Dec. 10, 1948). The UDHR is generally regarded as having acquired the status of customary international law, and the United Nations' General Assembly has stated that some of its provisions "constitute basic principles of international law." Lawrence O. Gostin & Benjamin E. Berkman, *Pandemic Influenza: Ethics, Law, and the Public's Health*, 59 Admin. L. Rev. 121, 143 (2007) (internal quotation marks and citation omitted).

[2] International Covenant on Civil and Political Rights, Dec. 1966, 999 U.N.T.S. 171.

[3] International Covenant on Economic, Social and Cultural Rights, Dec. 1966, 993 U.N.T.S. 3.

[4] *Cf.* Trevor Buck, International Child Law 47 (2005) (stating the CRC "has established itself as the central international instrument on children's rights"); Jonathan Todres & Daniela Villamizar Fink, *The Trauma of Trump's Family Separation and Child Detention Actions: A Children's Rights Perspective*, Wash. L. Rev. 95 (2020) 377, 408–09 (2020) ("Arguments under other treaties that the United States has ratified . . . are important; however, as the most comprehensive treaty on children's rights, and one of a small number of treaties that unify civil, political, economic, social and cultural rights, a CRC lens offers critical, more comprehensive insights"); Claire Fenton-Glynn, Children's Rights in Intercountry Adoption: A European Perspective 4 (2015) ("Using the United Nations Convention on the Rights of the Child as the foundation for analysis,

The CRC's hold on the international legal community in connection with children's issues has inhibited the theoretical exploration needed to construct a sound framework, and it has rendered most normative discussion of children's rights sui generis rather than founded upon general principles. This chapter aims to shake that community free for open reconsideration of children's normative position, without artificial constraint. It does so by identifying the many ways any group-specific charter of rights can actually disserve the group and by showing all to be true of the CRC.

To be sure, subsequent chapters will consider whether and how some rights of children should differ from those of autonomous adults, in their content or strength, considering children's distinctive characteristics and needs. There is no blanket rejection here of the idea that rights might appropriately differ across groups. However, reference to existing legal rules and authoritative interpretations of them will primarily look to general human rights instruments. This approach will be jarring to many. The child advocacy world appears to have forgotten that the general human rights conventions do apply to children as well as adults, and that legally they trump the CRC. Yet in many ways in many contexts, including international migration, the UDHR, ICCPR, and ICESCR, along with interpretive statements about them from international organizations and states, provide clearer and stronger legal bases for protecting the moral rights of children that ensuing chapters will develop. And they offer a better positive-law point of reference for theoretical exploration of children's moral rights. At best, the CRC might provide support for assuming widespread acceptance that particular general human rights do have a certain application to children, but in no case should the CRC be invoked to constrict application of general human rights to children.

1.2.1 A taxonomy of special-rights dangers

There is no necessary connection between receiving special rights and being better off than one was, or would be, without them. The connection could fail for at least seven reasons:

1. the special rights substitute for, yet are of less value substantively to the right-holder than, general rights previously held or otherwise available;
2. what the special "rights" guarantee, though assumed by others to be conducive to the right-holders' well-being, is actually bad for them, at least in

this book provides an examination of the application of children's rights in the field of intercountry adoption.").

some circumstances, and either the rights cannot be waived or the right-holders have no control over their assertion;
3. when a charter's subjects do not themselves craft it, because they are unable to control or perhaps even contribute to the drafting process, those who do create it might use it as a mechanism for creating or reasserting rights of their own that can operate to the detriment of the supposed beneficiaries;
4. special rights invite sui generis ad hoc "reasoning" about what the targeted group is entitled to, rather than extending to its members the same basic principles that authoritative bodies have developed in applying general human rights to traditionally privileged individuals (e.g., autonomous males with resources) in similar contexts;
5. enforcement of the special rights is relegated to a separate institution with lesser power to effect compliance than is held by institutions enforcing general rights;
6. interpretation and enforcement of the special rights fall to persons or institutions whose interests or aims are to some degree in conflict with those of the right-holders;
7. the special-rights charter creates an impression that the targeted group has received all the protections and benefits its members are due—that is, that the work of giving material expression to their moral status and claims on the rest of the world is completed, so no further efforts are required and any claim for something more is inherently suspect, overreaching.

An illustration of these possibilities outside the child welfare context is the coverture regime that once governed marriage in Western society, variants of which can still be found in some parts of the world. Though wives had some right against physical and sexual violence by their husbands under coverture, it was lesser and weaker relative to the right people in general had against violence by other persons. This can be viewed as granting the wife a "special" right to personal integrity vis-à-vis her husband, substituting for a stronger right she possessed against him before marrying or would possess even in marriage if the special law for marital rape did not exist, making her worse off rather than better, illustrating Problem 1. Insofar as the legal system has formally or informally channeled reports of spousal violence into civil legal proceedings or nonlegal responses such as counseling, to the exclusion of a criminal-law response, it has arguably diminished wives' rights against violence relative to what unmarried women possess (Problem 5). Because wives' separate identities disappeared as a legal matter under coverture, such that they could not bring suit on their own behalf, enforcement of any rights they retained upon marrying was left to their husbands, who in some contexts had interests or views contrary to those of their wives (Problem 6). During that era, some even suggested that husbands' dominion over their wives and authorization to chastise them physically were matters of moral *duty* that husbands owed to their wives, aspects of the protection and guidance to which marriage entitled a woman, so that she could escape the burdens and dangers of the market, the workplace, the political arena, and her own supposed irrationality (Problem 2).[5]

The risk that a body of group-specific special rights will make its ostensible beneficiaries worse off relative to what would otherwise be the case is especially pronounced when the right-holders do not participate in the process of creating the special rights and have no reliable proxy in that process. Today, international negotiation of conventions is highly inclusive of autonomous adults; every affected group can have input. But when negotiations concern rights for non-autonomous persons, such as children or adults of diminished cognitive capacity, persons other than those having the special rights bestowed on them are in control, and there is no guarantee they will faithfully represent the subjects of the new charter. Perusing the CRPD, for example, reveals that its protections are principally about physical access and accommodation of sensory impairments; little in it addresses the particular needs of cognitively different persons, yet it creates the impression that persons with disabilities as a whole have received their due (Problem 7).

All these pitfalls of special rights might be more likely in the international law context, if there is less popular accountability for the actions of a nation's delegates to international organizations than for officials at home enacting analogous domestic laws. But at any level of government, these dangers should give pause to advocates for vulnerable groups, particularly any group that cannot effectively speak for itself. In practice, advocates often look for the most expedient corrective for perceived problems. They might not consider whether existing general rights could eventually provide the legal ammunition they need to force change, and whether pursuing that is the better long-term strategy. Or they might have tried and failed, in the process creating adverse judicial precedents, so now believe a new bill of rights for Group X is the only means of accomplishing their aims. Even in that situation, though, they should consider the long-term downside of putting the group in a separate legal category, perhaps relegated to a separate enforcement system with lesser powers and inclined to unprincipled decision-making.

[5] *See, e.g.*, William Blackstone, Commentaries on the Laws of England, vol. I, at 445 (1765) ("[T]he law thought it reasonable to intrust him with this power of restraining her, by domestic chastisement . . . ; upon which we may observe, that even the disabilities which the wife lies under are for the most part intended for her protection and benefit: so great a favourite is the female sex of the laws of England.").

1.2.2 Recommendations for children's advocates in the United States

In that light, given that the United States has not taken the CRC plunge, advocates might consider developing American constitutional doctrine as a more promising route to serving children's needs. Unlike international law, and unlike domestic law in some other countries, U.S. federal law has just one fundamental-rights document, the Constitution. Its rights provisions ostensibly apply to all persons without limitation. Thus, when minors or their advocates assert in federal courts rights against state acts or omissions, they usually invoke the same rights adults invoke for themselves, such as the right to free speech or to intimate association.[6] This has the advantage of establishing a starting point of rights equal to those of adults and imposing on the state the burden of explaining why children should possess those rights to a lesser extent than adults do.

Of course, this does not guarantee proper calibration of children's rights; in any legal regime, non-autonomous persons are at a disadvantage in ensuring proper respect. The U.S. Supreme Court arguably has too readily diminished youths' constitutional rights in some contexts. Moreover, the Court has generally purported to interpret the U.S. Constitution as a negative-rights instrument, protective of individual liberty and self-determining powers as against state interference, and not a positive-rights instrument creating entitlements to protections and benefits.[7] That tends to favor interests of autonomous persons, who are more self-sufficient, over those of non-autonomous persons.[8] One might therefore suppose that American children would benefit from a constitutional amendment affording them, in particular, certain rights. But a better long-term strategy might be to continue pressing claims based on existing constitutional provisions and simply use them more effectively. For example, advocates should

[6] *See, e.g.*, A.R.L. v. Norfolk Dept. Hum. Serv., 4:20-cv-00110 (E.D. Va. 2020) (suit by "next friend" of two-year-old child in foster care asserting her procedural and substantive Fourteenth Amendment rights against government destruction of her intimate association with foster parents); Tinker v. Des Moines Indep. Cmty. Sch. Dist., 393 U.S. 503, 514 (1969) (holding that students' wearing of armbands in public school to protest the Vietnam War came within protection of First Amendment doctrine); *In re* Gault, 387 U.S. 1 (1967) (extending procedural protections from the adult criminal context to juvenile delinquency cases).

[7] *Cf.* Tamar Ezer, *A Positive Right to Protection for Children*, 7 YALE HUM. RTS. & DEV. L.J. 1 (2004) (explaining the weakness of positive rights, relative to negative rights, in international and American jurisprudence).

[8] In fact, though, the Court has ascribed some constitutional rights to adults that are in reality positive rather than negative rights, while mistakenly characterizing them as negative, some of which in effect denigrate children—in particular, a right of biological parents to the state's conferring legal-parent status on them and a right of legal parents to the state's conferring on them various legal powers to control children's lives, in both cases regardless of whether the right is consistent with children's well-being. For critique of the Court's decisions regarding parentage and parental control-rights, respectively, *see* JAMES G. DWYER, THE RELATIONSHIP RIGHTS OF CHILDREN (2006); and JAMES G. DWYER, RELIGIOUS SCHOOLS V. CHILDREN'S RIGHTS (1998).

recast what the Court has treated as positive-right claims of children as negative-rights claims. They could challenge states' explicit statutory authorization of corporal punishment of children, reframing the right asserted as one against something the state is doing (legally privileging and empowering parents to do something to children that is otherwise legally impermissible) rather than as one demanding state help in escaping purely private action. In addition, advocates can aim to demonstrate how basic principles the Court has proclaimed in its application of constitutional provisions to adults extend also to children and explicitly challenge the Court's tendency to sui generis treatment of children.

The recommendation for advocates for any vulnerable group in the international realm, then, is that they consider, before pursuing or endorsing a special-rights convention, whether existing general human rights enactments contain provisions that could, if favorably interpreted, give the group all that the advocates seek. If so, they might focus their efforts instead on developing a jurisprudence of those general rights provisions that is beneficial to the group. Promoting a special rights convention is likely to be advantageous only when a group has special needs that universal human rights, even on the best interpretation of them, cannot protect. And in that situation, advocates should limit the scope of any group-specific document they promote to provisions truly needed to address the special needs, rather than aiming for comprehensiveness, making clear in that document (as the CRC does, fortunately, though this is routinely overlooked) that it in no way supplants or diminishes the group's general rights embodied in other charters.

This, I suggest in what follows, is what international advocates for children should have done in the 1980s and beyond, instead of devoting tremendous energy to drafting and promoting the CRC, which has some positive aspects but is overall seriously problematic from a child-centered perspective, especially in connection with migration. The recommendation for the future is that advocates now shift their efforts to a strategy of returning to the original general-rights instruments—in particular the ICCPR and ICESCR—and developing arguments and legal causes of action from the provisions of those instruments. Relatedly, I will throughout the book urge political and moral theorists to cease sui generis treatment of children, in international and domestic contexts, and instead begin normative analysis of children's predicaments with generally applicable moral principles.

1.3 CRC as Embodiment of the Special Rights Fallacy

All the ways identified in Section 1.2 by which special rights can make their target group worse off are true of the CRC. There are unqualifiedly positive provisions in the Convention, but they largely replicate provisions in the general human rights conventions. For example, the statement of a right to education in the CRC is taken largely verbatim from the ICESCR, so the sole gain on that count is commitment in theory by more nations (those party to the CRC but not the ICESCR) to respecting that right. I therefore emphasize here negative aspects of the CRC.[9] I first identify two overarching problems with the Convention, then concerns with particular provisions, focusing on those relevant to migration.

1.3.1 Overarching problems with the CRC

The CRC treats children throughout as objects of others' rights, and in all aspects of their lives it makes children's interests susceptible to sacrifice for the sake of others.

1.3.1.1 Children as objects of others' rights

Though styled as a children's rights charter, the CRC is replete with references to rights of parents, cultures, and nations—in particular, rights to possess and control children. For example:

- Article 3(2) requires that state efforts to provide children with protection and care be pursued "taking into account the rights and duties of his or her parents."
- Article 5: "States Parties shall respect the responsibilities, rights and duties of parents or, where applicable, the members of the extended family or community as provided for by local custom . . ."
- Article 14: "States Parties . . . shall respect the rights and duties of the parents . . . to provide direction to the child in the exercise of his or her right . . ."

This is an instance of Problem 3: self-serving provisions inserted by the drafters. The CRC makes children objects of the rights of others under international law (as opposed to saying that children themselves have rights that could accomplish similar, but more child-focused, ends—i.e., rights to relationships with or surrogate decision-making by particular private parties when that is in their best interests). This feature of the CRC cannot rationally be defended as indirect protection of children, as the CRComm has attempted to do.[10] Rather, it denigrates

[9] For a more balanced but still child-centered assessment of the CRC, *see* Elizabeth Bartholet, *Ratification by the United States of the Convention on the Rights of the Child: Pros and Cons from a Child's Rights Perspective*, 633 Annals of Am. Acad. Pol. & Soc. Sci. 80 (2011).

[10] *See* "Statement of the Committee on the Rights of the Child on article 5 of the Convention on the Rights of the Child" (Oct. 11, 2023), https://www.ohchr.org/sites/default/files/documents/hrbodies/crc/statements/CRC-Article-5-statement.pdf (last visited Sept. 26, 2024).

their personhood, directs moral attention away from them, and provides warrant for sacrificing their welfare to some extent in many instances. Conceptually, the only purpose parental rights serve is to further the interests of parents, and specifically, satisfaction of their desire to dictate the course of children's lives.[11] Further, those rights of others limit the rights that the CRC ostensibly accords to children; states are to implement children's rights "taking into account" these rights of others. Such an admonition is unintelligible except as a constraint on efforts to do what is best for children.

This pronouncement of side constraints that emanate from the wishes of other private parties or collective entities is extraordinary for a rights charter. Imagine if the CRPD similarly were sprinkled with references to the rights of guardians or family members of mentally disabled persons—for example, "States will give elderly persons of diminished capacity protection and care, taking into account the rights of their adult offspring." Or if CEDAW or another women's rights document contained numerous passages reminding decision makers not to go overboard, because they must also respect the rights of husbands and religious communities, as well as the nation's need for women's reproductive capacities. The CRC does also speak to adult *responsibilities* regarding children; Article 18(1) states: "Parents . . . have the primary responsibility for the upbringing and development of the child." But this reads more as a denial of state responsibility and power—that is, as signatory nations' pronouncing a self-protective preference for privatizing dependency, while also reiterating parents' pride of place, rather than as a declaration of duties owed to children.[12]

Repeated reference to rights of others suggests a conception of children as not so much distinct persons with robust claims against the state but rather appendages of certain adults or objects of possessory rights—of parents, of ethnic groups, of nations—appendages and objects who simply ought to receive more consideration than they have been receiving and special protection against some especially bad practices (death penalty, military conscription, exploitation for labor or sex). There is almost no recognition in the Convention that children's interests could ever be at odds with those of their parents, parents' kin or community, or nation, and no clear statement of a right to protection from harm *by those other entities*, even though maltreatment by parents and other relatives might in most countries be more common than state mistreatment of children.

[11] *See* James G. Dwyer, *Parents' Religion and Children's Welfare: Debunking the Doctrine of Parents' Rights*, 82 Cal. L. Rev. 1371, 1424–46 (1994).

[12] *Cf.* Laura A. Rosenbury, *Federal Visions of Private Family Support*, Vand. L. Rev. 67 (2014) 1835.

The CRC makes just two references to maltreatment by parents. Article 9 says:

> State Parties shall ensure that a child shall not be separated from his or her parents against their will, except when . . . necessary for the best interests of the child . . . in a particular case such as one involving abuse or neglect of the child by the parents . . .

The dependent clause implicitly acknowledges removal from parental custody might be appropriate, but it conspicuously does not state that children have a right to this when it is best for them—the provision states a permissive exception rather than a command. And the mandate in the independent clause reads as a statement of parental possessory entitlement.

Article 19 admonishes states to "take all appropriate . . . measures to protect the child from all forms of . . . maltreatment . . . *while in the care of parent(s)*" (emphasis added). This can be read implicitly to rule out protecting children *by separating them* from abusive or neglectful parents. Further, it leaves out other, quite common situations, of potentially greater relevance to international migration, in which parents are unable to provide adequate care and so voluntarily separate from their children, leaving them in an orphanage or abandoning them somewhere else. The CRC imposes no specific duty on state parties to act in these other circumstances in children's best interests—for example, by determining and facilitating the best permanency plan among all that are practically available. Article 20 merely expresses vaguely that children not in parental custody are "entitled to special protection and assistance," admonishes states to "ensure alternative care" of some kind for children "in accordance with their national laws," and lists several things such alternative care "could include," if states so choose. Further, it emphasizes that choice among alternative forms of care should pay "due regard" to "the desirability of continuity in a child's upbringing," but omits any direction that decision makers consider whether *dis*continuity in upbringing is best for a child's well-being. The choice should also respect "the child's ethnic, religious, cultural and linguistic *background*," which reads as a statement of community ownership and imposed identity rather than as prescribing consideration of whether a given child *self-identifies* with any ethnicity, religion, culture, or language or instead is too young to be said meaningfully to do so.

The only clearly expressed rights of children pertaining to their relationships with parents, kin, community, or nation are rights to remain tied to them, such as:

- Article 7(1): "right from birth . . . to know and be cared for by his or her parents."
- Article 8(1): "right of the child to preserve his or her identity, including nationality, name, and family relations as recognized by law."

- Article 9(3): "right of the child who is separated from one or both parents to maintain personal relations and direct contact with both parents on a regular basis."
- Article 30: "right, in community with other members of his or her group, to enjoy his or her own culture, to profess and practice his or her own religion, or to use his or her own language" ("his or her own" presumably meaning, at least for young children, that of parents).

Other provisions order signatory nations to direct children's education so as to foster in them respect for their parents and for the culture and "national values" of their native country, to register and ensure a nationality for all children born in their territory (Art. 7(1)), and to prioritize keeping unparented children in their native land, however horrible the conditions there, over any solution entailing emigration (Art. 21).

Of course, there are situations in which any of these provisions *could* serve children's true interests—indeed, might be immensely important for some. Their inclusion in the CRC might principally reflect reaction to past practices that were genuinely harmful to children—in particular, forced separations by hostile actors with no child welfare motivation. But such proclamations are also easily manipulated to serve interests of adult members of cultural or ethnic groups at the expense of children's welfare, and it is difficult to read them otherwise than as aimed at reassuring state parties about their power over "their" children, parents' retention of traditional entitlements, and the international communities' respect for local culture(s). The rights accorded children are predicated on a supposedly overriding, always present, and unqualified interest in perpetuation of existing family ties and place of residence. As discussed further in Chapter 3, the patent reality is that these interests vary greatly across persons, based especially on age and past experience, and across family circumstances and locations. In the case of infants, there arguably is nothing to preserve.[13] And in some situations, for children of any age, perpetuating ties and residence could be affirmatively harmful to children. So these provisions exemplify Problem 2, that having certain rights might actually be bad for some holders at some times, if they have no control over enforcement and no trustworthy surrogate.

And again, there is no contrary right in the CRC to *sever* ties when *that* is welfare-optimizing for a child. The CRC manifests no recognition that a child might have a right *not* to have a culture-dictating identity imposed, that some cultures impose on some children an identity that undermines their self-respect,

[13] *Cf.* Elizabeth Bartholet, *Permanency Is Not Enough: Children Need the Nurturing Parents Found in International Adoption*, 55 N.Y.L. Sch. L. Rev. 781, 783 (2011) ("Those attacking such adoption as in conflict with children's heritage rights are speaking a language of a past in which it was common to see people as essentially defined by their race and national origin.").

and that even positive aspects of culture might not be a significant factor in a human's life until later stages of development and never the primary factor. Likewise with ties to a nation; some countries provide great numbers of children with a highly adverse living environment, with little or no prospect for improvement by internal migration. Yet the CRC similarly fails to accord children an independent right of exit. There is only, in Article 10(2), this passage:

> A child whose parents reside in different States shall have the right to maintain on a regular basis . . . personal relations and direct contacts with both parents. Towards that end and in accordance with the obligation of States Parties under article 9, paragraph 1, States Parties shall respect the right of the child and his or her parents to leave any country . . .

The obligation under Article 9(1) is to "ensure that a child shall not be separated from his or her parents against their will."

Thus, if children can plausibly be said to have any right to emigrate under the CRC, it is limited to situations when they are leaving with a parent, at the parent's election, for the purpose of maintaining contact with a parent. It is a far weaker and narrower right than that which the ICCPR provides to all persons. It is, in effect, just a special application of a "right" to remain with one's parents (whether that is good for a child or not). Moreover, the CRC nowhere acknowledges that some children might be better off separating from a country because of what might be called "national maltreatment"—that is, a state's inability or unwillingness with respect to some children to ensure them hospitable circumstances ("national neglect"), or deliberate practices injurious to children arising from the nation's dysfunction, political or military aims, or ideological commitments ("national abuse"). Nor that millions of children are currently unparented, living in institutions or on streets, with no domestic prospect of becoming parented.

1.3.1.2 Police power decision-making about central aspects of children's lives

A second overarching problem with the CRC is that an up-front omnibus provision implies that interests of other people or of a nation collectively can properly factor into all decisions about children's lives. The Convention does not require that any—let alone all—choices concerning matters at the core of children's lives, such as who raises them and where they will attend school, from among available alternatives, rest solely on their best interests. Language to that effect was proposed and rejected. Instead, Article 3(1) states: "In all actions concerning children . . . the best interests of the child shall be *a primary consideration*." "A" implies that other considerations can also be primary in any given case, "primary" implies that states may also allow any number of secondary considerations to influence all their actions "concerning children," and "consideration" is weaker than "requirement," "basis of decision," or "standard." John Eekelaar and John Tobin conclude that the language ultimately adopted for this provision clearly reflected the view that a child's interests should not be considered an overriding factor.[14]

The CRC thus effectively prescribes a "police power" approach to all decisions regarding children's lives, an approach that entails balancing the interests of all persons affected in any way, as the state ordinarily does when acting as agent for society as a whole, simply admonishing that in conducting such balancing states should make children's interests "a primary consideration," whatever that means. It does not, for any decisions, prescribe a parens patriae approach, under which the state acts as agent solely for a non-self-determining person. (This distinction will be further explored in Chapter 6.) In that sense, it does not aim at all to confer on children rights equivalent to those that autonomous (or non-autonomous) adults possess, which, with respect to core aspects of their lives such as with whom they live and what education they receive, are not compromised by interests or supposed rights of others. We adults are not required to do any balancing of our interests against interests of third parties when we enter or exit relationships or choose a form of education, nor to constrain such choices for the sake of societal aims. But with state decisions about comparable aspects of children's lives, under the CRC children's interests need not be even *the* primary consideration.

These two general features of the CRC—ascribing rights to others over children and prescribing police power decision-making as to all aspects of children's lives—treat children instrumentally, authorizing state assumption of control over core aspects of their lives for the purpose, in part, of serving other people's interests or supposed rights and collective aims. Chapter 6 will explain why this is morally unjustifiable; the point here is simply that the CRC has this denigrating aspect.

Many countries have long ostensibly adopted the approach domestically of considering only what is best for children, in some contexts, such as allocation of parenting time at divorce and approval of an adoption. This makes it all the more significant that the CRC eschews the parens patriae model of decision-making and action altogether. The CRC might even be read to encourage signatory nations to retreat from any such child-focused decision-making they might have used in the past and instead to balance children's well-being against other individuals' interests or claims or even corporate societal interests—for example,

[14] *See* John Eekelaar & John Tobin, "Article 3: The Best Interests of the Child," *in* John Tobin, ed., The UN Convention on the Rights of the Child: A Commentary 73–107, 75 (2019).

distributing children in divorce or adoption proceedings so as to compensate adults for admirable behavior (e.g., military service) or social disadvantage.

These general departures from what arguably should have been a singularly child-centered document, as well as the more specific ones detailed in Section 1.3.2, partly reflect the reality that the Convention was a product of negotiation and compromise among adult representatives of nations with widely divergent agendas and different degrees of willingness to go down the road of recognizing children as bearers of rights—in particular, to assenting to rights that might require change in domestic law and practice.[15] For example, Islamic nations were highly resistant to attributing to children a right to freedom of religion, and some African countries opposed any language that too clearly proscribed female genital alteration.[16] And yet children already had rights under international law—in particular, under the ICCPR (conferring numerous negative rights on "everyone") and the ICESCR (conferring numerous positive rights on "everyone"),[17] including rights to religious freedom and bodily integrity! The CRC was (and remains) unnecessary to accomplish that. It and the Hague Convention on the Protection of Children and Co-operation in Respect of Intercountry Adoption (Hague Convention) explicitly disavow any displacement of those universal-rights treaties,[18] and the universal-rights treaties themselves explicitly prohibit derogation from their edicts by entry into other treaties.[19] This raises the question why, in the face of resistance from many countries as to many provisions, necessitating such compromises, proponents of children's rights persisted with a special-rights agenda, the outcome of which has in practice, even if not technically in law, diminished children's rights in some important ways.

[15] *See* Sara Dillon, International Children's Rights (2010), 15 (saying the Working Group that drafted the CRC "operated on the basis of consensus" rather than majority vote, giving any participating country a de facto veto), 16 (describing politically driven obstructionism in the CRC drafting process), 18–19 (identifying points of especially acute disagreement, as to which compromises had to be reached).

[16] *See* Signe Howell, The Kinning of Foreigners: Transnational Adoption in a Global Perspective 169, 171–72 (2007) (explaining that differences in culture and morals between member nations made it difficult to "articulate worldwide moral standards for the treatment of children").

[17] That these terms were intended to include children is also supported by provision in ICCPR's Rules of Procedure for a representative to assert rights on behalf of any person "unable to submit the communication personally." Rules of Procedure of the Human Rights Committee, U.N. Doc. CCPR/C/3/Rev.6, R. 66, 72, 78, 90 (Apr. 24, 2001).

[18] *See* CRC, art. 41 ("Nothing in the present Convention shall affect any provisions which are more conducive to the realization of the rights of the child and which may be contained in . . . (b) International law in force for that State."); Hague Convention, art. 1 (requiring party States to "ensure that intercountry adoptions take place in the best interests of the child and with respect for his or her fundamental rights as recognized in international law.").

[19] ICCPR, art. 5(1) ("Nothing in the present Covenant may be interpreted as implying for any State, group or person any right to engage in any activity or perform any act aimed at the destruction of any of the rights and freedoms recognized herein or at their limitation to a greater extent than is provided for in the present Covenant."). A party to the ICCPR must also comply with its equal treatment stricture, so refrain from "any act" that withdraws an ICCPR right from a particular group, which would include children, on a discriminatory basis.

On balance, then, the CRC appears a strategic error on the part of advocates for children, making children worse off—overall or at least with respect to some matters—even at the time of promulgation, because it was (falsely) viewed then, as now, as supplanting any other international law that might previously have applied to children. Moreover, since that time, the international legal community has treated the CRC as a more-or-less complete statement of what children are entitled to, supplemented with just three later optional and not very popular protocols, and the CRC dominates conversation outside the United States about children's rights. In that way, it embodies Problem 7, creating an impression that it is the last word on what children deserve. Add to all this, the CRC's notoriously weak enforcement mechanism—the CRComm's "reviews" of self-study reports that countries are supposed to submit every five years (but often do not)[20]—and the jurisprudentially insular, ad hoc, and often perfunctory nature of guidance the Committee gives countries on the meaning of CRC provisions,[21] and we can check off every problem identified with special-rights charters.

1.3.2 Problematic provisions in the CRC

As to specific CRC provisions, some mirror language in general-rights conventions, so could potentially be just as robust. However, authoritative interpretation of them lies exclusively in the hands of the CRComm, which generally does not endeavor to conform its guidance to ICCPR or ICESCR jurisprudence. So these provisions in the CRC are likely to be understood as different from and weaker than the similar provisions in the general-rights conventions, illustrating Problem 4. For example, CRC Articles 13 and 14 pronounce a right of children to freedom of thought and expression similar to that in the ICCPR, but state parties and the Committee must give content to that right bearing in mind the CRC's requirements to respect the right of parents, kin, and cultural communities to provide "direction and guidance in the exercise by the child of the rights recognized in the present Convention" (Arts. 3, 5, and 14) and to ensure children's education develops in them respect for "national values," whatever those happen to be (Art. 29). Within that normative framework, what right does a young girl have under the CRC to speak against a nation's cultural practices that her parents, extended family, and adult community members

[20] *See* David M. Smolin, *Surrogacy as the Sale of Children: Applying Lessons Learned from Adoption to the Regulation of the Surrogacy Industry's Global Marketing of Children*, 43 Pepperdine L. Rev. 265, 302–03 (2016).

[21] *See* Jonathan Todres, *Making Children's Rights Widely Known*, 29 Minn. J. Int'l L. 109, 117–22 (2020).

support—including genital mutilation, exclusion of girls from schools, and forced marriages?

Other CRC provisions relate to topics that general human rights instruments address but articulate children's rights in those domains with different language that diminishes the protection. For example, CRC Article 19, rather than declaring a *right* of children not to be hit intentionally, a right they presumptively hold under the ICCPR (e.g., Article 9's right to security of the person), vaguely requires signatories simply to "take all appropriate . . . measures to protect the child from all forms of physical or mental violence." It leaves to interpretation when incursions on a child's body amount to "violence," and any interpretation, again, must avoid transgressing supposed rights of parents and communities and must respect culture. No other group of persons has their right against battery qualified by ascription of rights to other individuals or communities or compromised for the sake of respecting culture.

Turning to provisions of special relevance to children's right to emigrate, recall that the only explicit hint of such appears in the context of ensuring both of a child's parents, if there are two, contact with the child. Thus, if parents decide to emigrate, their home state should not prevent them from taking their children. As far as the authors of the CRC are concerned, children have no independent right of exit, regardless how intensely they wish to do so or how critical it is to their well-being. In cases of war or natural disaster when thousands of adults die and leave children parentless and in danger, the question never arises whether children have a right to leave, even if outside sources of care exist.

Additional, implicit reference to emigration appears in Article 21, relating to international adoption (IA), which has been highly controversial since the beginning of the CRC drafting process. It first suggests states need not permit adoption—international or domestic—at all; it addresses its mandate concerning adoption to "States Parties that recognize and/or permit the system of adoption," with no indication that state parties *ought* to recognize or permit it. The drafters saw this as a necessary capitulation to countries adhering to Sharia law, which does not permit adoption per se. The consequence is that under the CRC no parentless children have a right to enter into a normal legal family relationship with persons who wish to become their parents, care for them, and give them a loving home, even if the children intensely desire to do so. Correspondingly, no state is in violation of any duties under the CRC if it consigns all unparented children to life in institutions with no possibility of leaving unless and until their birth parents (who might be dead or have no intention of reuniting with them) come to retrieve them, even though the severe developmental harm this inflicts on children has been widely known at least since the 1990s.

Article 21 goes on to direct that, if a state does happen to allow adoption, then "inter-country adoption *may* be considered as an alternative means of child's care, *if* the child cannot be placed in a foster or an adoptive family or *cannot in any suitable manner be cared for in the child's country of origin*." One widely adopted interpretation of this language is that IA is permissible *only* if every available option for a child in his or her country of origin is completely unsuitable, as determined by local authorities.[22] Many refer to this as a "subsidiarity principle," but it is a mandate from above rather than preference for local decision-making, so it would better be termed a "Categorical Domestic Preference" (CDP). Under the CDP, it would not suffice that an adoption entailing emigration is clearly in the child's best interests and profoundly better than any available alternative, so long as there is any minimally "suitable" form of care available domestically. The CRComm and UN Children's Fund (UNICEF) have adopted this interpretation and have read "suitable" to include long-term institutional warehousing,[23] and on that basis have successfully pressured developing nations to truncate or shut down entirely their IA program.[24] The Committee does so by commenting on country reports, UNICEF by conditioning financial assistance.[25] It is not entirely clear what has motivated them to do so, but a postcolonial hostility to practices that smack of wealthy countries' exploiting poor countries, or that are viewed as insults to the dignity of poorer nations, appears to be a major part of the explanation, filtered through UN funding decisions and pressure from some human rights bodies.[26] Those motivations are not about the welfare of

[22] *See* Philip Alston et al., "Article 21: Adoption," *in* TOBIN, *supra* note 14, at 795–801.

[23] *See, e.g.*, BUCK, *supra* note 4, at 155 (stating the *travaux preparatoires* for the CRC reflect the view that IA should be a last resort); Bartholet, *supra* note 9, at 92 ("UNICEF calls for policy changes designed to limit international adoption to last-resort status"); Elizabeth Bartholet, *International Adoption: The Child's Story*, 24 GA. ST. U. L. REV. 333, 339 (2007) ("All this law [the CRC and Hague Convention] has tended to function generally to restrict rather than to facilitate international adoption.").

[24] MARK MONTGOMERY & IRENE POWELL, SAVING INTERNATIONAL ADOPTION: AN ARGUMENT FROM ECONOMICS AND PERSONAL EXPERIENCE 5 (2018) ("Officially, UNICEF approves of international adoption, but virtually every adoption professional we have asked confirms that the organization consistently acts to undermine it."); Richard Carlson, *A Child's Right to a Family versus a State's Discretion to Institutionalize the Child*, GEO. J. INT'L L. 47, 937, 987–90 (2016) (describing the history of UNICEF's stance toward IA); Bartholet, *supra* note 9, at 93 (noting UNICEF called for elimination of private intermediaries, which in some countries play a crucial role in IA, and that "[s]uch foster care as now exists in poor countries is often quite terrible, 'a euphemism for cottage industry-level institutionalization'").

[25] *See* BUCK, *supra* note 4, at 154 (noting CRComm has criticized South Korea for not making IA a last resort); Bartholet, *supra* note 23, at 341–42 (stating UNICEF has used its regulatory power tied to financial assistance to discourage IA).

[26] *See* Elizabeth Bartholet & David Smolin, "The Debate," *in* JUDITH L. GIBBONS & KAREN SMITH ROTABI EDS., INTERCOUNTRY ADOPTION: POLICIES, PRACTICES, AND OUTCOMES 233, 247 (2012) (indicating that UNICEF benefits financially from getting impoverished countries to restrict foreign adoption); Bartholet, *supra* note 9, at 92 (noting that the Human Rights Consultative Committee opposed Madonna's adoption of a child from Malawi by "arguing that under the Convention on the Rights of the Child institutional care was preferred to international adoption"); Guidelines for the Alternative Care of Children, G.A. Res. 64/142, U.N. Doc. A/RES/64/142, at ¶ 11 (2010) ("All decisions concerning alternative care should take full account of the desirability, in principle, of maintaining the child as close as possible to his/her habitual place of residence, in order to facilitate contact and potential reintegration with his/her family and to minimize disruption of

unparented children; the concerns are either entirely irrelevant to the well-being of children who emigrate to join a family elsewhere or, at most, of merely trivial and speculative significance far outweighed by the child's need for real family life and other basic goods.

The agencies have modified their position somewhat recently,[27] but IA has continued to disappear as an option for children around the world. Some nations adopt the CDP without pressure, out of hostility to receiving nations, but can cite the CRComm's interpretation of the CRC in support. It is not clear, for example, that Russia violated the CRC by shutting down adoption by Americans in 2013, even though it has meant many thousands of children, including many who are disabled, will never have a family life, or much of a life at all.[28] It is not clear that the CRC provides a basis for condemning Eritrea for its policy of refusing to allow foreign adoptions unless at least one adoptive parent is of Eritrean heritage and has completed national service,[29] which is tantamount to not permitting IA at all. Yet Eritrea has long been one of the most impoverished nations on earth and likely at any given time to have tens of thousands of children unparented because of famine, disease, and violence, with no prospect of domestic adoption. Its blocking children from exiting to become part of a family forces those children to live and die in miserable and dangerous circumstances despite the willingness of people in far more hospitable places in the world to welcome them into a family.[30]

his/her educational, cultural and social life."). *But see id.* ¶ 22 ("[A]lternative care for young children, especially those under the age of 3 years, should be provided in family-based settings."); *id.* ¶ 23 (prescribing "an overall deinstitutionalization strategy"); Elizabeth Bartholet, *International Adoption: Thoughts on the Human Rights Issues*, 13 BUFF. HUM. RTS. L. REV. 151, 161 (2007) (stating many countries' leaders believe IA reflects poorly on their ability to look after 'their own' abandoned children).

[27] *See* Alston et al., *supra* note 22, at 800 (noting that "in light of growing evidence demonstrating the detrimental effects of institutions on child development, the 'last resort' position of inter-country adoption vis-à-vis 'institutions' has been increasingly disavowed by the relevant international bodies").

[28] *See* David M. Herszenhorn, "In Russia, Ban on U.S. Adoptions Creates Rancor and Confusion," N.Y. TIMES (Jan. 15, 2013) ("Deputy Prime Minister Olga Golodets noted that Russia currently has a database of 128,000 orphans eligible for adoption but only about 18,000 prospective families willing to adopt . . . Alla V. Prozorova, an adoption facilitator . . . who has worked in the field of international adoptions for 14 years, said . . . 'People who are involved in this problem—I mean even higher-level authorities—they know only Americans really volunteer to adopt special needs children . . . No Italian, no French, no Germans.' ").

[29] *See* U.S. Dept. of State, Bureau of Consular Affairs, "Intercountry Adoption, Country Information: Eritrea," https://travel.state.gov/content/travel/en/Intercountry-Adoption/Intercountry-Adoption-Country-Information/Eritrea.html (last visited Jan. 24, 2025) (listing requirements to adopt a child from Eritrea into the United States and showing zero adoptions in the last two years reported).

[30] *See* OHCHR, "Human Rights Situation in Eritrea Remains Dire and the Authorities Choose to Maintain Practices which Perpetuate the Crisis, Special Rapporteur Tells Human Rights Council," https://www.ohchr.org/en/news/2024/06/human-rights-situation-eritrea-remains-dire-and-authorities-choose-maintain-practices (last visited Sept. 27, 2024).

Use of CDP by forces hostile to IA for non-child-welfare reasons is a specific instance of the problem that interpretation and enforcement of special-rights charters for non-autonomous or otherwise disempowered persons are likely to be left in the hands of public officials, governing institutions, and private organizations who purport to be agents for the targeted group, ostensibly promoting their welfare and enforcing their rights, but who in reality serve other people and other agendas and end up causing great harm to members of that group (Problem 6).[31] This problem exists in every legal system, and the CRC increased its occurrence in the international realm. The CDP has caused an inestimable number of children who could have been adopted to remain in institutional facilities, many in horrendous conditions, or living on the streets, or to die from treatable diseases, because IA was not considered for them when they were younger.[32]

In sum, though the CRC might in some ways have improved the lives of some children in some parts of the world,[33] it also has harmed a great number of children in particular ways. No one can reasonably deny that creating special rights for children presents this danger, that children might as a result have less protection than they would in the absence of those special rights. This is true simply as a conceptual matter.

1.4 Advantages of Invoking General Human Rights

Appeal to *universal* human rights, at least as a starting point, presents numerous advantages over reliance on special-rights conventions. For the most part, these are the obverse of the pitfalls the latter present. Because general rights charters and jurisprudence are typically developed with autonomous adults in mind, and their authors belong to that group, the rights proclaimed tend to be broad and bold. Regarding international movement, the general-rights documents clearly announce a strong right against obstacles to emigration. As further elaborated in Chapters 2 and 3, the UDHR and ICCPR establish a presumption against

[31] *See also* Herszenhorn, *supra* note 28 (stating Russia's ombudsperson for children is among the strongest defenders of the government's decision to prohibit Americans from adopting Russian children). I call attention to a domestic example of this phenomenon in James G. Dwyer, *Faux Advocacy in Amicus Practice*, 50 Pepp. L. Rev. 633 (2023).

[32] I leave aside here the role that the Hague Convention on Inter-Country Adoption plays. UN agencies deem the CRC more authoritative. *See* Buck, *supra* note 4, at 157. On conditions in child-holding institutions, *see* sources cited in James G. Dwyer, *Inter-Country Adoption and the Special Rights Fallacy*, 35 U. Pa. J. Int'l L. 189, 203, 204 (2013). I am not suggesting there are sufficient adoption seekers to provide families for all children of the world living in orphanages or on streets.

[33] *But see* Dillon, *supra* note 15, at 6 ("[T]here seems to be no area of children's rights where solid improvement can be cited as a result of the UNCRC. . . . [A]ll negative indicators seem to be worsening, some dramatically so.").

restrictions for every person and impose on the country of origin the burden of proving any restriction necessary to serve one of a short list of permissible aims. They implicitly declare to each state: "You do not own the people who live on your territory, and you need exceedingly compelling reason to stop them from leaving."

By contrast, the CRC implicitly supposes states have an entitlement to retain children, expresses no clear right of children relating to migration, and demands no justification whatsoever on the part of state parties, for blocking emigration by children without parents. They suggest a conception of the state as arrogant owner of children, for whom it is supererogatory to listen to pleas made on their behalf that the state relinquish its hold on them so they can join a new family—a conception well exemplified by Russia's behavior in 2013. But one would be hard pressed to find any country, international legal authority, or scholar offering any normative defense of viewing children as such. As Chapters 3 and 5 will discuss, nations arguably have *less* claim on children, to whom no choice regarding residence can plausibly be attributed and who might have received little so far in state-conferred benefits, than on adults.

Further, invoking universal human rights would check illicit sui generis reasoning about children. Interpretation of these rights occurs in a variety of settings involving people of many sorts, including autonomous adults, and adjudicative bodies typically aim for consistent interpretation of rights provisions across contexts. A presumption in favor of equal rights for all persons operates, and different treatment requires justification. The CRC illicitly skips that justificatory step; the CRComm need never consider whether children do or should have rights equivalent to those which adults possess in analogous contexts.

Related to this point about generalizing interpretations and justifications, appeal to general human rights instruments can also put important empirical issues in a different light. For example, the CDP as applied to unparented children ostensibly rests on child-centered justifications—primarily, the supposed interest of children in growing up within the culture of their state or local community of origin. Invoking the ICCPR right of every person to leave his or her country of origin places this concern in a broader context and invites consideration of whether it is sufficient reason to stop anyone and everyone from emigrating. It would be implausible to say it is so with respect to any adult who wishes to leave his or her country to marry someone in another part of the world. International tribunals would undoubtedly reject as a justification for confining such a person paternalistic concern that she would suffer by separating from her culture. They would do so not only because of a general aversion to paternalistic restrictions on autonomous adults (much of the world is not averse to such paternalism) but also because the concern is highly speculative, certainly simplistic, and relatively insignificant as an empirical matter compared with the benefits many stand to gain by emigrating. In some contexts, asserting such a basis for restricting adults' freedom of exit, which many seek to exercise with their children, would even be perverse—that is, if a primary motivation for exiting is to escape oppressive aspects of a society's culture. Chapter 3 will consider whether children in fact have different interests at stake than adults in relation to cultural continuity, as an empirical matter. The point here is simply the legal and conceptual one that a general-rights approach would put the burden on any state treating children differently to demonstrate that the children's needs are different in a way that supports that treatment, rather than simply citing culture to justify any practices that confine children to circumstances clearly detrimental to them in other respects.

Another advantage of invoking general human rights, at least the negative-rights provisions of the ICCPR, is potentially greater enforceability. Enforcing human rights is, as a general matter an uphill battle, fighting against (1) the principle of state sovereignty over internal matters, (2) the explicit statement in UN Charter (Art. 2) that it does not authorize the UN to intervene in "matters which are essentially within the domestic jurisdiction of any state," (3) the inapplicability of treaties per se, or any particular provisions of treaties, to any state unless it chooses to be bound, (4) the non-amenability of any state to the jurisdiction of any adjudicative body absent the state's consent, and (5) the general inability of international tribunals effectively to compel states to do anything. Still, there are soft-law compliance inducements, such as sanctions and reputational loss, to which most states respond, and they are more likely when a respected international body issues a formal judgment of treaty violation.[34]

In this respect, the CRC appears significantly weaker than the ICCPR, which it has de facto supplanted.[35] These two treaties (as well as the ICESCR) are structurally similar, with a core document containing substantive commitments and a process for oversight (periodic review of performance by a committee), and then an optional protocol by which states can consent to the oversight committee's receiving and expressing its views regarding individual complaints against them. A comparative judgment of efficacy should look at such variations as number of parties to the underlying convention, relative importance of those parties, whether a treaty provides for state-versus-state complaints, the number

[34] Andrew T. Guzman, *International Tribunals: A Rational Choice Analysis*, 157 U. PA. L. REV. 171 (2008) (identifying many ways international tribunals are effective even if not in the way we ordinarily expect of domestic courts).

[35] *See* John J. Garman, *International Law and Children's Human Rights: International, Constitutional, and Political Conflicts Blocking Passage of the Convention on the Rights of the Child*, 41 VAL. U. L. REV. 659, 681 (2006) ("[T]he CRC is essentially a toothless agreement with no formal enforcement mechanisms on participating states."); DILLON, *supra* note 15, at 4 ("Nowhere is the gap between international 'norm production' and effective remedies more striking than in the case of children's rights.").

and nature of reservations made, parties to any provision or protocol relating to procedures for complaints by individuals, and powers of the oversight body. The CRC looks relatively good in terms of ratification; it is universal except for the United States. But the general treaties are not far behind—currently over 170 parties to both the ICCPR (including the United States) and the ICESCR (but not including the United States). On several other factors, the CRC and general-rights covenants are equivalent; none include a standing commitment to submit to the jurisdiction of the International Court of Justice (ICJ); all now provide in one way or another for states to opt in to systems of state-versus-state complaints to an oversight committee (and a similar number of states has done so under the CRC and ICCPR, around fifty); those systems operate similarly (including a domestic exhaustion requirement, which is a substantial obstacle to individual complaints);[36] and a similar number of reservations have been entered for all three (assessing the relative substantive significance of those cannot be attempted here).

What most distinguishes the CRC from the ICCPR in terms of enforceability is the potential for effective individual complaints about rights violations. First, the CRComm commands less respect than the UN Human Rights Committee (UNHRC), just as juvenile courts in domestic legal systems command less respect than "adult courts." Second, only fifty-two states have become parties to the Third Optional Protocol to the CRC,[37] consenting to individual complaints against them, which did not even exist until 2012. In contrast, nearly two-thirds (116 as of 2024) of all nations have ratified the analogous First Optional Protocol to the ICCPR, which came into force in 1976.[38] So consider, for example, the IA situation in Guatemala. It was for many years an important sending state, but it foreclosed that route of emigration for unparented children in 2007. It has been a party to the ICCPR First Optional Protocol since 2000, so a complaint alleging a violation of the ICCPR right to exit the country could be filed by advocates for such children with the UNHRC. The UNHRC could declare Guatemala in violation of the treaty, advise it to institute procedures for recommencing IA, and request a follow-up report on steps taken. To ignore the UNHRC would risk significant reputational loss for the nation; Guatemala would appear a human

[36] Optional Protocol to the ICCPR, art. 2, Mar. 23, 1976, 999 U.N.T.S. 302; UN Human Rights Council, *Optional Protocol to the Convention on the Rights of the Child on a Communications Procedure: resolution/adopted by the Human Rights Council*, July 14, 2011, A/HRC/RES/17/18, https://www.refworld.org/docid/4e72fbb12.html (last visited Sept. 27, 2024) [hereinafter CRC TOP], art. 7(e).

[37] Child Rights Connect, "Ratification Status," https://opic.childrightsconnect.org/ratification-status/ (last visited Sept. 27, 2024).

[38] *Status of Treaties, Optional Protocol to the International Covenant on Civil and Political Rights*, UN Treaty Collection, https://treaties.un.org/pages/ViewDetails.aspx?src=TREATY&mtdsg_no=IV-5&chapter=4&clang=_en (listing 116 state parties to the Optional Protocol and 35 signatories, including many actual and potential large sending countries).

rights scofflaw and an unreliable treaty partner. This could have significant adverse material consequences. On the other hand, Guatemala has never signed or ratified the CRC Third Optional Protocol, so the CRComm cannot accept complaints against Guatemala by advocates for children trapped there. (On top of the substantive obstacle that the CRC confers no right of exit on unparented children.) Likewise with many other states that have dramatically reduced their IA programs in recent decades; they have consented to individual ICCPR complaints against them, but not individual CRC complaints.[39]

Further observations on the overall weakness of CRC enforcement: the basic original document (i.e., without the protocols) provides only for review of self-study reports that state parties are supposed to submit every five years to the CRComm. Many countries fail to file their reports on time, but the Committee has no power to impose any sort of penalty. The Committee also has no authority to "order" any change in any country's practices. It merely offers suggestions for improvement.[40] It also has no means itself of rewarding good behavior other than by saying positive things in its evaluation (though UNICEF can base funding decisions on nations' CRC record). Further, state parties are more likely to try to disguise their failings rather than reveal them in the report, and the CRC has no means to investigate whether treaty violations are unreported. This reporting system is thus, as to any country affirmatively harming children in it its territory, equivalent to counseling as the sole state response to domestic violence: every once in a while, the dominant party checks in with a supposed expert to tell them how things are going and to receive advice on how to do better, and the counselor has to rely on the individual's willingness to be forthright and responsive. There is an appearance of addressing problems, but little reason to expect behavioral change. Like a counselor, the Committee must worry that if it dared to issue a particularly strong admonition, it would reveal its own impotence and cause the offending party simply to withdraw from the process.

A reporting requirement is itself valuable. Because of it, nearly all nations are now expected to devote attention specifically to children and systematically assess progress in improving their well-being, then accept external assessment

[39] Some parents who were on the brink of taking children home from Russia—children with whom they already established a relationship when that country imposed a ban on American adoptions—filed complaints with the European Court of Human Rights. The Court's decision, coming four years after the ban interfered with dozens of adoptions for children who had already established relationships with the Americans they expected to become their parents, ultimately focused principally on the discriminatory nature of Russia's conduct vis-à-vis adoption applicants, rather than on the rights of children, because the lawyers who filed the case failed to develop an adequate children's-rights-based case. *See* A.H. and Others v. Russia, Nos. 6033/13 and 15 others, § 383, Jan. 17, 2017 (2017).

[40] CRC, art. 45(d). The Committee can ask the U.N. Secretary-General for a study of any particular areas of concern, CRC art. 45(c), but the Secretary-General would have no authority to take any coercive action based on perceived CRC violations.

of their efforts. This process might result in positive changes, because it gives policymakers new information or makes them worry about their international reputation. That is a point about process, though, not about the substantive rights children should have, and this book is principally concerned with the latter. Additionally, such self-assessment focused on children, or on vulnerable populations more generally, could have been the subject of an optional protocol to universal-rights covenants, which themselves command special solicitude for children.[41] Further, the assessment process necessarily reinforces the substantive prescriptions of the CRC, and given that some CRC provisions are substantively highly problematic, actually antithetical to children's well-being because designed to serve others' interests, the process itself can harm children. Thus, for example, state parties—including such nations as North Korea, Yemen, and Russia—must report to the Committee on their efforts to protect parents' rights to control children's lives, to teach children that their nation's culture in all its dimensions is good, to hold unparented children in institutions for so long as there is any chance of placing them in a local home, and so forth.

Finally, invoking general-rights conventions on behalf of children could trigger a profound attitudinal shift in the global community in a direction favorable to children. Asserting rights of children under the ICCPR to leave any country and change their nationality, for example, would be jarring to the international children's rights community and to individual nations. It might disturb entrenched views among politically driven bodies that now claim a monopoly on authoritative interpretation of children's rights, such as UNICEF and the CRComm. Demoting the special-rights conventions in the policy framework of nations and international organizations should also serve children by reminding everyone that children are not an inferior species begging for charity, nor any nation's possessions, but rather persons of equal moral status and with the same moral claims as adults. That includes freedom to pursue available opportunities for their betterment, wherever those opportunities might be, uncompromised by others' self-serving agendas. Tapping into universal human rights in any context should also inspire those working on other child welfare issues at the international level to consider always what additional and potentially more effective legal avenues might be open to them in general human rights documents. There could be a wholesale reorientation of international children's rights practice and scholarship. The lesson could extend as well to advocacy for other vulnerable populations that might be disserved by group-specific conventions.

[41] ICCPR, Article 21(1) states: "Every child shall have . . . the right to such measures of protection as are required by his status as a minor, on the part of his family, society and the State."

1.5 Conclusion

The primary aim of this chapter was ground clearing. It explains why the CRC will neither frame nor guide the book's analysis. Both the trumping feature of universal human rights treaties and the substantive critique of the CRC put the onus on anyone who insists the latter is authoritative in any sense to present a normative argument for forcing reasoning about children's moral rights in connection with international migration into the prescriptions of that cramped, denigrating, objectifying special-rights charter. To the extent the theory-building in the chapters to follow makes any reference to positive international law, then, it will be principally to general human rights treaties, and to the CRC only insofar as any of its provisions go beyond the general to add true benefits for children. That was, after all, its only permissible purpose.

The positive case the book constructs will not, though, be grounded principally in law, but rather in political and moral philosophy. It will sometimes look to law just for confirmation that certain normative principles are widely endorsed. Consistent with this chapter's criticism of treating children from the outset as in a distinct category, where principles specific to them and attendant sui generis reasoning prevail, the theory-development to follow will begin at each step with general normative principles presumptively applicable to all human beings. In addition, though, the analysis to follow will be distinctive insofar as it proceeds, *after* examining principles developed with autonomous adults in mind, to consider whether children's moral rights are stronger or weaker, or simply different, in some respects than those which adults have against nations and the international legal order in connection with their movement across borders to improve their lives and life prospects.

2
The Right to Emigrate

2.1 Introduction

The rights most obviously relevant to any person's migration are the right to leave the country where one currently resides and the right to enter another. This book's theorizing begins by examining the first of these and, more broadly, a person's relation to country of birth. State prevention of emigration happens to be a major obstacle to improved circumstances for a great many children around the world today. The most prevalent example is foreclosure of international adoption (IA) for children who are unparented and living in orphanages or other state institutions. But states might in some circumstances also block exit of older youth trying to leave on their own but with parents' blessing—for example, Mexico to curry favor with the United States, Russia to prevent potential future soldiers from escaping, a genocidal regime that would rather kill than allow departure. The right to leave therefore merits substantial separate attention.

This chapter first analyzes the right to leave per se and then whether other rights incidentally support it because their realization is more likely or complete, perhaps only possible, if a child emigrates. It then explores theoretical underpinnings of the right and the conditions for it to arise. Chapter 3 will consider what legitimate justifications a state could have for infringing the right and whether the justifications differ in content or strength as between adults and children, or as between older youth and the youngest children.

For reasons given in Chapter 1, general human rights treaties, rather than the CRC, will frame this book's discussion of children's *legal* rights regarding international migration. Analysis of *moral* rights need not be constrained by *any* legal documents; it can consider children's relation to states and international organizations abstracted from current positive law. Theoretical literature on moral underpinnings of existing international human rights, though, can inform normative analysis. A review of existing international legal norms can also provide evidence of a global consensus on the content of a moral right, including the right of exit. Section 2.2 therefore describes the basic right to leave in international law and how it can be infringed. Section 2.3 identifies other recognized human rights that support the right to emigrate, insofar as emigration is conducive to their fulfillment. It devotes particular attention to the right to family life,

International Migration of Children for a Better Life. James G. Dwyer, Oxford University Press. © Oxford University Press 2025.
DOI: 10.1093/9780197752333.003.0002

which is especially important for young children, yet has a more complex connection with emigration than some other rights.

Section 2.4 then reviews the theoretical literature on the right to leave and considers whether normative bases for the right differ in content or strength as between adults and children. Finally, Section 2.5 grapples with questions the theoretical literature largely overlooks—namely, whether particular individuals have a moral right to emigrate *only* if their other, more basic rights are unfulfilled in their current location and, relatedly, whether a right to emigrate arises for particular individuals only if the interests to be served cannot be satisfied by relocating domestically (as the Categorical Domestic Preference discussed in Chapter 1 might suggest). International law accords the right to leave in blanket fashion and allows for consideration of individual circumstances only in justifying infringement, but moral theory might support ascription of the right only to a subset of all people and only in limited circumstances.

2.2 The Right to Emigrate in International Law

The Universal Declaration of Human Rights (UDHR) begins with "recognition of the inherent dignity and of the equal and inalienable rights of *all members of the human family* . . . ,"[1] and then unqualifiedly states: "Everyone has the right to leave any country, including his own . . . ." Virtually identical language appears in the more binding ICCPR, in Article 12, and in regional treaties.[2] Likewise, the Convention on Rights of Persons with Disabilities (CRPD), which applies to persons who are non-autonomous because of mental disabilities, pronounces for them in Article 18 rights "to liberty of movement, to freedom to choose their residence . . . to obtain, possess and utilize documentation of their nationality . . . or to utilize relevant processes . . . needed to facilitate exercise of the right to liberty of movement . . . [and] to leave any country, including their own." The UDHR further proclaims, relatedly: "No one shall be . . . denied the right to change his nationality,"[3] making clear that the right to leave encompasses a right to leave permanently and forever dissociate oneself from one's country of birth.[4]

[1] *See also* UDHR, art. 1 ("All human beings are born free and equal in dignity and rights."); art. 2 ("Everyone is entitled to all the rights and freedoms set forth in this Declaration, without distinction of any kind . . .").

[2] *See* James G. Dwyer, *Inter-Country Adoption and the Special Rights Fallacy*, 35 U. Pa. J. Int'l L. 189, 267 (2013) (citing the American Convention on Human Rights and the European Convention for the Protection of Human Rights and Fundamental Freedoms) (ECHR); African Charter on Human and Peoples' Rights, art. 12 ¶ 2, June 27, 1981, 1520 U.N.T.S. 217. *Cf.* Case of Diamante and Pelliccioni v. San Marino, ECHR (App. No. 32250/08) (2011), ¶ 204 (holding that children also possess the ECHR right to leave a country).

[3] UDHR, art. 15, ¶ 2.

[4] The CRPD (art. 18) and some regional instruments contain similar pronouncements. *See* Dwyer, *supra* note 2, at 211 (citing American Declaration of the Rights and Duties of Man).

Hundreds of millions of people around the globe today wish they could do so, in pursuit of a better—even minimally adequate—existence.[5]

Importantly, non-autonomous persons can and plainly do possess legal rights just as much as autonomous persons do. Governmental actors can fulfill individual rights by respecting persons' choices, but also by effecting what it reasonably supposes a nonchoosing person would choose for themselves if able or by deferring to the judgment of appropriate fiduciaries for such persons. Such proxy decision making occurs for autonomous adults in the real world (e.g., when they are temporarily unconscious or unavailable, when attorneys or other fiduciaries exercise independent judgment while acting in their behalf, etc.). And it occurs for non-autonomous adults and for children, when the state provides or requires provision of certain goods and when guardians act in their behalf. This model is as applicable to the legal right to emigrate as to any other right.

Accordingly, any nation that prevents any children from leaving its territory, when the children wish to do so or when it is in their best interests to do so, patently infringes a human right of those children. An "infringement" means simply denial of whatever a right presumptively guarantees; it is not necessarily wrongful but requires justification. When an infringement lacks adequate justification, then it is wrongful and a "violation" of the right. With respect to the right to leave, infringement might not take the form of direct prohibition; states also infringe the right when they create unwarranted practical obstacles to leaving, such as refusing to provide a passport or other document that it requires people to present at border crossings.[6] With children in families, a state might prevent a child's emigration indirectly by refusing to allow their caregivers to leave. With unparented children, states might do so by preventing contact or communication between children and adults wishing to help them migrate, or by refusing to participate in administrative processes that could effect an orderly transfer of custody to persons abroad.

The right of children to leave, not a supposed right of states to control people on its territory, should be the starting point for analysis of these various policies and practices. It is useful, though, to distinguish the right to leave—which admits of some exceptions, some justified infringements—from the right against arbitrary detention,[7] which is even stronger under international law, treated as a

[5] *See* Charlotte Edmond, "Which countries do migrants want to move to?" WORLD ECONOMIC FORUM (11/22/2017) (reporting that "14% of the world's adults—nearly 710 million people—said they want to permanently migrate to another country" and that 20% of them want to migrate to the United States and 35% to other Western nations).

[6] *See, e.g.*, Alice Huling, *Domestic Workers in Malaysia: Hidden Victims of Abuse and Forced Labor*, 44 N.Y.U. J. INT'L L. & POL. 629, 659 (2012) ("the right to leave any country . . . [is] effectively denied when employers keep their workers' passports and the immigration laws are such that individuals cannot exit their workplace without their papers.").

[7] UDHR, art. 9 ("No one shall be subjected to arbitrary arrest, detention or exile.").

"peremptory norm"—a category of especially important rules that do not allow for exceptions (as one might expect from a prohibition that has arbitrariness built into it).[8] The prototypical form of detention is holding in a prison-like facility persons who otherwise could be and would be living freely in the community. We see this occur with youths in receiving nations, particularly the United States, but not much as a means for home states to prevent exit. They can simply stop people from going through a border checkpoint, and if they do this while allowing the individuals wanting to emigrate complete freedom to travel or relocate within the nation's borders, then this does not match the prevailing understanding of "detention."

Moreover, some legal authorities might regard the right against detention as always inapt in the case of young children, even if they are living in a state institution and practically unable to leave, given that young children must always be in someone's custody. Preventing emigration for adoption purposes might in effect force many children to remain in state custody—for example, in a public orphanage, when they could be living more freely in another country. But so long as the nation in question legally authorizes placement of a child in any suitable and available home within the country, denial of exit is *conceptually* less restrictive than de jure confinement to an institution, even if there is no available home domestically, though practically speaking it then amounts to the same. Analogously, if an adult were living in some country's state-run homeless shelter because she had no family in that country and no income, and if she had an opportunity to marry and live with someone in another country but was denied the freedom to emigrate, we would not characterize her situation as one of detention. We would simply say her home state is infringing her right to leave the country. So infringement of the right to emigrate, which is not a peremptory norm, rather than the right against arbitrary detention, seems the best way also to conceptualize the wrong done to children whose only or best opportunity for a minimally decent life is in another country and who suffer loss of that opportunity because of their native country's policies regarding international relocation.

Nevertheless, the right to leave is a quite strong right in international law today, as evidenced by the widespread condemnation states incur if they deny exit to adults without legitimate cause,[9] and by the very limited nature and

[8] Restatement (3rd) of Foreign Relations Law of the United States §§ 102 cmt. k., 702 cmts. d–i (1987).

[9] *See* Kieran Oberman, *Can Brain Drain Justify Immigration Restrictions?*, 123 Ethics 427, 431 (2013) (citing the former Soviet Union and East Germany as states condemned for violating the right to emigrate); Cox News Service, *Soviets Sought Pledge Athletes Couldn't Defect*, Ottawa Citizen, May 17, 1984, at 1 (indicating the Soviets' request that the Reagan administration return to Soviet custody any Soviet athletes who sought to defect during the Los Angles Summer Olympic Games was "promptly rejected as morally and politically objectionable"); Yevgenia Pismennaya & Yekaterina Kravchenko, *Jackson-Vanik Amendment Could Be Lifted*, Moscow Times, Apr. 26, 2010 (discussing 1974 federal U.S. law that "limited trade with countries of the socialist bloc that stopped their citizens

strict construction of justifications for infringement that human rights treaties do allow.[10] ICCPR Article 12 states that restrictions are permissible only insofar as they are "necessary to protect national security, public order (ordre public), public health or morals or the rights and freedoms of others, and are consistent with the other rights recognized in the present Covenant." Importantly, the "other rights" recognized in the ICCPR include the Article 2 right of all persons to equal enjoyment of all Covenant rights "without distinction of any kind." Chapter 3 examines which rationales for emigration denial international tribunals have accepted or should accept. The current chapter is devoted to the prior questions of why the right exists and has such force, questions to which theorists have paid little attention.

One other preliminary note is just that the scope of a nation's infringement of the right to leave, in terms of whom it covers, can vary. Some deny the right pretty universally. North Korea, for example, prohibits and prevents all its nationals from emigrating, characterizing it as treason. The concept of treason generally entails an intent element—namely, a deliberate betrayal, and one might think infants cannot have such an intent. Yet North Korea does not differentiate in the prohibition or in its avowed justification between those who are autonomous and those who are not, nor even between those who are autonomous and betrayal-minded versus those who are autonomous but lack that state of mind (e.g., leaving regretfully to rejoin loved ones). Some other nations, though, deny exit only or principally to a subset of citizens over whom the government wishes to maintain control—for example, dissidents, high-skill workers, Olympic athletes, or potential soldiers.[11] Some older minors might fall into one of those categories.

In addition, nearly all nations proscribe emigration of children specifically, in certain circumstances, and they have received much support from the international community in doing so. Perhaps the most defensible circumstance is when a parent aims to separate a child from another parent permanently, often called "abduction" (though sometimes custodial parents have good reason to flee and might not trust the local courts to protect the child). This might be understood to fall within the ICCPR Article 12 exception for protection of others' rights, insofar as it safeguards the right of parents and children to maintain their relationship with each other, or it might be interpreted as effectuation of a child's

from emigrating"). Sometimes objection to border-closing is dwarfed by condemnation of other things a state is doing at the same time—for example, engaging in a war of aggression, as in the case of Russia in 2022–2024, or forcing minors into military service.

[10] *See* Thomas Kleven, *Why International Law Favors Emigration over Immigration*, 33 U. Miami Inter-American L. Rev. 69, 72–73 (2002).

[11] The Cuban Health Ministry's Resolution 54 in 1999, for example, targeted health professionals for denial of exit permits.

right not to leave. As discussed further in Chapter 3, the right to leave is bivalent, including the right to stay if a person or their proxy so chooses, as against efforts by a state or private actor to force a departure. Under the Hague Convention on the Civil Aspects of International Child Abduction, state parties commit to locating and facilitating return of such children, or to prevent their departure in the first place.

Another, rather uncommon, but similarly motivated circumstance of denying exit to children is when a private organization or an agency of another country's government attempts to remove children to spare them from disaster. For example, after the 2010 Haiti earthquake, an American missionary group removed thirty-three children from an orphanage in an isolated village and was taking them by bus to the Dominican Republic when Haitian officials blocked them. If the missionaries were removing willing adults, the officials presumably would not have blocked their exit; if they had, it would clearly have been a human rights violation. In the case of children, though, ensuring they did not lose connections with parents and other family—if they had any—*might* have been adequate justification.

The most common situation of emigrating blocking, though, is precluding IA, and that has quite different motivations, which Chapter 3 discusses. Apart from the circumstances described thus far, any restriction on children's emigration is likely to be incidental to a state's determination to prevent exit by persons who are parents or guardians. In such cases, the child's right might be redundant, but not necessarily so; it might be best for the child to leave even if the parent is unable to, and the parent might well prefer that to both being stuck in place.

2.3 Other Relevant General Human Rights

The relative strength of the right to emigrate, reflected in the narrowness of permissible reasons for infringement and vehement condemnation of impermissible infringement, might seem surprising. Ability to change one's location, in and of itself, is not a particularly important human interest. The underlying interest might be characterized in various ways, but if it is simply wanting a "change of scenery," that is not comparable to interests directly grounding most other human rights, such as that against torture. Significantly, indices of human well-being in different nations do not include mobility as a measure, but rather focus on core physical needs, such as not being killed or malnourished or abused, and on basic developmental goods such as education, parenting, and mental health.[12]

[12] *See* David Stoesz, *Review of Amartya Sen, The Idea of Justice*, 21 Res. on Soc. Work Prac. 249 (2011).

The explanation must be that the right of exit is of great instrumental or indirect, rather than inherent, value to persons. It is important because other, more important interests one has—such as avoiding torture—might be satisfied only by moving to a different location.[13] Drafters of international instruments would have been aware that historically when states blocked persons who were trying to leave, those states typically were also inflicting great harms, material suffering, and denial of basic liberties. Including a right to leave in those instruments would afford persons a relatively quick and simple way to escape violation of their other, basic rights.

The human rights that supply an indirect basis for objecting to emigration restrictions are numerous. We might classify them into five types: negative rights against harm-inflicting conduct, incursions on basic liberties, and discrimination, and positive rights to provision of basic survival and developmental goods and to due process. The UDHR pronounces rights to, inter alia, "security of person" (Art. 3) and freedom from torture (Art. 5); freedom of expression, assembly, and religion (Arts. 18–20); "economic, social, and cultural rights indispensable for his dignity and the free development of his personality" (Art. 22) and "education" (Art. 26(1)); and "a fair and public hearing by an independent and impartial tribunal" in determination of one's rights (Art. 10). Every person is entitled to respect for such rights "without distinction of any kind" (Art. 2). The ICCPR embodies recognition by nearly all nations that individuals are entitled to freedom from degrading treatment, attacks on honor, arbitrary detention, involuntary servitude, and arbitrary deprivation of life (Arts. 6–10, 17), as well as freedom of movement, speech, and cultural practice (Arts. 12, 18–22, 27). The ICESCR's list of positive rights includes "the right of everyone to an adequate standard of living . . . including adequate food, clothing, and housing" (Art. 11(1)), "the fundamental right of everyone to be free from hunger" (Art. 11(2)), "the right of everyone to the enjoyment of the highest attainable standard of physical and mental health" (Art. 12(1)), and "the right of everyone to education" (Art. 13(1)).

The connection between migration and many of these other rights is straightforward. If one's home state is routinely violating negative rights against state violence or prohibits public criticism of the government, someone residing there might achieve greater safety and liberty by moving to another country. If one is born in a place with too little food or no schools, one might avoid starvation or

[13] *Cf.* VINCENT CHETAIL, INTERNATIONAL MIGRATION LAW 80–81 (2019) (describing discussions leading to inclusion of the right to leave in the UDHR); European Commissioner for Human Rights, "Issue Paper: The right to leave a country" (Council of Europe, 2015), 4 ("The right to leave a country, whether it is one's country of citizenship or current presence, is a necessary prerequisite to the enjoyment of a number of other human rights, most notably the right to international protection from torture, inhuman or degrading treatment or punishment.").

illiteracy by emigrating. A woman in a society with terribly oppressive norms for treatment of females could have her right against gender discrimination fulfilled by crossing a border and taking up new residence in a more egalitarian society. The very purpose of enacting human rights treaties is to address the fact that in some states some of these rights go unfulfilled, at least for a substantial number of people. Yet all such rights are substantially fulfilled in some other states. Therefore, being able to leave the former sort of location in order to enter one of the latter makes fulfillment of certain basic rights possible. Having a *right* to leave is thus valuable insofar as anyone else has the inclination and practical ability to block one's exit; one would want them to be under an enforceable duty not to obstruct one's migration. (Of course, ability to enter another place is also part of the equation.)

The widely recognized right to family life is another that the right to leave might serve indirectly. It merits separate and deeper treatment because it is so pertinent to child migration and because its connection to migration is more complicated. It appears to entail both negative and positive duties on the part of states. ICCPR Article 17 imposes on states a negative duty not to interfere with persons' privacy, family, home, or correspondence. One could read that article as also imposing on state parties a positive duty to protect against private conduct that interferes with these things.[14] It states: "Everyone has the right to the protection of the law against such interference." Similarly, ICESCR Article 10 declares that state parties "recognize" that the family "should be accorded . . . widest possible protection and assistance." Regional treaties also pronounce a right to family life.[15]

These iterations of the right in international treaties sound like the concern is only with existing relationships.[16] When people in existing relationships are co-residing, the connection to a right to leave is unclear. Perhaps if one party to a relationship wishes to emigrate and can do so but the government aims to prevent the other from leaving, then the right to family life would be relevant. The clearer connection with family life, though, exists when family members are currently separated, with some in one country and others in another, but who

[14] *Cf.* Case of Diamante, *supra* note 2, at ¶ 173 ("Although the essential object of Article 8 is to protect the individual against arbitrary interference by the public authorities, there may in addition be positive obligations inherent in an effective 'respect' for family life. These obligations may involve the adoption of measures designed to secure respect for family life even in the sphere of relations between individuals, including both the provision of a regulatory framework of adjudicatory and enforcement machinery protecting individuals' rights and the implementation, where appropriate, of specific steps.").

[15] *See e.g.*, ECHR, art. 8 ("Everyone has the right to respect for his private and family life, his home and his correspondence."); African Charter on Human and Peoples' Rights, art. 18 ("The family shall be the natural unit and basis of society. It shall be protected by the State . . .").

[16] Likewise, CRC Article 7(1) ("right to know and be cared for by his or her parents") reads as preservation of existing parent-child relationships, not encompassing formation of new.

wish to reunite, and in that case blocking emigration for one set or the other can obstruct family life.

Yet for nearly all people, the interest in preserving existing family relationships is likely to be at least partly *contrary* to relocation, because emigrating from one's country of birth typically entails leaving some family members behind. "Family" is generally understood to include any biological or legal relatives, and it is unusual for an entire family in that sense to emigrate all at once. Persons desiring to emigrate typically anticipate that they will suffer the pain of separation from some loved ones because of relocating transnationally. If they are not seeking to rejoin other family members who are elsewhere, or to form new relationships, but rather to go alone for other reasons, such as employment opportunities, a state might be thought to breach its duty to protect family life by facilitating their departure.

Some general-rights treaties do suggest a right also to form new relationships, but curiously characterize the right as belonging to adults specifically, rather than using the usual "all persons" language. In fact, the only new relationship contemplated is marriage, though perhaps also becoming parents by procreation within marriage. ICCPR Article 23(2) states: "The right of men and women of marriageable age to marry and to found a family shall be recognized." The UDHR and ECHR contain similar language.[17] The American Declaration of the Rights and Duties of Man is anomalous in suggesting a broader scope, one that could encompass children and other types of relationships; its Article VI announces without any age qualification that "[e]very person has the right to establish a family. . . ." Professor Elizabeth Bartholet of Harvard Law School has argued forcefully that states violate this right of children by foreclosing international adoption, blocking children's exit and therefore ability to become a member of a family rather than an inmate of an institution.[18] Bartholet and a coalition of experts on IA drafted legislation that would require the U.S. State Department to include unnecessary institutionalization of children who could be adopted in its annual report on human rights violations around the world.[19]

That the global treaties limit any right of relationship formation to marriage is peculiar, not only because that implies there is no right of adults to form other types of relationships with other adults (although there is a recognized right to freedom of association more broadly, encompassing also political and cultural association) but also because it implies that the millions of unparented children in

[17] *See also* UDHR, art. 16 ¶ 1 ("Men and women of full age . . . have the right to marry and to found a family."); ECHR, art. 12 ("Men and women of marriageable age have the right to marry and to found a family").

[18] *See* Elizabeth Bartholet, *International Adoption: The Human Rights Position*, 1 Global Pol'y 91 (2010).

[19] *See* Elizabeth Bartholet, *Advocating for the Child's Human Right to Family*, Adoption Advoc. 109 (July 2017).

the world have no right to state efforts to find parents for them, despite their fundamental need for parental care. (The CRC also pronounces no such right.) The ICCPR (in Art. 24(1)) and the ICESCR (in Art. 10(3)) refer only vaguely to states' obligation to afford special protection and assistance to children given their vulnerability. Perhaps this omission reflects the fact that awareness of the importance of parenting to child development was not as widespread when those treaties were drafted. In contrast, the CRPD, promulgated much later, in 2006, commits state parties to keeping disabled children out of institutions and instead in family settings in the community, by adoption if placement with kin is not feasible.[20]

In addition, though, further complicating the connection between family life and emigration: Even if there is a right of all persons to join or form a family, it might support a right of emigration only if no opportunity for such exists in-state. I discuss the possibility of a "domestic exhaustion" limitation on the right to emigrate in Section 2.5.2. Here I will just note that if there is such a limitation, it would seem to apply most commonly in the case of adults seeking to form new family relationships, so long as local law does not prohibit the type of relationship they seek (e.g., same-sex intimate partnership) and so long as there is not an anomalous shortage of potential partners (e.g., if war has drastically reduced the male population). Under normal circumstances in any country, even the poorest, there is an ample supply of potential, willing adult intimate partners. In contrast, countries with great numbers of unparented young children living in institutions typically have a great shortage of people willing to enter parent-child relationships with children who are not their offspring.

2.4 Theoretical Underpinnings of the Right to Emigrate

Theorists also regard the right of exit as great in strength, even "the first and most fundamental of man's liberties."[21] Yet the right of emigration has received far less scholarly attention than the right of immigration. This might be in part because existence of a moral right of exit seems intuitively obvious, like a moral right to breathe.

Yet the right is not so easy to defend. This is partly so because it is more difficult than generally supposed to distinguish the right of exit, in terms of the individual interests it protects and the national interests with which it might conflict, from a right of entry, which is generally viewed as weak or nonexistent. Both rights

[20] *See* Eric Rosenthal, *The Right of All Children to Grow Up with a Family Under International Law: Implications for Placement in Orphanages, Residential Care, and Group Homes*, 25 Buff. Hum. Rts. L. Rev. 65, 73–75 (2019).

[21] Chetail, *supra* note 13, at 77.

relate to a situation when persons want to move from Point A to Point B, points that happen to lie in territories of different states and separated from each other by a national border. Typically, a single motivation underlies exercise of either type of right, and when it is a pull factor, such as opportunity for family reunion or formation, it would seem equally compelling against each nation involved. Either of the nations might wish to prevent the movement, and there is much overlap in the reasons states have for wanting to prevent exit or entry—in particular, that the migration in or out could, if done by a large enough number of people, adversely affect the society. Chapters 3 and 8 will discuss those reasons.

What might most clearly distinguish the two rights is a connection to state legitimacy.[22] Political theorists today deem respect for the right of exit a necessary condition for the legitimacy and sovereignty of a nation or any subnational political entity. A regime cannot demand respect in the community of nations unless people are free to vote for or against it "with their feet."[23] Then the continued presence of people within the territory constitutes, some say, implicit approval.[24] A state is supposed to serve the welfare of its people, and the best indicator of whether it is doing so might be that people are content to remain. This rationale could extend to non-autonomous persons, if we view reliable proxies for them, including caretaking parents, as decision makers whose vote to stay or go can count as an endorsement or rejection. In fact, confining children within one's borders arguably threatens state legitimacy more than does confining adults, because in the former case the state is not only creating subjects by force but also taking control of humans' very formation, by which a state might prevent emergence of a preference to leave.

Another aspect of a state's legitimacy is the justifiability of its exerting force over people within its territory, and a right to leave might support a finding of justifiability if anyone who chooses to stay when free to leave is deemed to consent to the state's regime of regulation. Anna Stilz summarizes Locke's view of implicit consent: "Only if citizens have the ability to renounce their civic obligations, by leaving the territory, can we say they are truly bound when they decide to stay."[25]

This state-legitimacy approach to grounding a right of emigration is problematic in several ways. Most obvious and familiar is that relocation is too difficult practically for most people to warrant an inference from their not doing so. We should not be surprised that most Guatemalans do not try to leave, considering

[22] *See* Kleven, *supra* note 10, at 70 ("Excessive constraint on immigration might make a regime seem unjust but not illegitimate.").

[23] *See* Ilya Somin, Free to Move: Foot Voting, Migration, and Political Freedom 21–23 (2020).

[24] Daniel Sharp, *The Right to Emigrate: Exit and Equality in a World of States*, 24 J. Ethics & Soc. Phil. 371, 377 (2023) (discussing Lockean views).

[25] *See* Anna Stilz, "Is There an Unqualified Right to Leave?," *in* Sarah Fine & Lea Ypi, Migration in Political Theory: The Ethics of Movement and Membership 57–101, 68 (2019).

the arduous and treacherous ordeal involved in getting to a land of safety and opportunity. So a formal right of exit cannot be a sufficient condition of state legitimacy, though it might be a necessary one. More to the point here, insofar as the rationale for the *legal* right or privilege of exit rests on a state's interest in bearing the aspect of legitimacy, which it gains by popular endorsement, its normative foundation is not a moral right of individuals. Indeed, that state interest is difficult to situate in any common moral framework. Likewise, arguments for a legal right of emigration that point to pragmatic benefits, such as collective global economic gain from free movement, or removing temptation for states to move (further) in an authoritarian direction more broadly,[26] do not support an individual *moral* right.

The moral force of state legitimacy, rather, seems derivative—the flip side of individuals' moral right against indefensible subjugation and interference with pursuit of life plans.[27] Exerting power over other persons is, within the liberal political tradition, permissible only based on agreement within a voluntary association, and an association is voluntary only so long as individuals are free to not associate. Unless I have done something to forfeit my basic moral right as an autonomous person to self-determination, a state cannot reasonably expect me to submit to its laws and bear civic burdens if it has forced me to live in its territory, such that I have not willingly entered into a social contract. The state violates autonomous persons' fundamental right of self-determination by forcing them into a political and social association with other inhabitants of its territory and destroying opportunities for life elsewhere.[28] Thus, forced transport of adult Africans to America and prevention of their exit after arrival would have been wrongful even if within America they were not enslaved but rather accorded rights and respect equal to that of European Americans, even if their lives were thereby vastly improved in material terms, and even if the motivation were entirely altruistic. It would still run roughshod over their moral agency.

The underlying individual interest the right of emigration protects, on this view, is respect for and ability to exercise one's autonomy—but specifically, as to political and civic association, rather than as to movement or location per se. Such interest in freedom of dissociation exists for autonomous persons in all circumstances, not varying from one country to another, nor based on relative quality of life in one place or another. The right allows people to choose with whom they will enter a social compact, as well as where they will live, work, and participate in social and cultural life. Humans have imperfect rationality

[26] *See, e.g.*, Michael Blake, "The Right to Leave and What Remains," *in* Michael Blake & Gillian Brock, Debating Brain Drain: May Governments Restrict Emigration 195–97 (2015).

[27] *See* Somin, *supra* note 23, at 23–30.

[28] *See generally* Jane McAdams, *An Intellectual History of Freedom of Movement in International Law: The Right to Leave as a Personal Liberty*, 12 Melb. J. Int'l L. 27 (2011).

and sometimes make choices not in fact best for them—as evidenced, perhaps, by later regret. But the overriding value of autonomy precludes even paternalistic restrictions on life-determining choices of autonomous persons. People realize their full humanity by expressing and acting on endogenous preferences, and they develop their rational faculties by learning from the consequences of choices they make.

All that said, the underlying interest in exercising autonomy in that way should not be assumed absolute or at the top of a hierarchy of human interests. Insults to autonomy are common in any person's life and do not render the life miserable, and specifically there are innumerable limitations on our travels and choice of residence that we take for granted and do not experience as oppressive. Someone permitted "free range" within a state's territory, including ability to relocate from one local political unit (e.g., Vermont) to another (e.g., California), out of respect for their autonomy, is having the basic interest in free association respected to a substantial degree. It is not clear that one must have such freedom at every jurisdictional level to enjoy sufficient choice, respect, and contentment; indeed, exit from the global community is presently impossible. And were one to survey people about their willingness to trade off the right to exit for other rights or benefits that might be denied, the list of human interests that most would rank higher than freedom to emigrate would likely be long (remaining alive, freedom from violence, freedom to worship and form a family, a large pension, etc.). The results of the survey might not be uniform; even some of the best-off North Koreans might be so offended by the state's attitude in prohibiting exit that they would give up all the goods and special privileges they now enjoy, and risk capture and execution, to escape the political subjugation. But most people, I think, would say such persons' complaint about their situation is far less compelling than that of North Koreans who are starving, regularly beaten by police, and forced to work at painful jobs in horrible conditions for a hundred hours per week.[29]

Moreover, this basis for a right of emigration seems not to extend to non-autonomous persons. Young children and incompetent adults need to belong to some polity but are deemed incapable of meaningfully choosing for themselves which one; someone must impose the associations on them for their own good, and that makes doing so permissible. Thus, if current autonomy were the sole value supporting the right of emigration, a state would not undermine its legitimacy nor violate a right of emigration per se by keeping children born in its territory within its borders until they grow up. For adults with intellectual disability

[29] *See* Human Rights Watch, "World Report 2023: North Korea," https://www.hrw.org/world-report/2023/country-chapters/north-korea (last visited Sept. 27, 2024).

or mental illness that renders them permanently non-autonomous, a right of emigration would never exist.

Within the philosophical literature on moral status, many theorists make a move to avoid the implication that children have no moral claims whatsoever because lacking autonomy, from presently existing autonomy to potential for autonomy. That would save the day for most children (but not those with such disabilities or incurable fatal diseases that they will never become autonomous, nor permanently non-autonomous adults). Even if states must also respect "potential for future autonomy," however, that would not translate into a right of emigration for any children unless conditions for development of that potential are lacking in a state's territory. As to some countries, we might well conclude that the conditions are lacking. Even if it is not impossible for an individual child there to grow into an autonomous adolescent and adult, the odds might be so poor that this value suffices to ground a right of emigration for all children living there, or for those with the worst odds. Threats to bare survival—violence, famine, disease—might be so great, and educational opportunities so lacking, that a nation might reasonably be declared too hostile to children's fundamental interest in developing into an autonomous person.

That move to potential for autonomy as a basis for moral respect is difficult to defend, however; it appears ad hoc and strategic rather than well-grounded theoretically. It seems no longer about respecting persons as they are here and now but instead about revering some attribute for its own sake. If, however, there are other bases for ascribing moral status to non-autonomous persons, as prevailing practice and pluralist accounts of moral status suggest,[30] then states should respect whatever interests such persons have, and it is not at all illicit to ascribe current interests in future existence of certain states. Indeed, many of autonomous persons' currently recognized human rights serve to enable a future eventuality. We have a right to associate in part so that we can form new relationships, a right to seek asylum so we can become citizens and residents of some other country, a right against deliberate pollution of our environment so we enjoy health many years later in our lives, and a right to education so we can have new capabilities and employment opportunities in the future. However, children's interest in becoming autonomous supports a right of emigration in a way very different from that for adults who already are autonomous; it is about achieving some good rather than being master of one's political associations today, personal development rather than exercising personal sovereignty as against the state.

Additional support for a right of children to emigrate lies in other, more concrete and current interests. These are the interests underlying other recognized

[30] *See* James G. Dwyer, Moral Status and Human Life: The Case for Children's Superiority (2011).

human rights, which indirectly support the right to emigrate. Most of these clearly belong both to non-autonomous persons and to autonomous persons. Some might appear *stronger* for autonomous adults than for children. For example, freedom of expression is valuable in part because it allows us to convey to the world beliefs we have come to through independent thought and an identity we have formed over a prolonged period. These things seem not applicable to young children, or less so. Speech does serve those purposes for children at some point in their development to some degree, though, and in addition it serves other, developmental interests that are important. Being able to share one's thoughts and get responses from others validates one's personhood and facilitates ego and superego development. But the expression is less likely with children to be of a sort that triggers government suppression and therefore a need to emigrate. Economic opportunity, too, might seem important principally for adults, though we can view schooling as a stage on the path to economic self-sufficiency and prosperity; jobs and education are two preconditions for satisfaction of the same human interest, and either might be lacking in a person's home state.

Other human interests that commonly motivate migration are clearly important for both adults and children—in particular, basic physical survival needs, medical care, and avoiding pain and terror. The right to leave serves as what Daniel Sharp terms a "safety valve," a means of escape "for those whose states violate or fail to protect their basic rights."[31] This valve arguably is more important for children. This is in part because of their lesser ability to alter local circumstances.[32] And it is in part because the impact of these adverse experiences is greater. Absence of food and hydration doesn't merely induce an experience of suffering in children, it stunts their bodily and cognitive growth. Illnesses with lifelong effects, such as polio and malaria, will tend to plague children longer because they have more years ahead and because the diseases stunt development, so access to health care is arguably of greater importance for them. And children are less able than adults to anticipate, comprehend, process, and cope with experiences causing pain and terror.[33]

One supportive human right is more clearly of greater importance to children than to adults—namely, the right to family life. It is vital for children in a way that existing human rights documents do not clearly recognize. Paulo Barrozo contends that the right to family life, in fact, should for children be accorded a foundational status among all human rights because it is "a pre-condition for the

[31] Sharp, *supra* note 24, at 373.

[32] *Cf. id.* at 382–85, 388–89 (explaining why the right to leave is especially important for those in positions of social subordination and vulnerability).

[33] *See, e.g.*, Daniel S. Pine et al., *Trauma, Proximity, and Developmental Psychopathology: The Effects of War and Terrorism on Children*, 30 Neuropsychopharmacology 1781–92 (2005).

enjoyment of most other human rights."[34] For adults, the relationships that the right to family life might encompass range in significance from extended family ties to marriage to parenthood. The last two are of great subjective importance to most, but no relationship interest of adults can compare to, and none are fundamental in the same way as, young children's need to be parented. This point will be importantly relevant at other points in the book as well.

Fundamental to a flourishing life for humans is formation in infancy of a secure attachment to one or more consistent, nurturing caregivers. The empirical literature on this developmental phenomenon is now robust, including the many ways a person's life is substantially diminished by failing to form a secure attachment to at least one parent in early childhood. And it must be a parent figure, not a changing cast of characters who merely feed, clothe, and occasionally comfort a child. Awareness of attachment began with study of children who spent their early years in orphanages, where they received minimally adequate physical care but never experienced real, loving, attentive parenting. Their caregivers were a rotating staff of overworked nurses who devoted little attention to them and did not respond to cries of need with sufficient speed and care to make the child experience the world as a safe, nurturing place rather than harsh and full of suffering. And the children could not identify particular individuals as reliable sources of security and need-satisfaction, because none were consistently present. The children developed an anxious disposition toward the world that undermined their sense of self-worth, capacity later for close relationships, and trust in other humans. Failure of attachment and lack of the nurturance that underwrites it also inhibit development of the body and the brain and multiply the likelihood of mental illness, attention disorder, and other obstacles to healthy functioning in adolescence and adulthood. The conditions in which children are unable to form a secure attachment—in particular, institutions—are also ones ripe for active abuse, because staff are typically under stress and do not bond with the children, so the children are likely to be seen solely as a burden, even more aggravating when they express needs. Abuse also causes lasting cognitive and psycho-emotional impairment.

In the migration context, this reality is of special relevance to unparented young children, including both those who have been rendered parentless (true orphans) and those who cannot be reunited with capable parents (because their parents are not capable or cannot be located). The need for parenting continues well past early childhood, though, and might remain for young people, at least until adolescence, far more important than are adults' desires for intimate partnership or to serve as parents, and certainly more important than adults' desire

[34] Paulo Barrozo, *Finding Home in the World: A Deontological Theory of the Right to Be Adopted*, 55 N.Y.L. Sch. L. Rev. 701, 731 (2011).

simply to live in a society whose values coincide with theirs or where there is opportunity for new associations with a greater diversity of people.[35]

Children also have some relationship interests that are less vital—for example, in knowing and associating with extended family members and preserving friendships. Those might usually cut against emigration. Knowing and remaining close to siblings is often of greater significance, especially for those who have lost their parents. What is of ultimate importance for young children, though, is having and living in the care of capable parents, and that can constitute a compelling reason for emigrating—to acquire parents if now unparented, or to rejoin existing parents—but also a compelling reason against emigrating—to remain with or rejoin parents who live in a child's current state of residence *if* they are now able to care adequately for the child.

To summarize: Children might have only interests that indirectly give rise to a moral right of migration, whereas autonomous adults' interest in self-determining choice among available social contracts directly generates that right. This structural difference seems to make children's moral right of migration more contingent; it exists only for children whose relevant interests are not satisfied in their current location. On the other hand, children's interest in being parented is far weightier than the interests of adults that lead directly to a right to emigrate—that is, in being respected as autonomous persons and free to exercise their capacity for autonomous choice in one, albeit important, way (which social contract one will enter).

This all might cash out thus: All adults should at all times possess an effective legal right to leave any country, whereas international law need ascribe such a right to children only in certain circumstances. But when children do have the right because they are unparented in their current location or because their other basic needs are unmet, it is a stronger right than that of adults who simply want to exercise their autonomy. For both children and adults, the right to migrate exists and is as strong as one can imagine when their very survival is at risk, though perhaps still stronger for children because they would otherwise have more years of life left to live.

Section 2.5 will examine more closely whether this view of the right to migrate as contingent for children, and contingent in its strongest form for both adults and children, is correct. I have sometimes thus far referred to a right to migrate rather than a right to emigrate, because one of the pertinent questions to be addressed is whether someone might in some circumstances have the former but not the latter—in other words, whether it might be that in order for a given child

[35] *Cf.* Blake, *supra* note 26, at 198 (citing opportunity for new social relationships as an interest potentially grounding a right of exit, but then focusing on freedom of political association as the firmer ground).

in given circumstances to have a right to emigrate it would have to be the case that a relocation domestically would fail to satisfy the interest now unfulfilled in their current location.

2.5 Conditions for Having a Right to Emigrate

Apart from adults' interest in exercising autonomy, the various normative bases for a legal right to emigrate identified in Sections 2.3 and 2.4 are contingent. They do the necessary work if conditions where a child now lives are contrary to fundamental human interests and if the solution is relocation to a different country. But we should ask whether *only* a child currently in seriously adverse conditions has a right to migrate. And whether any person, whether autonomous or not, has a right to emigrate *only* if there is not opportunity for much-improved circumstances domestically, by transformation of the place where the person is living or by domestic relocation.

2.5.1 Must one be suffering for the indirect bases of a right to emigrate to work?

"Change of scenery" in a geographical sense, I have suggested, is not the stuff of human rights for anyone, any more than is the benefit of a broader range of restaurants in one's city. Diversity of experience is valuable, to be sure. Some degree of it might be necessary to human flourishing, to developing one's intellectual and creative abilities, to enjoying a satisfyingly expansive conception of the world and one's place in it. But one can have a tremendous variety of experience without changing one's place of residence. Any locality with population above some very low number is likely itself to offer meaningful variety of topography, activities, and personalities. Further, people can enjoy additional diversity of experience by traveling, if they have the means. So might it be that only a subset of children has a right to change where they live—that is, only those whose current place of residence is truly stultifying or for other reasons falls below some standard of livability? We might wonder: Would Sweden violate any moral right of Swedish children by declaring that they legally may not leave the country? Answering this question is not vital to this book's aim, which is to consider whether migration should be an option available to children now trapped in horrible circumstances. But doing so, or at least offering reasons for one answer or another, might generate additional insight.

There is something attractive about the proposition that only some children have this right. If international migration is a limited good, there is intuitive appeal to giving priority to those in the worst circumstances. This might seem a point more pertinent to *im*migration policy, if the limited good is space in a country that ensures children in general a decent life (no nation does this perfectly, of course; there will always be threats by individual bad actors, and many "advanced" nations tolerate highly adverse circumstances in particular localities). But perhaps some nations with high quality of life, such as Sweden, would contribute to a global system of just distribution of improved circumstances by keeping children now living in their territory at home, not allowing them to take an immigration spot in, say the United States, by leaving Sweden, so that there are more spots in the United States for children from countries where circumstances are dire, such as Haiti.

Some other nation might distinguish among children within its territory based on comparative need for internal reasons. It might be able to tolerate only so many departures of its young people. An exit token might be a limited good for that reason, and perhaps it would be just and wise for a nation to permit only those currently in truly bad circumstances to leave, without violating any right of those in good circumstances. So, one might think, children born into the slums of Calcutta have a right to relocate, but those born into a wealthy Jain community in Maharashtra have no such right.

There is a practical objection to this idea, as there usually is to ideas inconsistent with current practices. The number and variety of conditions that can prevent flourishing for children, collectively or as individuals, might be so great as to belie any attempt even conceptually to distinguish those who have the right from those who do not. A child might be born in a safe place with adequate housing and food but suffer greatly because of local attitudes toward, or lack of conditions for supporting, a particular disability, sexual orientation, race, and so forth. Individual experiences can also impact one's ability to thrive in a particular place—for example, conflicts or tragedies a person or family has endured there. Perhaps in theory a Location-Based-Misery Meter could be attached to each individual applicant for emigration and tokens given to those registering in a "red zone." If so, we might conclude that no moral right is violated if those with little reason to leave are not permitted. Indeed, one might think parents should be discouraged from transplanting children on a whim, given the value of stability in a child's life. We might also want to consider the probability of misery-reduction elsewhere; if a person suffers from a terminal illness, it might be that palliative care is better elsewhere but no cure exists anywhere, so the value of emigration is less compelling than if a great gain in long-term life prospects is likely to be achieved by relocating.

An objection more normative in nature might arise from general unease with disparate treatment by the state. A need-based view of the right to leave, though, is similar in animating spirit to asylum-granting standards for exigent immigration in receiving countries, and it would have an egalitarian, corrective-justice aim. Freedom to exit might justifiably depend on demonstrated hardship in place of origin just as freedom to enter does. Perhaps what is most troubling about emigration quotas, then, is not the idea of discriminating among applicants but rather the idea that a home state should have the power to trap anyone within its borders. This is in part because freedom of exit is a condition of state legitimacy, but also in part because it appears to treat persons instrumentally or as possessions. It suggests that if someone does not have a compelling reason for leaving, then the state can force them to stay so they contribute to the local economy or because the state views them as belonging to it. Maybe even being owned by Sweden is an insult to human dignity. Chapter 3 will address this issue in greater depth.

2.5.2 If one is suffering, must there be no domestic solution?

Supposing a given person is among those now suffering from unfulfilled basic needs, a further question arises—namely, whether a moral right exists to move permanently out of a particular part of the earth's land surface, defined by political boundaries, only if relocation within those boundaries cannot sufficiently improve the person's situation. Chapter 3 will address potential justifications for infringing the right if it exists, and they have partly to do with interests of the state or other individuals and partly, at least in the case of children, with interests of the right-holders themselves that are contrary to emigration. Here the question is whether interests that one might satisfy by emigrating are insufficient to support a right to do so if one might satisfy them sufficiently or as well by moving to another location within one's native land. Later chapters will consider whether this possibility affects one's normative position relative to other states where one might want to go, or relative to the international community. Here we are asking whether, supposing a person can enter some other country where circumstances are much better, it matters to the home state's duties to that person whether there is an equally good, or at least adequate, domestic destination.

Autonomous adults, recall, have an interest in respect for and exercise of their autonomy. Insofar as that entails having a range of choices as to residential location, a state might reasonably say, at least if its territory is sufficiently large and varied, that people do not need freedom to move out of the country to have a sufficient range. No one in the world has limitless choices. The combination of zoning laws and existing property ownership substantially shrinks the range for everyone at the local level, and we generally do not view it as an incursion on our autonomy that our residential choices are limited to residential zones where someone is willing to sell or lease a property. In fact, such limits arguably are a precondition for anyone's exercise of autonomy, because it is "only once we have rules about property, uses of public space, and so on that we can freely pursue our projects"; boundaries and exclusions are necessary to "coordinate our uses of the spatial world" within a society and, it would seem, also across societies.[36] (It is a different matter, of course, if one has no means of affording a place to live.)[37] Our autonomy is compatible with limitations on choices so long as some reasonable number and variety remains for us, and nearly all nations of the world might be thought to offer such when it comes to suitable residential locations.

However, our autonomy-related interests are not only about variety of residential settings; more fundamentally, they include ability to choose which social contract we will enter, which national community we will join. That requires freedom to relocate to a different country. Autonomous adults therefore appear to have a moral right to emigrate regardless of how materially hospitable conditions are within their native country or what another country might have to offer.

For non-autonomous persons, on the other hand, the interests underlying a right to migrate are those protected by other human rights; migration is merely instrumental to meeting those needs. One might therefore suppose that if the needs can be met within their native country, such persons have no right to move outside it. Some human rights problems are likely to extend throughout a nation—for example, denial of civil liberties and cultural norms aimed at subordinating women. Thus, in any country, interests in basic legal freedoms and nonsubordination might support international migration for all. Lack of other goods, however—for example, adequate housing, food, schools, and marriage prospects—is often more localized. And as between a transnational relocation and a domestic one equally good in terms of securing such goods, the choice seems not to implicate an interest important enough to give rise to a fundamental human right.

Indeed, human rights in general aim at improving welfare relative to a condition of severe deprivation, getting all persons above some threshold level of adequacy as to any good. A moral right to leave one's country might arise, therefore, only when there is no possibility of rising above that threshold by relocating within one's country. A "sufficientarian" interpretation of the right to form new family relationships, for example, would on this view mean that the right almost never provides indirect support for adults' right to emigrate. There are typically countless potential intimate partners within one's home state, including

[36] Stilz, *supra* note 25, at 61.

[37] *See* Jeremy Waldron, *Homelessness and the Issue of Freedom*, 39 UCLA L. Rev. 295 (1991).

some with whom one could procreate and thereby realize an ambition to be a parent. Only if a state were to prohibit a particular individual from forming new relationships altogether, or were to prohibit for anyone the only kind of intimate relationship they wish to have, then a right to form a family might be realizable only by emigrating. But the common case would be that an individual seeking to emigrate for the ostensible purpose of marrying could find a partner domestically. Typically, such an individual either already has in mind a specific person who lives abroad as a potential partner, but (we are here assuming) does not yet have a full-fledged relationship so could shift their attention to a co-national without great suffering, or they just want to live elsewhere and see marriage as the route to that end. In that latter case, perhaps best exemplified by the huge "mail-order bride" business, the home state might say the right to family life does not support the request for permission to leave. That right guarantees merely opportunity for forming *some* intimate partnership, not the best-available-in-the-world partnership nor a partnership with a particular individual of one's choosing (e.g., having found them online).

The same might be said of unparented children, if there are ample opportunities domestically for adoption. A country thus might—indeed, many do—defend preventing exit of unparented children by claiming there is opportunity for family life domestically, so it is respecting negative rights by not preventing realization of *that* opportunity and positive rights by affirmatively seeking new families in-country for such children. Critics might therefore need to show that in fact little or no opportunity for normal family life exists domestically or that the country's search efforts are inadequate.

To some extent, a Categorical Domestic Preference like that which the CRComm and UNICEF have promoted in the adoption context could also undercut invocation of other human rights by autonomous persons, or on behalf of non-autonomous persons, as support for a desire to emigrate. Realization of various negative rights against specific harms, such as police brutality, and positive rights to receive specific goods necessary to a minimally adequate life, such as food and education, might also be far more likely and complete by migrating to another country, yet not impossible within one's home state.

Further, rights to provision of basic goods one lacks, including state protection from private harms such as sexual abuse and forced marriage, are generally conceived as positive rights and regarded as weaker than negative rights. The ICESCR expresses them vaguely and qualifies them with language, in Article 2, providing that a state should undertake to provide the enumerated benefits and opportunities "to the maximum of its available resources, with a view to achieving progressively the full realization of the rights." The drafters and signatories of these pronouncements likely presupposed such rights would be effectuated, if at all, by ensuring that everywhere in the world these goods exist for everyone, not by facilitating international migration. They might have supposed this simply because they had in mind states' entire populations and so only envisioned satisfaction of needs by improving conditions where people currently live. Thus, if the motivation for emigration is nonfulfillment of positive rights, rather than systemic violation of negative rights, one might suppose domestic relocation an adequate remedy.

At the same time, no universal-rights treaties pronounce such a jurisdictional limitation—that is, that individuals must have their rights fulfilled in their native country or that the state of their current nationality is empowered to force them to seek fulfillment domestically, rather than leaving them free to choose for themselves among relocation destinations otherwise available, including another nation. In fact, ICESCR provisions could be interpreted as not merely assertions of positive right—that is, rights to assistance—but also as assertions of a negative right—namely, against state parties' obstructing any person's opportunities for *better* fulfillment, for comfort rather than bare survival, including via transnational migration. Fulfillment by crossing borders might even be more convenient than doing so by a domestic move—for example, if one's current location is just a few miles from the territorial boundary with another country.

Further, from a moral theory standpoint, a "subsidiarity" condition on rights, requiring that there be no reasonable opportunity for fulfillment domestically, appears simply groundless. There is no apparent basis for building into the right of free movement or the other rights that support it any sort of domestic preference or other geographical limitation. If one is currently in a place where basic needs are unmet, one has a moral right to leave it, to relocate to any other available place where those needs will be met, period. Constraint on where one goes to do that should not be presupposed. There is no moral basis for applying to humans' lives a general presumption that they should never leave their native land, that they "belong" where they started life, or that their country of birth has a claim on them simply by virtue of their having been born there, such that they must justify exiting as the chosen means to getting relief from suffering. This is so not (just) because of a right to respect for autonomy or conditions for state legitimacy, but simply because a state claim to own people is a nonstarter. It is a common claim, historically, but without moral support. The mere possibility of a domestic solution thus cannot suffice by itself to justify constraining choice of relocation destination for anyone, any more than the possibility of a solution in Foreign Country X should in and of itself preclude migration to Foreign Country Y. Some other reason for constraint might, in combination with the availability of domestic opportunity, suffice, though, and Chapter 3 will examine other potentially legitimate reasons.

2.6 Conclusion

Autonomous persons have a moral right to emigrate regardless of whether they are suffering terribly where they now live. Non-autonomous persons have a moral right to migrate if remaining in their current location would undermine fulfillment of their more basic human rights, and when that is true, their right is stronger than that of autonomous persons in similar circumstances. Current location might threaten a child's fundamental interests because of bad local conditions or because persons who can fulfill fundamental needs (e.g., existing or potential parents) reside elsewhere. Further, there is no tenable basis for limiting the right against a home state categorically to domestic migration, regardless of the quality of available domestic alternatives. At most, the state of origin might have legitimate authority to enforce the fiduciary obligation that a private proxy decision maker for a non-autonomous person owes that person, by asking for demonstration that a foreign alternative chosen is better for the child, all things considered. (But also, a fiduciary proxy would also be at fault for choosing a domestic alternative when an available foreign one is much better, all things considered.) Chapter 6 will have much more to say about fiduciary decision-making for children. First, though, Chapter 3 asks what are the "all things" that should be considered and how much weight each carries when a home state attempts to justify infringing a child's right to leave.

3

Justifications for Infringing the Right to Leave

3.1 Introduction

Neither international law nor theoretical writing on migration treats the right to leave as absolute. Clear cases of permissible constraint include persons believed to have committed serious crimes who might attempt to flee and persons who could jeopardize national security by giving to an enemy nation information obtained in a position of confidence in government. Sometimes states block the doors to enforce positive obligations owed to society (e.g., military service) or to other private parties (contractual debts), without incurring condemnation.[1] Those cases generally involve only adults. Quite different rationales have been offered for infringing children's right to leave their homeland. This chapter considers any purported justifications that might apply to children but looks first at the defensibility of each as to persons in general, including adults. Section 3.1 identifies exceptions to the right that international law recognizes. Section 3.2 asks what theory supports.

3.2 Justifications Recognized under International Law

The ICCPR qualifies the "right to leave any country" by authorizing restrictions "necessary to protect national security, public order . . . , public health or morals or the rights and freedoms of others," so long as they are "consistent with the other rights recognized in the present Covenant."[2] This leaves much room for

[1] *See* Vincent Chetail, International Migration Law (2019), 82 (stating drafters of ICCPR agreed the right to leave "could not be claimed in order to escape legal proceedings or to avoid such obligations as national service, and the payment of fines, taxes or maintenance allowances."), 84; Jane McAdam, *An Intellectual History of Freedom of Movement in International Law: The Right to Leave as a Personal Liberty*, 12 Melb. J. Int'l L. 27 (2011).

[2] ICCPR, art. 12 ¶ 3. UDHR, art. 29 ¶ 2 lists, as an additional potential justification for infringing the rights it pronounces, "meeting the just requirements of . . . the general welfare in a democratic society." Drafters of the ICCPR rejected that utilitarian basis for denying the right to emigrate, which would have diminished the force of Covenant rights considerably. *See* Jeffrey Barist et al., *Who May Leave: A Review of Soviet Practice Restricting Emigration on Grounds of Knowledge of "State Secrets" in Comparison with Standards of International Law and the Policies of Other States*, 15 Hofstra L. Rev. 381, 388 (1987).

International Migration of Children for a Better Life. James G. Dwyer, Oxford University Press. © Oxford University Press 2025.
DOI: 10.1093/9780197752333.003.0003

interpretation, but the state bears the burdens of proof and persuasion. A nation that prevents just a particular group from leaving bears an additional burden; "the other rights recognized in the present Covenant" include a right to equal treatment, so the infringing state must not only demonstrate the necessity of its action to serving a compelling public purpose but also provide rational justification for targeting that group. If the rationale offered would apply to other persons, the state must either infringe the right of those other persons as well or infringe the right of no one. This is also a principle of moral philosophy—that reasons should presumptively be generalized to apply to all who are similarly situated in morally relevant ways.[3]

The jurisprudence on permissible infringements of the right to emigrate is sparse. It is possible, though, to discern established views about the permissibility of some reasons for denying freedom to leave and about general standards by which to judge restrictions and rationales not yet adjudicated. The principal sources are a document called the Siracusa Principles, generated in the 1980s by respected experts on international and human rights law, setting forth the UN's position on permissible derogation from ICCPR rights generally,[4] and published decisions of international human rights tribunals and domestic courts.

3.2.1 The Siracusa Principles

The Principles' general guidance makes clear that (1) exceptions are disfavored, (2) the ICCPR must itself authorize the exception, (3) state parties and tribunals should interpret any exception narrowly, and (4) states must apply an exception in the least restrictive manner feasible to satisfy its rationale. The third of these counteracts the inclination of state leaders to invoke extremely broad interpretations to try to defend actions that are entirely unprincipled.

Thus, any nation preventing any children from emigrating should have to account to the UNHRC, presenting objective evidence that this is necessary to serve one of the few exceptions the ICCPR enumerates, narrowly interpreted, and demonstrating that it applies the restriction also against

[3] *See, e.g.*, Charles E. Caton, *In What Sense and Why "Ought" Judgements Are Universalizable*, 13 Phil. Q. 48, 55 (1963) ("the logic of the notion of a reason or a justification is such that, if a person puts forward certain considerations as reasons for an 'ought'-judgment, he must also be prepared to put forward the same reasons for the same judgment about a different but not dissimilar case-he must, that is, on pain of unintelligibility"); A.K. Rogers, The Theory of Ethics 191–92 (1922) (noting that when endeavoring to "show definite reasons, that a reasonable being is bound to admit, why the principle applies in the one instance and not in the other . . . the reasons must be themselves general ones.").

[4] United Nations Economic and Social Council, The Siracusa Principles on the Limitation and Derogation Provisions in the International Covenant on Civil and Political Rights, annex, U.N. Doc. E/CN.4/1985/4 (Sept. 28, 1984).

adults whenever that would serve the asserted aim and that it cannot protect the state interest embodied in that aim by means other than obstructing a child's departure.

The Siracusa Principles also provide guidance on each enumerated exception. National security is unlikely ever to be a reason for confining children within the home state's borders. The public health exception addresses "serious threat to the health of the population or individual members of the population." This most straightforwardly applies to communicable diseases, and a state invoking this rationale should show both that the danger to individual well-being or public health is substantial and necessitates denial of emigration and that it applies the same restriction to all persons or can convincingly explain any disparate treatment.

The remaining exceptions seem more promising bases for preventing children from leaving. "Public order" is "the sum of rules which ensure the functioning of society or the set of fundamental principles on which society is founded."[5] The Principles observe that public order necessarily entails respect for human rights, so a state could not invoke "fundamental principles" that entail denying human rights to some. Thus, a nation could not prohibit married women from emigrating without their husbands on the grounds that husbands' ownership of their wives is a fundamental principle in, and necessary to the functioning of, that society. Likewise with a principle that children belong to fathers, which some nations might invoke to refuse cooperation in child abduction cases. So, too, a fundamental principle that treats children as property of other persons in any other way, or of a group or the nation; it, too, would conflict with the universal right to be treated as a person with inherent dignity[6] so could not legally be invoked to justify denying freedom to emigrate.

One legitimate fundamental principle on which any society might be founded is the social contract-related principle of "fair dealing," under which members of a society have a duty to reciprocate for benefits they have received.[7] This principle underlies general acceptance of a military-service obligation as valid reason for preventing exit. The principle has also been the subject of most philosophical writing on emigration, with a focus on "brain drain," and I discuss that literature in Section 3.3.2.

[5] *Cf.* Barist et al., *supra* note 2, at 405 (stating ICCPR drafters substituted "public order" for "public safety" assuming the former to be more restrictive).

[6] *Cf.* ICCPR, art. 16 ("Everyone shall have the right to recognition everywhere as a person before the law."), art. 26 ("All persons are equal before the law and are entitled without any discrimination to the equal protection of the law.").

[7] *See* LAWRENCE C. BECKER, RECIPROCITY 73, 81 (1986) (observing that the norm of reciprocating for benefits received exists in nearly every human society).

Relatedly, a nation might allude to "functioning of society" more broadly and warn of social disintegration were a large portion of its population to exit. It would be implausible, though, for a nation to suggest it would cease to function if a very small percentage of children leave, especially if it has an overpopulation problem, and especially if the children who would leave are currently entirely dependent on the state for care and living in an environment not conducive to healthy development toward productive participation in economic and civic life, as is true of children living on the streets or in state institutions. Moreover, any threat that larger loss of population poses to societal functioning would appear to arise at least as much from departure of able adults as from departure of children, so the equal-treatment requirement precludes denying only children freedom to leave on that ground.

"Public morals" is similar to fundamental principles; the Siracusa Principles explain that the state must "demonstrate that the limitation in question is essential to the maintenance of respect for fundamental values of the community." Any society's foundational values would include the importance of family, but families are more likely to be disrupted by departure of adults than by departure of children (who usually either leave with parents or are unparented, though unaccompanied minors crossing borders on their own are an exception). Foundational values might also include, though, special solicitude for vulnerable persons, which most clearly pertains to non-autonomous persons, but then the state would have to demonstrate that preventing their emigration protects their well-being objectively assessed rather than the opposite. That might be true when, for example, parents seek to relocate or simply travel abroad with a child to impose on the child treatments deemed harmful in the home state (female genital mutilation, conversion therapy, etc.).

Finally, as to rights and freedoms of others, the Principles opine that these might include some that do not arise from the ICCPR itself but from other sources, such as domestic contract law. The law of some nations recognizes rights in family relationships that a nation might cite to justify blocking some persons from leaving, including husbands' rights to control their wives and parental rights regarding children. The Principles state, however, that the ICCPR itself is assumed "to protect the most fundamental rights and freedoms" and that Covenant does not pronounce such other-regarding control "rights" per se. It does, in Article 18, commit states to respecting a limited "liberty" of parents "to ensure the religious and moral education of their children in conformity with their own convictions," but it would be disingenuous to invoke that as a basis for blocking emigration of children whom the state has failed to connect with any parents or who are leaving with their parents' approval.

The only other guidance the Principles offer is that a restriction on human rights "shall not be used to protect the State and its officials from public opinion or criticism." This suggests no state could legitimately defend restrictions on emigration of any nationals by complaining that their leaving embarrasses the state or its leaders or exposes them to criticism.[8]

3.2.2 Adjudication of obstacles to exit

The UNHRC adjudicates ICCPR-based complaints. It has issued only a dozen or so decisions on the right to leave, and none involving children. Most have involved a state's denying a passport to an adult national living at home or abroad. With one exception, the UNHRC found a violation in all cases in which the charged nation had in fact inhibited its national from moving across national borders.[9] A common government motivation is retribution against critics of the regime, and in no case did the UNHRC even entertain the idea that criticism of government could constitute a threat to national security, public order, or rights of others. This reinforces the point that fear of embarrassment is never a legitimate justification. The one decision that upheld a passport denial involved an adult citizen of Finland who failed to report for compulsory military service when called.[10] The UNHRC noted agreement among the Convention state parties that national service obligations can be "necessary for the protection of national security and public order." In two cases, the UNHRC found an Article 12 violation where departure was prohibited because of criminal charges but the state had allowed the criminal proceedings to drag on for many years.[11] Pending legal proceedings can justify denial of freedom to leave, the UNHRC acknowledged, but not indefinitely. The restraint becomes unjustified when disproportionate or "proceedings are unduly delayed," which might be said of prolonged state efforts to attempt a domestic adoption for children in orphanages.

The European Convention on Human Rights contains a provision like ICCPR Article 12. The European Court of Human Rights (ECHR) has accepted enforcement of a financial obligation—taxes or debt to another private party—as legitimate justification for preventing emigration. But it has required that the restraint be proportional and necessary and that it contain clear guidance as to how the person can discharge the obligation, finding in most cases this

[8] *Cf.* CHETAIL, *supra* note 1, at 82 ("refusing to issue a passport to a political dissident is undoubtedly a violation of the right to leave any country").

[9] *See, e.g.*, Ruzimatov v. Turkmenistan, Communication No. 3285/2019 (2022), ¶ 6.2 (unexplained and prolonged detention of family members of person accused with illegal money transfer); Petromelidis v. Greece, Communication No. 3065/2017 (2021), ¶ 9.9 (fourteen-year travel ban excessive for ensuring appearance at criminal proceeding). For earlier decisions, *see* James G. Dwyer, *Inter-Country Adoption and the Special Rights Fallacy*, 35 U. PA. J. INT'L L. 189, 233–36 (2013).

[10] Peltonen v. Finland, 2 U.N. Rep. of the Human Rights Committee 238–43, PP2.1, ¶ 8.4, U.N. GAOR, 49th Sess., Supp. No. 40, U.N. Doc. A/49/40 (Sept. 21, 1994).

[11] *See Ruzimatov*, *supra* note 9; and González del Río v. Peru, U.N. Rep. of the Human Rights Comm. 17-21, Nov. 1, 1993, U.N. Doc. A/48/40 (Part II).

requirement was not met. The ECHR has also held that complete denial of the right to leave in order to help another nation enforce its immigration restrictions is inherently disproportionate and grossly overbroad, insofar as it prevents entry into all other countries of the world regardless of their immigration rules.[12] In one case addressing a child's emigration right, the Court held that withdrawal of a child's passport for six months to ensure compliance with a custody order, in light of a mother's plan to relocate to another country, was within the "ordre public" and "rights of others" exceptions.[13]

Lack of adjudications involving children might reflect a couple of things. First, states block children from leaving in only a few contexts: custody disputes between parents and two situations in which children are unparented—international adoption and group evacuation from crisis (as in Haiti). In the latter two contexts, at least, it might be practically difficult for anyone who believes the children should be able to leave to mount a legal case—collecting evidence about a child's situation and the behavior of state actors, exhausting domestic remedies, and so forth. Second, as observed in Chapter One, since the CRC's promulgation, the child advocacy world has forgotten children are persons under general human rights conventions, and the CRC recognizes no independent right of children to emigrate. Significantly, in one high-profile legal challenge to a state's restriction on international adoption, against Russia before the ECHR, the legal claims asserted were rights of potential adoptive parents, not of children—a lost opportunity to advance the legal position of institutionalized children.[14]

In sum, very few reasons for denying the ICCPR right to leave a country have been recognized as legitimate under international law. They do not include the reason underlying the Categorical Domestic Preference (CDP) now imposed on unparented children warehoused in state institutions—namely, a state's belief that a person whose emigration it wishes to block could perhaps at some point have a minimally decent life within the home state, even though they currently do not.

3.3 Critical Assessment of Particular Justifications

Theorists have paid no separate attention to children's right of emigration. Analysis of adults' right to leave has been almost entirely focused on developing states' efforts to combat "brain drain" or exit of other high-value adults,

[12] Commissioner for Human Rights, "Issue Paper: The right to leave a country" 19–20 (2013).

[13] Case of Diamante and Pelliccioni v. San Marino, ECHR (App. No. 32250/08) (2011), ¶¶ 213–15.

[14] A.H. and Others v. Russian Federation (ECHR, 2017).

such as athletes, who can earn far higher incomes in developed nations but are viewed by home states as owing a debt of repayment for investments in their training. The literature does, though, suggest some general principles helpful in analyzing a fuller range of potential rationales for preventing exit. I group these rationales by whose interests they aim to protect: (a) other nations, (b) home state, (c) remaining residents of home state, (d) emigrants themselves.

Preliminarily, I will suggest that the strength a justification needs to have, in terms of moral force and evidentiary basis, differs depending on which human interests emigration would serve. I explained in Chapter 2 that the right to emigrate has limited inherent value and mostly derives its force from other human rights it contingently serves. If someone wishes to relocate from a relatively peaceful, stable, democratic society with a decent standard of living to another solely because it offers broader opportunities or somewhat higher salary in a chosen field of work, the home nation should perhaps have a less demanding burden of justification, as a matter of political morality, for thwarting exit than would a nation blocking departure of people seeking to escape dire circumstances. A boy escaping death threats by a Guatemalan gang or an infant languishing in a Guatemalan orphanage who could be adopted by a loving family in the United States has truly fundamental interests at stake, and so the state's burden of justification is at its highest. In contrast, a recent graduate of a Canadian medical school who simply wants the higher salary that migration to the United States would enable has much less weighty reason for emigrating, so Canada would have a correspondingly lower burden of justification for infringing the right to leave.

3.3.1 Protecting the rest of the world

Preventing spread of deadly disease is a legitimate end, but denying exit must be a necessary means.[15] A more common situation is when one nation solicits assistance from others in preventing people from entering the former's territory, where immigration control is insufficiently effective.

The United States would prefer that Central American countries block exit of their northward-bound nationals. The EU was happy to have Turkey house Syrian refugees and prevent their movement north. The moral justifiability of this presumably depends in part on whether the destination nations are morally justified in blocking immigration. If the United States does no wrong in

[15] Gregory P. Campbell, *Global H1N1 Pandemic, Quarantine Law, and the Due Process Conflict*, 12 San Diego Int'l L.J. 497, 516–18 (2011).

stopping people from crossing the U.S.-Mexico border into the United States, when they lack permission to enter (see Chapter 8), it is hard to see how it could be wrong for Mexico to do the same but from the other side of the border, if its sole reason is to help the United States accomplish its aim. It also depends, though, on how comprehensive the infringement of the right is. If the United States pays Honduras a billion dollars to institute a complete ban on emigration, so that Hondurans also could not travel south, for any reason, nor north to join family in Belize, the ban would outrun the justification. Particularly given the threats to safety, health, and freedom in Honduras, its government should adopt as means to any legitimate end those least restrictive of the right to leave. There is an ostensible tension with the requirement of equal treatment, but that requirement applies as between persons or groups that are similarly situated, and those who do not plan to try to enter the United States illegally are differently situated from those who do. Honduras might also need to distinguish those who aim to enter the United States illegally from those who have or are likely to receive permission to enter.

3.3.2 Protecting the home state's interests

A state's interests in enforcing its criminal law and tax or contractual financial obligations are generally accepted as bases for denying freedom to leave, but they are rarely pertinent to children. More pertinent but also more problematic are invocations of debt to society, national pride, and resisting perceived neocolonial exploitation.

3.3.2.1 Debt to society

Formalized recoupment of investments made in persons' development by imposing a national service obligation, such as military duty, receives little objection in law or academic writing. Such duty typically arises legally only upon reaching adulthood, yet if the rationale rests merely on past benefits the nation has bestowed, it is unclear when the moral duty arises. Might not fourteen years of state-subsidized upbringing suffice, even if the duty cannot be fulfilled until years later? Surely the rationale weakens the younger a person is, though; there seems no plausibility to saying a child of three owes such a duty and could be prevented from leaving for that reason until he or she fulfills the duty. This is in part because of the lesser state investment and in part because of the lengthy period till service would begin. As to the latter, even with a sixteen-year-old, if the person cannot begin to fulfill it till age eighteen, a nation might be expected to find a less restrictive way of enforcing the duty than blocking exit for an extra two years.

In any case, this rationale for blocking exit is unpersuasive if it rests solely on benefits bestowed. If a duty of repayment is memorialized in a contract, that presents a stronger case. A talented young adult might agree to work locally for a fixed number of years, perhaps for the government itself, in exchange for the state's providing professional training. Most theorists accept this contractual obligation as a basis for denying emigration, or at least for imposing financial liability for breach.[16] Some would require an explicit contract, others might extend the argument to an implicit contract, when the recipient knows that service is expected in return for state support. In either case, though, the individual would need capacity for contracting, so this justification cannot support preventing children from emigrating.

Theorists disagree about the permissibility of blocking talented and trained people from emigrating, or even imposing a tax on exit, when there is no contract. If the justification is simply that their leaving per se would make the country worse off than if they remained, then, as Michael Blake notes, one would need to justify treating the native differently than a temporary visitor (or forcibly enlist the latter also). A stronger justification focuses on the country's lost investment and defeated expectation, and this seems the only rationale defended in the philosophical literature that could potentially apply to children. Professional training is likely to be pertinent only to adults, though, and athletic training only to a very small number of minors, and probably only adolescents. Further, lost investment can be addressed with a tax; if that can still be extracted after a person emigrates, then recoupment cannot justify denying freedom to leave. Thus, the justification in the case of children would have to be based on basic education and defeated expectations; the state would argue that it invested in children's schooling on the assumption that this would result in a certain future workforce, and it rested its overall economic planning on that assumption.

Any plausibility this argument has diminishes the less a society has invested in an individual, so generally less so the younger a person is, but it can apply to some degree to a person of almost any age, so it is worth delving into arguments for such a "quantum meruit" obligation. Several practical objections immediately come to mind. First, some nations get as good as they give; some leave, but also some arrive from other countries. The argument might therefore have purchase only with nations that experience a net negative flow of potential workers. Those are likely to be the nations providing the worst living conditions, though, so the argument remains relevant for the nations of particular concern

[16] *See, e.g.*, GILLIAN BROCK & MICHAEL BLAKE, DEBATING BRAIN DRAIN: MAY GOVERNMENTS RESTRICT EMIGRATION? (2015) (offering contrasting views on preconditions for enforceability of such contracts); Ayelet Shachar, *Picking Winners: Olympic Citizenship and the Global Race for Talent*, 120 YALE L.J. 2088, 2126 (2011); Kieran Oberman, *Can Brain Drain Justify Immigration Restrictions?*, 123 ETHICS 427, 431 (2013).

in this book. Second, though, those nations generally invest the least in children in absolute terms. Additionally, their leaders also are less likely to do long-term economic planning or to expect their child residents to want to stay as adults; they must be aware of widespread desire to relocate. Further, if leaders do invest highly in the most talented, it might well be with the expectation that they will serve the nation's elite, not the people generally, in which case the fairness argument loses much of its bite.

A final practical objection I will note is that a state's investment in persons' development generally correlates positively with likely uncoerced payoff. The older a person is when they leave a country of birth, the more likely they are to retain social connections there and send remittances and visit.[17] And the more intensive the investment, the more sizeable the wealth transfers. An extreme example would be a seventeen-year-old baseball prodigy who moves from Colombia to the United States after receiving expensive training and coaching. At home, he might provide only entertainment, but in the United States he can quickly become a multimillionaire. Ilya Somin identifies other ways emigration of the talented can improve material conditions in sending countries: enabling residents to see the great potential benefits of education and to learn more about life in freer and more democratic societies, strengthening the society's connections with more developed countries and generating a flow of ideas for innovation.[18]

On a more normative front, even if emigration creates an unfairness to poor nations, it is unclear who, if anyone, should compensate or sacrifice to prevent it. Kieran Oberman suggests the persons who received the training have the obligation, ascribing to them causation of their compatriots' worsened situation.[19] But there is a stronger case for saying the receiving nations, which also play a causal role, should bear that burden. The most advanced countries further widen the already huge economic gulf between themselves and the least advanced by inducing the most capable to migrate from the latter, freeriding on the latter's investments in upbringing and training. They exploit the permanent residents of poor countries, including the non-elite, who lose whatever share of their already meager resources they contributed to schools and social supports. Notably, this could be true to some extent even with exodus of low-skill laborers; though many residents of receiving nations view them as a threat and an economic burden, those nations actually experience a net financial gain from the influx of workers to pick their vegetables, build and clean their houses, and contribute to the public treasury. One might analogize the phenomena of brain- and

[17] *See* Michael J. Trebilcock & Matthew Sudak, *The Political Economy of Emigration and Immigration*, 81 NYU L. Rev. 234 (2006).

[18] Ilya Somin, Free to Move: Foot Voting, Migration, and Political Freedom 116 (2020).

[19] Oberman, *supra* note 16, at 435.

brawn-drain to stealing equipment (medical technology, computers, farm tractors) from a poor neighboring country.

As redress, receiving countries might be expected to pay a tax to sending states for each professional or laborer they import, instead of making the individuals pay. They might do this by a treaty allowing sending states to capture some or all of the tax on immigrants' income. The practical problem with this solution is that the tax, regardless of what form it takes, would create a hindrance to emigration, by diminishing the willingness of other nations to welcome those who carry this tax liability. A receiving state might neutralize the impact on the public treasury by imposing a special immigrant tax on employers, but then the employers either will be less inclined to hire the foreign professionals—thereby destroying opportunities for some—or will pay the immigrants less—thereby relocating the tax back to the immigrants.

It is much more difficult to justify taxing the individuals, let alone denying them freedom to leave their home country de jure. From an individual-rights perspective, a state's desire to hold persons on its territory because of the value it expected to recover from them seems improperly to treat them instrumentally, as possessable assets rather than persons with inherent dignity. That the state has subsidized their personal development does not necessarily alter the state's apparent attitude of indifference to the individuals' longing to chart their own course in life by their own lights, which likely will include not only higher income but also a more stimulating professional environment and a different cultural experience.

With adults, perhaps the state need not be viewed that way; it could deny exit while still respecting the individuals as moral agents. From the state's perspective, those individuals are making an immoral choice, to be unjustly enriched at the expense of needy compatriots, whereas those who remain repay society's investment in them by laboring, paying taxes, participating in civic and cultural institutions and practices at home, and so forth.[20] However, as with imposing the cost on a receiving nation, this might be addressed with a tax rather than a prohibition on exit.[21] To the point here, this line of reasoning is simply unavailable in the case of children, especially young ones, if we assume there is no moral agency to be respected or disrespected.

Further, one might think that, at least absent actual agreement to compensate, and perhaps especially if individuals never asked for the investment, persons seeking to emigrate from the poorest countries are *less* morally bound than other

[20] *See* Gillian Brock, "Brock Responds to Blake," *in* Brock & Blake, *supra* note 16, at 242.

[21] *Id.*, 252. *See also* Erick J. Sam, *Emigration, Secession, and the Structure of International Taxation*, 15 Wash. U. Juris. Rev. 203 (2023); Devesh Kapur & John McHale, *Should a Cosmopolitan Worry about "Brain Drain"?*, Ethics 123, 305–20, 317–19 (2013).

potential contributors to national welfare.[22] Blake contends that the burden of redressing or mitigating global inequality should not be foisted disproportionately on particular individuals, especially not on people who encountered greater challenges than most in developing their talents and abilities, and especially not in the form of tethering them to a place and forcing them to serve a particular population.[23] He writes: "We cannot balance our moral ledgers by placing such a strong duty precisely on those people who have the least protection, the worst institutions, and the lowest prospects."[24] That no one else is compensating the poor nation for its investment does not change those persons' normative position; they have neither a primary obligation nor a fallback obligation, but rather no obligation. And, as Oberman puts it, "[t]o coerce people to get them to labor for others, without first establishing that they have a duty to labor, is to come too close to treating them merely as a means to be acceptable."[25]

Poor societies might have a moral claim to global wealth redistribution in their favor, but that claim applies against other states, other states' nationals (e.g., exploitative corporations), and international organizations, not against individuals simply because they happen to have begun life in those societies, and not in a way that defeats their ability to develop the best possible plan of life for themselves. Blake observes that persons who escape an adverse childhood environment and realize great material success might be less admirable if they never "give back" than persons with similar histories who do give back, but they have not breached a moral duty, so their having resided there cannot justify blocking or taxing their exit, directly or indirectly (by taxing their employer or new home state).

Our intuitions about domestic migration support Blake's view. Within a federation like the United States or the EU, the fact that some jurisdictions have fewer resources than others does not lead people to think talented individuals raised in the former have a moral obligation to stay put or, if they relocate, to send part of their earnings back to their hometown. To say someone who grew up in West Baltimore and received free education in neighborhood public schools and then at the University of Baltimore has an obligation to live and work in Baltimore would impose on them a duty that individuals who grow up in Palo Alto do not bear, simply because of the arbitrary fact of birth location and the reality of

[22] *Cf.* Shachar, *supra* note 16, at 2126 ("Her home country may plead with her to stay or make promises to further invest in her development as an athlete, but as a cold legal matter, it cannot force her to stay."); Michael Traynor, *The Restatement (Third) of Restitution & Unjust Enrichment: Some Introductory Suggestions*, 68 WASH. & LEE L. REV. 899, 900 (2011) ("A person who confers an unrequested benefit voluntarily will usually not be able to recover in restitution; and the law will not impose liability on an innocent recipient to a forced exchange").

[23] Michael Blake, "The Right to Leave: Looking Back," *in* BROCK & BLAKE, *supra* note 16, at 125–29.

[24] *Id.*, at 169.

[25] Oberman, *supra* note 16.

unequal resources, for which they bear no responsibility. We do sometimes have special duties because of arbitrary facts, such as proximity to someone in urgent need (e.g., to save an infant who has fallen into a lake beside which we alone are standing).[26] But in those instances one is uniquely positioned to assist and can do so at little cost to oneself.

In contrast, people exiting an impoverished community are not better positioned to improve the fortunes of that community than are people born in wealthy places (who could quickly relocate to a poor place or send some of their income to poor communities) or than wealthy jurisdictions (which could send money to the poor community that it can use to retain or lure high-skill people). (Gillian Brock suggests greater familiarity makes one better able,[27] but indebtedness and family neediness likely cut in the other direction, and anyway this would be true only of certain professions and less true the younger a person is when leaving.) Moreover, the cost of severely limited opportunity is quite high.

And so domestically, to the extent we mitigate disparities in local standard of living, we do so by wealth redistribution at the national and state levels, with people in wealthier communities, regardless of origin, taxed more to help those in poorer communities, including by using public funds (e.g., through loan forgiveness, tax credits) to attract professionals to work in underprivileged areas. A comparable global system of wealth redistribution might be largely lacking, but that is not the fault of those born in poor nations who wish to leave.

Finally, theorists generally agree that nations whose governments violate human rights to a substantial degree can have no claim on those wishing to leave. A precondition for enforcing even an explicit service contract is "a minimal level of state adequacy," including being "sufficiently rights-protecting."[28] We can conceptualize this as having a stronger right to leave the worse circumstances are in one's home country, or as a breach of the social contract. The idea can be broadened to include not only violation of negative human rights but also failure to ensure basic goods—another way of looking at the reality that many countries invest little in their people's development, some led by an exploitative elite. A given child in dire circumstances—the child on whom this book focuses—is likely to have received precious little in benefits from his or her country. By a local standard of wealth, the amount spent might be significant even if just for a primitive school and minimal health care, but by any standard this is not the sort of investment in human development that cries out for payback. A fairness rationale thus seems especially inadequate to justify blocking a child's exit from a home state where destitution, deprivation, and danger prevail.

[26] Brock, *supra* note 20, at 249.
[27] *Id.*
[28] *Id.*, 276–77.

3.3.2.2 Gratuitous financial gain

A nation might receive payments from outside sources for blocking its exits. One nation might offer another money to stop the flow of immigrants to the former. UNICEF has sometimes made its aid to poor countries contingent on their shutting down international adoption. Practically, the gain would be offset by lost remittances and, with international adoption (IA), greater institutional-care costs. Even assuming a net gain, and even assuming the receiving state's leaders would use the money to benefit the society generally, the instrumental treatment of persons is unconscionable. Receiving payment to hold people captive is akin to slavery and trafficking. Normatively, it is no more defensible with nationals than with non-nationals—for example, if Russia offered Turkey a million euros each for retaining any Russian who vacations in Istanbul and is on a list of undesirables, or if Turkey decided to refuse departure to German tourists and demand ransom or more favorable trade terms from Germany.

3.3.2.3 National pride

An actual reason, perhaps the most common, for blocking the exit of unparented children is bolstering national pride.[29] South Korea first constricted international adoption in the late 1980s when Western media coverage of the Seoul Olympics called attention to the many children leaving to be raised in other countries. North Korea used this to humiliate its capitalist neighbor, which reacted by imposing a strong domestic placement preference, even though domestic adoption opportunities were minuscule relative to the number of abandoned children in South Korean orphanages.[30] Russian President Vladimir Putin indicated that his support for the 2013 ban on American adoption of Russian-born children arose from his view that the practice is demeaning for Russia.[31]

[29] For evidence of its commonness, *see* MARK MONTGOMERY & IRENE POWELL, SAVING INTERNATIONAL ADOPTION: AN ARGUMENT FROM ECONOMICS AND PERSONAL EXPERIENCE 152–53 (2018); Ann Smith, *We Have the Right Tools: An Examination and Defense of Spending in International Adoption*, 58 HARV. INT'L L.J. 485, 513 (2017) ("Critics of international adoption have expressed concerns that the nations who send children abroad may be stigmatized by their perceived inability to care for their own children."); REBECCA J. COMPTON, ADOPTION BEYOND BORDERS: HOW INTERNATIONAL ADOPTION BENEFITS CHILDREN (2016); Elizabeth Bartholet, "The International Adoption Cliff: Do Child Human Rights Matter?," *in* ROBERT L. BALLARD ET AL. EDS., THE INTERCOUNTRY ADOPTION DEBATE: DIALOGUES ACROSS DISCIPLINES 193–200, 197–98 (2015) (discussing China and the African Child Policy Forum); Rachel J. Wechsler, *Giving Every Child a Chance: The Need for Reform and Infrastructure in Intercountry Adoption Policy*, 22 PACE INT'L L. REV. 1, 35 (2010) (discussing Georgia); Dwyer, *supra* note 9, at 238–39 (citing other sources).

[30] *See* Donald Kirk, "South Korea Tries to Recall a U.S. Adoption," CHRISTIAN SCIENCE MONITOR, Jan. 23, 2013; MONTGOMERY & POWELL, *supra* note 29, at 42–43.

[31] *See* David Herszenhorn & Erik Eckholm, "Putin Signs Bill that Bars U.S. Adoptions, Upending Families," N.Y. TIMES, Dec. 27, 2012 ("'There are probably many places in the world where living standards are better than ours,' Mr. Putin said. 'So what? Shall we send all children there, or move there ourselves?'").

This motivation is inherently illicit, another way of treating persons instrumentally, and it violates the ICCPR's equality constraint on justifications unless a nation is prepared to deny adults as well the ability to emigrate whenever that reflects poorly on the nation. Innumerable adults leave developing nations to form family relationships with persons in a country offering a far higher quality of life. There is typically no shortage of potential husbands for women in sending countries, so the desire of innumerable Belorussian, Chinese, Venezuelan, and so forth women to find a husband in Western Europe or America, and advertising themselves openly on Internet meeting sites, reflects poorly on men and the state in those nations. Yet those nations do not stop the women from leaving, nor from using marriage websites to meet foreign men, and if they did, would be widely condemned for treating women as property. Analogously, if a man forcibly holds his girlfriend captive because her departure to pursue better marriage prospects would wound his pride, his conduct is abuse, pure and simple, not commendable or even tolerable.

Finally, the CDP ideology itself contributes to the self-image problem for poor countries. The shame has two components: (1) the precept that the home state bears a moral obligation to provide homes itself for all children born on its territory, and (2) a judgment that a country is failing to fulfill that obligation. No international law shapers or academics have provided a theoretical basis for (1). Yet IA opponents, self-righteously portraying themselves as allies and defenders of poor nations, relentlessly hammer those nations with the message that they have this obligation and that they may not fulfill it by facilitating IA, despite knowing the poor nations lack the means to fulfill the obligation any other way. They create the predicate for shaming those nations. Jettison the obligation, and there can be no basis for shame. Or affirm the obligation but impress on those nations that they may and should use all available means of fulfilling it, including IA.

3.3.2.4 Preventing neocolonialism

Some critics of wealthy states' immigration policies, which in part favor high-skill workers, charge them with further exploitation of poorer nations, a new form of colonialism. Some scholars make a similar allegation regarding IA, and leaders of some developing countries have explained decisions to restrict or prohibit the practice as protest against as a modern-day form of imperialist resource stealing.[32] For them, intercountry adoptions "epitomize the exercise of influence and control by the more powerful nations who are seen as 'robbing' Third World countries of their children."[33] Left-wing commentators echo

[32] *See* Dwyer, *supra* note 9 (citing examples).

[33] John Triseliotis, "Inter-country Adoption: In Whose Best Interest?," *in* MICHAEL HUMPHREY & HEATHER HUMPHREY, INTER-COUNTRY ADOPTION: PRACTICAL EXPERIENCES 119–37, 131 (1993).

the characterization of babies as a national resource and international adoption as theft (but also, oddly, accuse adoptive parents of commodifying children by paying fees levied by orphanages and adoption agencies).[34] Extremists characterize it as genocide, destroying communities and cultures by removing the next generation.[35]

Those leveling a neocolonialism charge uniformly fail to explain how an exploitation charge could apply to countries with an overpopulation problem and circumstances where a state is incurring the cost of institutional care that only produces bad outcomes for the children and, in turn, the society. None of the critics offers any evidence that any sending countries or cultural communities have suffered from departure of children from orphanages. On the contrary, there is ample evidence that sending countries benefit economically from IA, because it reduces spending on institutions, injects foreign currency through adopters' travel expenses and fees paid to local agencies, and triggers voluntary contributions and purchases of local products by adopting parents and, eventually, adopted children.[36] Ultimately, the imperialism charge collapses into assertion of national pride, dismissed in Section 3.3.2.3.

Generalizing this justification shows how inapt it would be even if it had empirical basis. A neocolonial exploitation charge would be more plausible regarding international marriage, a phenomenon principally consisting of Western men extracting a valuable "resource" (i.e., educated young women) from poor countries. A nation might well suffer from departure of a substantial portion of its healthy, educated young women, especially a nation like China that is experiencing a serious shortfall of marriageable women and a declining birthrate, yet no one suggests this is a valid reason to block or even inhibit their emigration. The idea that a state has a moral right or permission to warehouse unparented children so as to have more future laborers reflects a condemnable objectification of persons far worse than what adoption agencies are accused of doing if they profit at all by facilitating family life for children.

[34] *See* Twila Perry, "Continuing Dilemmas of International Adoption," *in* Jonathan Todres & Shani M. King, The Oxford Handbook of Children's Rights Law (2020), 329, 330 ("adoption of children of color from Global South countries represents further exploitation of a resource of countries that may have already experienced a history of colonialism and exploitation at the hands of the West."), 341–42; Dwyer, *supra* note 9, at 239–40 (quoting other sources).

[35] *See* Alice Hearst, "Children, International Human Rights, and the Politics of Belonging," *in* Martha Albertson Fineman & Karen Worthington eds., What Is Right for Children?: The Competing Paradigms of Religion and Human Rights 329, 330 (2009) ("[M]any groups view placement of children outside their boundaries as tantamount to genocide."). The same sort of view appears in the U.S. domestic context, underlying opposition to White people parenting children labeled as Native American or Black. *See* James G. Dwyer, *The Real Wrongs of ICWA*, 69 Villanova L. Rev. 1 (2024) (responding to defenders of the Indian Child Welfare Act who express this view).

[36] *See* Dwyer, *supra* note 9, at 240.

3.3.3 Protecting those left behind

Departure of some persons might impact adversely, or even violate rights of, others left behind.

3.3.3.1 General welfare of persons in poor nations

In addition to the lost-resource and debt-to-society rationales addressed in Section 3.3.2, one might posit negative impact on sending nations because emigration lessens the motivation of governments to improve circumstances within them. First, a sending state's own government might make less effort to improve conditions domestically if there are fewer suffering people agitating for reform. Perhaps the more children crowded into orphanages or living on streets, the more inclined the government will be to create a child-welfare system that helps parents and creates a robust foster care program.[37] It would be odd, of course, for a country to defend infringement of the right to leave on the grounds that it is trying to motivate itself to improve conditions domestically. But perhaps an international authority should impose restrictions on emigration from certain countries with that aim—that is, to keep disgruntled people at home agitating for reform. Second, some suggest developed countries and their nationals would send more money to a developing country if they were not taking away its people. Wealthy nations might believe they have an imperfect duty of foreign aid but can satisfy it by welcoming migrants instead of helping to improve conditions in the sending countries.

The normative flavor of these arguments is more consequentialist than deontological. No one suggests those left behind have a moral *right* to hold hostage those who can leave. Even on consequentialist grounds, though, the arguments are unpersuasive. The empirical premise is doubtful, regarding motivations of various actors in counterfactual situations. Some autocrats simply kill or imprison critics who do not flee. Persons thwarted from pursuing dreams might become despondent rather than dissident. If no desperately poor adults left Haiti, the government might try harder to create jobs and social supports, but it might instead feel more overwhelmed by the needs. If India never lost any of its eleven million street children to migration, it might make a greater effort to provide housing for them all, or it might give traffickers a legal holiday. There is no reason to believe Ethiopia improved aggregate welfare among unparented children by shutting down its IA program in 2017, or that any nation has provoked an improvement in the domestic child-welfare system or increased aid from developed countries by limiting IA to older and disabled orphans.[38]

[37] *See id.*, at 241–42 (citing commentators making this argument).

[38] *Cf.* Compton, *supra* note 29, at 154–55 (describing lack of success in increasing domestic adoption in traditional sending nations).

The more plausible empirical hypothesis is that exit by some of the most desperate people gives those remaining a better chance of getting assistance. There are fewer people with a claim on scarce resources, and the exodus draws attention to conditions in the nation, which might motivate the existing regime there to improve conditions for reputational purposes and international organizations (IOs) to give more aid. Those left behind might agitate for reform so they do not lose more loved ones. Ilya Somin contends that "foot voting" against a regime can send it a powerful message about need for improvements.[39] All of these have happened in past instances. For example, exodus from East Germany in the communist era created both internal and external pressures for reform.[40]

As for receiving countries, the press of desperate immigrants might trigger larger foreign aid packages to sending nations, to help stem the flow. In addition, whereas their nationals who welcome immigrants (employers and adopters) generate sizeable remittance flow, being unable to hire or adopt from a particular poor country because it refuses exit is not going to motivate those private parties to send donations to that country; the result will be indifference at best and at worst an impression that the country is so corrupt that aid would be wasted. There is, of course, no basis for ascribing to them a special moral obligation to send donations simply because they once had a thought about possibly hiring or adopting.

But again, even if the empirical premise were plausible, an implicit normative premise is highly problematic—namely, that persons' right to leave a country (or, presumably, political subunit of a country, community, private organization, family, etc.) is properly overridden by the aim of preventing a worsening of the situation of those who remain. A Benthamite who thinks moral rights nonsense anyway might find that acceptable. From the deontological perspective that pervades human rights law and policy, though, it looks like not giving rights their due and not respecting the humanity of the right-holder, instead endorsing instrumental use of some in service to others, holding the former hostage, treating them as mere means.

A somewhat different argument points to the substitutability of people and concludes that allowing some to migrate denies spots to others. For example, David Smolin maintains that open IA policies hurt older and special-needs children in orphanages because they are passed over in favor of healthy infants.[41] Limiting IA to the former or imposing a three-year "holding period" for the latter corrects for this seeming unfairness. The empirical premise here, too, is

[39] *See* Somin, *supra* note 18.

[40] *See* Michael Blake, "The Right to Leave and What Remains," *in* Brock & Blake, *supra* note 16, at 196.

[41] David Smolin, "Smolin's Position," *in* Judith L. Gibbons & Karen Smith Rotabi eds., Intercountry Adoption: Policies, Practices, and Outcomes 242–43 (2012). He also asserts, paradoxically, that intercountry adoption is generally bad for older children, because very disorienting. *Id.*, 238–39, 240.

questionable. The policy might result in some hard-to-place children being adopted who otherwise would not be, but it might instead cause a great number of potential adopters—who perhaps initially doubt their ability to care for special-needs children but would consider adopting such children after meeting them—simply to look to other countries from the outset or give up altogether on the idea of adopting, with a net negative effect on such children.

As for normative underpinnings of the argument, Smolin does not explain why those passed over under an open policy ought to receive priority. Perhaps those with greater need have a stronger claim, but it is unclear that a five-year-old has greater need for adoption than a one-year-old, or that any disabled child has greater need than any nondisabled child. Nor does Smolin defend applying his implicit normative principle only to children; the equality constraint on infringing rights requires Smolin to distinguish in morally relevant ways the situation of unparented children from the situation of women in the same country who wish to form a family relationship with someone in a more affluent country, or anyone who applies for a competitive job in another country. Extending a neediest-first principle to those other contexts would suggest only women who have the poorest domestic marriage prospects or suffer the most in their home country for other reasons should be permitted to emigrate to marry, and only those adults least able to earn a livable wage in their home state should be permitted to leave to take jobs in affluent nations. Others should be held back until they are the neediest among those remaining. Presumably this line of moral reasoning would apply domestically too; the more capable one is of forming relationships and working high-paying jobs, the more one has a moral duty not to take those opportunities, or government would be more justified in stopping you from doing so, enabling the less capable or more needy to do so instead. Should Smolin have forgone his opportunity to be a law professor in favor of someone less capable or more needy?

What political theorists would likely say in these adult contexts is that basic liberties are not properly subject to a neediest-first allocative principle. Material goods, perhaps; when food or medical services are in short supply, it seems fitting to give first to those with greatest need if they can be saved. But all persons should enjoy the same basic liberties, despite existing inequality in opportunities for exercising them, and freedom to change one's residence and nation is a basic liberty. A government might try to use its resources to even out opportunities for exercise, or to mitigate hardship for those unable to exercise them, but it may not simply deny the liberties to some as a means of redressing underlying inequalities. Prohibiting some from speaking cannot be a solution to others' lesser ability to amplify their views.[42] Addressing unequal practical

[42] *See, e.g.*, JOHN RAWLS, JUSTICE AS FAIRNESS: A RESTATEMENT 42–44 (2001) (concluding that all persons should have equal liberties, and that only in the case of political liberties (voting, running for office, influencing office holders) must states attempt to equalize ability to exercise).

ability to exercise formally equal liberties by creating a regime of formally unequal liberties would be perverse.

As in the debt-to-society context, some suggest a compensation scheme for the supposed harm to those left behind, as an alternative to restraints on anyone's basic liberties.[43] Make an employer contribute to a jobs program in the employee's home state. Make Western men pay into a fund for unmarried women left behind, as a condition for securing an exit permit for a fiancé.[44] Make an adopter donate a substantial sum to the orphanage (as is already common).

Charging a price to persons who give others opportunity to migrate (foreign employers, husbands, and adoptive parents) is in tension with the complaint coming from many of the same people that the foreign bride phenomenon and IA constitute commodification of persons and even human "trafficking." Putting aside self-contradiction, this compensation idea is inherently problematic. Empirically, a tax prices out or discourages some potential transactors. At the margin, some people who could otherwise have left bad life circumstances for much better ones are denied that opportunity to exercise the right to leave. Proponents of the idea implicitly assume that Westerners wishing to marry or adopt abroad have unlimited money and that demand is inelastic, but the current high cost of both already deters many people.[45] So the tax would effectively deny some their basic liberties in order to benefit others, just as the outright denial of liberty to some does. Or it could be viewed as imposing on some a prohibitive added cost of exercising their human right to leave; in theory, they could pay the price themselves, so a potential husband or adoptive parent is not discouraged, but they lack the means to do so.

Normatively, it looks, from the perspective of those who lose opportunities, like foisting the cost of helping the very worst off onto the next-worst off, which cannot possibly be justifiable. Among all ways to improve the situation of hard-to-place persons suffering lack of family life, states would be choosing the least fair way, worsening the position of those least able to endure a worse situation. From the perspective of the foreign parties, it looks like no good deed goes unpunished. Even if one assumes some negative impact in the aggregate on those

[43] *E.g.*, Shani King, *Challenging Monohumanism: An Argument for Changing the Way We Think About Intercountry Adoption*, 30 MICH. J. INT'L L. 413, 464–65 (2009) (noting some countries require donations by adopters to orphanages and suggesting this should help assuage critics of international adoption); John Triseliotis, "Inter-country Adoption: In Whose Best Interest?," *in* MICHAEL HUMPHREY & HEATHER HUMPHREY EDS., INTER-COUNTRY ADOPTION: PRACTICAL EXPERIENCES 132 (1993).

[44] *Cf.* Gulnoza Saidazimova, "Turkmenistan: Marriage Gets Cheaper as Turkmenbashi Drops $50,000 Dollar Foreigners' Fee," RADIO FREE EUROPE, Jan. 10, 2005.

[45] *See* Wechsler, *supra* note 29, at 30 (explaining that costs for international adoption are prohibitively high for many).

left behind, an individual employer's or husband's or adopter's negative impact would be minuscule, so any levy above that is gratuitous penalty or arbitrary imposition of forced charity on people solely because they are susceptible to the coercion. To critics of IA, the foreign-bride industry, and "drain," it might seem everyone who adopts, marries, or hires someone from a poor country is a neocolonial exploiter, so there's nothing problematic about punishing them. But such ideology-driven insults should not influence human rights law, let alone political theory. The critics could themselves be charged with exploiting the most vulnerable people in the developing world, using them to advance a political view and agenda, by promoting policies that consign helpless children to a life in institutions, indifferent to the impact their armchair banner-waving has on real people.

What a state might do instead is to use its general revenues—from a progressive income tax or foreign/international aid—to incentivize third parties abroad or domestically who create opportunities for exercise of basic liberties, making it more attractive for them to give the opportunity to those otherwise unlikely to be selected. For example, it might require foreign-bride companies to waive fees for communicating with older or disabled or less educated women, waive any fees it charges for providing exit documents for such women, and even reimburse men for the travel and visa costs they incur in pursuing a relationship with such women. The state might also pay for expenses such women incur in presenting themselves favorably to potential husbands—clothes, photography, language lessons, and so forth. Something like this occurs in the domestic adoption context; some states waive fees and provide greater adoption subsidies and services for those who adopt hard-to-place children, and they go to extra efforts to communicate the availability of those children to potential adopters. The subsidies alter the relative "price" of those women or children who are inherently "easier to place," adding an opportunity cost for potential husbands and adoptive parents, but in and of themselves are not a tax, let alone a denial of the basic liberty. It might be difficult politically, of course, to adopt policies aimed at getting more of one's nationals—especially women—to leave.

3.3.3.2 Rights of individuals left behind

A right of others that a nation might invoke to deny emigration to someone is an imputed right of family members to maintain a relationship and have a say in the would-be emigrant's life. Presumably that nation would have to identify family members of a particular émigré who oppose the departure, or at least family members who *might* exist and *might* object. This basis would not serve, therefore, in cases where the pertinent family members knowingly consent to a person's leaving, as is usually the case with spouses, children who accompany parents, and older children who travel on their own to another country. Further, it would be difficult to apply when family members holding equal rights under local law disagree. For example, if in a society a father and a husband have equal rights over a woman, they might disagree about whether she should move to another country to escape oppressive conditions.

More common is a custody dispute between parents when one wishes to relocate with a child and the other objects. In such cases, one family member's imputed control rights would seem to cancel out the other's rights. It is common for a court or other state agency to say it is protecting a parent's relationship right by blocking relocation, but in doing so the agency fails to see how it is impinging upon the relationship of the other parent, the one who does emigrate and will thereafter have less or no contact. (And it is no answer to say the one emigrating effectively waives his or her right, because the other could also be seen as waiving her or his right by refusing to emigrate also if the child leaves.) Some countries resolve such conflicts with gendered priorities. I will not undertake analysis of the justifiability of such. Countries with gender-equality norms default in case of conflict to the child's best interests, which might be viewed as ascribing to the child a right to proxy decision-making of best location for him or her all things considered.

The context in which this "rights of others" justification might make sense, if it ever can, is where all family members who exist or might exist and who have a legal right to contact or control are opposed to a person's departure or at least have not consented. A husband might alone have rights to possess and control his wife under local law and refuse his permission for the wife to relocate, and the nation might block her exit for that reason. A single parent might have left his child at an orphanage two years ago, with no intention of taking custody again, yet be unwilling to consent to an adoption, or be unlocatable, yet local law might view an IA as a violation of his rights.

It is not enough, though, in international law or normative theory, that domestic law gives some persons other-regarding rights of this sort. The legal rights must be morally defensible ones, perhaps even grounded in moral rights, and must be consistent with others' human rights and with sound moral principles. The notion that anyone has an *entitlement* to possess and control the life of *any* other human being is morally repugnant and inconsistent with human rights principles set forth in international treaties—specifically, to equal treatment and respect for inherent dignity. To ascribe to husbands rights over their wives violates both principles, and so too does ascription to guardians of *rights* to retain and control their incompetent adult wards or to parents rights over children.[46] This is quite different from saying caretakers for non-autonomous

[46] *See* James G. Dwyer, *Parents' Religion and Children's Welfare: Debunking the Doctrine of Parents' Rights*, 82 CAL. L. REV. 1371, 1405–23 (1994).

persons should have certain legal decision-making authority in regard to those persons lives *because that is best for them*, and so is a way for the state to discharge duties of care and protection that it owes *to the non-autonomous persons.* Treating any persons as objects of others' entitlements, such that third parties owe duties to the latter to accord them power over the former, is an insult to the former's humanity, regardless of whether they are autonomous. It was as true of African children whom White Americans enslaved as of enslaved African adults. Two individuals might be said to share a right to maintain a relationship with each other when both choose that or, if one person is non-autonomous, when the autonomous person wants it and it is in the non-autonomous person's best interests as determined by an appropriate proxy. But there can be no legitimate entitlement when one is trying to escape the relationship, as in dissolution of an intimate partnership, or in the case of non-autonomous persons when it is in their best interests to exit a legal relationship with one guardian and form a new one.[47]

Accordingly, there is no moral purchase to a claim that parents who have relinquished custody or are incapable of caring for a child are entitled to keep the child nearby, regardless of whether that is in the child's best interests, or are entitled to block the child's relocation to join a functional family. Yet the migration context in which commentators most often invoke such family rights is IA. Most unparented children in developing countries have one or two living parents. IA critics place tremendous weight on this and assume, without evidence, that any living parent would prefer a child not leave the country or be adopted, and assume, without defense, that the parent is entitled to this.[48] From this they conclude that children should remain in destructive institutional care indefinitely, in case a parent might ever want to reclaim the child, however unlikely that is.[49] This presumably would preclude domestic adoption as well as international adoption. This line of thought is as repugnant as reasoning that a state is justified in blocking a woman from emigrating against the wishes of a father or husband who has abandoned her, because he might want her back. Significantly, it is not followed regarding children in the U.S. domestic context; if parents bring a child to a social services office and ask to be relieved of responsibility, then disappear, the agency legally can and should start the process of terminating the parent-child relationship then and there, so that the child can join a new family. It is not clear why the normative situation of parents in developing countries should be any different.

[47] *See* James G. Dwyer, The Relationship Rights of Children (2006).

[48] *Cf.* Philip Holmes, "Don't Suspend Inter-Country Adoption," Republica, Feb. 24, 2010 (longtime child-welfare worker in Nepal observing that nearly all children in Nepalese orphanages "were driven out of their homes by stepparents").

[49] *Cf.* Compton, *supra* note 29, at 12–14 (discussing rate of return to parents in certain countries).

A related objection to IA is that some children's parents who do consent to adoption are defrauded (false promises of continued contact) or financially induced to do so.[50] The competing rights would then be ones against deception and coercion. This is the leading justification today for shutting down IA programs. For how many children these practices are a but-for cause of their placement for IA is a subject of perennial debate.[51]

The vulnerability to fraud and financial inducement, though, points to an additional problem with the children's pre-adoption situation—that is, parents' radical disempowerment, which must more generally diminish their ability to care for all their children. That is tragic, but it is the reality for a great number of children. Many parents in such conditions sell their older children into marriage or slavery,[52] so that is a likely future fate for a young child prevented today from joining another family by adoption. A parent might, in fact, reclaim a child from an orphanage just for that purpose, as an asset to be sold. Also likely for such children is one day becoming themselves parents so destitute that they are forced to sell their children, and so on generation after generation. Some parents might rationally and lovingly conclude that they best serve their child by allowing him or her to leave when young to join a family in another country, rather than holding on to the child only to give them a tragic fate, and we ordinarily suppose parents know best what is in their child's interests. Parents and older children in those countries might wonder how it is that they are better off as a result of their "protectors" imposing cumbersome procedures designed to ensure parents receive no money in the process of separating from their youngest children, or are not able to have someone else care for a child except by placing the child in an institution.[53] Children who are adopted internationally after their birth parents

[50] *See* Claire Fenton-Glynn, Children's Rights in Intercountry Adoption: A European Perspective 87–88 (2014); Dwyer, *supra* note 9 (quoting other sources).

[51] *See, e.g.*, Fenton-Glynn, *supra* note 50, at 90–91 (contending it is prevalent); Elizabeth Bartholet, *International Adoption: Thoughts on the Human Rights Issues*, 13 Buff. Hum. Rts. L. Rev. 151, 185–91 (2007) (arguing it is rare and overdramatized); Jini L. Roby & Stacey A Shaw, *The African Orphan Crisis and International Adoption*, 51 Soc. Work 199, 200 (2006) (reporting no documented cases of "adoption trafficking" into the United States from Africa); Lynn D. Wardle, *The Hague Convention on Intercountry Adoption and American Implementing Law: Implications for International Adoptions by Gay and Lesbian Couples or Partners*, 18 Ind. Int'l & Comp. L. Rev. 113, 144 (2008) (finding "abuses existing in a small-but-sensational minority of international adoptions").

[52] *See* Siddharth Kara, Sex Trafficking: Inside the Business of Modern Slavery 8, 15 (2009).

[53] *Cf.* David M. Smolin, *Intercountry Adoption and Poverty: A Human Rights Analysis*, 36 Cap. U. L. Rev. 413, 434 (2007) ("Should hungry or malnourished birth parents, and their remaining children, be turned away with nothing, solely to protect the purity of their consents?"). Smolin contends that when any birth parents in the poorest countries propose to relinquish a child for adoption, they should be offered money sufficient to enable them to retain their children, to ensure poverty is not the only reason they give up a child. He suggests this cost be passed on to adoption applicants and speculates it might amount to an additional $3,000 per adoption. *Id.* The proposal has theoretical appeal, but as explained, there are normative and practical problems with imposing a tax on adopters. Foreign governments would be even less inclined to pay for this. And it would incentivize parents to offer their children for adoption even when not otherwise inclined to do so.

were paid or falsely promised later reunification might wonder how they would have been better off if they had continued living with their birth parents. The fraud is more clearly a harm to the parents than is financial inducement, but it, too, is difficult to make a basis for a child-centered rationale for shutting down IA programs.

To be clear: I am not endorsing baby buying or child stealing. And of course, everyone wishes no families were in such desperate circumstances. But they exist, they will continue to exist, and history shows that forcing children to remain in them does not leverage greater international or domestic efforts to eliminate them. It cannot suffice to tell a child who is dying of starvation along with her AIDS-infected parents, and who has been raped several times while walking the five-mile road to the water spigot, that the state did not permit her parents to place her for international adoption immediately after her birth because it was worried about their vulnerability to fraud or their capacity for uncoerced decision-making and hoping rich countries would feel sorry for her and send billions of dollars, euros, or pounds in aid.

The most effective and appropriate way to address concerns about fraud and financial inducement, as well as the even less common phenomenon of kidnapping children in order to sell them to an orphanage or adoption agency, is obvious and has been noted by others: Liberalize adoption from orphanages in all nations so that there will be so many children available there is no profit for unscrupulous people or agencies in scouring the countryside looking for parents who can be manipulated. The "child buying" reason for foreclosing foreign adoption suffers from the usual problem with prohibiting highly desired transactions for fear of harmful side effects—namely, that by shrinking supply it drives up the price where the transactions remain legal, incentivizing illicit means of facilitating transactions, and gives rise to an illegal market where they are prohibited. The natural oversupply of children whose parents are dead or truly unable to provide a minimally decent life—estimated to be in the tens of millions worldwide—would, if not artificially limited, eliminate any financial incentive to approach parents who are living and capable of raising their children, or to risk criminal prosecution for kidnapping.[54] Within a global framework, UNICEF's successful pressuring of many nations to curtail international adoption *is itself the cause of the profit-driven problems* with IA. It has caused millions of "true orphans" (both parents deceased) in the world, warehoused in institutions, to be unavailable for adoption. It has thus made fraud, coercion,

[54] *See* Richard Carlson, *A Child's Right to a Family versus a State's Discretion to Institutionalize the Child*, 47 Geo. J. Int'l L. 937, 938, 994 (2016).

baby buying, and kidnapping *more common* in nations that remain open to IA, because it makes such practices more lucrative.

Given the extraordinarily high success rate for IA,[55] it appears the real concern relating to money is not child well-being but the hypothetical long-term happiness of biological parents. Lamentations about financial inducement of parents are entirely parent-focused.[56] Yet that supposition about parental suffering has not been documented, overlooks the suffering parents might experience when their children languish in orphanages or starve before their eyes, and in and of itself cannot justify denying a right to children. Desperate parents themselves might be much better off in the long run by placing their child for adoption, knowing that their child will not endure the same fate they have, and not having to face later the more tragic choice whether to sell them into labor or sexual exploitation. Some such parents fully recognize that and want their children adopted abroad.[57] Critics of IA have not explained why such parents are wrong and should be prevented, nor documented that children are better off when the option is foreclosed.[58] And if parents' decision is rational, it is unclear what is wrong if in the process parents also receive money that might allow them to feed their other children or themselves.

Yes, it is horrible for us in the West to think that any parents and children could be better off by separating, perhaps permanently, or that a young woman could be better off leaving her family, friends, favorite places, and culture to marry a man she hardly knows and go live with him in a place where she does not know anyone else at all. But there are many places in the world where horrible is the human condition, and shutting down IA or international marriage is not going to change that. Moreover, our horror emanates from our own Western perspective, experience, values, and ideas of normalcy, which might not be the same as those of people in other cultures. We imagine ourselves in their position, but we

[55] *See generally* COMPTON, *supra* note 29; MONTGOMERY & POWELL, *supra* note 29, at 9, 24 (physical and cognitive development improves dramatically relative to siblings and other peers remaining in the home country); Wechsler, *supra* note 29, at 4 (describing improvement in quality of life); Martin T. Stein et al., *International Adoption: A 4-Year-Old Child with Unusual Behaviors Adopted at 6 Months of Age*, 114 PEDIATRICS 1425, 1431 (2004) ("For the vast majority of children who are adopted today, the prognosis is excellent. In cases in which the developmental-behavioral outcome is problematic, diagnostic consideration should be given to factors that are not related to the adoption history.").

[56] *See, e.g.*, Perry, *supra* note 34, at 342–43 (critiquing IA from feminist legal theory perspective focused on unfairness to mothers); FENTON-GLYNN, *supra* note 50, at 87–92, 102.

[57] *See* MONTGOMERY & POWELL, *supra* note 29, at 7.

[58] *See, e.g.*, FENTON-GLYNN, *supra* note 50, at 44–45. Fenton-Glynn also contends IA is problematic because it causes fewer children to be adopted from sending countries' domestic foster care system. *Id.*, 47. But she (a) provides no evidence of that effect, which is unlikely, and (b) offers no explanation for why, if true, it is problematic.

should not assume we really understand their position. As with cultural experience, connection to biological relatives is something on which people in some parts of the world do not place the same importance we do.[59] The experience we impute to them might not match their reality.

A final concern about IA I will address here, though it is not clear whether it is about harm to parents or to children or simply about some people's disgust at the role money plays in human affairs, is "profiteering."[60] UNICEF and the CRC have placed great emphasis on eliminating or minimizing profits for adoption agencies and intermediaries. It is quite unclear, though, whom any profiting from IA harms, other than adoptive parents who pay the fees and children who remain unparented because the high cost of adoption deters other would-be adopters. And as with payments to parents, an obvious and less restrictive means of reducing profit is opening IA and increasing exponentially the number of children allowed to join families abroad by adoption, rather than shutting down IA programs wherever "excessive profit" is perceived.

Apart from the illogic of this objection, it would not stand up upon being generalized to cover formation across national borders of family bonds more generally. The proliferation of international dating websites suggests there is much money to be made in the aggregate by charging fees to men in wealthy nations to meet online and communicate with women in poorer nations (just as companies like Match make money by facilitating domestic dating). Yet no country has enacted legislation to ban marriage of its citizens to foreigners or to deny the right to emigrate for marriage purposes, on the ground that these marriage agencies are driven by profit motives. Or on the ground that the women creating profiles on international marriage websites are motivated by their poor economic circumstances in their country of origin rather than simply by a desire for adventure or special attraction to Western men. International employment agencies also profit from bringing people together. And a lot of people make a lot of money helping people become parents by producing their own biological offspring, yet no one suggests that needs to stop.

[59] *See* MONTGOMERY & POWELL, *supra* note 29, at 125 ("selling babies to other families has a long history among Chinese peasants"); 128 ("it is widely believed that baby selling was common not only in China and Guatemala, but in Cambodia, Vietnam, Romania, and Ethiopia as well"); COMPTON, *supra* note 29, at 87–88 ("In some cultures, adoption or fostering is even the norm. . . . In this cultural setting, foster parents are considered preferable to biological parents. After weaning, children move to the home of the 'social parent' (foster parent), who then takes responsibility for rearing and educating the child.").

[60] *See, e.g.*, FENTON-GLYNN, *supra* note 50, at 95–98; Ann Laquer Estin, *Families Across Border: The Hague Children's Convention and the Case for International Family Law in the United States*, FLA. L. REV. 62, 47, 88 (2010) ("it is essential to build protections against profiteering").

3.3.4 Paternalistic protection of the would-be emigree

Human rights treaties generally do not contemplate paternalistic justifications for infringing a person's rights, perhaps reflecting a supposition of autonomy in right holders despite the avowed universal extension of the rights. The exceptions to the ICCPR right to leave, in particular, do not explicitly include protecting the right-holder's own welfare. The language closest to authorizing it would be "public health."

Yet even as to autonomous adults one can imagine situations where a state would not be faulted for restricting persons' freedom to relocate for the purpose of protecting them. Zoning laws uncontroversially prevent people from setting up a home too close to polluting factories, and a country that blocked emigration by particular routes (e.g., rafts in a turbulent sea) out of genuine concern for people's safety would not be condemned for doing that (though they might be condemned for making local conditions so horrible that people are that desperate to leave). Indeed, given ICESCR parties' obligation affirmatively to *promote* persons' well-being in numerous ways, one might suppose individuals sometimes have a moral right to such state intervention, even against their expressed wishes. And that is presumably truer of non-autonomous persons. A child might assent to relocation alone or with some adult (abusive parent, trafficker) in a particular instance even though it is quite plainly bad for them to do so, and a home state might then have a moral obligation as well as permission to restrain the child if aware of the danger. It is worthwhile to consider, then, what paternalistic concerns justify infringing which persons' right to leave.

3.3.4.1 Protecting a person from violation of other human rights

A home state certainly is justified in trying to protect any nationals against violations of their rights by other private parties or other states. Preventing their relocation might sometimes serve that purpose. When autonomous persons do not wish to leave but are forced by others, the state would not infringe the person's migration right by blocking their exit; rather, it would be enforcing their right *not* to leave. Such cases rarely present themselves to border officials, however. More commonly, a person expresses a desire to leave with other persons even though the state suspects the others of harboring intent to harm, as with human traffickers, because she has been deceived about the others' intent or feels obligated to serve her family by submitting to exploitation.[61] Most states are legally committed to supporting efforts to end the modern slave trade.

[61] Kara, *supra* note 52, at 8–9 (discussing Ukraine), 52 (Nepal), 90–91 (Nigeria), 155–59 (Thailand).

"Trafficking" has a specific meaning in international law. It is:

> [T]he recruitment, transportation, transfer, harbouring or receipt of persons, by means of the threat or use of force or other forms of coercion, of abduction, of fraud, of deception, of the abuse of power or of a position of vulnerability or of the giving or receiving of payments or benefits to achieve the consent of a person having control over another person, for the purpose of exploitation.[62]

The last phrase is critical; the objective of a person transporting someone else across national boundaries must be to subject the person to exploitation for there to be trafficking. The treaty to combat trafficking defines "exploitation" thus:

> Trafficking shall include, at a minimum, the exploitation of the prostitution of others or other forms of sexual exploitation, forced labour or services, slavery or practices similar to slavery, servitude or the removal of organs.[63]

The basic idea is clear: exploitation means treating people instrumentally and benefiting from infliction of harm upon them, typically enslavement. Accordingly, the U.S. State Department has issued a bulletin clarifying that international adoption is not trafficking even when improper conduct plays a role in making the child available for adoption.[64] Likewise, international marriage is not trafficking if undertaken for the normal purpose of voluntary intimate association, even if it involves "the recruitment, transportation, transfer, . . . or receipt of persons, by means . . . of the giving . . . of payments or benefits to achieve the consent of a person having control over another person," as might be true with women from cultures where a bride price is expected. Misusing "trafficking" to denigrate practices not fitting the definition is not innocent. People active in international efforts to eliminate slavery lament the widespread overuse of the term because it dilutes the seriousness of and distracts attention from the truly horrible, ill-intentioned conduct that the treaty targets.[65] Yet many who are

[62] Protocol to Prevent, Suppress and Punish Trafficking in Persons, Especially Women and Children, G.A. Res. 55/25, art. 3(a), U.N. Doc. A/RES/55/25 (Nov. 15, 2000).

[63] *Id.*

[64] *See* U.S. Dep't of State, "Human Trafficking Defined," https://www.state.gov/reports/2023-trafficking-in-persons-report/; U.S. Citizenship and Immigration Services, Training Module, "Detecting Possible Victims of Trafficking," at 23–24, https://www.uscis.gov/sites/default/files/document/foia/Trafficking_LP_RAIO.pdf. *See also* David Smolin, *Intercountry Adoption as Child Trafficking*, 39 Valparaiso U. L. Rev. 281 (2004). Some take the view that sale of children preceding an adoption constitutes trafficking, but again there must be harm to children in the transaction, and harm of a particular kind, for it to constitute trafficking. Likewise, if someone kidnaps a child then demands ransom, we would not say trafficking occurs when the parents pay to recover the child. An exchange of child and money does not necessarily fall within the concept of trafficking.

[65] *See, e.g.*, Kara, *supra* note 52, at 38 ("Confusion over what trafficking is results in blunted purpose, diffracted focus, and the exclusion of important components of trafficking-related crimes.").

offended by the existence of international marriage websites or by intercountry adoption of children toss out the word "trafficking" for rhetorical effect.[66] They thereby undermine the campaign to stop real trafficking of women and children.

Real traffickers, unsurprisingly, do not try to become the legal spouse or parent of their victims, which would involve getting a government agency to approve and memorialize the relationship and incurring legal obligations to the victim, and they generally do not want infants. Richard Carlson notes regarding international adoption that it is "safer in some respects than intra-state adoption because it involves an extra layer of safeguards," being "subject to separate oversight by two states, not one."[67] To be sure, *false and unfulfilled* promises of marriage *are* used to lure women into prostitution, and some husbands sell their child brides into sex slavery if dissatisfied with them as wives, but these things generally occur domestically and are not connected to the international marriage sites Western men use.[68] Much recruiting is done also with false offers of employment.[69] Further, a shocking amount of trafficking begins with open and explicit transacting with parents, those so poor that they knowingly sell their older children into brutal captivity.[70] Traffickers operating internationally try to manipulate single women and teens into accompanying them willingly, with promises of good work and good pay, or threats, and failing that forcibly smuggle them by clandestine means across national boundaries. As for adoption of children, books about trafficking, tellingly, do not even mention it.[71]

Because trafficking in the true sense entails undermining the autonomy of adult and adolescent victims, one might say the victims' right to emigrate is at its weakest; the right is not much serving their interest in exercising and receiving respect for their autonomy, and it is not serving other interests they have. For these reasons, theorists generally agree there is no moral right to consent to one's enslavement.[72] Alternatively, we might say the state has a sufficiently compelling reason for infringing the right to leave and detaining at the border anyone who border officials sincerely believe to be a trafficking victim. From either perspective, the case for blocking departure arguably is stronger with minors, because of their less well-developed autonomy, greater vulnerability, and longer expected future life.

[66] *See e.g.*, Smolin, *supra* note 53.

[67] Carlson, *supra* note 54, at 981.

[68] *See, e.g.*, Kara, *supra* note 52, at 7, 9, 49, 51, 71.

[69] *Id.*, 7–8, 181.

[70] *Id.*, 63 (discussing India), 70–71 (Nepal), 148–49 (Albania), 160 (Thailand), 168–69 (Vietnam), 169 (Cambodia).

[71] *See, e.g.*, <UBT>Jonathan Todres & Angela Diaz, Preventing Child Trafficking: A Public Health Approach (2019); Kara, *supra* note 52. *See also id.*, at 6 ("Acquisition of sex slaves primarily occurs in one of five ways: deceit, sale by family, abduction, seduction or romance, or recruitment by former slaves.").

[72] *See* David Archard, *Freedom Not to Be Free: The Case of the Slavery Contract in J.S. Mill's On Liberty*, Phil. Q. 40, 453–65 (1990).

What if a person is not being trafficked when leaving the home state but risks falling prey to traffickers after leaving? This is a real danger for women and minors migrating alone; a substantial percentage from Central America are grabbed or seduced by traffickers along the route north—to such an extent, many parents have daughters receive long-term contraceptive injections before beginning the journey.[73] Officials in their home states are aware of this. Would they be justified in stopping at the border people at risk of predation after leaving?

The known probability seems to matter. If home state officials perceive a 100 percent chance a woman or girl will be seized immediately after crossing the border, it could reasonably view that as equivalent to arriving at the border in the control of traffickers. At the other extreme, if there is less than a 1 percent chance, that seems insufficient to justify blocking exit; if *any* chance of ending up in slavery suffices, then why not any chance of being injured in a car accident or drowning during a sea crossing or incurring any other harm? That would eviscerate the right to leave. Conditions in the home state for a person also seem to matter. If the risk at home of getting shot, starving, incurring female genital mutilation, or being sold into marriage while still a child is very high, it would be paradoxical to refuse exit based on less severe or lower-probability harms abroad. Also part of the equation is gain in quality of life if the intended destination is reached, and for those currently in the worst circumstances, that is substantial.

For an autonomous adult, the home state should inform of risks but defer to the émigré's assessment of whether they are worth taking, unless their rationality or autonomy appears greatly compromised. If someone is already in the control of traffickers or highly likely to become so after crossing the border, their expressed wish nevertheless to leave would seem to reflect such a malfunctioning of the autonomous will. But a small likelihood that a trafficker might use an international marriage website to identify and arrange meetings with potential victims does not make it patently irrational for a woman to create a profile on such sites and arrange initial meetings with men who contact her, so would not justify a nation's closing that particular emigration path, as the Philippines once tried to do.[74] For a fourteen-year-old, something closer to a substituted judgment or best-interest assessment might be fitting, an objective balancing of risks and benefits associated with leaving or remaining, in light of their magnitude. If the youth faces a high likelihood of being killed in the home state, it cannot

[73] *See* Marjorie S. Zatz & Nancy Rodriquez, Dreams and Nightmares: Immigration Policy, Youth, and Families 122–24 (2015).

[74] *Cf.* Roxanne Sims, *A Comparison of Laws in the Philippines, the U.S.A., Taiwan, and Belarus to Regulate the Mail-Order Bride Industry*, 42 Akron L. Rev. 607, 616–17 (2009) ("The Philippines legislature intended for Republic Act No. 6955 to protect Filipino women from being sexually and economically exploited by international marriage brokers."). The law might well have been a self-interested reaction by male legislators to the exodus of women from the country. It proved ineffective. *See id.*, 616–18.

suffice to justify infringing his right to leave that there is, say, a 5 percent chance of being seized or of incurring other severe harms along the journey. In contrast, a home state might stop a youth from undertaking a perilous journey across the Mediterranean Sea in a raft or through Mexico atop a train if he is not escaping horrors but just dreaming of riches or hurting from rejection by a teenage crush.

A final point about IA in connection with trafficking: the more a country creates obstacles to adoption of unparented children or of children in the care of parents who are abjectly incapable of providing adequate care, the more likely children are to end up in the slave trade. Older children who live on the streets after parents abandon them or after many years in an orphanage are prime targets for traffickers. A father who concludes he is unable to care for his ten-year-old child after the mother dies and who finds that no family or community member is available to foster the child might prefer to place the child for adoption into a good family, even if that means the child will move to another country. However, if his country makes that impossible through licensed and regulated agencies or intermediaries, he might hand the child over to anyone who approaches with a stack of currency and empty promises. Most child trafficking cases originate with such transactions.[75] Guatemala, which shut down its international adoption program in 2008 because of some reports of illicit payments and defrauding of parents in connection with true adoptions (i.e., not trafficking), is now a major site of human trafficking of many sorts.[76]

3.3.4.2 Mistreatment in receiving countries

In any nation, immigrants can be especially vulnerable to abuse in public or at home, perpetrated by government or private actors. They are typically in a precarious financial situation, unfamiliar with some dangers and how to avoid them, afraid to report any harms they incur for fear of being deported. Most are moving from a place where they were in the racial majority to one in which they will be in a racial minority, and developed countries generally have a chronic problem of mistreatment, sometimes brutal, of people of minority race. Religious bigotry can also give rise to overt hostility.

In some places or contexts, youth might be more vulnerable than adults, because less able to protect themselves. In others, youth are likely to receive special solicitude and protection from public officials and private parties. Unauthorized immigrant women are at substantial risk of domestic violence at home and sexual

[75] *See* Counter Trafficking Data Collaborative, "Recruiter Relationship Adults and Children," https://www.ctdatacollaborative.org/dataset/age-data-story/resource/160b51ae-ac39-40ef-a490-e578e771090f (last visited Sept. 21, 2024), (showing trafficking originates with a transaction between recruiters and parents in 45% of cases and between recruiters and spouses of the child (who typically will have purchased the child from parents) in 13% of cases).

[76] *See* U.S. Dept. of State, "2024 Trafficking in Persons Report: Guatemala," https://www.state.gov/reports/2024-trafficking-in-persons-report/guatemala/ (last visited Sept. 28, 2024).

harassment and coercion at a job. The problems appear not sufficiently severe and prevalent, though, for any sending nation to deny exit permits to any group or to prohibit operation of agencies that facilitate international relocation, especially given that the home state cannot predict where its nationals will end up and given the dangers likely to exist in the home state. The prevailing response to concern about the vulnerability of foreign brides entering Western nations has not been to shut down intercountry marriage agencies or to deny exit permits to women but simply to mandate background checks of the Western men and disclosure to the women of their fiancée's marital and criminal history.[77]

Ironically, the one example of sending nations infringing the right to leave on a pretext of guarding against abuse in a receiving state pertains to the emigration route that appears safest—international adoption. A child who emigrates via IA is immediately under the protective care of natives and citizens in the destination country, people who have demonstrated their devotion to the welfare of the new immigrant by making great sacrifices to navigate an arduous process and pay substantial fees, and who likely live in a safe neighborhood with good childrearing resources. Rates of maltreatment in adoptive homes in the United States are minuscule, much lower than the rate for children raised here in biological families, whereas the rate of maltreatment and child mortality in institutional care in poor countries' is quite high.[78] Rates of maltreatment and return-to-agency by adoptive parents are also far higher with domestic adoptions in sending states, so this consideration clearly cuts against the CDP.[79] And for the vast majority of children who, once placed in an institution, remain institutionalized until old enough to choose to leave on their own, there is the additional substantial developmental harm that comes from lack of loving, nurturing parents.

Thus, a survey would likely reveal that all or nearly all people would have the intuition that, if they were to be born again tomorrow reincarnated as a child in a desperately poor country whose parents are deceased or unable to care for them,

[77] *See, e.g.*, International Marriage Broker Regulation Act of 2005, 8 U.S.C. § 1375a (2012).

[78] *See* Compton, *supra* note 29, ch. 6; Christopher Balding et al., *Who Wants to Adopt and Who Wants to Be Adopted: A Sample of American Families and Sub-Saharan African Orphans*, 30 Health Pol'y & Plan. 1320 (2015) (finding maltreatment rate in IA homes half that of the general population and high rate of maltreatment and child mortality among orphans who remain in sub-Saharan Africa); Kathleen Ja Sook Bergquist, *International Asian Adoption: In the Best Interests of the Child?*, 10 Tex. Wesleyan L. Rev. 343, 348 (2004) ("Early adoption research documented the successful adaptation of minority children into their white middle class families, and more recent studies have indicated that these children do well in school, attach to their adoptive families, and have relatively few psychosocial or behavioral problems in comparison to their white peers."); Signe Howell, The Kinning of Foreigners: Transnational Adoption in a Global Perspective 103–07 (2006) (showing the vast majority of adopted children develop well); Triseliotis, *supra* note 43, at 131. *See also* Christopher Balding, *International Child Adoption Law and Empirical Analysis*, Whittier J. Child. & Fam. Adv. 13, 51 (2014) (showing pronounced health and development risks for orphaned children not adopted).

[79] Compton, *supra* note 29, at 104–05.

they would want immediately to join a family in an advanced nation rather than remain in any institution or mercenary foster placement in their home state, and rather than joining a new family in some other part of their native country. If readers try that thought experiment (inspired by John Rawls' "veil of ignorance" heuristic), imagining themselves being born again and in such a situation, they might deem that choice a "no-brainer." To infringe unparented children's right to leave with lesser justification than there is with any other group of people in impoverished countries, considering both current circumstances and prospects in a new country, is both independently unsupportable and a violation of the right to equal treatment.

An objection to IA that is difficult to categorize, but might translate into a mistreatment concern, obliquely impugns adopters' motives. The typical allegation is that IA has been transformed from a practice done for charitable reasons, in reaction to the publicized plight of children orphaned by wars, to a practice serving the desires of adults in affluent nations who want to have children but are unable to procreate or adopt infants domestically.[80] "Supplying a child for the parents rather than supplying parents for the child" is the common refrain. This simple story, if it reflects any real evolution in IA, is hardly a complete account of adopters' motivations. It omits, for example, mention of the thousands who by choice adopt special-needs children and the thousands who adopt even though they already have biological offspring and could produce more if they wished.[81] In reality, the allegation seems a reaction to behavior of for-profit adoption agencies rather than to anything adoptive parents have done,[82] and the denigration of the parents by people who likely have done nothing so selfless in their lives is condemnable.

The normative-analytical problem with this complaint, however, is the unexamined, implicit, and bizarre premise that it is worse for people to adopt children when they truly desire a relationship with the children rather than solely because they feel sorry for the children. That would impugn every couple who

[80] *See, e.g.*, Smolin, *supra* note 41, at 242–43; Bergquist, *supra* note 78, at 350 (alleging "a shift from a child-centered to parent-centered focus in adoption"); Triseliotis, *supra* note 43, at 119–20, 131–32; Eur. Parl., Recommendation 1443: International Adoption: Respecting Children's Rights PP 1–3 (2000), 1–3 ("The purpose of international adoption must be to provide children with a mother and a father in a way that respects their rights, not to enable foreign parents to satisfy their wish for a child . . . The Assembly therefore fiercely opposes the current transformation of international adoption into nothing short of a market regulated by the capitalist laws of supply and demand, and characterized by a one-way flow of children from poor states or states in transition to developed countries").

[81] *See* Herszenhorn & Eckholm, *supra* note 31; Wardle, *supra* note 51, at 115 ("[F]ew international transactions . . . compare with the selfless, charitable, and compassionate act of responsible adults taking stranger children from foreign countries and cultures into their homes, as members of their own families, and assuming the obligation to feed, clothe, house, teach, love, nurture and protect the children").

[82] *See* Carlson, *supra* note 54, at 992–93.

intentionally procreates. Today, advocates for children have greatest concern in IA with people who adopt primarily out of a sense of religious mission. No one has argued explicitly that the supposedly self-serving desire to provide loving care to unparented children is a good and sufficient reason to stop IA, but the purpose of alleging it is clearly to add to other supposed reasons for viewing international adoption in a negative light.

Yet if we place international adoption into the larger context of emigration for purpose of family formation, and we ask what justifications might suffice for infringing anyone's right to leave their country of origin for that purpose, it immediately becomes apparent how ironic is this charge. No doubt, if one surveyed women who have come to the United States for marriage to American men and asked, "Would you rather that your husband married you because he really wanted a wife and fell in love with you, or instead because he felt sorry for you or believed he had a religious duty to help poor people?," the uniform answer would be the former. A similar survey of adoptees would undoubtedly produce a like result—that is, they would rather have been adopted because their parents really wanted to have a parent-child relationship rather than because their parents pitied them or felt obligated. The former motivation is more likely to coincide with parents' having a very positive view of the child, as a blessing rather than burden, and any child should prefer that. A reciprocal desire or need seems a healthy and normal basis for a family relationship. A final point to consider is that such reciprocity is lacking in the case of couples choosing to create a baby for themselves to raise; that seems to be all about satisfying the adults' desire, yet biological parents proceed to do this without incurring the criticism adopters suffer.

3.3.4.3 Loss of culture

International relocation typically involves change in dominant cultural milieu. How this change affects a migrant varies tremendously. There is no evidence that it is a substantial hardship for a significant percentage of migrants. There are several reasons why.

First, most follow a path created by previous migrants from their native land to a diaspora community that carries on their homeland's cultural practices. Nearly all Western societies today have a substantial immigrant population and cultural diversity, even in smaller towns.

Second, a great many adults migrate precisely to escape their home nation's culture, because they experience it as terribly oppressive, supporting systemic violations of human rights. Siddharth Kara writes:

> More than poverty, military conflict, or other social disasters, what drove rural women into the clutches of sex traffickers was a primary factor everywhere

> I investigated sex trafficking: Millions of women lived in a world that overwhelmingly disdained them. In Sindhupalchok, females were systematically beaten, raped, denied basic rights, and brutally exploited by men. Desperation to escape this tyranny delivered them to slave traders. I encountered similar dynamics in every developing country I visited. . . . [A] young woman named Uma told me that her husband had recently accused her of being a witch. As punishment, he and every man in the village gang-raped her. A few days later, her husband married a younger woman. Uma had no rights, no education, and no way to support herself without a husband. As a witch, not even her parents would accept her. . . . Family after family, woman after woman, child after child. The stories of violence fell upon me in waves. Countless children were raped by grown men. Countless husbands tortured their wives. Countless crimes passed without investigation. . . . When I asked the women of Sindhupalchok why the men treated them as they did, I invariably received the same two answers: "This is our culture." "Men want women as slaves."[83]

As Elizabeth Bartholet notes, it would be ludicrous to tell women escaping such cultures that they should stay where they are, that they will only make themselves worse off by leaving, because they will lose their culture.[84] So, too, it is ludicrous, even sadistic, to say an unparented girl in Uma's village should be kept locally, whether adopted or institutionalized, rather than adopted internationally, because we must protect her interest in being immersed in "her culture." It might also be ludicrous to say a boy in that village needs to remain so that he does not suffer loss of "his culture"—that is, his opportunity to rape, beat, and enslave women. To any objection that outsiders should not presume to judge someone else's culture, I say: Listen to the oppressed within that culture themselves. Also, that it is self-contradictory to say, "outsiders cannot judge the value of a culture" but at the same time "(I judge that) the culture of the developing country is valuable for the children born there."

Moreover, culture includes more than assumed roles in society. It can include: condemnation and denigration of any who diverge from any norm deemed important—sexuality, ability, and so forth; disregard for human life generally; deference to illegitimate powers, such as gangs and militias who assert their will arbitrarily and have their own cult figures, rituals, and ways of expressing respect; and routine repression and abuse, especially of children,

83 Kara, *supra* note 52, at 76–78. *See also id.*, 129–30 (describing Kanun culture in Albania). *See also* Harriet Zurndorfer, *Escape from the Country: The Gender Politics of Chinese Women in Pursuit of Transnational Romance*, 25 Gender, Place & Culture 489 (2018); Blaine Bookey, *Enforcing the Right to be Free from Sexual Violence and the Role of Lawyers in Post-Earthquake Haiti*, 14 CUNY L. Rev. 255, 259–63 (2011).

84 Elizabeth Bartholet, *International Adoption: The Human Rights Position*, 1 Global Pol'y 91, 97 (2010).

particularly those most vulnerable (e.g., those institutionalized).[85] Culture, like weather, is hardly inherently good.

To the extent changing cultural surroundings is at all difficult for anyone, it is more likely to be so the older a person is at the time of emigration. Older people have more fully absorbed and formed their lifestyle, worldview, and personal identity in the native culture, and they might be less adaptable. Perhaps a home state should have concern about elderly people whose offspring pressure them to relocate internationally, but that does not seem to be a common phenomenon. At the other end of the age spectrum, babies simply do not have a culture. Ascription of one to them is metaphysical rather than factual,[86] and it is contrary to the human right to choose one's own culture and form one's own identity based on one's own experience of life; it is an insult to the child's individual humanity.[87] This is why we regard it as insulting to Americans of non-European ancestry to assume they must have very different lifestyle and cultural practices than other Americans, or to ask them questions with phrases like "your people." The irrationality of the ascription based on place of birth is easily illustrated; compare a child born to German parents while they are on vacation in Romania with a child born in Berlin to Romanian parents living in a Romanian immigrant community. Is the former intrinsically more Romanian than the latter? Or imagine a four-year-old child living in an Indian childcare institution since birth, placed there as a "foundling," who is suddenly discovered to be the offspring of deceased Spanish citizens and therefore a national of Spain; would anyone worry about the child's loss of culture if Spain asked to have the child transported to Spain for adoption?

Significantly, children of any age brought by their parents to a new land typically manifest no lasting problems from culture change, but rather feel comfortable in new surroundings more quickly than the parents do. Would we worry about a child born in the United States to American parents if the child were adopted by a French couple and went to live in France, that the child would suffer from not being immersed in American culture? A romanticizing of the poor appears to underlie this concern about culture; only developing countries have a culture that matters, and it matters infinitely. There is also often a related racial essentializing at work that is, as Bartholet observes, reactionary rather

[85] *Cf.* Eric Rosenthal, *The Right of All Children to Grow Up with a Family Under International Law: Implications for Placement in Orphanages, Residential Care, and Group Homes*, 25 Buff. Hum. Rts. L. Rev. 65, 81–82 (2019) (describing the "culture" of abuse in institutions housing children and persons with disabilities in poor nations).

[86] *See* Compton, *supra* note 29, at 8–9, ch. 4.

[87] *Cf.* Dwyer, *supra* note 35 (discussing the "identity violence" the Indian Child Welfare Act inflicts on children living in mainstream American society who have no connection to a tribal community and predominantly non-Indian ancestry); Elizabeth Bartholet, *Permanency Is Not Enough: Children Need the Nurturing Parents Found in International Adoption*, 55 N.Y.L. Sch. L. Rev. 781, 785 (2011) (referring to the cultural identity objection to international adoption as "the false romanticism surrounding birth and national heritage").

than progressive—"speaking a language of a past in which it was common to see people as essentially defined by their race and national origin."[88]

Many persons adopted as children transnationally do develop curiosity at some point about life in the place where they were born. Even many second- or third-generation Americans put their ancestral lands high on their list of vacation destinations. Curiosity about place is easily satisfied. Adoptive parents commonly provide information, experiences, and networks to help with this, and for most adoptees that appears to suffice.[89] One-third of international adoptees later in life make pilgrimages to their nation of birth, but they have the same primary focus as persons adopted domestically who make similar searches and trips—namely, meeting their biological parents and/or extended biological family. Not the place, but people. Cultural experience is at most a secondary aim. After their excursion, they are more likely to say they are glad not to have grown up in the culture of their native land, that they are happy to have grown up as Swedes or Italians or Americans.[90] Researchers who interview international adoptees find the vast majority feel little sense of cultural loss and little desire to learn more than they already have about the culture of their country of birth.[91]

For any adoptees who do express some sense of loss, there is no evidentiary basis for supposing this more pronounced than the many other ways in which all of us feel some things missing in our lives. The empirical literature simply does not support the weight given to culture by IA opponents.[92] Nor is there any basis for deeming any feeling of absence such a detriment to adoptees' well-being as to outweigh the dramatic improvements to their lives in other ways arising from adoption.[93] Sara Dillon aptly states:

> In order to be consistent with the international rights of children, legal regimes must reflect a hierarchy of human needs, with consistency and depth of

[88] *See, e.g.*, Elizabeth Bartholet, *International Adoption: A Way Forward*, 55 N.Y. L. Sch. L. Rev. 687, 692 (2010–2011).

[89] *See* Howell, *supra* note 78, at 32, 76–79 (describing pamphlets, associations among families, organized trips back to country of origin, etc.); *id.*, 106 (describing adoptees who categorically reject the notion that they are incomplete unless they connect with the culture of their country of birth). *See also* Signe Howell, "The Backpackers That Come to Stay: New Challenges to Norwegian Transnational Adoptive Families," *in* Fiona Bowie ed., Cross-Cultural Approaches to Adoption 227, 238 (2004) (describing similar phenomenon in Norway).

[90] *See* Barbara Yngvesson, Belonging in an Adopted World (2010), 148 ("I like Ethiopia, but what I like about it is the people, while the culture isn't exactly—if I could choose—it isn't the country I would choose to be from"), 162 ("I could very easily find a job in Korea . . . But I don't want to. I don't want to live in Korea."), 171 ("I am glad I grew up here").

[91] *See* Howell, *supra* note 78, at 80, 111–21 (finding, based on interviews with adoptees returning to Norway from "motherland tours," that most come back "fully confirmed in their Norwegianness"); Bartholet, *supra* note 84, at 97 ("Science provides no basis for believing that children are better off if raised in their community of origin.").

[92] *See* Compton, *supra* note 29, ch. 4.

[93] *Cf. id.*, 78–79 (noting view of some observers that efforts to give children a community and cultural experience tied to their adoption from another country might serve interests of adoptive parents more than interests of the children); Bartholet, *supra* note 84, at 93–96 (2010) (citing evidence of horrible conditions in orphanages in countries that have shut down IA).

> care placed at the top of the hierarchy. National legal regimes should not be constructed on the belief that complex relationships with cultural environments are the equivalent of the psychological problems that arise from long-term residence in institutional or other inadequate care.[94]

Tellingly, the ICESCR itself implicitly treats culture as of little significance to individuals. It and the ICCPR proscribe state oppression of cultural groups, but the ICESCR in its conferral of individual rights mentions last "the right of everyone [t]o take part in cultural life"—not even identifying the individual with a culture but rather guaranteeing opportunity to participate in whatever culture is available. This follows enumeration of truly fundamental rights in the ICESCR, to freedom of employment, an economic social safety net, special protections for children, food, housing, health, and so forth, and the ICCPR's rights to protections against killing, slavery, arbitrary or inhumane detention, due process, freedom of movement, thought, speech, and religious practice, and so forth—any of which some persons might have fulfilled only by migrating transnationally.

Discussions with citizens of sending countries reveal that they themselves do not believe people born there lose anything significant by separating from the country at an early age and being raised in a different culture; many express puzzlement with Westerners' preoccupation with "roots."[95] Millions of adults in poor countries leave or try to leave every year, with little or no concern about loss of culture, and that should tell us something about the relative importance of cultural heritage to human welfare. Hundreds of thousands of women have traveled to the United States in the hope of giving birth here and thereby securing U.S. citizenship for their child, so that the child can upon reaching adulthood (or sooner) leave their native land and families and come to live in the United States.[96] The cost-benefit analysis tips even more so in favor of migration for infants, both because they have less to give up culturally (especially if they have been languishing in lifeless institutions) and because they can more easily adapt to a new culture, language, and living situation. Western commentators who ascribe to foreign-born children needs they do not have, and on that basis urge that

[94] Sara Dillon, *Making Legal Regimes for Intercountry Adoption Reflect Human Rights Principles: Transforming the United Nations Convention on the Rights of the Child with the Hague Convention on Intercountry Adoption*, 21 B.U. Int'l L.J. 179, 238 (2003). *See also* Tanya M. Washington, *Throwing Black Babies Out with the Bathwater: A Child-Centered Challenge to Same-Sex Adoption Bans*, 6 Hastings Race & Poverty L.J. 1, 47–49 (2008–2009) (describing congressional finding that not being adopted is more harmful than any difficulty transracial placement might entail).

[95] *See, e.g.*, Howell, *supra* note 78, at 209 (discussing Ethiopia), 215 (China), 220 (Romania).

[96] *Cf.* Cindy Chang, "In Suburbs of L.A., a Cottage Industry of Birth Tourism," L.A. Times, Jan. 3, 2013 (describing L.A.'s growing number of "maternity hotels," where foreign women stay for the sole purpose of giving birth in the United States).

certain policies dictate children's life course, are carrying out their own form of oppressive imperialism.

In short, cultural loss does not come close to a valid paternalistic justification for infringing anyone's right to leave their country of birth. In fact, it is not unique to international relocation; domestic relocation in many developing countries can involve a starker discontinuity in culture. A ten-year-old who has been living in the Andean Highlands of Peru speaking Quechua is likely to need longer to adjust to a new life if adopted by a Spanish-speaking couple in Lima than would a ten-year-old child from Tijuana or Tegucigalpa adopted into a family in San Diego. An infant in either situation would need no time whatsoever.

In any context, those facilitating relocation should be sensitive to the possibility of temporary cultural disorientation with older children and, for any children, the longer-term possibility of developing a self-conception that is in some way different—whether it be feeling less connected to the new nation or more connected to an ancestral nation—from that of the typical native-born child. Legal processes for approving the migration, including the vetting process for IA and a court hearing in a custody dispute between parents, can provide an occasion for mandating education about this.

3.3.4.4 Loss of family ties

Finally, we come to a real loss that many actual emigrants expressly lament—daily physical contact with family members and friends back home. If there is any plausible justification for imposing a CDP on anyone in any circumstances, this would be it. This interest in kinship ties, however, can vary considerably from one individual to another, depending on such things as the nature of relationships formed in the home state and with whom one migrates.

For any émigré who has been immersed in already established relationships with family and friends back home, pain of separation from them is likely. However, this is far less pronounced today than it once was, as developments in electronic communication and proliferation of devices for it limit the deprivation to loss of physical contact, just as with domestic migrations. Videos of refugees arriving in Greece or Italy by raft show them immediately opening their cell phones to "face-time" with family members back home. Again, that millions of autonomous persons choose to emigrate despite full awareness of the costs, including physical separation from loved ones, suggests this cost is far outweighed by dangers escaped and opportunities anticipated.

Any migrating adult or adolescent is likely to have this emotional cost of separation to some extent. Young children who migrate with their families, on the other hand, might have little experience of loss. They remain with the persons who matter most to them (assuming the receiving state does not separate them, as the Trump administration intentionally did for a while with children crossing the U.S.-Mexico border). And they are likely to remain in communication with kin and friends left behind. They might also be reuniting with family members who preceded them, and they are likely to form new relationships in their new community, which is often mostly people from the same home country.

In parental relocation or abduction cases, where a child would emigrate with only one parent, the child presumptively has a strong interest in continued contact with a parent who remains in the home state and a corresponding interest in adherence to procedures aimed at determining whether that is so and how to protect the interest. A state would therefore be justified in blocking the child's exit if its courts function properly in deciding whether departure or remaining is on the whole best for the child (a determination that should take into account living conditions in the home state) and if no court has authorized the separation from a remaining parent. But in that case, we could simply say the state is enforcing the child's right not to emigrate, as in trafficking cases. The analysis is the same as with domestic long-distance domestic moves, except that putting a national border between child and parent might increase the difficulty of visitation. As in domestic relocation cases, cultural and religious differences regarding child welfare might arise, and in the international realm as well a liberal view supports the position that adjudicative bodies should rely on empirically verifiable assumptions about children's temporal interests.

The experience of children who emigrate in the custody of adoptive parents must vary based on the extent to which they had established relationships with biological family members and how long they were separated from those relatives before the adoption (e.g., because residing in an orphanage for months or years). Presumably, most have little or no memory of parents or other kin; would-be adopters are unlikely to seek adoption of a child who remembers and expresses longing to return to his or her parents or other relatives, at least if those persons are alive and reachable. The child's kin-related interest is therefore that of anyone adopted domestically as a baby or infant—namely, none initially, and later in life curiosity, perhaps a longing to know and connect. It might generally be somewhat more difficult with international adoption than with domestic to trace the kin, but in today's world the only additional difficulty lies mostly in taking a long flight; otherwise, someone adopted by a family in Mogadishu is likely to find it at least as challenging as someone adopted by a family in Munich to track down a birth mother who left them at an orphanage in a northern Somalian village before fleeing to a refugee camp in Ethiopia.

Some critics of IA nevertheless insist sending countries pursue domestic placement with kin before approving an adoption of an unparented child by a foreigner, and so they do.[97] However, there are costs inherent in the search

[97] *See, e.g.*, Smolin, *supra* note 41, at 240–241; King, *supra* note 43, at 466; FENTON-GLYNN, *supra* note 50, at 24 (listing countries with waiting periods).

for kin or for a domestic placement more broadly. A major downside is delay, as drafters of the Hague Convention recognized.[98] Infants need attachment figures in place as early as possible for their healthy development, so the longer they live in an institutional setting, the more they suffer developmentally.[99] Children in orphanages are there because there was no kin network in place for them to help or substitute for their parents; if there were kin aware of the child and inclined to step in when parents struggle, the child would not end up in an orphanage in the first place. Many cultures within developing countries have a tradition of communal care for children, by kin and by biologically unrelated community members, but poverty, disease, war, internal displacement, and other tragedies make it impossible for many communities to sustain this tradition.[100] Insistence that a government agency pursue kin seems to presuppose no one else has done so before the child ends up in an institution. Yet it seems more plausible to assume that any parents who bring their child to an orphanage have first exhausted other possibilities. And that when parents have died, if that results in the children being taken into custody by a state agency, either there were no kin nearby or there were relatives who were aware of the death but were unable to undertake care of the child. The hope underlying a search therefore must be that a child has some kin who are unaware of the child's plight yet are willing and able to take the (unknown) child into their home. The unlikelihood of that prospect is apparent, and so the search will probably be protracted and ultimately unsuccessful. Moreover, in such cases, there is not the benefit for the child of familiarity generally assumed with kincare.

Bartholet has proposed, as a compromise solution to the delay associated with seeking kin or other domestic placements, that countries engage in "concurrent planning," and she co-authored federal legislation committing the United States to promoting this practice.[101] Sending countries would search for a good domestic placement but at the same time complete as many steps as possible toward a foreign adoption, so that if a good domestic placement does not arise, as

[98] *See* Hague Conference Permanent Bureau, "The implementation and operation of the 1993 Hague International Adoption Convention: A guide to good practice" (Hague Family Law 2008), 22 ("States should also ensure that efforts to achieve this goal [exploring domestic options] do not unintentionally harm children by delaying unduly a permanent solution through intercountry adoption. States should guarantee permanency planning in the shortest time possible for each child deprived of his/her parents.").

[99] *See* Fenton-Glynn, *supra* note 50, at 25 (describing study finding attachment disorders more common among children not adopted until after twelve months of age); James G. Dwyer, *The Child Protection Pretense: States' Continued Consignment of Newborn Babies to Unfit Parents*, Minn. L. Rev. 93, 407, 415–35 (2008).

[100] *See* Roby & Shaw, *supra* note 51, at 200; Celia W. Dugger, "Aid Gives Alternative to African Orphanages," N.Y. Times, Dec. 5, 2009 (reporting that "children placed in institutions are often seen as the lucky ones" by families too poor to provide education or adequate food).

[101] Children in Families First Act of 2013, S. 1530, 113th Cong. (2013); Bartholet, *supra* note 51, at 193–94.

is likely, the foreign adoption can go forward immediately. This approach might sound more costly for sending countries, but it is not necessarily so. If searches for domestic adopters or kin guardians usually fail, the alternative to conducting both processes for each child concurrently will usually be to do them both anyway but sequentially. As a result, most children remain longer in a state-funded institution, some destined to remain in that institution throughout childhood because of missed opportunity for foreign adoption, having become older and more damaged while held in institutional limbo.

An additional problem with emphasis on domestic placement is that nonparent kin or other co-nationals interested in adopting are likely to live in circumstances as adverse as those of the parents, and that can lead to deprivation and even abuse. They might view the children as burdens or assets more so than beloved objects of affection, protection, and concern. In some parts of the world, many kin are as exploitative as child-labor traffickers. They take in a child not out of compassion but out of mercenary motivation (e.g., if they will receive payments to do so) and/or a desire for free labor.[102] The so-called "foster-care system" in Haiti is infamous for turning orphans into relatives' indentured servants.[103] Some kin might sell a child to traffickers. And kin might be less able or less inclined than foreign adoptive parents to assist a child in maintaining ties to birth parents.

Further, connection to kin is, as a factual matter, even when a positive thing, only one variable in a child's overall well-being, and in many cases its possibility is outweighed by the quality of care particular kin are capable of providing (e.g., if they are living in abject poverty) and problems in the community or nation where the kin live (e.g., famine, war, disease, oppression). Countless children who remain in the poorest parts of the world ultimately lose all connection with their families anyway because forced when adolescents or young adults to migrate domestically for survival, ending up in exploitative conditions that result in isolation from or shunning by their family and home community, or early death.[104]

For those adopted internationally, studies suggest ties to biological family are less important to them than CDP supporters assert.[105] Longing to know a birth parent can be strong. But children in orphanages are generally ones whose

[102] *See, e.g.*, Montgomery & Powell, *supra* note 29, at 13 ("a number of African orphanage directors have told us that—ironically, in light of the Subsidiarity Principle—children placed with extended or local families are more likely to end up being treated as servants").

[103] *See* Richard Carlson, *Seeking the Better Interests of Children with a New International Law of Adoption*, 55 N.Y.L. Sch. L. Rev. 733, 762 (2010–2011) ("In Haiti, what might pass for foster care is actually a form of indentured servitude."); Jim Loney, "Haiti 'Restavek' Tradition Called Child Slavery," Reuters, Feb. 18, 2010.

[104] Kara, *supra* note 52, at 62, 76, 169.

[105] *See* Howell, *supra* note 78, at 111–21 (showing many adopted children not concerned with biological ties to family).

parents have died, are unable to care for them, or have created an unsafe home environment[106] *and* whose biological kin, as noted, were also not available to care for them—in other words, children whose only alternatives to international adoption even in theory are just domestic nonkin placement (adoption or foster care) and, far more likely, continued institutionalization with no kin contact. Even if connecting with biological kin is important to some adoptees, there is no evidence that any conclude they would have been better off remaining in their country of birth and being raised among their kin. The tendency to conclude from the search that the adoption was a mistake is patently illogical. Adoptees become integrated into a kin network with their adoptive family, and that network of relationships becomes constitutive of their identity.[107]

Finally, I note again the ever-increasing ease of communication and travel. A policy of encouraging adoptive parents and birth families to allow agencies in sending countries to relay communications between them would enable many children more readily to connect to birth parents or kin who are alive and want contact.[108] Any adoptive parents who see their child struggling with the disconnection are likely to welcome the opportunity for that. The fears about contact with biological kin that some who adopt domestically have are likely to be far less or entirely absent for those who adopt internationally; in the latter case, kin cannot readily show up at one's door, and they are unlikely to have the personal dysfunctions, such as addiction and mental illness, that plague the families in affluent nations who lose children to foster care and adoption.

3.4 Conclusion

Any state that prevents any person's departure from its territory bears a burden of justification. The weight of the burden is at its greatest when exercise of the right to leave would serve fundamental interests—survival, healthy development, basic liberties and opportunities—as is true in the real-world contexts this book addresses. With respect to exit by children in particular, no proposed justification that appeals only to the interests of the home state or of persons left behind in the home country has any purchase. Even if blocking children's exit could serve other interests, there is no plausible major premise linking such an empirical supposition with a conclusion that the state's negative duty not to

106 *See* Holmes, *supra* note 48 (questioning the wisdom of pursuing family reunification in a society where great numbers of children are driven out of their homes by stepparents).

107 *See, e.g.*, Howell, *supra* note 89, at 232–33; Howell, *supra* note 78, at 74.

108 *Cf.* Malinda L. Seymore, *Openness in International Adoption*, 46 Colum. Hum. Rts. L. Rev. 163 (2015); Wechsler, *supra* note 29, at 37–39 (proposing an international agency that would oversee and coordinate intercountry adoptions and maintain a central database with information about adoptees, their birth parents, and adopters).

block exit is morally overridden. And, to the contrary, there is the moral principle precluding such instrumental treatment of persons; a home state may not use some children, at least not to the extent of severely diminishing their life options, to serve other individuals or society collectively. Further, the equality side constraint on infringement of human rights would require doing the same for all groups to whom the underlying aim could apply. If allocating the right to leave were permissible, as between adults and children, states generally should favor children, subject to exceptions for extraordinarily needy adults.

The strongest rationales for infringing children's right to leave are paternalistic, appealing to the interests of would-be emigrants themselves, but they will rarely suffice. When they do, it would be more accurate to say the child's right not to emigrate is being protected. One real-world context in which this might be pertinent is a custody dispute between parents. Another is when children are temporarily separated from parents in a crisis and someone proposes to take them away en masse permanently and without trying to locate their parents, as occurred in post-earthquake Haiti. But when the benefit of emigrating is escaping substantial threats to fundamental aspects of well-being, which can include lack of family life, the costs of leaving would have to be great indeed, and substantiated rather than merely imagined, to outweigh it. In the IA context, supposed concerns for children's welfare are hollow and mainly serve to provide cover for quite different, ideological motivations. The consequences of giving those concerns undue credence have been tragically ironic. Drastically shrinking the number of children available for adoption has increased the payoff for any bad actors, and it has multiplied the number of youth who age out of institutional warehousing to life on the streets, where they are highly vulnerable to true trafficking.

Finally, availability of opportunity for improved circumstances domestically carries no independent weight as a justification for infringing the right to leave. If a domestic opportunity is superior on other grounds (safety, necessities, availability of parents, education, ability to remain connected to family and culture) to all foreign opportunities, then a state might block emigration, simply as a means of enforcing a best-interests selection among all opportunities. But forcing a preference for a same-nation solution per se on anyone is illicit, insofar as it treats individuals as property of the nation rather than rights-bearing persons.

4
Citizenship as Liability

4.1 Introduction

The next three chapters examine the nature of children's relationship with the nation in which they reside. This chapter and the next focus on formal legal status, and Chapter 6 examines the nature of the state's role when it assumes control over aspects of children's lives that for adults are a matter of self-determination, including residential location.

A person's legal status in relation to a nation can have several forms. Citizenship is membership of the fullest sort.[1] Alternatively, one could be a resident noncitizen (sometimes called "alien") or a nonresident noncitizen who happens to be present at a given time on the nation's territory—for example, holding a temporary visa for tourism or employment purposes or having entered without legal permission. Or one might have neither physical nor legal connection with a particular nation.

Today in Western societies there is heightened attention, some hostile and some compassionate, to persons deemed "alien" in the country they currently inhabit, especially if they have not gone through the prescribed process for entry. Western European countries struggle to cope with masses of desperate people arriving from Africa, the Middle East, and Eastern Europe, fleeing war, government oppression, and destitution. In the United States, a primary political focus for many years has been the stream of migrants from all over Central and South America crossing the U.S.-Mexico border without permission, a stream that has swelled in recent years because of increased violence and persistent poverty in many Latin American countries. Less publicized mass migrations occur in other parts of the world, sometimes from one impoverished nation to another simply

[1] Some nations historically have had both "citizens" and "nationals," with slightly different packages of rights and privileges pertaining to the two. For U.S. law's treatment of residents of its territories, *see* Irina D. Manta & Cassandra Burke Robertson, *Adopting Nationality*, 98 Wash. L. Rev. 483 (2023). There is no inherent practical distinction between the two statuses, however, and in some other nations they are indistinguishable. The international law community has historically used "nationality" in its instruments and decisions, because of its focus on states as actors in the international realm and its view of individuals as represented by a nation in that realm. But scholars see that changing, with increasing reference to citizenship in law and scholarship, reflecting a general modern elevation of the individual in international jurisprudence. *See* Peter J. Spiro, *A New International Law of Citizenship*, 105 Am. J. Int'l L. 694, 695 (2011). This book will treat them as functionally equivalent and, because it is more familiar in the English-speaking world, and has a more singular meaning, principally refer to "citizenship," using "nationality" when alluding to treaties that use the term.

International Migration of Children for a Better Life. James G. Dwyer, Oxford University Press. © Oxford University Press 2025.
DOI: 10.1093/9780197752333.003.0004

because the latter is safer, with varying reactions locally to the influx of people, who typically are unable to sustain themselves independently.

With no prospect of safe return to their home countries, or of securing any assistance from the government of their home states, yet welcome only temporarily or not at all in destination nations, such migrants practically have no nation to call their own. They are "effectively" or "de facto" stateless even if formally still citizens of the nation they fled. Their plight has triggered not just intense public debate but also an explosion of scholarly literature on statelessness and an intense focus from international human rights organizations. De facto statelessness also befalls many people because, though citizens, their home state fails to provide them documentation needed to prove their citizenship.[2]

In addition, many persons are de jure stateless, truly lacking citizenship anywhere, even if living in their native land. Causes include national laws that limit citizenship to those descended from past inhabitants who were registered at a particular time (e.g., before a foreign occupation); collapse or disappearance of a state (e.g., breakup of Yugoslavia, island nations sinking in the rising seas); denaturalization (as Russia did to those who fled the Bolshevik Revolution, as Nazis did to Jewish Germans, and as many nations have done to political dissidents); and the happenstance of being born in a country adhering to the *jus sanguinis* approach to citizenship, under which one inherits citizenship from one's parents, if one's parents are not citizens of that state (or the mother might be a citizen but domestic law allows inheritance of citizenship only through a father).

In all quarters, the view prevails that possessing a "nationality" (the term generally used in international law to connote national membership)—any nationality—is an unquestionable desideratum, a salvation for those now lacking it because thought to be a precondition of access to a host of state-conferred benefits, rights, and opportunities.[3] In a global environment of refugee crises, controversies over illegal immigration and ascription of second-class legal status to members of ethnic minorities within some nations, the human rights community uniformly and vociferously calls for all humans to have a nationality and for

[2] Whether registration and documentation constitute rather than provide evidence of citizenship is disputed. *See* Kelly Staples, "Recognition, Nationality, and Statelessness: State-Based Challenges for UNHCR's Plan to End Statelessness," *in* Tendayi Bloom et al. eds., Understanding Statelessness 173–88, 178–79 (2017). It would seem a matter local law determines.

[3] *See, e.g.*, Laura van Waas & Melanie J. Khanna eds., Solving Statelessness (2017) (collection of papers by different authors making exaggerated claims about the necessity of nationality in order to have any rights); Ayelet Shachar, *Citizenship as Property*, 35 Pol. Theory 253 (2007) (tying numerous life advantages available in affluent countries to citizenship when in fact they flow simply from residing in such countries, and asserting that citizenship gives rise to "the complementary right not to be excluded from any additional attendant rights and privileges" as if no citizens are excluded from, for example, the franchise).

statelessness to be banished.[4] The UN High Commissioner for Human Rights labeled statelessness a "curse" and issued a rallying cry for its elimination by 2024. The U.S. Supreme Court has characterized involuntary denaturalization as a punishment "more primitive than torture" and banned it.[5] Thus, when someone moves from a condition of statelessness to being a national/citizen of any state, regardless of which one, this is viewed as a profound improvement in his or her life and well-being. The presumptive means of ensuring every human being has the status of citizen is for every nation to commit to conferring its citizenship on anyone within its territory who is otherwise stateless.

This chapter advances the contrarian view that some people in some circumstances would be better off if not citizens of the country in which they reside, even if otherwise stateless, and that this is more likely true for children. Section 4.2 explains why the human rights community and legal authorities at the national and international level hold up "having a nationality" as a basic human right and fundamental good, but then also why it is really not so important today. Section 4.3 offers full consideration of potential downsides to being a national of some state. Section 4.4 considers whether for some persons the costs of being claimed by a particular state can outweigh the benefits, such that those persons would be better off stateless. It concludes that this is certainly true, and more likely to be so for children than for adults. This calls directly into question not only the wisdom of the campaign to end statelessness but also the permissibility of states imposing their citizenship on individuals, particularly those who cannot meaningfully consent. Chapter 5 addresses those questions.

4.2 The Value of Citizenship

Citizenship is a type of group membership. As a conceptual matter, belonging to any group could be a good thing or a bad thing compared to alternatives, or could make no difference. For example, being a member of the group "Inmates of Angola Prison" seems undesirable overall, though it might have some benefits (e.g., free room and board). Being a nonmember as to all groups of a particular kind could be benign (e.g., political parties), presumptively bad (e.g., families), or presumptively good (e.g., gangs). The assessment depends on what membership offers and an individual's particular circumstances and needs. Groups of some types compete with one another (e.g., football teams), and belonging to

[4] *See, e.g.*, Melanie J. Khanna & Peggy Brett, "Making Effective Use of UN Human Rights Mechanisms to Solve Statelessness," *in* van Waas & Khanna, *supra* note 3, at 13–45, 17 (noting that in 2012 alone the UN Human Rights Council issued seven resolutions specifically mentioning statelessness or the right to a nationality).

[5] Afroyim v. Rusk, 387 U.S. 253 (1967); Trop v. Dulles, 356 US 86, 102 (1958).

a particular one can have personal significance or material advantages. On the other hand, membership in one group might have implications for how other groups treat one when associating with them (e.g., a warring clan), and being a member of no group could be advantageous in some situations (e.g., a free-agent football player). These many complications in valuing membership generally go unrecognized in the literature on citizenship.

This section describes international efforts to end statelessness and explains why scholars and human rights advocates deem belonging to some nation—any nation—in this legal sense a universal need. It then argues that the value of citizenship varies vastly from one nation to another and in general is greatly overstated. It is not a necessary formal condition for enjoying basic rights, and in practice it is not a sufficient condition either.

4.2.1 The human right to nationality

Historically, conferral of nationality was entirely within the discretion of each state, with no basis in international law for directing a state to treat any particular persons as its nationals.[6] Today conventions, declarations, and resolutions pronounce an obligation of all nations to work cooperatively to eliminate statelessness and impose a duty on individual states to confer their nationality on certain persons.[7] That includes imposing nationality on newborn children.

This positive duty of conferral is uniformly thought to arise from physical connection between individual and state. Most commonly, an individual's formal right to have a particular state confer on them its nationality arises from the fact of having been born within the state's territory. In some circumstances, though, a right might arise from presence later in life, typically when it has been prolonged or a person has no practical option for living in another country of which they are a national, as in cases of asylum.

Yet the significance ascribed to physical connection, in international law, is never so great as to trigger an absolute right and corresponding duty. They are always conditional on the person not possessing nationality in another state. They are never dependent, however, on the relative desirability of belonging to a particular polity, nor the mere fact that a person does or does not desire it,

[6] *See* Myers S. McDougal et al., *Nationality and Human Rights: The Protection of the Individual in External Arenas*, 83 Yale L.J. 900, 914–15 (1974) ("Hague Convention on Nationality, which only makes customary international law explicit, . . . stipulates that '[i]t is for each state to determine under its own law who are its nationals' ").

[7] *See* Olivier Willem Vonk et al., " 'Benchmarking' Legal Protection Against Statelessness," *in* van Waas & Khanna, *supra* note 3, at 163–90, 168.

even though the desirability varies immensely from one nation to another. There seems to be at work implicit and undefended premises that nationality even in the most inhospitable nation on earth is preferable to being stateless and that there is no conceivable basis other than physical connection for imposing a duty on a nation to confer its nationality (*jus sanguinis* conferral is therefore always optional).

Thus, the 1961 Convention on the Reduction of Statelessness, to which nearly half of states are parties, provides in Article 1 that any contracting state must "grant its nationality to a person born in its territory who would otherwise be stateless," either by automatic operation of law or upon application. Article 2 addresses "foundlings"—that is, children whose place of birth is unknown and who are discovered without any caregivers or identifying papers, requiring each contracting state to presume such a child discovered on its territory was born in its territory and to parents who are its nationals.[8] In other words, every country should claim as its own any child of unknown parentage found in its territory, with no consideration of whether the child would be likely to assent to that if capable of understanding the consequences. For example, a baby deserted in a bathroom at La Aurora International Airport in Guatemala City with no information about state of origin must become a Guatemalan citizen, period, and then likely spend his or her entire childhood in an institution. The background assumptions must be that at any point in a person's life any nationality is better than no nationality and that the only possible bases for ascribing nationality are physical presence at some determinative time or else genealogy. A "best available nation" rule for citizenship presumably would far better serve unparented, stateless children, but that has never even been considered. Guatemala may and must claim that child, not Switzerland.

Regional treaties contain a similar commitment to ensure every human being is claimed by some nation. The American Convention on Human Rights, in Article 20(2); the African Charter on the Rights and Welfare of the Child, in Article 6(4); and the European Convention on Nationality, in Article 6(2), all impose on state parties a duty to confer nationality on any minor children born on their territory who do not automatically acquire some other nationality (e.g., by birth to a citizen of some other country with a *jus sanguinis* rule). Other international instruments, such as the CRC (in Article 7(1)) and the UDHR (in

[8] The 1930 Convention on Certain Questions Relating to the Conflict of Nationality Law [Nationality Convention] stated without qualification that party states must impose their nationality on certain children. Article 14 stated: "A child whose parents are both unknown shall have the nationality of the country of birth. . . . A foundling is, until the contrary is proved, presumed to have been born on the territory of the State in which it was found."

Article 15) pronounce more vaguely a right of every person to possess a nationality, without specifying on whom the correlative duty falls or when.

In addition to endowment with nationality in the first instance, *preserving* nationality per se—that is, not falling from the position of being a citizen of some state to the condition of being stateless—is a basic human right under international law. Treaties allow for loss of citizenship as to a particular nation, but only so long as the individual acquires nationality status in another. This is so even when a person wants to renounce an existing citizenship. Article 7 of the 1930 Convention on Certain Questions relating to the Conflict of Nationality Laws provides that an expatriation permit issued by a state "shall not entail loss of the nationality of the State which issues it, unless the person to whom it is issued possesses another nationality or unless and until he acquires another nationality."

Another incident of supposing nationality an unqualified good is that international law does not clearly impose any negative duty on states ever *not* to confer or impose their citizenship upon a person, even a person who lacks both physical connection with the state and descent from a citizen of the state, and even if the person does not consent to the conferral. Inroads on state discretion as to citizenship ascription have been focused on state power to withhold or withdraw citizenship.[9] Some scholars opine that there are situations when a nation should not declare certain persons its citizens, and for some the conviction is so strong that they insist there actually are limits that would render involuntary conferral entirely ineffective.[10] But apart from a couple of decisions from nineteenth-century bilateral claims tribunals, there appears to be no actual legal authority saying so, nor documentation of an *opinio juris* that could underwrite a finding of customary international law.[11] If a state's claiming someone as its citizen conflicts with interests of another state, that state might have basis for complaining about it and for refusing to recognize the conferral if it is not based on a genuine connection the person has with the state claiming him or her.[12] But

[9] *See* Spiro, *supra* note 1, at 694 ("international law has had little to say about the citizenship practices of states and the terms on which states determine the boundaries of their memberships"), 716 ("most leading commentators on citizenship theory . . . continue to characterize nationality practice as largely outside the ambit of international law").

[10] *See, e.g.*, Michelle Foster & Helene Lambert, International Refugee Law and the Protection of Stateless Persons 119–21 (2019); Peter J. Spiro, *Citizenship Overreach*, 38 Mich. J. Int'l L. 167, 175 (2017); McDougal et al., *supra* note 6, at 902, 918–30.

[11] If there is an emerging rule of customary international law that states may not impose nationality on the unwilling, its recognition would seem to require grappling with the situation of nonautonomous persons and international treaties compelling states to impose their nationality on any stateless persons present on their territory. Scholars who recoil at the idea of involuntary citizenship appear oblivious to the fact that it befalls nearly every human being during childhood.

[12] *See* Lichtenstein v. Guatemala (Preliminary Objection), I.C.J. Rep. 1953, 111, Second Phase, I.C.J. Rep. 1955, 4.

otherwise, states, it seems, are legally free to declare as their citizens anyone they choose and then try to use that to their advantage however international law or politics allows.[13] In particular, there is no clear right of the individual against being claimed and labeled,[14] as is evident from the fact that in most instances people acquire citizenship involuntarily, as infants.

Thus, there is no clear legal impediment to, for example, North Korea announcing that everyone in the world, whatever other nationality they might have, is now (also) its citizen. The impact of such action would likely vary across persons depending on whether they are citizens of another nation and, if so, whether that nation is prepared to defend them against any efforts by North Korea to control or exploit them. So suppose North Korea were to declare, more modestly, that all currently stateless people of the world, who have no other nation to defend them in international fora, are now its citizens. Or perhaps just particular groups of stateless persons who are unwelcome in the nations where they reside. And suppose North Korea then purported to assert protective representation of those new citizens in their country of residence, challenging their treatment by the host nation. Or suppose it asked the host nation to transport those people to North Korea or permit North Korea to remove them, which some nations might be quite willing to do. Nothing in international law clearly precludes this from happening; indeed, it would be consistent with the international commitment to end statelessness. As a party to the ICCPR, North Korea is ostensibly obligated to respect individuals' right to leave and to change nationality, but these individuals might have nowhere to go and no other nationality to claim, and in practice North Korea overtly flouts with impunity this obligation to allow emigration from its territory.

[13] *See* Nationality Convention, art. 1 ("It is for each State to determine under its own law who are its nationals."), art. 2 ("Any question as to whether a person possesses the nationality of a particular State shall be determined in accordance with the law of that State."); RUTH DONNER, THE REGULATION OF NATIONALITY IN INTERNATIONAL LAW, 2ND ED. 17 (1994) ("any limitation on the right of States to frame their own nationality law must be shown . . . nationality falls within the reserved domain of State authority . . . International tribunals, applying international law, cannot, unless there is a conventional basis of jurisdiction, deal with questions of nationality. Nationality may only be handled as a problem of the choice of law, when a tribunal has to decide what nationality law to apply . . .").

[14] FOSTER & LAMBERT, *supra* note 10, at 119 ("In principle nationality is a matter not regulated by international law. The right of a State to use its discretion in this matter may only be restricted by obligations which it has undertaken to other States, that is to say by express derogations contained chiefly in treaties."), 148 (interpreting the obstacle to uninvited imposition of citizenship as the right of other states to refuse recognition if they so choose), 159–64 (describing decisions of national and municipal courts holding to that effect). *See also id.*, 119–21 (citing ILC Draft Articles on Nationality of Natural Persons in relation to the Succession of States with Commentaries, which excludes cases of stateless persons from a general prohibition on a state's "attribute[ing] its nationality to persons concerned who have their habitual residence in another State"); and prior discussion of the 1961 Convention.

4.2.2 The benefits of belonging

Citizenship and nationality have no fixed meanings and carry few inherent benefits. Their incidents vary over time and across nations, reflecting the freedom and power international law generally affords states not only to determine who are their citizens or nationals but also to define what that status entails in rights, privileges, and duties.[15] What the Harvard Research on the Law of Nationality stated in 1929 remains true:

> Nationality has no positive, immutable meaning. On the contrary its meaning and import have changed with the changing character of states. Thus, nationality in the feudal period differed essentially from nationality, or what corresponded to it, in earlier times before states had become established within definite territorial limits, and it differs now from what it was in the feudal period. It may acquire a new meaning in the future as the result of further changes in the character of human society and developments in international organization.

In addition to change over time, there is at any given moment much variation across the globe. Absent a voluntarily undertaken treaty obligation, sovereign states are free to attach any or no benefits to citizenship, so high variability is unsurprising.

One benefit almost universally limited to citizens is the right to vote. Realistically, this is likely low on the list of importance for most persons lacking citizenship in their country of residence, especially if they could not expect to wield much influence with the franchise. But the symbolism of casting a ballot might be of psychological significance for those whose basic survival needs are met.

Another good traditionally dependent on nationality per se is state advocacy for one's protection against harmful conduct by governments of other nations—for example, while traveling abroad. This has always been gratuitous on the part of one's state, though. International law was originally a set of rules only for relations between and among nations, and international diplomacy and adjudication were means for states to vindicate their corporate interests and rights, as against incursions by other states. States claimed the authority to redress a wrong done by another state to one of their citizens—by complaint

[15] *See* Maximilian Koessler, *"SUBJECT," "CITIZEN," "NATIONAL," AND "PERMANENT ALLEGIANCE,"* 56 YALE L.J. 58, 63 (1946) ("since the list of the concrete rights and duties that constitute 'citizenship' in this specific sense, differs according to the country in question, it has also been said, 'there is no universal definition of citizenship'"), 70 ("The concept of nationality is no more than a formal frame, surrounding a picture of changeable character.").

before an international tribunal, direct retaliatory action, or diplomatic negotiation—based on their own state interests, not as agents for individuals with "rights" to redress.

Thus, stateless persons have no reason to expect advocacy on their behalf from any nation in combatting ill treatment by any government. No nation would have standing to complain in international fora about another's treatment of those persons, nor license to intervene directly. Myers McDougal observed in 1974:

> [T]he principle that a state can provide protection only in cases of deprivations suffered by its own nationals is well established. The only "link" generally accepted for purposes of establishing standing to protect against deprivations is, thus, that of nationality. The fiction that sustains this inhibiting practice is that an injury to the individual is an injury to the state of his nationality.... As developed under customary international law, a claimant must possess the nationality of the espousing state from the moment of deprivation, through the presentation of the claim, and often to the time of settlement. Thus, a claimant whose nationality is changed or lost after suffering a deprivation cannot obtain remedy.[16]

Today international law, via human rights treaties, gives individuals a limited opportunity to act on their own behalf, to complain to a human rights committee of a limited range of behaviors by one of a limited number of states (those who are parties to the treaties and the optional protocols thereto). But the committee has no power to order states to change their behavior or compensate individuals they have harmed.

The benefit of citizenship per se most cited is a right to reside permanently in a nation.[17] ICCPR Article 12(4) promises: "No one shall be arbitrarily deprived of the right to enter his own country." This suggests a right also not to be forced to leave one's own country in the first place. For a significant minority of humans, this right to remain is of profound practical value, because the government where they now reside wishes to expel them. Lacking a right to remain makes them vulnerable not only to expulsion but also to exploitation and abuse while they remain; the tentative nature of their residency can make it difficult for them to find work, and if their presence is illegal, others can use the threat of

[16] McDougal et al., *supra* note 6, at 906–08. *See also id.*, 994 ("It is through 'nationality' only that the individual acquires much of what access he has to transnational processes of authoritative decision.").

[17] *E.g.*, Adam Omar Hosein, "Refugees and the Right to Remain," *in* David Miller & Christine Straehle eds., The Political Philosophy of Refuge (2020); Radha Govil, "The Sustainable Development Goals and Solutions to Statelessness," *in* van Waas & Khanna, *supra* note 3, at 47–69, 49.

reporting them to authorities to coerce them.[18] The degree of vulnerability can vary depending on what other status a person has; typically, someone present illegally is subject to deportation without other cause, whereas someone with a proper visa might be excludable only for cause, and a legal resident might have due process rights even if not a substantive right as strong as that of citizens. Additionally, simply having a home somewhere, a place where one has a right to live if not welcome anywhere else, seems valuable in the abstract.

Further, those able to remain in a nation are likely to find that some employment opportunities there directly depend on citizenship. In some instances, this is true de jure; a narrow set of jobs is legally available only to citizens, typically for reasons of national security.[19] Additionally, nations might impose burdens on employers who hire noncitizens—for example, extra paperwork, background checks, or liability insurance—and thereby make noncitizens less attractive applicants for positions. Employers might be reluctant to hire aliens also because their lack of citizenship makes it more likely they will leave the country, by choice or compulsion. Self-employment can also be more difficult for noncitizens, because some countries do not allow them to own real property.

Obstacles could exist also in access to education, housing, and welfare.[20] Often such obstacles arise only indirectly from lack of citizenship; receipt depends on presenting official identity papers, such as a birth certificate, and the state issues them only to citizens.[21] Other times it arises from lack of proof of citizenship. The UN Refugee Agency reports: "In more than 30 countries, children need nationality documentation to receive medical care. In at least 20 countries, stateless children cannot be legally vaccinated."[22]

Citizenship can underwrite more intangible goods as well. If it enables greater stability and social acceptance, then it facilitates integration into a community and development of a personal support network. Scholars and courts have

[18] *See, e.g.*, Amal de Chickera & Joanna Whiteman, "Addressing Statelessness Through the Rights to Equality and Nondiscrimination," *in* VAN WAAS & KHANNA, *supra* note 3, at 99–128, 107 ("stateless people have reported being exploited by, for instance, employers who know that it is particularly difficult for them to find work and so they may be more willing to work illegally on a low wage").

[19] *See, e.g.*, Katja Swider, "Why End Statelessness?," *in* BLOOM ET AL. EDS., *supra* note 2, at 197 (discussing modest limitations on rights of stateless persons in Latvia); Cabell v. Chavez-Salido, 454 U.S. 432 (1982) (upholding state statute precluding non-citizens from becoming peace officers) Foley v. Connelie, 435 U.S. 291 (1978) (upholding a statute prohibiting aliens from working as police officers). *But see* Sugarman v. Dougall, 413 U.S. 634 (1973) (holding unconstitutional exclusion of aliens from state civil service).

[20] *See, e.g.*, Volker Turk, "Introduction," *in* VAN WAAS & KHANNA, *supra* note 3, at 7–10, 8; Govil, *supra* note 17, at 54–56; Chickera & Whiteman, *supra* note 18, at 106.

[21] Chickera & Whiteman, *supra* note 18, at 115–16 (observing that parents in Nepal are increasingly required to show a child's birth certificate for the child to attend school).

[22] UNHCR, "I Am Here, I Belong: The Urgent Need to End Childhood Statelessness," https://www.unhcr.org/ibelong/i-belong-i-am-here/ (last visited Sept. 29, 2024).

recognized a psychological benefit, a feeling of belonging and equal standing.[23] Conversely, being an "alien" is stigmatizing and can feel demeaning.

4.2.3 Limits on the value of nationality in law and practice

All that said, citizenship does not in practice guarantee anything. A nation might confer only very limited rights, and many fail to respect the legal rights they purport to confer—as to everyone or as to those belonging to a disfavored group. Likewise, employers and the public discriminate against and disdain members of some groups regardless of their citizenship status.

International law commitments tied to citizenship per se are quite narrow, largely limited to political participation. Even that commitment is unrealized in many nations. Many lack a functioning democracy. The ICCPR right to reside is not tied to citizenship and anyway might be merely theoretical for citizen members of a minority whom the government would like to expatriate. To accomplish this, the state might disingenuously invoke one of the few exceptions to the right. Kenya, for example, has expelled citizens of Somali descent on pretense of serving national security. Or it might apply extralegal compulsion to leave; many states target unwanted groups, defined by ethnicity or political opposition or something else, with treatment so oppressive and harmful as to induce them to leave "voluntarily." Tutsis in the Democratic Republic of the Congo, for example, have been subjected to a variety of legal and extralegal measures to expel them. If a country is not a party to the ICCPR or other treaty that commits it to conferring such right, its government might simply deny that citizenship entails it, insisting that national sovereignty gives it unqualified power to decide who may live within the nation's territory.

In addition, having some nationality naturally does not ensure ability to remain where one is living if one is not living in the territory of the state that has conferred the nationality. In fact, having citizenship elsewhere renders one more susceptible to deportation, if the nation of which one *is* a national is willing or obligated to permit one's entry. In contrast, a stateless person might be able to

[23] *See, e.g.*, Govil, *supra* note 17, at 49, 56 (referring to a sense of "marginalization" as well "anger, resentment, frustration and depression"); Laura Bingham & Liliana Gamboa, "Litigating Against Statelessness," *in* VAN WAAS & KHANNA, *supra* note 3, at 129–61, 137 ("the European Court of human rights has taken up nationality cases under . . . article 8, which protects an individual's private life, including individual identity, dignity and personal autonomy."); Open Society Justice initiative v. Cote d'Ivoire, African commission on human and people's rights, Communication 318/06 (May 27, 2016), ¶ 140 ("dignity and legal status are fundamentally interdependent"), ¶ 141 ("failure to grant nationality as a legal recognition is an injurious infringement of human dignity"); Yean and Bosico v. Dominican Republic, Inter-American Court of Human Rights (2005), IHRL 1514 (2005), ¶ 179 ("The Court considers that the failure to recognize juridical personality harms human dignity, because it denies absolutely an individual's condition of being a subject of rights . . .").

remain because no other nation has an obligation. The 1954 Convention on statelessness, in Article 31, prohibits parties from expelling stateless persons who are lawfully present in their territory "save on grounds of national security or public order"—the same protection the ICCPR affords to citizens. Thus, because Belgium does not recognize the Taliban regime, it treats refugees from Afghanistan as effectively stateless, and they are therefore not susceptible to forced return to that country or deportation more generally.

Moreover, if effective, the right to remain is of value only if one wishes to remain in that place, which presumably would depend at least in part on its living conditions. Remaining allows one to take advantage of goods and opportunities in that territory, such as they are. It can also provide the benefits of continuity in lifestyle and relationships and ability to form and execute a plan of life, if local conditions are at least minimally adequate for such things. For any persons desperate to escape horrible conditions, however, including radical disruption of social existence and life plans, the right to remain is valueless.

As for benefits in relation to employment, services, social welfare programs, and social acceptance, if the state in any given nation is now refusing to confer citizenship on a despised ethnic minority, it is wishful thinking to suppose that, were the government finally forced by the international community to confer nationality on members of that group, those individuals would suddenly have equal access and treatment.[24] Human rights organizations decry the predicament of "asylum seekers, refugees and undocumented migrants living in harrowing and life-threatening conditions,"[25] but if the cause of this is ethnic hatred, what reason is there to think the plight of such people would substantially improve merely by becoming citizens of the country where they are now present? Their becoming citizens might make it more difficult for the government, practically or in terms of appearances vis-à-vis the outside world, to explain discriminating against them, especially as to political rights. However, such a government is already violating its obligations under any human rights treaties to which they are parties, which do not permit discrimination based on nationality, so there is little reason to think it will change its disposition toward a despised group. Private individuals and organizations have even less reason to change their disposition.

Many nations in fact now effectively treat some of their own citizens just like noncitizens. One common way of doing this is simply denying them the documentary proof of citizenship they need to secure benefits, opportunities, and liberties. A state might do this as a matter of deliberate policy, or more likely it will make it

[24] *See* Staples, *supra* note 2, at 179–80 ("'even for those who have received their citizenship cards, life has not changed'").

[25] *See* Human Rights Watch, "No Healing Here: Violence, Discrimination and Barriers to Health for Migrants in South Africa," 5 (2009), https://www.hrw.org/report/2009/12/07/no-healing-here/violence-discrimination-and-barriers-health-migrants-south-africa (last visited Sept. 30, 2024).

practically difficult or impossible for some to navigate the process for obtaining documents. Kenya, for example, long made the process of applying for identification cards far more difficult for Nubians, an ethnic group present in Kenya for over a century after being forcibly relocated there by the British colonial regime.[26] The Dominican Republic has done the same to nationals of Haitian descent.

Further, some citizenship-based benefits, such as diplomatic advocacy, are optional for the state; they have no clear legal obligation to provide them to anyone.[27] Many never do so, because disinclined or dysfunctional. It is difficult to imagine, for example, that whoever is in power in Haiti at a given moment would devote any attention to mistreatment of Haitians abroad, with that country perennially in chaos.

In practice, states vary enormously in the extent to which they confer on an equality basis any benefits they ostensibly guarantee their citizens. Some countries, the poorest or those most beset with chaos from internal conflict and government instability, provide little or no benefit to anyone. Somalians, for example, are largely dependent on international organizations for fulfillment of their basic needs—security, health care, education, food. Those organizations naturally draw no distinctions among people based on citizenship. Other countries' governments provide significant benefits but only on a discriminatory basis to preferred groups, even as among citizens. For example, some states' laws confer greater powers, privileges, and opportunities on favored religious or ethnic groups, some grant greater liberties to men than to women, and some would likely decline to exert diplomatic pressure to help any of their political dissidents in exile.[28]

Conversely, as scholars increasingly acknowledge, the birth and growth of human rights in international law has considerably shrunk the ostensible marginal value of

[26] *See* Children of Nubian Descent in Kenya v. Kenya, African Committee of Experts on the Rights and Welfare of the Child, Decision 002/COM/002/09 (2011).

[27] McDougal et al., *supra* note 6, at 906 ("states are still regarded as having an option with respect to whether they will protect their nationals, for international law imposes no duty on the state to do so. Hence individuals are left to the arbitrary whim or caprice of state officials . . .").

[28] *See* Dimitry Kochenov, *The Right to Leave Any Country Including Your Own in International Law*, 28 CONN. J. INT'L L. 43, 61–62 (2012). No Convention has received universal ratification, but no nation has refused to sign all treaties conferring rights on children without nationality-based discrimination. Every nation other than the United States has ratified the CRC, and the United States has ratified the ICCPR, a protocol to the CRC that aims to end use of minors as soldiers, a treaty prohibiting child labor, and the Convention against Torture and Other Cruel, Inhuman or Degrading Treatment or Punishment. The United States has also *signed* the CRC and the ICESCR, and a signature per se obligates a nation to refrain from "acts which would defeat the object and purpose of a treaty." Vienna Convention on the Law of Treaties, art. 18. In addition, there is growing sense among international law scholars that "widely ratified multilateral conventions or treaties which have established human rights prohibitions . . . actually form confirmation of customary international law binding upon all states, not just the signatories," though this idea has primarily been discussed in connection with the most serious international-law crimes—genocide, torture, and slavery—that are, anyway, the subject of *jus cogens* norms, binding on all states whether they agree to it or not. *See* Roozbeh B. Baker, *Customary International Law in the 21st Century: Old Challenges and New Debates*, 21 EUR. J. INT'L L. 173, 174 (2010). *But cf.* Bill Ong Hing & Lizzie Bird, *Curtailing the Deportation of Undocumented Parents in the Best Interest of the Child*, 35 GEO. IMMIGR. L.J. 113,

being citizens relative to being noncitizen residents of a country. International law obligations to recognize and respect basic human rights are not tied to nationality, but rather simply to humanity. Under treaties and declarations, states bear duties to "every person" without regard to national origin or legal status. Both the ICCPR and the ICESCR have sweeping antidiscrimination provisions, guaranteeing their rights to all persons "without distinction of any kind, including. . . national or social origin . . . birth or other status." The United Nations High Commissioner for Refugees (UNHCR) has opined that this precludes discrimination against stateless persons per se as well, and the 1954 statelessness convention makes this explicit as to some goods, such as "public relief" and elementary education. This antidiscrimination principle might even have jus cogens status in international law, so it is not dependent on a state's ratification of any treaty.[29] For the negative rights that principally constitute the ICCPR, the scope of application is universal not only as to persons protected but also as to place of conduct, so nations engaged in official action abroad must respect the negative human rights of all persons, not just their own citizens.

The ICESCR, in Article 2, does suggest developing countries have a lesser obligation to fulfill some economic rights as to non-nationals, given their limited resources.[30] However, by implication, refusal to provide for non-nationals for nonresource reasons is impermissible, and there is no excusing lesser provision for non-nationals by nations with the means to provide for all in their territory. In addition, that Covenant has a special provision regarding children with its own, unqualified antidiscrimination clause; Article 10(3) commits states to take "special measures of protection and assistance . . . on behalf of all children without any discrimination for reasons of parentage or other conditions." And the CRC, which contains more detailed provisions about benefits state parties should provide to children, nowhere allows for favoring of children who are nationals over those who are not. Regional treaties also proscribe nationality-based discrimination, and without qualification.[31] Some specialized treaties do as well.[32]

147 (2020) (arguing that the rights set forth in the CRC must be regarded as customary international law and that its best-interests principle is a jus cogens norm).

[29] *See* Eric Fripp, Nationality and Statelessness in the International Law of Refugee Status 281 (2016) (describing 2003 decision of the Inter-American Court of Human Rights).

[30] ICESCR, art. 2(3) ("Developing countries, with due regard to human rights and their national economy, may determine to what extent they would guarantee the economic rights recognized in the present Covenant to non-nationals.").

[31] *Cf.* Andrejeva v. Latvia, App. No. 55707/00 (ECHR 2009) (concluding that Latvia's denial of pension benefits to a lifelong resident who became stateless after the collapse of the Soviet Union violated Article 14 of the European Convention on Human Rights).

[32] *See, e.g.*, International Convention on the Protection of the Rights of All Migrant Workers and Members of Their Families, art. 30 ("Each child of a migrant worker shall have the basic

These various instruments drastically lessen the rights permissibly tied to citizenship. Benefits states permissibly accord only to their citizens now are ones beyond fulfillment of basic human needs—principally, political rights (voting, standing for election), and performing certain public functions. Rights now guaranteed to all include even the right to remain, at least after one has been settled for a substantial period; the UN Human Rights Committee has opined that the ICCPR Article 12 right to remain in or return to a country that is "his own" was intended to be broader than "of which he is a national," to include persons lacking nationality in the country where their life has been centered, persons who have "special ties" such that they "cannot be considered to be a mere alien."[33] And as previously noted, stateless persons are practically undeportable, because no other nation need admit them.[34]

In most of the world today, then, all persons are, at least in theory, guaranteed numerous negative and positive rights against states simply by virtue of their humanity, and they have access to fora in which they can assert those rights themselves without the aid of any state.[35] Citizenship is no longer *the* right to have rights; simply having the status of human now entitles one to many domestic-law rights. Thus, when children of Haitian descent brought a claim against the Dominican Republic in the Inter-American Court of Human Rights for its failure to give them documentary proof of nationality required to attend school, the Commission might have responded that the Dominican Republic simply may not require such documentation as a condition of school attendance. As a signatory to the American Declaration of the Rights and Duties of Man and a party to the ICESCR, the Dominican Republic is bound to respect the right of "everyone" to education. When young adults in Côte d'Ivoire and Georgia complain of the inability to pursue their career dreams because employers are only able to hire citizens,[36] one should ask why those countries have policies causing such denial of opportunities in contravention of their treaty obligations. Those nations are parties to the ICESCR, which provides in Article 6(1): "States Parties to the present Covenant recognize the right to work, which includes the right of everyone to the

right of access to education on the basis of equality of treatment with nationals of the State concerned.").

[33] UN Human Rights Committee (UNHRC), CCPR General Comment No. 27: Article 12 (Freedom of Movement), Nov. 2, 1999, CCPR/C/21/Rev.1/Add.9, ¶ 20.

[34] *See* Kelly Staples, Retheorizing Statelessness: A Background Theory of Membership in World Politics 107 (2012) (citing authorities recognizing this reality)

[35] Even in the 1940s, Koessler observed "a trend toward permitting private persons to raise international claims without the intermediate agency of a state," a trend that, if continued, "would render the institution of diplomatic protection obsolete, if not formally abolished." Koessler, *supra* note 15, at 71.

[36] *See* UNHCR, *supra* note 22 (presenting case studies in various countries).

opportunity to gain his living by work which he freely chooses or accepts, and will take appropriate steps to safeguard this right." Denial of employment opportunity in the private sector cannot plausibly be justified by lack of state resources.

Continued emphasis on nationality in fact seems to undermine the progressive aims of elevating the status of the individual in international law and of predicating protections of welfare and freedom on individual worth rather than sponsorship by a state. It perpetuates an arguably retrograde belief about the normative significance of citizenship. Katja Swider observes: "[I]nsisting that stateless persons access human rights through the 'gateway of nationality' normalizes the situation where the nationality status can be required for accessing human rights, which is contradictory to the ideal of human rights as accessible to any human being."[37] Further, pushing nations to eliminate statelessness incidentally discourages each from treating noncitizens so well that they feel no need to undertake the naturalization process.

There is, unsurprisingly, little evidence that becoming citizens appreciably improves the living conditions of long-oppressed groups and plenty of evidence that they continue to suffer oppression even if the government begrudgingly confers nationality.[38] States currently use denial of citizenship not as an end in itself but as a tool for accomplishing invidious discrimination against persons with certain affiliations or characteristics.[39] The evidence is consistent with the hypothesis that the animosity still exists and inhibits access to benefits even after citizenship is conferred. As Lindsey Kingston notes, "most stateless populations lack legal nationality because they are part of a marginalized group that faces systematic discrimination and oppression from the start," and "the acquisition of legal nationality alone will not ensure their access to human rights."[40] Those who characterize statelessness or lack of citizenship in one's nation of residence as *the*

[37] Swider, *supra* note 19, at 205. *See also* Amal de Chickera and Laura van Waas, "Unpacking Statelessness," *in* BLOOM ET AL. EDS., *supra* note 2, at 53–69, 58–59 ("To contend that protection and enjoyment of rights is not forthcoming, either because the individual is stateless or because he or she does not enjoy an effective nationality, is to undermine the nature of rights as inherent to every human being and revert to the pre-justiciable human rights world order, in which the individual only had a place vicariously, through this or her state. In today's human rights worlds, the statelessness treaties are no longer the only instruments that benefit stateless persons.").

[38] *See, e.g.*, B.K. Blitz, "The State and the Stateless," *in* BLOOM ET AL. EDS., *supra* note 2, at 70–84, 77 (saying of Nubians in Kenya: "Citizenship has not improved access to housing rights, sanitation, water, or education for the participants interviewed."), 78 (describing problems the Estate Tamils experienced in Sri Lanka even after being accorded citizenship).

[39] Even denials of citizenship that result from gendered rules can reflect hostility to particular groups. Those rules typically stipulate that a child may inherit citizenship only from a citizen father. As a result, a child of a citizen mother and a foreigner father cannot become a citizen. Such a rule might reflect some xenophobic view about men who immigrate—for example, that they are likely to be from a particular ethnic group. It could, though, truly be about gender, reflecting an aversion on the part of male legislators to entry of men who will take jobs and wives away from native men if they enter and stay, and a belief that denying citizenship to their offspring is one way to discourage them.

[40] Lindsey N. Kingston, "Worthy of Rights: Statelessness as a Cause and Symptom of Marginalization," *in* BLOOM ET AL. EDS., *supra* note 2, at 17–34, 17–18. *See also* Chickera & Whiteman, *supra* note 18, at 107.

cause of suffering for marginalized groups make the basic error of conflating correlation and causation.

The fullest empirical treatment is a 2011 edited volume collecting studies from eight countries.[41] The studies reveal that finally receiving citizenship does not substantially change life for anyone. Minority groups previously well treated despite lack of citizenship, such as the Tatars returning to Crimea after Ukraine became an independent state, or the Russian-speaking people of Estonia after its independence, are, of course, still well treated after receiving citizen status. Minority groups previously oppressed because of ethnic hostility, on the other hand, continue to be mistreated and denied public and social benefits. If they gained anything, it was principally just the ability to vote in elections. Gaining the franchise is not entirely inconsequential; it has symbolic value and can eventually lead to material improvements, as one's group becomes better able to form political alliances with other groups to influence public policy. But oppressed peoples continue to be oppressed even with citizenship; they live as second-class citizens.

For example, in Kenya, Abraham Korir Sing'Oei found "structural barriers still consign the Nubians to the same state of poverty and destitution that they were seeking to escape through their struggle for citizenship. In this case, citizenship has not brought relief."[42] In Bangladesh, Katherine Southwick likewise found that for the Urdu-speaking population, "legal victories are not enough," because of "the political, social, economic and administrative obstacles that frustrate implementation of the group's rights as citizens."[43] Distilling the eight studies, the editors conclude:

> Seven of the eight researchers identified discrimination or marginalization as ongoing problems. . . . [T]he underlying problem or cause of statelessness

[41] Brad K. Blitz & Maureen Lynch eds., Statelessness and Citizenship: A Comparative Study on the Benefits of Nationality (2011).

[42] Abraham Korir Sing'Oei, "Citizenship in Kenya: The Nubian Case," *in* Blitz & Lynch eds., *supra* note 41, at 45–65, 61. *See also id.*, at 55–60 ("their acquired civic recognition has not impacted their economic status, which has yet to improve although they were . . . able to vote for the first time . . . The historical marginality of the community that denied them opportunities for social development, notably access to education, still undermines the fuller participation of Nubian individuals in the affairs of [Kenya] . . . [T]here are many who are unemployed . . . for simply being Nubians . . . The relationship between Nubians and the land they occupy remains tenuous, a reflection of the inability of juridical citizenship to secure stronger recognition of property rights for a minority group."); P.P. Sivapragasam, "From Statelessness to Citizenship: Up-country Tamils in Sri Lanka," *in* Blitz & Lynch, *supra* note 41, at 84–96, (quoting several Tamils saying their lives have not improved by becoming citizens of Sri Lanka).

[43] Katherine Southwick, "The Urdu-speakers of Bangladesh: An Unfinished Story of Enforcing Citizenship Rights," *in* Blitz & Lynch, *supra* note 41, at 115–41, 136. The experience of marginalized groups in some countries is more complex, because their status and regard by the majority has been ambiguous or changing over time. The Bidoon in Kuwait and Bahrain are one example, treated like full members of the society under one government then seeing a later regime withdraw many of their

> was at best swept under the carpet and at worst further frustrated by the process of acquiring nationality in practically every case.... Irrespective of trends in international law, the granting of citizenship itself is not sufficient to ensure the protection of human rights and to act as a unifying force for social integration. Indeed the findings of this research study call into question some of the claims made by cosmopolitan scholars—most of whose work is based on European investigations and studies from advanced economies—over the potency of citizenship. The ending of direct discrimination on the basis of nationality does not undo structural effects or other modes of discrimination.[44]

With respect to positive benefits, states might incur little criticism for continued denial to some, given the conditional nature of positive-rights commitments in treaties. Because those commitments are only to "progressive realization" as able, states can explain the deprivation of some as the natural consequence of having to start somewhere while building capacity to provide for all.[45]

Further, denial of some legal rights might be of less practical significance than generally supposed. Voting is just one form of political participation, and noncitizens are free to engage in other forms—for example, organizing with others in a similar situation and engaging in political expression or mustering resources to influence politicians. In addition, nations or political subunits within nations might choose to confer voting privileges on noncitizens, as some cities in the United States (San Francisco, Washington, DC, New York City, etc.) have done. Someone unable to own land despite the ability to pay might accomplish something functionally similar by creating a trust or entering a contract with someone who is able to own land. Permissible limits on employment opportunities are very narrow, leaving a plethora of other jobs available, including some analogous to those not available.

In addition to treaty commitments to respect numerous rights of all persons, endogenously driven humanitarian expansion of welfare states in more developed countries also has made citizenship largely irrelevant to daily life for noncitizens there, at least so long as they are permitted to remain. Swider observes among noncitizens in Latvia, for example, a general lack of interest in naturalizing,

rights and opportunities. *See* Abbas Shiblak, "Arabia's Bidoon," *in* BLITZ & LYNCH, *supra* note 41, at 172–193.

[44] Maureen Lynch and Brad K. Blitz, "Summary and Conclusions," in BLITZ & LYNCH, *supra* note 41, at 194–208, 202–04.

[45] *Cf.* Chickera & Whiteman, *supra* note 18, at 109 ("the principle of progressive realization allows developing countries to limit the enjoyment of economic rights by non-nationals in certain circumstances").

because the host government treats them so well.[46] In the United States, though some jurisdictions once refused undocumented immigrant children admission to public schools or tried to charge them tuition, the Supreme Court ruled that this discrimination violated the U.S. federal Constitution.[47] As a result, in any U.S. state today, children can attend the local public school regardless of legal status. The Court had previously held unanimously that denial of welfare benefits based on alienage was unconstitutional.[48] In addition, at least prior to the second Trump Administration, by federal statute anyone legally present in the United States could obtain health insurance under the Affordable Care Act; children legally present could participate in the Children's Health Insurance Program (CHIP); their parents could receive Temporary Assistance for Needy Families (TANF), food stamps, and other welfare benefits; and emergency or urgent-care medical facilities would never turn away children based on legal status.[49] This does not mean all immigrant children actually have received all available benefits, but the things that create practical obstacles to doing so (needing to work for the family to survive, fear of interaction with government agencies) arise from causes other than children's legal status (parents' status, poverty, lack of information, etc.).[50]

The American example invites one important caveat to the presentation of reasons why citizenship is of little practical importance. In affluent Western nations that are "destination countries" for refugees, provision of basic goods is offered to all, and a robust law enforcement regime suppresses interethnic hostility. However, deportation back to a country with dramatically poorer living conditions is a serious and ongoing threat for noncitizens, especially those who entered illegally, and this deters many from taking advantage of the benefits provided for all, insofar as that entails contact with agencies and persons who might report them to immigration authorities. Were such persons to be given citizenship, they would no longer fear removal, because the government respects the right of citizens to remain, and then they could begin to take full advantage of all opportunities their new nation offers. For that population, citizenship clearly matters. (I will suggest, though, that it is primarily citizenship for adults in this population that is crucial.) In contrast, for the noncitizen populations in the studies of statelessness, expulsion either was not a concern or it was a concern that would not be alleviated by conferral of citizenship.

46 Swider, *supra* note 19, at 199.
47 Plyler v. Doe, 457 U.S. 202 (1982).
48 Graham v. Richardson, 403 U.S. 365 (1971).
49 *See* Peter J. Spiro, *The (Dwindling) Rights and Obligations of Citizenship*, 21 Wm. & Mary Bill Rts. J. 899, 904–06 (2013) (describing federal and state legislation extending various financial support programs to immigrants).
50 *See* Frank D. Bean et al., Parents Without Papers: The Progress and Pitfalls of Mexican American Integration (2015), ch. 9.

In sum, then, as a practical matter nationality is neither a necessary nor a sufficient condition for receiving basic goods, services, and opportunities. It is close to irrelevant, and focus on it arguably is misplaced. Even regarding the supposed psychological benefit of membership, the value appears overstated, given that nationality does not guarantee social acceptance. And in addition, unlike basic material goods, this benefit arises solely by comparison to others—that is, from the fact that some persons have been declared to belong there, while others have not. If *no one* in one's cohort bore a particular status or label, then not having it would be unlikely to affect one's sense of belonging or worth, to make one feel second-class. And ultimately, we might question the idea that having a state regime claim you as one of its minions is a necessary source of human dignity.

4.3 Potential Downsides to Citizenship

Some who write about statelessness acknowledge that nationality and citizenship can entail not only legal rights and privileges but also legal duties—for example, to pay taxes on income worldwide rather than just domestic and to serve in a nation's military or other public service role.[51] However, a full catalogue of the potential downsides to being a national of a particular state is necessary to assess its net value. In addition to the positive obligations of financial contribution and service, being a citizen of a particular nation can entail imposition of additional negative duties, denials of some rights and liberties, and various forms of unfavorable treatment by other nations and private or public international organizations. Under international law, states are empowered to impose on any whom they claim as their nationals any duties and disabilities not clearly proscribed by international legal instruments to which they are bound or by universally applicable international legal norms. Other states and international entities are also legally free to treat those persons, based on their nationality, in any unfavorable ways not clearly proscribed by their international-law obligations. Moreover, today stateless persons receive many protections under international law, and being claimed as a national by a state makes one ineligible for these protections, in part because the rules reflect respect for the claim that one's state of nationality should control one's fate.

This susceptibility to some adverse treatment by all nations of the world, and this exclusion from some benefits afforded stateless persons, on account of being a national of a particular state, we might characterize in a general way as a

[51] *See, e.g.*, McDougal et al., *supra* note 6, at 902 ("It is a distinguishing characteristic of nation-states that they claim a special competence to impose upon their members unique burdens with respect, for example, to taxation, military service, and subjection to civil and criminal jurisdiction").

"liability," in the sense jurist Wesley Hohfeld articulated—that is, vulnerability to having one's rights, duties, and privileges altered, possibly contrary to one's welfare or wishes, by another entity that holds a "power" over one.

4.3.1 Treatment by the state of one's nationality

In feudal times, residents of a land were "subjects" of the ruling lord and owed him perpetual allegiance, which involved an expectation of monetary contribution and military service and precluded change of allegiance to another land or lord.[52] To a great extent, it was the desire of American colonial populations for independence that first eroded the notion that one must always remain tied to the nation of one's birth and the conception of society's members as subjects. Choice of "citizen" for the U.S. federal Constitution was a deliberate rejection of that servile view of the individual.[53] Thomas Jefferson invoked the writings of Locke, Blackstone, and others to support a claim of entitlement to expatriation and a view of government as servant of the people rather than vice versa.[54] Mass immigration to the new world in the nineteenth century created additional pressure for international recognition of a right to transfer allegiance; the United States did not want, for example, German immigrants to remain beholden to their motherland.[55] Today the right to change nationality is well established and might partly explain why nations make belonging less burdensome; they must compete with other nations for the allegiance of those capable of relocating. Yet still, citizenship, so long as one retains it, comes with incrementally greater obligations, limits on liberty, and susceptibility to government power.

4.3.1.1 Duties

Conscription has been a common practice throughout the world. Still today many nations expect all citizens (or all male citizens) to perform military or civil service for some years upon reaching adulthood, even in peacetime. Dual citizens might be subject to service obligations in two nations.[56] Any nations that

[52] *See* Jane McAdam, *The Right to Leave as Personal Liberty*, 12 Melb. J. Int'l L. 12, 38 (2011).

[53] *See* Koessler, *supra* note 15, at 59–60 (1946).

[54] McAdam, *supra* note 52, at 39. Others in the founding generation, such as Alexander Hamilton, resisted this then-novel idea of a right of expatriation, arguing for continued adherence to the common law doctrine of perpetual allegiance. *Id.*

[55] *Id.*, 40–42.

[56] *See* Michael Tae Woo, *Dual Citizenship and Mandatory Military Service in the Republic of Korea*, 108 Iowa L. Rev. 2049 (2023). The Protocol Relating to Military Obligations in Certain Cases of Double Nationality (1930) presented a partial solution, excusing any dual national from service to a nation if he "habitually resides in" and is "most closely connected with" another of which he is a national. But only a couple dozen states signed it. Many nations have instead or also executed bilateral agreements aimed at ensuring no individual is forced to fulfill such a duty to more than one nation, but those are quite limited in scope and many nations have no such agreements.

do not now have a draft could institute one when circumstances make it appear necessary. Whether noncitizens residing in a country bear such a duty varies by nation, but the dominant approach is to impose it only on citizens. This is the case, for example, in South Korea and Greece and Brazil. The United States is unusual in casting a wider net; nearly all males on U.S. soil must register with the Selective Service (exempted are immigrants for the first year of residence and those here on temporary visas). But U.S. citizens are liable to the draft even if living abroad, whereas persons who are neither U.S. citizens nor living in the United States owe no service obligation to the United States even if they previously lived in the United States.

International law authorizes states to tax their citizens' income regardless of where they reside or work and to impose an "exit tax" on those intending to establish residence in another country and renounce their original citizenship.[57] A non-national who departs from a country to work elsewhere, in contrast, has no such continuing obligation to that country.

International law also recognizes a power of states to apply their laws to their citizens for conduct outside their territory, whereas they have criminal and civil jurisdiction over non-nationals only as to conduct committed or causing effects within their territory.[58] For example, the U.S. Foreign Corrupt Practices Act allows for punishment of American citizens for conduct they engage in entirely within the territory of other nations. If one were instead stateless, that possibility of criminal prosecution under that statute would not exist. Being a citizen of a particular nation also makes one more susceptible, if currently abroad, to extradition to that nation for criminal prosecution.[59]

4.3.1.2 Legal Disabilities

International law pronouncing rights to free movement and to leave any country, discussed in previous chapters, does not differentiate between nationals and non-nationals. However, governments have felt far freer, more justified, in detaining their own nationals for a broader range of reasons.[60] Correspondingly,

[57] *See* Laura Snyder, *The Myths and Truths of Extraterritorial Taxation*, 32 Cornell J.L. & Pub. Pol'y 185, 250 (2022) ("While U.S. citizens can remove themselves from the physical territory of the United States, they can never remove themselves from the fiscal territory of the United States."). Snyder argues that U.S. extraterritorial taxation is so burdensome that it effectively violates human rights to migration and free choice of employment and causes U.S. citizens to experience various forms of inequality of treatment and opportunity. *Id.*, 248–63. Snyder notes, however, that the United States is unusual in this respect; most other nations choose to tax citizens residing abroad to a much lesser extent. *Id.*, 268–69. And in the United States, the foreign tax credit and foreign earned income exclusion mitigate the burden substantially. Also, the United States has entered numerous bilateral tax treaties to avoid "double taxation."

[58] *See* Charles Doyle, "Extraterritorial Application of American Criminal Law: An Abbreviated Sketch," 3 (Congressional Research Services, 2023).

[59] *Id.*, 5.

[60] *See* McAdam, *supra* note 52, at 56 n. 196.

international bodies are generally more deferential to states' treatment of their own nationals, as reflected, for example, in humanitarian law.[61] One basis for blocking a citizen's exit generally accepted as legitimate is to enforce the service and financial obligations citizens bear. But even when that justification is absent, the UN Human Rights Committee has observed, states make it more difficult for their own citizens to exit, by: imposing procedural, bureaucratic, and financial obstacles to obtaining a passport; demanding assurances of return such as affirmations by employers and family members, money deposits, and restrictions on family members traveling abroad at the same time; and shaming applicants by telling them they are harming their country's good name or honor by going abroad.[62] Some states, such as Nepal, require citizens to apply for an exit visa and pay a fee to travel abroad or emigrate, and they might deny the application of anyone deemed valuable to the regime, on any pretense; this presumptive control over citizens gives them means of surreptitiously infringing liberties when they cannot do so legitimately.

Conversely, being a national of one's state of residence could conceivably make one more vulnerable to expulsion, if the state treats nationals' right to remain as weaker than that of persons in its territory who are only nationals of some other state(s) but holding a visa, or who are stateless. This greater vulnerability might be de jure, or it might be a matter of persons' citizenship giving a government motivation to expel—for example, because they enjoy rights as citizens exercise of which could impede the aims of those in power (e.g., political participation or property ownership), or because it hopes they will denationalize themselves and cease to have any positive claims on the state (e.g., to recognition and protection of their property rights).

In addition, certain liabilities can attend dual nationality. McDougal identified several:

> A multiple national . . . may be subjected to the civil and criminal jurisdiction, which follows a national wherever he goes, of two or more states; he may be subject to the laws relating to treason, enemy status, military service and security clearance of more than one state. More than one state may have jurisdiction to tax him, to expropriate his property, to impose restrictions on his trading activities, and to restrict disposition of his property. More than one state may discriminate against him; he may be discriminated against on different grounds in different communities. He may be subjected to physical and psychological insecurity in more than one state. He may be subjected to compulsory education

[61] *See* Vanessa Holzer, Refugees From Armed Conflict: The 1951 Refugee Convention and International Humanitarian Law 51–53 (2015) (discussing Geneva Convention IV, on protection of civilians).

[62] UNHRC, *supra* note 33, ¶ 17.

> in more than one state. More than one state may seek to impose restrictions on his practice of certain professions. More than one state may assert jurisdiction with respect to his family life, including marriage, children's up-bringing, education and welfare. Finally, more than one state may seek to restrict his religious affiliations and activities.[63]

An additional disability for citizens stems from rights of territorial control that governments possess under international law, which they can use to exclude potential sources of assistance to their nationals. Like an abusive parent, a state blocks both exit of "its people" and entry by those who wish to help them. A recent UN report found nations blocking human rights monitoring and humanitarian aid in a "shocking" number of cases, imperiling millions of lives.[64] Abusing other states' nationals or stateless persons in this way risks complaint by the other states or the UNHRC. But other nations lack standing to complain in international fora about a nation's mistreatment of "its own."[65] And though international law now imposes on states a duty to permit aid from outside sources in some circumstances (see Chapter 9), there is authority suggesting the duty is stronger regarding aid to noncitizens.[66] Moreover, the 1954 statelessness convention requires parties to "accord to stateless persons the same treatment as is accorded to aliens generally," which would include deference to other states' effort to provide aid.

Other nations also presumptively lack lawful freedom to use force against a nation to enable entry of outside sources of assistance to its own citizens. Article 2(4) of the UN Charter prohibits a state's use of force against another state, and the idea that a state's violation of its own citizens human rights creates an exception to this fundamental principle is only slowly gaining acceptance, and only in contemplation of the most extreme cases, such as genocide.[67] The freedom of other states to intervene forcibly is clearer when the aim is to protect persons who

[63] McDougal et al., *supra* note 6, at 982.

[64] *See* "'Shocking Increase' in Denial of Access to Life-Saving Humanitarian Aid for Children in Conflict Zones Worldwide, Security Council Hears, as Delegates Discuss Solutions," UN Security Council Meeting Report, SC/15651 (Apr. 3, 2024).

[65] This holds true even in cases of dual nationality. *See* McDougal et al., *supra* note 6, at 981–82 ("Traditional doctrine holds that one state of nationality cannot protect an individual against another state of his nationality.").

[66] *See* Holzer, *supra* note 61.

[67] *See* Taylor B. Seybolt, Humanitarian Military Intervention: The Conditions for Success and Failure (2007), 2 ("human security as a justification for military intervention under certain circumstances has gained widespread acceptance"), 5–6 (explaining that when one state intervenes in another to protect persons other than the former's own citizens, the action falls in the category of humanitarian military intervention, whereas protecting one's own citizens residing in the target nation falls in a different category requiring less justification).

are not the target state's own citizens. This is partly because other states have a recognized "right to rescue" their own citizens.[68] But another rationale is a negative inference that would apply also in the case of intervention to protect stateless persons—namely, that so long as intervention does not aim to annex territory *or* to usurp government authority over a state's own nationals, it does not violate "the territorial integrity or political independence" of the target state.[69] That rationale is not universally accepted,[70] but it receives serious attention and has greater purchase when the proposed intervention is an evacuation of persons who are not citizens of the target state rather than establishment of an ongoing operation.[71]

Finally, a less tangible downside to citizenship, a counterpoint to the psychological benefit of belonging, is a sense of being owned by a nation, which some people at some times have wished to avoid. During and after World War II, for example, some refugees denaturalized by their fascist home nations contended that they should not have to seek nationality status in their new country of residence to enjoy full human rights there. Eric Fripp writes that "eminent intellectuals . . . wrote to U.N. Secretary General Trygvie Lie . . . [that] 'sheer force of events has given them the feeling of belonging to a community larger than one nation . . . citizens of the world . . .' [and] the situation of postwar refugees offered unprecedented opportunity 'to let the ideal of world citizenship subsist . . . in courageous experimenting and in a genuine respect for the human person.'"[72] The International Relief Organization was dismissive of their plea, but the sense of an unclaimed or untethered self that those refugees expressed might appeal to many people in the world today, whether refugees or not.

4.3.2 Treatment by other nations

Being a national of one state can also cause other states not to try to assist. In terms of representation in international fora, traditionally one's being a national of State X has meant no other state could seek via formal legal action to guard one against harmful conduct by State X or by any other state.[73] Even if one were a dual national, the other state could not bring a complaint against State X in

[68] *See, e.g.*, Andrew W.R. Thomson, *Doctrine of the Protection of Nationals Abroad: Rise of the Non-Combatant Evacuation Operation*, 11 Wash. U. Global Stud. L. Rev. 627, 628 (2012).
[69] *Id.*, 636–37.
[70] *Id.*, 638–54.
[71] *Id.*, 654–67.
[72] Fripp, *supra* note 29, at xvi.
[73] *See* McDougal et al., *supra* note 6, at 906 ("The overwhelming trend of decision has been to permit the state of nationality, and only the state of nationality, to protect individuals.").

any international tribunal, because the individual in a sense belonged also to State X.[74] In the modern era, the "principle of effective nationality" has limited that norm in cases of multiple nationality to situations in which the allegedly offending state is the dominant nationality of the person. And the refugee conventions empower state parties to bring an ICJ action against any other state party for failure to comply, presumably including failing to respect substantive rights of refugees (who by definition are not nationals of the offending state).[75] But that bar does not exist in relation to any nation for a person who is stateless. A state inclined to help such a person might or might not be able to bring an ICJ action for that purpose, but regardless it could exert diplomatic pressure without incurring criticism for interfering with a state's treatment of one of its own.

In connection with expulsion from a country, being a national of another country makes this more likely. This is the other side of the right-to-remain coin. A country generally may expel anyone who is not its own national, particularly if they have entered the country illegally, subject to the principle of non-refoulement—that is, not returning someone to a place where they would incur persecution. But they have even less freedom legally and practically to expel someone who is stateless. The 1954 statelessness convention, in Article 31, commits state parties to "not expel a stateless person lawfully in their territory save on grounds of national security or public order" and only after provision of due process. Moreover, there is the practical obstacle that no other country is legally required to accept such persons; it is difficult to expel someone refused entry everywhere else. Thus, for example, if Russia had not revoked the citizenship of those who fled after the Bolshevik Revolution in 1921, some states to which such persons migrated might well have returned them.

As for entering a country of which one is not a national, most developed countries have immigration restrictions or quotas that vary by nation of origin. Thus, among those wishing to migrate to such a country, being a national of one state rather than another (or stateless) could be a hindrance. At times, a country might ban all nationals of certain states, as President Donald Trump did with his "Muslim ban" in 2017,[76] and as the U.S. Immigration Act of 1924 did to all who were nationals of an Asian country.

[74] *See, e.g.*, Hague Convention on Nationality (1930), art. 4 ("A State may not afford diplomatic protection to one of its nationals against a State whose nationality such person also possesses."); McDougal et al., *supra* note 6, at 981–82 ("Traditional doctrine holds that one state of nationality cannot protect an individual against another state of his nationality. If the party imposing deprivations happens to be a state of his nationality, the individual having multiple nationality may never get a hearing on the merits of his claim.").

[75] 1966 Protocol relating to the Status of Refugees, art. 4.

[76] *See* Trump v. Hawaii, 585 U.S. 667 (2018) (upholding the ban against statutory and constitutional challenges).

Even if one is able to enter a country of which one is not a national, possessing the nationality of a particular other country could be prejudicial, provoking surveillance or civil disabilities, for the same reason a country might wish to deny the person entry.[77] For example, in 2024, Finland moved to ban Russian citizens from purchasing property in its territory.[78] An immigrant's nationality could also invite social hostility and persecution, if perceived as allegiance to or sympathy with an enemy nation.[79] During and after World War II, many émigrés from Germany living in the United Kingdom, the United States, and elsewhere sought to renounce their German citizenship, preferring statelessness to being identified with Germany. Many altered their names in part for the same reason.

Further, acquiring citizenship where one resides can be more difficult or impossible if one is a national of any other country. Human rights prescriptions for conferral of *jus soli* citizenship are limited to persons who have no other nationality. And for most of history, multiple nationality was anathema to the international community. Many individual nations have had rules whereby they would refuse to confer citizenship on a person who was already a citizen of another country and who could not or preferred not to terminate that citizenship, and whereby they would revoke the citizenship of someone who became a citizen of another country.[80] Today, there is greater acceptance of dual nationality, but anyone applying for naturalization might still encounter a prohibition or at least procedural obstacles because of already having a nationality; many nations require such applicants to supply certain documents from the nation of their existing citizenship, which some have difficulty providing, whereas that is not expected of stateless persons.[81]

Beyond immigration, nations discriminate among foreigners in providing other benefits, with citizens of some other nations ineligible. Russia's exclusion specifically of Americans from its international adoption program is an example. Denial of tourist visas to nationals of certain other countries is common. If the benefit denied is not the subject of a human right to which the discriminatory nation is committed, there might be no violation of international law in this practice.

[77] *Cf.* ADL & Others v. Sec. of State for the Home Dept. [2024] EWHC 994 (adjudicating permissibility of electronic monitoring of immigrants).

[78] Whether human rights treaties permit such discrimination internally based on nationality is somewhat unclear. Fripp, *supra* note 29, at 257–81 (arguing they do not).

[79] For this and other examples, *see id.*, 146–52.

[80] *See, e.g.*, Lucy Hovel, "Ensuring That Today's Refugees Are Not Tomorrow's Stateless: Solutions in a Refugee Context," *in* van Waas & Khanna, *supra* note 2, at 71–97, 90 (noting Sudanese law stating Sudanese nationality "shall automatically be revoked if the person has acquired, de jure or de facto, the nationality of South Sudan.").

[81] *See* Swider, *supra* note 19, at 200 (discussing Armenian citizen seeking to naturalize in the Netherlands).

4.3.3 Treatment by international entities

Having the nationality of one's state of residence makes international bodies overseeing humanitarian and human rights treaties more deferential toward the state in its treatment of the person. With respect to international humanitarian law (IHL) protections for civilians, traditionally one is better off if stateless when mistreated by the state where one resides.[82] Additionally, because domestic governments have power to impose their laws on their citizens, whether at home or abroad, private or public international entities might refuse or prefer not to deal with citizens of certain nations. For example, Peter Spiro observes that because of "the administrative expenses of complex FATCA [Foreign Account Tax Compliance Act] controls, many foreign banks have turned away U.S. customers."[83]

4.4 Citizenship as Net Negative

Though conceptual and empirical complexities make objective quantification of citizenship's benefits and costs difficult, as a logical matter it is undeniable that the costs can outweigh the benefits for some people in relation to some states. For certain countries, no doubt, this is true for a great portion of their citizens. Section 4.4.1 spells out how that might be the case. Section 4.4.2 explains why it is especially likely to be true for children.

4.4.1 For any person

This is straightforward. The main benefit of citizenship in the place where one resides, if one wishes to remain there, is typically the right to remain. But this right now applies also to noncitizens who have resided in a nation for an extensive period, and the ability to remain exists de facto for stateless persons regardless of length of residence. In addition, a given state might not respect this right for anyone. Or it might do so, but the country is so inhospitable that the right is of no value, as it is presumably for the tens of millions trying to escape from poor or authoritarian nations to affluent Western democracies. Opportunities and social welfare benefits might not exist for anyone. Likewise with political rights; some nations ostensibly have elected governments but deny or block exercise of the franchise to some (e.g., Black Americans before the civil rights

[82] *See* Holzer, *supra* note 61, at 52–53.
[83] Spiro, *supra* note 10, at 171.

era), or they "fix" the results, and many do not even pretend. Further, nations struggling to create minimally adequate living conditions are unlikely to devote resources to diplomatic protection of their nationals living abroad or harmed by other nations. Contrary to what some who decry statelessness claim,[84] opportunity for advocacy by the UNHCR might be more effective for those in the worst circumstances than is the opportunity for diplomatic representation by the state of one's nationality.

On the other side of the equation, regimes that are nondemocratic, oppressive of some or all, and/or in a condition of turmoil and devastation might be especially likely to impose onerous burdens on nationals—in particular, extracting as much wealth from them as possible and forcing them to serve the regime's military aims or security interests. Many desperate émigrés are seeking not only to satisfy basic survival needs but also to escape enlistment in military or police service.

4.4.2 For children especially

These statements about benefits would typically be true for children as much as for adults. They have general human rights that are not dependent on their nationality, and some statements of the nondiscrimination principle are tied specifically to basic goods for children—for example, elementary education, in the 1954 statelessness convention. In addition, many typically cited benefits of citizenship per se, even if available to adults, are unavailable or of little value to children, thus diminishing the positive side of the value assessment to near zero. The main benefits to exiting statelessness and entering citizenship that Brad Blitz and Maureen Flynn identified were opportunities for employment, university education, and voting. Young children are not supposed to be working, they need primary and secondary education rather than post-secondary studies (which are more optional under human rights treaties), and states generally do not afford minors political rights whether they are citizens or not.[85] In part because of exclusion from political life, their being citizens does not have the same symbolic and psychological significance, or give them the same sense of full membership, as with adults; they suffer from second-class status regardless.

[84] *See, e.g.*, Staples, *supra* note 34, at 111–12.

[85] Some scholars have taken the view that children are incapable of citizenship because capacity for political participation is a prerequisite. *See* Jacqueline Bhabha, Child Migration & Human Rights in a Global Age (2014), ch. 2. This view reflects an undefended essentialist understanding of citizenship as necessarily entailing enjoyment of particular rights. As noted, citizenship has no fixed meaning; the positive law of a particular jurisdiction gives it the meaning the governing regime wishes it to have. Most nations deem children "citizens" even though not holding a right to vote.

Further, children might be less likely to benefit from any state efforts to improve welfare for all, because states presume to decide for themselves what serves the well-being of their nationals, and children are less able to express disagreement. Having claimed children as "theirs," nations proceed with greater apparent authority to pronounce what those children's interests are, and other nations are deferential. Yet some clearly do so disingenuously. Anne Bayefsky observes that when nations assert "cultural sovereignty," typically "the real interests of the state protagonists is not protection of cultural identity but non-interference, supremacy, and control."[86] As discussed in Chapter 3, this is common in defending shutdown of IA.

Additionally, the right to remain per se is generally of less value for children, even when effective. Jacqueline Bhabha contends that "the importance of residency rights for children" is underestimated, explaining that "the ties and influences that result from belonging to a particular territory are critical, even for very young children."[87] But then her illustration of the idea is entirely about the relative quality of life in one place or another, which has no inherent connection to the right to reside; indeed, it would cut against remaining in place for children in bad circumstances who have opportunity to move to better. The most important type of stability infants and young children need is undisturbed connection to the persons who are parenting them, and that might or might not depend on remaining in place. In terms of retaining ties to other persons in the social environment and remaining in familiar circumstances, these are largely nonexistent for infants and increase in significance only gradually. Elementary-school-age children have little difficulty relocating with parents. Peer socializing becomes more important in the later schooling years, to a point where teens can be upset about a family relocation, but such rootedness falls off for a time upon reaching adulthood; in young adulthood, many people, even having grown up in wonderful circumstances, choose to venture afield. At some point, often after becoming parents, the value of remaining in place grows again, and by old age is likely most pronounced. Hence, we see many elderly persons refusing to leave their village in Ukraine even as invading Russian forces approach.

One inherent value of a right to remain is the ability to make and pursue life plans. This value is also less or nonexistent for young children; they are not yet autonomous and do little consciously to conjure and begin executing a life plan. Their time horizon is short, and they typically have much of their early life course dictated by others, usually parents. Adolescents do begin to develop a life plan, but the aspects of executing it that depend on stability of residence usually do not

[86] Anne F. Bayefsky, *Cultural Sovereignty, Relativism, and International Human Rights: New Excuses for Old Strategies*, 9(1) Ratio Juris 42–59, 43 (1996).
[87] Bhabha, *supra* note 85, at 68.

take place till adulthood, after they have started a vocation or business. Higher education often requires going abroad.

The greatest potential value in having a right to remain for a child is being able to remain in a good place, if one happens to be in one, rather than being forced to migrate to a bad place. So it is potentially valuable for a child of Guatemalan parents who recently migrated to the United States, but not so much for a child residing in Guatemala. In any event, a formal right to remain is largely meaningless for children in many countries. A (rebuttable) presumption prevails, for good reason, that they are best off remaining with parents even if the parents are to be deported, or returning to parents who have remained behind in a less hospitable land. Bhabha documents that many U.S.-born children are effectively forced to leave the United States, despite being U.S. citizens, when their noncitizen parents are deported.[88] Conversely, if a child's parents are citizens, the child will be allowed to remain even if not a citizen (though this is rare). Adults who are U.S. citizens can bring or keep family members, but the family (re)union benefit does not attach to children's citizenship. David Thronson summarizes: "As a practical matter, immigration law's frameworks for family immigration subordinate children's status to that of their parents."[89] This is not universally true; the European Court of Justice has blocked deportation of parents in some cases because this would frustrate a child's right to remain, and the Inter-American Commission has suggested a citizen child's best interests must be considered in deportation actions against parents.[90] But such a policy really rests on a liberal impulse to let in as many people escaping from horrible situations as possible, rather than on any sound argument that child citizenship should give one family priority over others in affording the opportunity to live in a high-functioning society.

Laura Ferracioli contends that children need the right to remain so that the state of their residence at any given moment can properly ensure satisfaction of their needs.[91] But she provides no explanation of why that state must continue to be the same one, and she fails to acknowledge the drastic differences in capacity to care for children across nations. She does acknowledge that being parented is of primary importance and that children of parents who are citizens will be able to remain wherever the parents are, but then she points to the fact that many children are unparented and somehow deduces from this that children need an independent right to remain. That is counterintuitive. Being bereft of family in

[88] *See id.*, *supra* note 85, ch. 2, at 71 ("If children have no right to use their citizenship as a basis for exercising family reunion or shoring up family unity, then—if their parents face deportation—the children too risk constructive deportation, despite being citizens.").

[89] David Thronson, "Citizenship and Rights of Children," *in* Jonathan Todres & Shani M. King, The Oxford Handbook of Children's Rights Law 223–36, 231 (2020).

[90] *See id.*, at 230, and Bhabha, *supra* note 85, at 83–86.

[91] *See* Laura Ferracioli, Liberal Self-Determination in a World of Migration (2022), ch. 1.

Country X is actually a reason to leave Country X, because it typically signals the inability of that nation to provide for children in general (e.g., by having a system of foster care and adoption). Even absent that signal, there is simply nothing inherent in being in Country X at point in time T that creates a need for a child to remain in Country X at T + 1 to be cared for. For countless children, a decent life is only possible by international migration, at the earliest feasible time.

In short, then, transitioning from the status of stateless to the status of citizen entails little or no inherit benefit for children. And on the downside, some disabilities that citizenship entails are greater for children as a matter of law or practice. Children are universally regarded still as quasi-property, owned in part by their nation of citizenship, rather than as persons with rights and worthy of moral respect. For example, whereas adults in detention facilities or internment camps receive much attention from international humanitarian organizations and are deemed to have a right to outside assistance and monitoring, young children now held in state institutions cannot assert rights to contact with such organizations. Such organizations are themselves likely to be deferential to the state's handling of children, accepting assertions that the children belong to the state and are no one else's concern.[92]

Finally, regarding liabilities: children are better off in some respects. They are unlikely to be taxed, though they are in the same position as an adult who has neither wages nor wealth. And they are supposed to be immune from conscription (not universally true in practice, of course). On the other hand, some liabilities of citizenship more greatly impact children in practice—namely, the correlatives of states' powers to block exit and to block access to external sources of assistance, along with the inability of the UNHCR and other nations to advocate for them. The CRC has played a role in this, insofar as it has caused the international legal community to look there for articulation of children's rights, which in the case of emigration are greatly diminished, rather than to the ICCPR.

4.5 Conclusion

Swider, one of the few scholars to question the push for universal nationality, concludes from a review of case studies: "Pursuing the elimination of statelessness as a policy goal per se, without regard to preferences and the human rights situation of the affected persons, cannot be justified by reference to the interests of those persons."[93] This is most clearly true with respect to children. Moreover,

[92] *See* Sara A. Dillon, *Time for a Truth-Based Policy: Humanitarian Access to Children Living Without Family Care*, 27 Fla. J. Int'l L. 23, 41 (2015).
[93] Swider, *supra* note 19, at 191.

young children have no ability themselves to object to imposition of citizenship, and even older youth might be unable to renounce an on-the-whole undesirable citizenship—either because the conferring nation does not recognize minors' decisions as legally effective or because renunciation by anyone lacking another nationality is precluded under the statelessness Conventions.[94] It is time to recognize that citizenship or nationality can be a curse for a child, and so to think carefully about when, if ever, it is even permissible, let alone mandatory, for a nation to ascribe its citizenship to a child.

[94] *See* Hague Convention on Nationality, art. 7; 1961 Convention on the Reduction of Statelessness, art. 7(1)(a).

5
Claiming Persons as Citizens

> *"A child is born a subject of no country and government. He is under his father's tuition and authority, till he come to age of discretion; and then he is a free-man, at liberty what government he will put himself under; what body politick he will unite himself to."*
>
> John Locke, *A Second Treatise of Government*

> *"For my part I am not prepared for citizenship in the United States. I do not want it.... It takes greed of gain to make a successful citizen of the United States."*
>
> Walter Adair Duncan, father of the Cherokee social welfare system, in *Statehood* (1893)

5.1 Introduction

The supposition that it would be beneficial for all human beings if international law ensured conferral of a nationality on every person, without regard to which nationality for which persons, is implausible, Chapter 4 concluded. Yet absent this supposition, what justification could there be for current international law dictates, thrusting citizenship upon children everywhere and strongly discouraging—in some cases even proscribing—statelessness among adults even if they prefer it? Prevailing moral beliefs today rule out a view in which human individuals are simply subordinated to state interests, instruments for rulers' use. And, on the other hand, they endorse a two-sided moral right regarding political association—that is, a right to join and a right not to join. Yet rules of nationality today appear to reflect a combination of lingering pre-Enlightenment views of the individual's relation to the state and post-Enlightenment realpolitik, rather than genuine respect for persons. In the pre-Enlightenment world, God placed all persons under the governance of divinely ordained rulers, the better to serve God's plan for life on earth. In the post-Enlightenment world, states agreed to respect the complete dominion of other rulers over people on their territory in exchange for receiving the same deference, and states claimed people as they wished because they could, only occasionally experiencing conflicts in this regard with other states.

International Migration of Children for a Better Life. James G. Dwyer, Oxford University Press. © Oxford University Press 2025.
DOI: 10.1093/9780197752333.003.0005

This chapter develops a position regarding citizenship of children based on the contemporary outlook elevating the status of the individual, diminishing that of the state. The state is servant to the people, and every individual holds, as against the state and international institutions, basic rights to respect, integrity, and ultimate self-determination. The fact that universal citizenship serves the aim of dividing up the world neatly for state rulers to control has explanatory but not justificatory force. Because there clearly are situations when it is overall not beneficial—indeed can be a life-defeating burden—for a particular person, especially a child, to have a particular nationality, or any nationality rather than none, there ought to be a compelling defense of current citizenship law and practice. We need an account of when a nation is warranted in declaring someone to be its citizen and when it is appropriate for the international legal regime to push a person into possessing some nationality rather than none. Correspondingly, we should ask whether persons, and in particular children, have any moral right against imposition of citizenship on them.

The normative analysis is complicated by the indefiniteness of citizenship's content; as explained in Chapter 4, it can entail a different package of rights, duties, powers, and liabilities in different nations and within a single nation over time. Let us suppose citizenship entails the benefits treaties attach specifically to nationality—namely, a right to vote and hold political office as an adult and the opportunity to enjoy the state's representation in international fora and diplomacy should the state choose to give it. But also, that it entails the liabilities of having a particular state (1) control one's proof of identity and ability to migrate, and (2) hold power to demand that one contribute service and wealth to the state. This chapter will first consider whether a state may ever, consistent with respect for the moral status of the individual, brand autonomous persons as its nationals without their actual consent and thereby impose its specific package of benefits and liabilities. It will then examine children's normative situation. After concluding that no state can ever rightfully impose its citizenship on children, and especially not states that fail to provide minimally adequate living conditions for them, it considers what the world might look like if no state could claim any child as belonging to it—that is, if citizenship were limited to adults and all children were stateless.

5.2 Citizenship and Autonomous Persons

Free and informed choice by the individual would seem a necessary and sufficient condition for the permissibility of a state's ascribing its citizenship to autonomous persons. Liberal societies recognize an individual right of dissociation in almost every aspect of life, even when an association would have no practical consequences. Citizenship is a kind of association and status that in most nations entails special obligations (e.g., service and financial contribution regardless of residence) beyond those arising simply from being present within a society at a particular point in time (e.g., obedience to law, limits on liberty arising from others' basic rights), as well as special liabilities (state control over migration and behavior abroad, etc.). One might therefore suppose that, from a liberal perspective, no autonomous person should have that status forced upon them.

Further, because international relocation is typically quite difficult, states might be expected to allow for different types of affiliation between the nation and its residents, different levels of commitment, rather than insisting on an all-or-nothing regime of membership—that is, accept citizenship or leave. If an autonomous person prefers to have a second-tier status within a nation, that should be accepted as a legitimate choice. Conversely, one might suppose that if an autonomous person does accept a full-membership deal offered by a particular state, nothing further is required for the membership to exist. But it is not so simple.

5.2.1 Actual consent as a necessary condition

As to the necessity of consent, all societies accept that even some autonomous persons are sometimes appropriately forced into some kinds of group membership. But this is limited to exceptional circumstances that justify overriding the persons' will, typically because of their wrongdoing. States impose membership in the group "prison inmates" on people who have committed serious crimes. Imposing citizenship would be an odd response to crime; the opposite, involuntary denaturalization, makes more sense intuitively. But one might think the imposition justifiable to prevent wrongdoing of an unjust enrichment sort. That is one way to view the stance some take regarding brain and brawn drain. Chapter 3 concluded that even if some duty arises from receiving extraordinary benefits, an obligation not to leave would be disproportionate, at least absent a contractual commitment undertaken in conditions of fair bargaining. But perhaps for those who wish to remain in that society, it is fair and proportionate to insist that they accept and retain citizenship and its burdens rather than trying to live in some liminal status between alien and citizen. This is not a forfeiting of basic liberty so much as agreeing to repay a debt.[1]

[1] Important historical figures in international law jurisprudence have taken such a view. Vattel, for example, maintained that anyone who received education and protection from the state throughout childhood was obligated to pay back, including by military service, but otherwise free to emigrate. *See* Peter H. Schuck & Rogers M. Smith, Citizenship Without Consent: Illegal Aliens in the American Polity 47 (1985).

This possible debt-based exception to a voluntarist view would be at best very narrow, though, in terms of the number of people encompassed. As an empirical matter, the benefits received would need to be truly extraordinary, and an individual's contribution to the economy in adulthood comparatively small, to create concern about unjust enrichment. Economists tell us adults of average capacities contribute more to a nation's economy, simply by working and paying tax on domestic income, than they receive from standard state support for their development in childhood (schooling, health care, etc.) and spending on them in adulthood (infrastructure, protection, etc.). Individuals who received exceptional investment likely have exceptional ability to contribute. This helps explain why military service is voluntary and compensated in most developed countries; it is deemed supererogatory, beyond reasonable expectation. So whatever the normative plausibility of viewing compulsory citizenship as appropriate if necessary for persons to repay their debt to society, the factual scenario in which it is actually necessary for persons who remain in their native country seems unlikely.

Another possible justification for imposing citizenship without actual consent is that this is in the individual's best interests. Paternalistic impositions on autonomous persons are presumptively impermissible. Yet in the literature on state legitimacy, hypothetical consent views prevail, holding that a state legitimately wields authority over subjects even if they have not given actual consent to it doing so, if it can reasonably be posited that they would consent under certain counterfactual conditions (real alternatives, ease of relocation, full information, etc.). John Simmons defines legitimacy as "the complex moral right [a state] possesses to be the exclusive imposer of binding duties on its subjects, to have its subjects comply with these duties, and to use coercion to enforce the duties."[2] He identifies the source of legitimacy in "morally significant relations . . . between state and subject." Simmons, along with Locke and many other political philosophers in the liberal tradition, have contended that the only relations grounding legitimacy are consensual ones, but serious problems with reliance on actual consent arise: a government might brainwash subjects into consenting, most people have no real ability practically to go elsewhere, and most people have not actually consented. This has led many other theorists, including Kant, to think instead in terms of whether people would consent to a particular regime under ideal decision-making conditions. The aim is to preserve some modicum of respect for the individual as a self-ruling moral person while also salvaging state legitimacy.

One reason a person might consent to a state's authority under ideal conditions is that the state would serve them well and they have reason to prefer it over other

[2] A. John Simmons, *Consent Theory for Libertarians*, 22 Soc. Phil. & Pol'y 330–56 (2005)

nations that might also serve them well. We might suppose, as a corollary, that a state may impose its citizenship on individuals who hypothetically would consent to that under ideal conditions because they would perceive it to be in their best interests. Citizenship and being under legitimate rule are not the same thing; I might choose, even in ideal conditions, not to become a full member of the national society in which I presently live, while recognizing that the state governing that society properly exerts coercive force over me to some degree (i.e., making me obey its laws). Yet both are about the connection between state power and individual will. The point of focusing on consent, actual or hypothetical, is to say something about the normative position of the state in relation to the individual. And the citizenship question is also a matter of the state's normative position in an individual's life—that is, its having a particular set of rights against and power over the individual. If it is analytically licit to ascribe to persons hypothetical yet effective consent to the state's basic authority over them, on the grounds that the state will serve them well, then why not also hypothetical yet effective consent to the enhanced authority over them that citizenship entails, considering the extra benefits citizenship provides?

Contributors to the legitimacy literature rarely address whether legitimacy is a person-by-person matter, such that a state might be legitimate as to some but not others, or instead a single and separate determination, such that a state must be legitimate as to all its subjects if it is legitimate as to any. Those who insist on actual consent presumably would adopt the person-by-person view.[3] With hypothetical consent it is less clear.[4] Some of its proponents seem to assume that if *anyone* hypothetically would consent then all would,[5] but they do not defend this position, and there is reason to doubt that the judgment is generic and uniform. And it seems too demanding to say a state is illegitimate unless all actual persons, with their distinctive characteristics, needs, interests, and values, would consent to it in conditions that ensured fully informed and free autonomous choice. A state might treat just a few people unjustly, or a few people might have unusual values incompatible with the state's policy leanings. Should we say the

[3] *See* Amanda Greene, "Consent and Political Legitimacy," *in* DAVID SOBEL ET AL., OXFORD STUDIES IN POLITICAL PHILOSOPHY, VOL. 2, at 2 (2016) ("those in the voluntarist family believe legitimacy rests on actual consent, but an individual's consent renders the government legitimate only for that individual"); Simmons, *supra* note 2, at 354–55 ("Institutional legitimacy is a function for the rights arising from specific relations between those institutions and particular persons, considered one by one.").

[4] *Cf.* THOMAS NAGEL, EQUALITY AND PLURALITY 33 (1991) ("The search for legitimacy is a search for unanimity—not about everything but about the controlling framework within which more controversial decisions will be made.")

[5] For example, Copp encapsulates David Estlund's position on state legitimacy thus: "A state or kind of state is legitimate only if its coercive enforcement of law can be justified on a basis that no possible qualified person could reject or on a basis to which there is no possible qualified objection." David Copp, *Reasonable Acceptability and Democratic Legitimacy: Estlund's Qualified Acceptability Requirement*, 121 ETHICS 239 (2011).

state is therefore altogether illegitimate, that every individual has a veto over legitimacy? That would likely render every state entirely illegitimate.[6] The person-by-person perspective seems more sensible regarding legitimacy, and it seems obviously the right perspective to take regarding citizenship as well.

If so, that suggests a state is justified in exerting power over all individuals as to whom it is deemed a legitimate authority. But legitimacy theorists also typically fail to address what *degree* of power and authority the state should have once it is deemed legitimate—that is, whether it is *only* to coerce conformity to basic rules of civil society, to avoid harm to others and pay for services used, or whether it could extend to imposing citizenship and the additional duties and liabilities that that status entails. In other words, they do not ask whether individuals' actual or hypothetical consent might be calibrated to different levels of submission to authority. Consistent with their general heuristic, they presumably should say it is, that state legitimacy and authority as to a given person extends as far as that person did or would consent to. Or, from a slightly different angle, that the state may impose citizenship per se based on the same sort of consent underwriting its legitimacy. Within a hypothetical consent framework, one basis for finding "consent" to citizenship, then, would be a judgment that the person in question would, if rational and operating in ideal decision-making conditions, see acquisition of citizenship to be in his or her best interests; its incremental benefits exceed its incremental costs. As applied, this is close to paternalism, but the hypothetical consent lens respects the individual right to self-rule to the extent of allowing a person's own conception of the good to play a role.

Alternatively, if we assume a person reasonable, in the sense of accepting the burdens of justice, we might suppose that person hypothetically would consent to citizenship if it were a fair condition of residing in the nation. David Estlund has advanced something like this in his account of state legitimacy.[7] He contends we should find "normative consent" to a state's authority when it would be wrongful for the individual to refuse it—that is, when something gives rise to a duty to consent. Whether this is persuasive and fits comfortably within the hypothetical-consent family of theories are questions I will not address.[8] The basic idea it supports with respect to citizenship—that is, to the fullest form of

[6] Voluntarist-anarchists accept the conclusion that no existing state is legitimate, simply because there is not universal actual consent in any. Someone who allows for hypothetical consent might also embrace the idea that no existing state is legitimate. This might not render the notion of legitimacy useless; it can serve as an ideal against which actual states are assessed as more or less legitimate. For voluntarists, that would depend on what percentage actually consent. For proponents of hypothetical consent, the percentage better served by a regime relative to some alternative (comparativists say another available state, noncomparatives say a regime below some threshold of value for the individual).

[7] David Estlund, Democratic Authority: A Philosophical Framework (2008).

[8] A symposium issue of Ethics, vol. 121, iss. no. 2 (2011), was devoted to these and other questions about Estlund's book.

state authority over a person—is that it might be unfair in some circumstances for a person to refuse it. This is a narrower basis for imputing consent than a finding that the citizenship deal would be fair; that a proposed contractual deal is fair does not necessarily mean that refusing it would be unfair. But it seems a stronger basis. The basic concern is that a person is receiving ongoing benefits from residing in a state—including government spending on infrastructure and law enforcement, an economic safety net, and a regulatory framework enabling a thriving economy—without giving proportionately in return.[9] They are freeriding to some degree absent acceptance of the citizenship contract. It is not payback so much as pay-as-you-go.

Both a best-interests and a fair-expectation judgment, however, should consider actual circumstances in a nation for a given person—that is, how much a person is truly benefiting from a society and its government and what he or she is contributing in ways other than fulfilling duties of citizenship per se—for example, by working and paying taxes. A best-interests judgment should also take place against a background assumption of hypothetical free choice about nation of residence, lest a nation generate a best-interests finding simply by making noncitizenship extremely miserable, while making citizenship also a miserable condition just less so. Arguably, a fair expectation rationale should as well; it gains much of its intuitive appeal from presumed freedom to go elsewhere; "if you choose to live here, then here is the condition." We might say, however, that if a state grants the right of emigration (so it cannot be blamed for lack of actual options), it might justifiably impose citizenship on any persons who remain, even if their remaining is the result of situational constraints (e.g., needs of family members, no other country will allow immigration, etc.) rather than desire, if that person would consent to it under ideal conditions (including absence of such constraints), either because doing so is good for them or a fair condition of residence. A corollary would be that the individual possesses no right, when either condition (best interests or fair deal) is met, to remain without accepting citizenship. States, correspondingly, are under no duty to offer or tolerate different levels of membership, if an all-or-nothing regime of social membership is good or fair for all.

To illustrate, imagine someone migrates to the United States from a nation where living conditions are unbearable and renounces citizenship in that nation, becoming stateless. He receives legal permission to remain here for enough years to qualify for citizenship, and does remain, but after qualifying for citizenship chooses not to apply, mistakenly believing citizenship would serve no

[9] *Cf.* Anna Stilz, Liberal Loyalty: Freedom, Obligation, and the State (2009) (explaining the necessity of collective action to create a well-ordered and just society, with a state possessing authority to define and enforce individual rights, so autonomous persons can flourish in the way liberals envision—that is, to enjoy freedom and shape one's own life based on one's own values).

purpose for him and/or not wanting to devote time to the application process. The United States might be justified in imposing citizenship on such a person, not allowing him to remain stateless, on the paternalistic grounds that he will live a better life if able to enjoy the political rights, broader career opportunities, and so forth that attend citizenship. Or on a sound judgment that it would be unfair of him to refuse citizenship, with the duties and liabilities that entails, if he plans to remain and enjoy all the benefits that life in American society provides, because merely obeying the law and paying taxes on income earned from work in the United States do not add up to paying one's fair share.

Pushback against this conclusion will come from the standpoint of respecting autonomy. Because my ultimate interest is in the normative position of persons who are non-autonomous, I will not delve deeply into this, but some work done on hypothetical consent from this standpoint will help frame analysis of children's situation. David Enoch has helpfully identified different autonomy-related values at stake with paternalistic impositions and suggested there are degrees of insult to autonomy, dependent upon which values are violated or ignored.[10] One value is "sovereignty," a person's control over her own life simply because it is hers and no one else's. I and the state respect you as a distinct person of inherent moral worth who has a right of self-ownership by not overriding or supplanting your self-determining choices. That value is at stake no matter how trivial the decision (Enoch gives the example of putting salt on his dinner.) Another value is "non-alienation," being able to have your life go in accordance with your deep commitments. Enoch suggests non-alienation is the stronger of the two values, illustrating with five examples of autonomous adults who will die without a blood transfusion: (1) a conscious person who declines the procedure because of needle anxiety, (2) a conscious person who declines because a Christian Scientist, (3) an unconscious person with needle anxiety, (4) an unconscious Christian Scientist, and (5) an unconscious person with no qualms about blood transfusions. Intuitively, it seems worst to administer the procedure on grounds of hypothetical consent in case 2; it violates both sovereignty and non-alienation values. It seems worse in case 4 than in case 3 (in both of which the person cannot exercise sovereignty or experience anxiety anyway), possibly even worse than in case 1, because of the greater importance of non-alienation. Enoch writes:

> Sometimes, treating someone in a way that he doesn't consent to but that he would consent to under hypothetical conditions that filter our his superficial desires and emphasize his deep commitments does not amount to an attack on his self or to an affront to his ability to be the author of his life story—anyway,

[10] *See* David Enoch, *Hypothetical Consent and the Value(s) of Autonomy*, 128 Ethics 6 (2017).

not as much so as similar treatment of someone who wouldn't even consent under those conditions.[11]

Acting on hypothetical consent in case 1 might be permissible because the gain from the procedure is profound and the autonomy-related value overridden less significant; a life is saved at the cost of some anxiety and an isolated incursion on personal sovereignty, preserving the opportunity for many more years of life as an autonomous person, experiencing both values. Acting on hypothetical consent in case 5, which is most like the situation of a child (not able autonomously to choose now, no deep convictions against the procedure, and likely to value continued life greatly), seems most clearly permissible. It might even be morally obligatory. Arguably both values would be respected in some way in that case. The person is not able to exercise sovereignty now, so we would not be overriding her exercise of it, and she almost certainly would choose to have the procedure if conscious, so we honor her right of self-determination in a second-best way. We would honor it more by holding off until she regains consciousness, but if a decision needs to be made immediately, then that first-best option is not available. The non-alienation value is served by deciding in accordance with, rather than contrary to, her deeply held convictions—namely, that continued life is profoundly valuable and there is nothing immoral or sacrilegious about such treatment.

The immigrant in the example, who declines to apply for citizenship though eligible simply because not perceiving sufficient value in doing so, seems to have only the sovereignty value at stake. Like a person in need of medical care who declines it because he simply fails to comprehend its value or irrationally chooses to avoid a small cost rather than incur it for the sake of a substantial benefit. Paternalistic imposition seems less troubling than it would if the individual had a deep moral conviction that becoming an American citizen would be incompatible with their deeply held beliefs or self-conception (they might have chosen to enter the United States only out of desperation). In the latter case, the non-alienation value would also be at stake, and it seems the United States ought to have stronger reason for forcing citizenship upon the person as a condition of continued residence than in the former case, especially given that they likely lack practical freedom to go elsewhere. Simmons explains:

> The more personal form of Kantian justification—justification in terms of individuals' hypothetical endorsements—recognizes the need to take account of different viewpoints, so that justifications can hope to convince and motivate those to whom they are addressed, but without surrendering completely to

[11] *Id.*, 30–31.

> the eccentricities of individual uptake. [S]uch justifications aim for the middle ground between impersonal appeals to what is objectively right and personal legitimation by actual individual consent.[12]

Paternalistic reasons seem insufficient when non-alienation is at stake, even if the benefits of citizenship in a particular country are great; autonomous persons should be allowed to decide for themselves whether the benefits of political participation, diplomatic assistance abroad, broader employment opportunities, and so forth are great enough to outweigh their moral convictions (in addition to any costs attending citizenship, such as service obligations). Those paternalistic reasons might also be insufficient to defeat the sovereignty interest. The incremental benefit of citizenship is far less than that of a life-saving blood transfusion, at least if we assume the already established right of non-refoulement and/or *jus connectionis* right to remain that the UNHRC has read into the ICCPR. Further, the justifiability of infringing sovereignty based on hypothetical consent should take into account the possibility in this context of deferring the decision for some period, while the person in question acquires more experience living in the society without citizenship and learning about what benefits and costs formal membership per se entails.

Whenever the paternalistic reason is insufficient, the fair-expectation rationale would have to do some work. And it would need to be more compelling to defeat the non-alienation value than when only sovereignty is at stake. In either case, the analysis will resemble that for unjust enrichment; a fair expectation would presumably exist precisely when refusing citizenship but continuing to reside in a society would amount to substantial freeriding. As noted, that might only be so as an empirical matter when a person is receiving extraordinary benefits on an ongoing basis and/or contributing very little by working and paying taxes even though able to do more. Otherwise, as Simmons writes:

> While it may be more convenient for states to simply impose political duties on all within the territories they claim, it would certainly be possible (and perhaps even optimific) for states to enforce fair rules that severely limit the political duties of unwilling subjects (as well as the political benefits they receive), while still protecting and doing justice for their willing citizens. . . . If we can act morally without accepting membership in a political community, the Kantian cannot successfully argue that the state is for each of us "morally necessary" or that unwillingness to cooperate to produce shared political solutions is "unreasonable" or morally objectionable. It is, at worst, eccentric, or perhaps "unneighborly."[13]

[12] John Simmons, *Justification and Legitimacy*, 109 Ethics 739, 762 (1999).
[13] *Id.*, 766–67.

What Enoch adds is a reminder that the bypassing of autonomy that hypothetical consent entails, even if only the self-sovereignty value is at stake, is also a cost to the individual that should be weighed in calculating whether forced citizenship is a fair deal.

Rather than delve further into the complexities of hypothetical consent, I will close this discussion with the observation that any plausible argument for imposing citizenship on autonomous adults must presuppose that the citizenship package a given nation presents is of a certain net value for any person on whom it is imposed. It cannot be that every state of the world today may, based on hypothetical consent, impose its citizenship on all autonomous persons residing in the territory it governs. In some nations, the package has immense negative net value, such that (1) the cost is grossly excessive relative to any obligation that can reasonably be imputed to a person, and (2) individuals would not, if operating in ideal decision-making conditions, choose it for their own sake nor acknowledge that it is a fair imposition. A great many people in those nations wish desperately to leave and have no moral qualms about doing so but are practically unable for reasons other than denial of the right to emigrate. It is implausible to say they should recognize forced citizenship as fair simply because they will remain despite having the formal right to leave. If a nation routinely violates civil and political rights, makes no effort to protect its citizens' interests abroad, and offers no social supports internally, how could it reasonably expect, for example, military service from its residents, or even power to control their relocation? How could it justify extracting taxes from someone able to earn income from, for example, stock ownership in or work done remotely for a foreign company (or even from work domestically) if a corrupt government does not use the tax to fund public works? Even in the pre-Enlightenment, state-focused moral universe, political membership was regarded as a reciprocal arrangement, in which the individual owed allegiance and the sovereign in turn owed duties to protect and provide for his subjects.[14] How, then, in the modern era of moral respect for the human individual, can the international law community regard it as permissible, let alone obligatory, for North Korea, Syria, Sudan, Haiti, Afghanistan, Belarus, and so forth to impose their citizenship on any persons?

5.2.2 Actual consent as a sufficient condition

Should we ever override an autonomous person's decision *to consent* to this association and status? Here we should consider both the internal validity of actual consent, meaning the bindingness upon the individual, and the external

[14] *See* Schuck & Smith, *supra* note 1, at 12–16.

effect or recognition of the consent by third parties. Internally, we would start with respect for the individual's autonomy and allow that they can submit themselves to a bad deal if they wish, but also recognize that sometimes actual consent reflects compromise of autonomy due to brainwashing, coercion, and so forth, in which case the individual should not be bound, just as with ordinary contracting. An additional limitation is suggested by the literature on voluntary enslavement—namely, that one simply cannot give up one's right to exit an association or to be treated as a being of moral worth. Some states' "citizenship deal"—for example, North Korea—might amount to enslavement and abject denigration, such that no one should ever be deemed bound by actual consent to it even if given while autonomous and not subject to brainwashing, coercion, and so forth.

In addition, though, the rest of the world might be permitted to refuse recognition of a person's citizenship acquired by autonomous actual consent not on paternalistic grounds but because the person's joining contributes to serious harm to others, by strengthening and implicitly endorsing a bad-actor state.[15] The large-scale association that a given nation constitutes might generate negative externalities on an ongoing basis, and each individual's decision to join or remain in the association strengthens it and its adverse impact on other societies. A nation might detract from regional or global welfare because of internal conflict that destroys human potential and destabilizes the region, because of aggression against other states, or because it contributes to legitimizing or normalizing oppressive practices. Incidental harm to others can also occur domestically, if becoming or remaining a citizen emboldens a brutal dictator. Such a nation becomes stronger with a larger, compliant citizenry pledging its loyalty and committing to service obligations, more immune to intervention by outsiders. If so, perhaps autonomous individuals have an obligation to refuse or renounce citizenship in such nations—for example, Russia, to avoid implicitly and materially supporting its war of aggression against Ukraine, or Eritrea, so as not to endorse Isaias Afwerki's brutality against political opponents. This is one application of the widely endorsed general principle that one ought not participate in unjust institutions in such a way as to contribute to the injustice.[16] Other nations and international bodies might reinforce this moral obligation by refusing to recognize anyone's citizenship in such nations, instead treating them as stateless.

[15] *Cf.* Simmons, *supra* note 2, at 341 ("Typically, consent theorists hold that personal consent is not sufficient to bring about these results [a person has general political obligations to a state and the state legitimately rules that person] if consent is in important ways defective—for example, if it is nonvoluntary, unintentional, uninformed, or given to arrangements that violate others' rights.").

[16] *See, e.g.*, Thomas W. Pogge, *Cosmopolitanism and Sovereignty*, 103 ETHICS 48 (1992).

In other words, choosing a particular nationality is not an entirely personal choice; it supports a government and its actions and decisions. Yet whereas domestic law might prohibit joining some associations, such as criminal enterprises, international law now *compels* membership even in nations that are the most sociopathic globally, thereby strengthening them. Arguably, it should do the opposite; if it is feasible to identify nations unworthy of being chosen, international law could qualify the right to a nationality set forth in treaties with a modifier like "in a nation not on the list of outlaw states." The UN Secretary-General now maintains a list of nations deserving of "naming and shaming" reputational sanctions, with a particular focus on those which fail to protect children from various forms of violence and exploitations. Or international law could include among UN-imposed sanctions on a pariah state suspension of its citizenship-conferring powers under international law, relieving other nations of obligation to recognize its citizenship conferrals.

In sum, with respect to autonomous persons, actual consent is generally a morally necessary condition for ascription of citizenship. Imputing hypothetical consent can be more or less justifiable, but it appears rarely a sufficient basis for overriding an individual's autonomy in the context of citizenship conferral. Neither a paternalistic nor a fair-expectation justification for a general practice of imposing citizenship has any plausibility in a nation that inflicts more misery than benefit on its people. Or, we might say, an additional necessary condition for imposing citizenship is that a nation is currently worthy of being chosen, of receiving allegiance and support. Further, neither actual nor hypothetical consent is even a sufficient condition for citizenship to arise in nations whose governing regime no one should endorse, because of the great harm it inflicts.

Thus, in a world pocked with pockets of hell, statelessness should be seen as a valid choice for persons living in one of them, as is accepting an offer of citizenship from another nation elsewhere, should one be extended. For the authority governing a hellish territory to force national membership on persons trapped there should be regarded as a violation of a basic human right of dissociation, rather than something the state must do to fulfill the individual's supposed right to have a nationality regardless of which one it is. Given that the right to leave is well established, supported by the values of associational freedom, self-ownership, and the right to live by one's own conception of the good,[17] so too

[17] *Cf.* Fernando Tesón, *Brain Drain*, 45 San Diego L. Rev. 899 (2008) (arguing for a right of emigration based on self-ownership); Christopher Wellman, "Freedom of Movement and the Rights of Entry and Exit," *in* Sarah Fine & Leah Ypi eds., Migration in Political Theory: The Ethics of Movement and Membership (2016) (defending a strong right of emigration on grounds of freedom of association); Seyla Benhabib, *The Law of Peoples, Distributive Justice, and Migrations*, 72 Fordham L. Rev. 1761 (2004) (arguing the right to emigrate is required to ensure individuals can effectively pursue their personal conception of the good and thus a necessary component of Rawlsian liberalism).

should be a right against forced political association for those who, even if legally free to leave, are practically unable to do so.[18]

5.3 Citizenship and Children

Every day, millions of human beings come into existence, in a completely helpless condition, in all parts of an earth now divided into roughly two hundred discrete, self-governing political units. In what normative position does any such child stand relative to any of the planet's states? If one adopts a robust conception of citizenship in which its holders are entitled to participate fully in self-governance of the nation, then one might say no nation may rightly claim any children as its citizens unless and until it is prepared to, among other things, bestow that entitlement on them. But there is widespread use of a more modest conception that makes "citizen" equivalent to what "national" usually connotes—that is, someone with a special legal connection to a state, a type of formal membership in a society, even if not able fully to participate in the people's political self-determination. This must be what anyone means when referring to young children as citizens of some nation or other, as people in many countries do.

So, may the authority governing the territory where a child happens to have been born legitimately claim (i.e., based on morally defensible principles) the child as one of its formal members, one of the persons whom it will, to the exclusion of other states that might wish to, govern and control in the various ways citizenship entails? Or might some other state have a legitimate and competing claim, perhaps exclusive, based on the child's ancestry or ethnicity, or because it has greater need for more members, is far better equipped to care for the child, or has some other reason in its favor? Or is no state entitled to lay claim to any child as its own, as a presumptively permanent member of the polity it governs? Should all children instead be viewed as temporary residents of whatever nation they inhabit, with no formal legal tie to it or any other, like children not yet belonging to any family when placed in foster care after anonymous birth or abandonment at a "safe haven"? Some theorists have asked why persons who arrive in a nation by crossing a border should be treated any differently than persons who arrive by being born there. Here I reverse the question to ask why newborns should not be treated the same as new immigrants just arrived who, having renounced membership in their nation of birth, lack any citizenship until they meet the usual requirements for naturalization, including ability to make

[18] *Cf.* Simmons, *supra* note 2, at 356 ("societies must provide their 'captive,' nonconsenting residents (e.g., the consenters' children) with a reasonable set of options . . . for instance . . . a resident, nonmember status that is less burdened with objectionable obligations than is full membership").

an autonomous choice, to demonstrate understanding of the nation's political system and history, and to meaningfully commit to accepting and helping improve the society's fair terms of cooperation. We might begin to answer such questions by asking whether the conclusions as to autonomous persons extend to children.

5.3.1 Actual consent as a necessary condition

Anyone who believes actual, autonomous consent an absolute requirement for citizenship presumably would say no persons should be regarded as citizens until they are capable of such consent and actually give it. Some, though, might have a principled reason for deeming actual consent unnecessary for non-autonomous persons, in order to regard the state as legitimately exercising authority over them. If one believes any actual state legitimate, then presumably one would wish its laws to constrain minors as well as adults, for some of the same reasons. Such authority might extend even to imposition of citizenship, if there is some morally sound reason other than actual consent for doing so. Other forms of authority over children—for example, that of guardians and teachers—are deemed legitimate though they would not be regarding autonomous persons because not the result of autonomous consent.

Even as to autonomous persons, I considered whether actual consent might not be a necessary condition for imposing citizenship. One alternative basis considered was a debt to society, but that was plausible only in a narrow range of cases—extraordinary state investment coupled with disappointed expectations. Generally, no children receive extraordinary investment, and all have received fewer years of ordinary investment. However, they also generally are incapable in the short term of repaying society at all by working and paying taxes, so perhaps submission to citizenship and its attendant liabilities can serve that purpose until they reach adulthood. For children, a "fair deal" hypothetical consent rationale would look pretty much the same; especially if state investment in child-rearing is morally gratuitous, we might say a state acts reasonably in offering this deal: we will invest in exchange for being able to brand you as ours and enjoy control over your migration. Membership in a family might be thought of in a similar way; offspring are expected in adulthood to pay back parents in material ways for investment in their upbringing, but while the offspring are still dependent minors, parents derive immediate compensation in the legal power to claim a child, exert control over their life, exclude other claimants, and prevent other associations.

However, special affection plays a role in our intuitions about family belongingness; it can lead us to speak even of spouses as belonging to each other in some sense. Such bonds typically do not exist between state and individual. In addition, the payback rationale for parental entitlements simply does not work,[19] and it would not be accepted for guardians of an incompetent adult—that is, that their sacrifice gives rise to *entitlements* to perpetuate the relationship and control the dependent person's life, or with any other association. Those who sacrifice for children must simply hope for payback later, and that hope will be more realistic for a nation the more it does to make its society attractive to young adults. That, we might say, is the best deal a nation can expect; it invests, and in return it gets hope (and parents' greater willingness to live and work there). Not investing in childrearing in the first place might be a morally permissible option, but a nation that chooses that cannot realistically have any such hope.

Moreover, as with all potential rationales for imposing citizenship on adults, the quality of life in a particular country is of critical importance. A debt-based justification has no plausibility whatsoever in countries that provide little or no benefits, let alone those whose regimes affirmatively cause great suffering for children—by creating a climate of fear, killing family members, displacing families from their homes, siphoning off the people's wealth, institutionalizing unparented children, and so forth. It also cannot work as to any person whom the state prevented from accepting the opportunity in childhood to emigrate to a place where he or she would have had a much better life, thereby forcing the child to accept its (likely meager) benefits rather than those available elsewhere. A Self-Serving Samaritan who knowingly makes a needy person worse off than she could otherwise have been, by insisting that he provide the assistance rather than someone better able to do so, deserves no thanks. So, for example, persons who grow up parentless in institutions, because the state governing the territory where they were born foreclosed international adoption, owe their nation nothing. To the contrary, that nation owes compensation to those individuals for the harm inflicted.

Paternalism-based hypothetical consent would seem more legitimate as to non-autonomous persons. Many other types of decisions states make regarding them—some profoundly important, including placement in other types of affiliation—are justified in paternalistic terms, sometimes with the language of hypothetical consent, what a child would choose for themselves if able. We might say parentage laws, placing children into legal relationships with caregivers and attaching legal powers to the caregiver role, are justifiable to the extent they accomplish what a child might reasonably be expected to choose if able, or later endorse, in light of newborns' urgent need to enter a stable family association, and specifically a long-term relationship with a nurturing caretaker, within the first year of life. (We might deploy a Rawlsian heuristic for evaluating the content

[19] *See* James G. Dwyer, *Deflating Parents' Rights*, 40 LAW & PHIL. 387 (2021).

of existing parentage laws, viewed as state decision-making on behalf of infants, in which we imagine ourselves being born again in the future, in circumstances we know nothing about in advance, including who our birth parents will be.) Likewise, if a four-year-old needs medical care for bacterial meningitis, the law does not require the child's consent or even acquiescence, but rather simply dictates that it will be done, and one way of justifying this is in terms of doing what the child would most likely choose if able and under proper conditions of voluntariness.

Those types of decisions, though, differ from becoming a citizen in an important way. They involve something a child needs immediately for the sake of fundamental well-being, whereas citizenship is decidedly not such a thing. Young children need their state of residence to respect their rights as humans, including their right to self-determination later in life and their right against being forced to live in a place of extreme danger or deprivation. They do not need it to impose on them the legal tie, control, and branding that citizenship represents. Also counting against unnecessary imposition, potentially, are the autonomy-related values Enoch identified. For children who survive to adulthood, as with the unconscious adult who does awaken, some sovereignty will have been lost to the extent decisions have already been made for them, including a nation's having imposed its citizenship on them, especially if that has cashed out into forced residence in the nation. And for a great many—for example, girls in a nation where gender oppression is intense—the value of non-alienation might also have been defeated in a particularly painful way.

Domestic law in most jurisdictions does authorize parents and other adults to do things to children without their consent that are not essential to their well-being—in fact, even some things contrary to their well-being, such as corporal punishment. But, in the first place, that is often unjustifiable.[20] When justified, it is for reasons inapplicable in the case of citizenship—for example, that it is good for children if their caregivers, with whom they interact intimately and daily, to enjoy some freedom to structure and color their lives in accord with caregivers' own preferences and values. Caregivers are happier and feel a stronger bond with a child when they enjoy some degree of independent control over the child's daily life and share value-based experiences with them. But for matters more momentous yet not needing to be decided during childhood, presumptively domestic law should suspend the decision until the child becomes capable of autonomous choice for themselves.[21] Citizenship falls in that category; it can

[20] *See* Joan E. Durrant, "Corporal Punishment and the Law in Global Perspective," *in* James G. Dwyer, Oxford Handbook of Children and the Law 293–320 (2020); James G. Dwyer, *Parental Entitlement and Corporal Punishment*, 73 Law & Contemp. Probs. 189 (2010).

[21] *See* The Brussels Collaboration on Bodily Integrity, *Genital Modifications in Prepubescent Minors: When May Clinicians Ethically Proceed?*, Am. J. Bioethics 1 (2024).

wait till adulthood, and so it should. That citizenship in many nations is a life-defeating curse strengthens the conclusion.

To say citizenship can wait for autonomy to develop will spark practical objections of two kinds, addressed further on, having to do with a person's needs and experiences during childhood and with the practicalities of assigning citizenship at age of maturity. But if those can be overcome, the proper stance of international law with respect to new entrants to the world is that no nation can claim them; they should all remain free agents until they can make an autonomous choice.

5.3.2 Actual consent as a sufficient condition

The observations about sufficiency apply also to children. Because of the negative externalities citizenship can entail, international law should not condone, let alone command, claiming of children by disordered states or criminal regimes. It should instead prohibit placement of children, however compliant, into a proto-membership status that supports chaos and evil acts of destruction (Hitler youth being an extreme example of a widespread phenomenon). Even absent externalities, paternalistic overriding of a youth's expressed preference to become a citizen is more justifiable than in the case of adults. Autonomous persons might be free to choose citizenship in, for example, Yemen, despite its extreme poverty and horrendous human rights record, but little or no weight should be given to a ten-year-old child's expression of desire to belong to that nation, which could result in enlistment into the Houthi military at age fifteen or marriage at age twelve. Domestic laws in well-ordered societies generally do not give effect to a child's wish to do things likely to harm them, such as join a gang, work in a slaughterhouse, enter a casino, or marry.

5.3.3 Prescribing statelessness for children

The proposal here, then, is that no children should be citizens or nationals of any country. All children should be legally stateless. No nation should have a privileged claim to their presence or later allegiance. Persons should possess a citizenship only after becoming capable of choosing it for themselves autonomously, from among those available (see Section 5.5.2), and so choosing. This is not unheard of; there have been societies in which only adults were citizens—not just ancient Greece, but also some in more recent centuries.[22] Some European countries today have policies expressly allowing for children living in their

[22] *See* Maximilian Koessler, *"SUBJECT," "CITIZEN," "NATIONAL," AND "PERMANENT ALLEGIANCE,"* 56 Yale L.J. 58, 63 (1946) (citing Mexico as an example in the 1940s).

territory who are stateless—typically because the state does not confer its citizenship on children of immigrants based on their being born there—to remain such until they reach the age of majority, which might in part reflect recognition that citizenship is less advantageous for children.[23] Various political theorists, including Locke, have espoused the view that citizenship is something one should choose freely upon reaching adulthood, not something that should be imposed on anyone involuntarily, not even children. On the other hand, no theorist has presented an argument in favor of ascribing citizenship to infants as a general matter, as opposed to having all be stateless; it simply has not been considered.

The rest of this chapter will attempt to persuade that universal child statelessness could be a valuable and viable policy in practice as well as in theory. I close this section by noting that my proposal is not a cosmopolitan one for banishing national citizenship altogether. Many theorists have defended the parochial association that citizenship for adults constitutes,[24] and I am not challenging their view. I am simply proposing that citizenship be reserved for adults.[25] I also am not proposing "global citizenship" for children; I am suggesting the concept of citizenship is simply inapt for them.

5.4 Benefits of Eliminating Citizenship for Children

In addition to respecting children's right against forced political association and against being treated as possessions, eliminating citizenship for children would have several other benefits for children and some for societies as well. First, citizenship would cease to be a basis for discriminating among children. As explained in Chapter 4, human rights treaties prohibit discrimination based on nationality in connection with provision of basic goods such as health care and education, yet it still occurs, in the form of outright denial or higher cost for those lacking proof of citizenship.[26] In a world of universal child statelessness, discrimination on this basis among children would be not only legally impermissible and morally condemnable but also impossible. Whatever benefits a state wished to give children in its territory, it would have to provide without demanding proof of citizenship. Citizenship currently is like the star on Sneetch

[23] *See* Tamas Molnar, "A Fresh Examination of Facilitated Naturalization as a Solution for Stateless Persons," *in* Laura van Waas & Melanie J. Khanna, Solving Statelessness 225–58, 237–38 (2017).
[24] *See, e.g.*, Stilz, *supra* note 9 (summarizing other defenses and presenting her own).
[25] I also offer no opinion here about adults who either never become autonomous, or obtain but later lose the capacities that autonomy entails. Developing and adequately defending a position could fill another book.
[26] *See, e.g.*, Laura Ferracioli, *Citizenship for Children: By Soil, by Blood, or by Paternalism?*, 175 Phil. Stud. 2859, 2871 (2018) ("In some states, a lack of citizenship translates into higher insurance premiums as well as higher fees for schooling and health care services.").

bellies, a morally arbitrary mark used as pretext to denigrate and deny. And whereas Dr. Seuss's solution was random assignment of the mark, another solution, more sensible in the case of citizenship, is to get rid of the mark altogether, for everyone (or, in this context, for all children).

Of course, this would not eliminate all discrimination. As observed in Chapter 4, giving citizenship to currently stateless minority groups would not eliminate the hostility toward them. Undoubtedly, public and private actors in some places would continue to disfavor children and families belonging to certain cultural or racial communities. "No one is a citizen" is no different from "everyone is a citizen" in that respect. Universal child statelessness would not solve all problems facing children in such groups. But eliminating this basis for discrimination that historically has been viewed as legitimate, that is still sanctioned to some degree in human rights law, and that creates a need for documentation states have used surreptitiously to deny benefits and opportunities, should make adverse discriminatory treatment more difficult—practically and politically. Depending on locale, it might be harder to distinguish between members of different cultural groups than to distinguish between those who have national ID papers and those who do not. And condemnation by other nations and by human rights committees and observers is much more likely with racial, ethnic, or religious discrimination than with nationality discrimination.

A second benefit likely from eliminating citizenship for children, and from the attendant nation-selection process that young adults would undertake, is to make nations think, to a greater extent than they have in the past, about why anyone should choose them, what makes them attractive. They would become more cognizant of the need to compete with other nations for members, and they presumably would compete by providing better public services, especially for minors. Now nations can largely take for granted the permanent residence and allegiance of the great majority of people born in their territory, in part because they claim ownership and control over them, sanctioned by international law, and can thereby constrain their ability to leave. This no doubt facilitates some degree of state indifference and even abuse.

There is already, of course, the possibility that young adults will choose to emigrate and change their nationality, but having a pre-assigned citizenship creates some friction, attitudinal and practical resistance.[27] In a world where all youth are seen as "free agents," that friction should be less. Nations with negative

[27] *See, e.g.*, Peter J. Spiro, *Citizenship Overreach*, 38 MICH. J. INT'L L. 167, 172 (2017) ("U.S. citizenship is sticky at the back. Termination of citizenship on the individual's part can involve substantial fees. Expatriation is contingent on tax compliance and, in some cases, will implicate the recognition of capital gains."), 180 (observing that some nations "make expatriation contingent on the satisfaction of military service requirements, even for those born with nationality abroad"), 185–86 (describing various costs and administrative hurdles the United States places in the way of citizenship relinquishment).

population trends would feel freer to bid for young potential immigrants; that would be no offense to another state. An international system of nation selection by free agents should have the same virtues as a free market in other realms (schools, employment, cellphone service, etc.). More developed nations already have this phenomenon at the local and regional level. States and cities in the United States, for example, consciously endeavor to attract residents and businesses. States offer substantially reduced university tuition to young adults coming from elsewhere who take steps toward permanent residence. Imagine if, instead, Oklahoma could impose a sticky membership label on children born there, create administrative obstacles to their relocating to another state, impose burdensome service obligations on them in young adulthood, and claim a share of their income even if they move to another state. State leaders could then more freely adopt self-serving policies rather than investing in public services, knowing they have a semi-captive future workforce.

One objection to this image of freer and more open bidding for citizens is that it would exacerbate inequalities among nations, making the brain- and brawn-drain pipeline so much wider. As explained in Chapter 3, however, making people captive to a nation is not an appropriate response to this concern. Young persons, especially those who have had less advantageous childhoods, have no duty to shape their life course to help redress global injustice, and international law cannot justifiably make them instruments of remedial efforts, as if they are distributable resources. Further, regimes governing inhospitable places would experience greater pressure to improve conditions themselves locally, to end the corruption and ineptitude that having a captive population facilitates. Tyrannical regimes surely understand that the spoils of self-serving power diminish as the populace disappears.

A third, related benefit is enhancement of young adults' personal autonomy. Minimizing migration friction effectively expands residential and career options. Those who choose a nation other than where they grew up would not need to document a prior nationality nor complete an onerous process that the native state might require to be released. There would be no condition of being "owned" that one must escape to join the polity of one's choosing.

A fourth benefit is a likely increase in awareness of, attention to, and insistence upon better opportunities for young children elsewhere than their nation of birth. It should make more glaring the utterly irrational mismatch between the current dire situation of millions of unparented children in less developed nations and the desire of adults in more developed nations to welcome those children into their families, as well as the need of some developed nations' economies for a more robust young generation. Today many write off the mismatch as inevitable or as justified because the children belong to the state where they reside and the state is owed deference in its treatment of its citizens. Eliminating citizenship should undermine that view of the state's position in relation to such children. The state might better be seen as like a property owner who happens to find a child abandoned in its backyard, having a duty of care but no claim of possession or forced membership in the household. Authorities would not hesitate to remove that child to the best available home.

A final, societal benefit of my proposal is that youth might become more motivated to become more integrated in and valuable to their communities. I will endorse what Ayelet Shachar calls a *jus nexi* basis of citizenship conferral; persons who have resided in a state's territory for a substantial period and developed ties and shown dedication to the good of their community are entitled to citizenship. Shachar identifies as factors to consider both (1) aspects of life that would make it a hardship for a person to be forced to leave the country—family and community ties, social and cultural interests, development of a business or career, and so forth, and (2) things that make a person more deserving of the right to remain and to have a say in formation of laws that govern a society, or that make an individual more valuable to the nation, such as charitable or civic works.[28] This would expand a phenomenon, which seems highly salutary all around, now nascent in many locales in Western societies, of requiring volunteer hours for high school graduation. It gives youth who might not otherwise be motivated to seek it the experience and habit of giving to others, of contributing to the common good, which is good for their moral development and self-esteem and creates goodwill in the community.

A last, incidental point: a view of children as "free agents" could be appropriate in relation to other types of community as well—for example, religions, ethnic groups, and Indigenous tribes, rendering illicit any group's treating children as its property or resource. At the same time, it allows for all sorts of communities to retain great importance in human life; adults would still be citizens of particular nations and members of cultural, religious, and so forth communities of their choosing, and parents would still have great freedom to involve their children in the activities of such communities. Only the formal status of children in relation to those communities would change. That might lead parents to take a somewhat different approach to involving their children in culture and public life, if they understand future membership to be a choice rather than an inheritance or fate, and presumably an approach that is more respectful, that aims to make the experience more positive for children so they will want to remain.

[28] *See* Ayelet Shachar, "The Missing Link: Rootedness as a Basis for Membership," *in* SIGAL R. BEN-PORATH & ROGERS M. SMITH, VARIETIES OF SOVEREIGNTY AND CITIZENSHIP 124–46 (2013). Instantiation of the rule can avoid punishing individuals for disabilities, by applying broad conceptions of contribution and value and considering ability in assessing them.

5.5 Operationalizing a Regime of Universal Statelessness for Children

The proposal will raise practical concerns—in particular, as to how children's lives would be managed if none are legally assigned to a particular nation, and as to how the process of citizenship selection would go for the hundreds of millions who reach adulthood each year. On both those counts, my proposal is less a departure from the status quo than might at first appear.

5.5.1 Managing childrearing in a world of universal statelessness

The idea of universal child statelessness raises questions about distribution of welfare supports, children's residence and relocation, and legal identification.

5.5.1.1 Social supports

Human rights treaties commit state parties to respecting in some fashion the rights of all persons, without regard to citizenship or residence. But the implicit assumption has been that primary responsibility falls on some state to which the individual has a special connection. Whether that is state of nationality or state of residence has not been worked out explicitly, but state practice suggests it is the latter. Even as to noncitizen children in their territory who have a nationality elsewhere, when states provide for them, they do not thereafter send a bill to the other nation, and as to stateless children, none contemplate charging a state of prior residence.

States that now refuse to provide for noncitizen children on their territory, even as a backup to a child's state of citizenship or prior residence, even though able to do so, are in breach of treaty obligations. As discussed in Chapter 4, every state party to the ICESCR or CRC (i.e., all but the United States) has a duty to try to ensure all children have their basic needs met—either by providing for those children itself, without giving any priority over others, or by facilitating aid from outside (see Chapter 9). As noted, eliminating citizenship as a basis for discrimination should improve treaty compliance, and it would incentivize nations to do more for all children, knowing they are competing for future citizens (though increased cost will limit what they can do).

For any state not committed to positive-rights treaty obligations (i.e., not parties to the ICECSR or the CRC), if currently providing for all or for none, the change to universal child statelessness would have no effect. The United States already is providing for all children in most respects. If some other state in the future were party to neither, and were choosing to provide only for children who are its citizens, being forced to accept universal child statelessness would have the same effect as on states that are parties; it would lose the practical ability to discriminate on that basis, and competing incentive effects (cost of providing for more children versus need to compete) would likely have a neutral or positive effect in terms of social supports.

5.5.1.2 Residence and relocation

The right of young children to reside in the state of their nationality is now ineffectual in many nations, including the United States, because the legal status of parents is determinative. An "anchor baby" is not really an anchor here; the child will leave with deported parents. That would be true everywhere if all children were stateless; their right to protection of their relationship with their parents, if they have any, would be controlling, and parents' status would determine where they live. This would be best overall for those children whose parents are citizens of a country with an adequate quality of life; their relationship with their parents is presumptively more important to their welfare than an incremental gain in standard of living. But a great portion of citizen children whose parents are vulnerable to deportation would be sent to live in starkly worse conditions. Some European countries now allow for family-based immigration through child nationals, so those children whose parents are citizens only of a far less hospitable country would be worse off in this new regime. They and their parents would both be noncitizens of the nation where they wish to live and thus more vulnerable to deportation. But they could still apply for asylum. In addition, because these children would not be citizens of *any* nation, no other nation would have an obligation to accept them, at least not based on nationality, which might strengthen the family's plea to remain.

In any event, these situations of family-based rights through children ultimately rest on moral arbitrariness—that is, the fact of a child having been born inside the destination state's territory.[29] In a world where, to paraphrase Garrison Keeler, all nations were above average, no one would think it a good idea to give newborns a nationality different from that of their parents simply because they happen to have exited the womb while present in the territory of some state other than that of their parents' nationality. It is difficult to quarrel with those who find it irrational that from this arbitrary fact of birth location should arise a right for a whole family to gain entry, when millions of other families have no such right even if they have greater need or a stronger moral claim (e.g., because their native

[29] Laura Ferracioli's argument for a right of child citizens to "sponsor" parent immigrants appears circular. She argues for ascription of citizenship based on "the facts that a child is born in the territory of a state *and* that she is likely to reside in that state (a likelihood which can, for instance, be adduced from the residence status of her parents)," and then that because they are citizens children have a right to remain, and because they have moral status equal to adults they should have the same right adult citizens have to sponsor family members, including their parents. Ferracioli, *supra* note 26.

country was more damaged by actions of the destination nation), simply because they do not share that happenstance. Proponents of more liberal immigration policies in affluent countries applaud family-based immigration founded upon children's *jus soli* citizenship simply because they want more people admitted, not because there is any sound normative defense of that underlying citizenship conferral. They say children should not lose their right to remain just because of their parents' nationality status, but they never explain why the children ought to have that right in the first place. The only rationale for *jus soli* citizenship floating about starts with irrational statelessness-panic and an undefended assumption that the state where a child is born is the sole potential savior for any child who would otherwise be stateless.

Finally, with respect to residence, universal child statelessness would seem to make better off older children who are unparented and wishing to migrate internationally, such as unaccompanied minors who cross into the United States at a steady pace. Whereas now they are identified as belonging to some other nation and therefore highly susceptible to return there for that reason, in a regime of universal child statelessness all who manage to enter another country would not be deportable on grounds of alienage. If they have no parents, do not know their parents' whereabouts, or refuse to disclose information about their parents, deportation also could not be predicated upon family reunification. Thus, though they might not have a right of entry anywhere under current treaty law, and states correspondingly might have no legal duty currently to permit entry, states would be under a disability with respect to expulsion when entry nevertheless occurs, if neither family reunification nor nationality in another country were available as a basis for doing so. If a parentless child is on your territory, it matters not how they got there or from whence they came. They must be allowed to leave if they so choose or if a proper decision-making body determines there is a better life opportunity for them elsewhere, but they may not be expelled against their wishes and best interests, and they must be cared for so long as they remain.

This raises concern that it would incidentally incentivize increased migration and unauthorized border crossing by children without parents, meaning more families separated and more youths embarking on a perilous journey. How great the increase would be is unclear and likely to vary by region. That illegal southern border crossings in the United States plummeted after President Joseph Biden imposed a very low asylum-petition cap suggests families consider the probability of being able to remain when deciding whether to have young people make the attempt, at least when the costs of the attempt are high. Some paths, such as that through the Darien Gap in Panama and across Mexico, or boat crossings on the Mediterranean Sea, are so hazardous that willingness to undertake the journey must reflect truly horrible conditions in young people's native countries. Even if the new regime entailed substantially higher probability of remaining in the destination country, the hazardousness would still be a strong deterrent, so it seems unlikely many families would send their children off on them unless truly necessary for their well-being. An increase in entry of unaccompanied minors should therefore amount to life improvement for more youths.

The downsides of increased youth migration are (1) for the young people who lose their life, get trapped in trafficking, or otherwise experience harms along the way, and (2) the upset caused adult nationals in the destination state who believe unlawful entry by anyone harms them or the nation in some way. As to downside 1, as tragic as those outcomes are, losing a gamble does not make it an irrational gamble. And an obvious policy alternative would reduce the harms—namely, give all children a right to enter every nation. That would eliminate the cost of assistance with illegal crossings, and that savings might enable parents to put children in seats on trains instead of having them ride on top of trains. As to downside 2, there is reason to believe there is less hostility to "illegal" unaccompanied minors than to "illegal" adults (see Chapter 8). Some migratory paths, it is worth mentioning, are not so treacherous, and the consequences of the proposed new regime for youth would likely be different for those who face less of an ordeal, but we might assume parents generally do not send their children to other countries frivolously.

5.5.1.3 Documentation of identity

Presumably stateless children would not have a passport of any nation. So how would they travel? Some states issue another form of documentary proof of nationality for internal purposes and make presentation of that proof prerequisite to securing various benefits. That, too, would no longer exist. So how would children obtain medical care, schooling, and welfare benefits?

The first of these concerns is already partially addressed by the 1954 statelessness convention, Article 28 of which requires state parties to issue travel documents to lawfully present non-nationals, effective to enable exit and reentry. Likewise, refugee treaties since 1921 have committed state parties to issuing identity documents for travel purposes to refugees on their territories. The latter concern is addressed by the CRC, which in Article 7 commits all state parties to register every child immediately after birth, something most already endeavor to do without regard to nationality (in the United States, at the state level). The UN in 2015 created an interagency body to promote states' fulfillment of this obligation.[30]

Both concerns might be better addressed by a global child registry and identification system, replacing or supplementing states' own systems. If one

[30] *See* Radha Govil, "The Sustainable Development Goals and Solutions to Statelessness," *in* VAN WAAS & KHANNA, *supra* note 23, at 47–70.

steps back from current practices, it might appear odd that movement within Country Y and movement from Y to Z could require possession of a document issued by Country X, especially given that a person might have escaped from X because its regime was intent on causing the person great suffering. The UN High Commission for Refugees offers a model of a global registration system; it maintains a digital Population Registration and Identity Management Ecosystem, collecting biometric and biographic information (including family relationships) from as many of the world's roughly 120 million refugees as the agency can reach, in order to facilitate oversight of their care, reunite families, and enable movement to places where refugees can establish new lives. That office also serves in some fashion non-refugees who are stateless, including helping them obtain identity documents and citizenship, but its principal focus is refugees—that is, people displaced from their country of habitual residence and needing emergency assistance.

Commentators have noted, though, that protective activities for and legal processes for refugees have been decidedly adult-focused, even though half of all refugees are children.[31] For this reason, and because children staying in place are generally in a much different situation than refugees, and for other reasons, children would likely be better served by a distinct agency that focuses just on them, and all of them—including the vast majority who remain in their nation of birth. That agency would serve as a vital records office, in addition to carrying out monitoring, advocacy, and protective functions.[32] It would maintain a database of all the world's children and create means—documentary and electronic—for identifying them wherever they are at any given moment, even if they lose state-issued identification papers. All nations would have an obligation to ensure registration of both children born on their territory and any children who have migrated to their territory and were not registered elsewhere, and then to share their databases with this global vital-records agency. This would provide every nation's border control and other government agencies—including education and health departments—one uniform system of personal identification for all children. Private providers of services and goods to children, such as hospitals, could interact with those agencies to establish the identify of those whom they serve. Control over identity and documentation thereof would no

[31] *See, e.g.*, Jason M. Pobjoy, The Child in International Refugee Law 3–4, 46–47 (2017).

[32] There are already UN bodies devoted to children, of course. The CRComm's current functions are limited to reviewing country reports, issuing observations on complaints received, and offering interpretive guidance on CRC provisions. In theory, its remit could be expanded to add active monitoring, advocacy, proactive assistance, and registration. UNICEF currently provides advocacy and assistance in emergency situations. One might think the idea here best realized by subsuming these two agencies under an umbrella agency that also has a vital records office. However, a dramatically new way of conceptualizing children in relation to states calls for a new agency to serve them. CRComm and UNICEF are both in the thrall of the CRC and in some contexts more protective of states than of children.

longer be in the exclusive and unsupervised control of the potentially discriminatory and uncooperative regime holding power in a child's place of birth at a given time. In other words, a child's ICCPR rights to "recognition everywhere as a person before the law" (Art. 16), registration and a name (Art. 24), and access to public services (Art. 25(c)) would be less susceptible to the whims of a given state's current regime.

Such an international registry should also be more effective for monitoring the location of migrant children, who today might not carry a passport with them or might lose it on their journey, and for establishing what citizenship anyone acquires after reaching adulthood. It would also make private and public entities everywhere better able to establish any person's age, thus facilitating enforcement of laws precluding dangerous employment, marriage, incarceration, military enlistment, and so forth of children.[33] Even countries like the United States that are wary of sharing personal information and of internationalization generally should perceive benefits from such a system.

In addition, the Global Child Registry could include information about birth parents' identities and habitual residence, to facilitate reunion if a child becomes unparented at any point because of war, natural disaster, kidnapping, abandonment, or other cause and if parents are alive and able to care for the child. This would also help to combat child trafficking.[34] The registry could maintain a record of who has legal custody of a child (presumably parents, but not necessarily), so the child could travel freely to wherever those persons are permitted or entitled to go. At an appropriate age, youths could travel independently if those custodians give permission, with a right to return to the custodians. The right-of-entry function of a passport would thus also be obviated. Children would have a right to go wherever their parents or other guardians are at any given time.

More generally, a universal child statelessness regime would create a more direct relationship between children and international institutions. This should allow for easier monitoring of children's living conditions as well as their whereabouts if they migrate, which family members might value greatly, and this would facilitate international humanitarian efforts on their behalf if ever necessary. This should not be seen as a step toward an all-encompassing world government, which would present dangers of its own for children. Rather it would be a salutary dispersion of power over the lives of human individuals, further breaking up the monopoly power states historically have had,[35] focusing just on

[33] *Cf.* Molnar, *supra* note 23, at 413 (discussing difficulty of enforcing such protective laws when many children go unregistered).

[34] *Cf. id.* ("Unregistered children are also at greater risk of prolonged family separation, illegal adoption and trafficking, since the tracing and reunification of separated children is more difficult in the absence of records verifying a child's actual parentage.").

[35] *Cf.* Pogge, *supra* note 16, at 58 ("persons should be citizens of, and govern themselves through, a number of political units of various sizes, without any one political unit being dominant and thus

the early portion of persons' lives when they are especially vulnerable and have not yet given autonomous consent to membership in any nation. Sara Dillon contends that as to "children living out of family care," in particular, there should be "a clear international law principle of humanitarian access."[36] Such children are living in orphanages and other institutions—many decrepit and all depriving children of the crucial nurturing that parent figures provide—or on the streets. Viewed as belonging to that state, and so known only to the state, they are entirely at the mercy of the state, and the states that treat such children worst are also those most inclined to conceal the children's condition or very existence. Having a UN agency registering and monitoring their location and conditions should help dissolve the possessory aspect of that perceived belongingness and foster an alternative appearance of affiliation with a global community.

This enhanced connection to international institutions does not at all preclude immersion in a local cultural experience, to anticipate a communitarian objection. It simply shifts legal connections to some degree from national to international authority. Already children, regardless of citizenship, have the power to file claims directly with the Human Rights Committee and the Children's Rights Committee, complaining of action by any government that has agreed to respond to individual complaints. And already children who are stateless are supposed to have the right to file claims in domestic courts, against other private parties or against the state. Universal statelessness would not change this. But children should be better off if known to governments at all levels, so that there can be some vertical checks and balances in power exerted over their lives, and a global registration process could enable this.

5.5.2 Citizenship acquisition upon reaching adulthood

The few scholars who acknowledge the possibility of postponing conferral of citizenship till adulthood are dismissive, typically on grounds of administrability. Rogers Brubaker characterizes it as "an administrative nightmare," without explanation.[37] (He also rejects the idea because "states regard their citizens as bound to them," without explaining how that is morally relevant.) Yet on this score, too, the change universal child statelessness would occasion is not dramatic. It

occupying the traditional role of state. And their political allegiance and loyalties should be widely dispersed over these units: neighborhood, town, county, province, state, region, and world at large.").

[36] Sara Dillon, *Time for a Truth-Based Policy: Humanitarian Access to Children Living Without Family Care*, 27 FLA. J. INT'L L. 23, 30 (2015).

[37] ROGERS BRUBAKER, CITIZENSHIP AS SOCIAL CLOSURE: CITIZENSHIP AND NATIONHOOD IN FRANCE AND GERMANY (1992), ch. 1.

would amount to a switch from an opt-out system (freedom to renounce), which is widely endorsed,[38] to an opt-in system that similarly operates upon reaching adulthood and has largely the same result—the individual possesses a chosen nationality rather than an imposed one. (The only difference might be that statelessness-by-choice would be easier.) Some states in fact now require persons who acquired two or more nationalities in childhood to renounce all but one upon reaching adulthood. Universal child statelessness would mean that the first conceptual step of renouncing an existing citizenship is always unnecessary, and as a practical matter it would remove the ability of any nation to violate the renunciation right or to place impediments in the way of its exercise, as some now do. No international body or other nation should pay any heed to a nation's assertion that it has a prior claim on someone who has just reached the age of citizenship election. Those new adults would have unencumbered freedom to choose from among all nations that offer citizenship to them. Or to choose none, perhaps preferring self-identification as solely a member of a people not recognized as a state under international law, such as an Indigenous tribe.

Opting in is a common practice already, undertaken by those who naturalize after immigrating and by those eligible for citizenship in a *jus sanguinis* state that conditions conferral on applying for it. In fact, the 1961 Convention on Reduction of Statelessness allows for a state party to limit its conferral of nationality to adults and only upon application. Article 1 requires states to grant their nationality to anyone born on their territory who would otherwise be stateless, but it allows that a state might require an application for nationality to be made "by or on behalf of the person," and it provides that such a state may, if it chooses, allow for applications only after the person has reached age eighteen. So the proposal here is essentially that this already-permitted approach to initial citizenship become exclusive.

The practical worry must stem, then, simply from numerosity; an opt-in system might seem to entail having an enormously greater number of people having to do something with a government agency in order to possess citizenship. But interaction with government already occurs now for nearly all who are citizens from birth. Any child who needs a passport to travel abroad now must apply for it and prove the basis for it. That would no longer be needed; children could travel with parents using their birth certificate and/or proof of custody. Adults now register to vote and possibly also for the draft. Registration as a citizen could be combined with either of those.

[38] *See* Spiro, *supra* note 27, at 181–82 (noting widespread support among human rights experts for the UDHR's pronouncement of a right of adults to renounce their original citizenship in order to adopt another).

I will suggest that possessing an international-law *right* to citizenship in a particular nation might depend on having an established social connection with it, and that suggests a somewhat fact-intensive inquiry. But we already have models of this—namely, youth qualification for in-state tuition at public universities, noncitizen qualification for state-funded healthcare, and the naturalization process—which collectively suggest the added administrative burden would not be overwhelming. Acquiring a driver's license might be a more arduous process for individuals and the government than establishing a *jus connnectionis* basis of citizenship upon reaching adulthood.

5.5.2.1 Grounds of selection

The main normative question is whether any nation *must* offer its citizenship to particular persons. Or might some be left with no options? Or only options that entail radical dislocation? One possible answer is that the current right to nationality would arise upon reaching adulthood rather than at birth, with similar content—that is, with ultimate responsibility for fulfilling the right falling on the nation where the child-cum-adult is living, which would usually mean the nation of birth but often not. That nation must confer its citizenship unless the child has access to another.

The conditional "if the individual has no other," though, could cause much greater hardship for a new adult than for a newborn, whenever there is another option, because the former is likely to have created a life and formed attachments within the nation where they are living when coming of age. A nation wanting to get rid of certain individuals when they reach adulthood could freely do so if any other nation on the planet were willing to take them, and most likely there would always be at least one, not necessarily a very attractive one. Forced displacement is threatening to the basic welfare, autonomy, and identity of a young adult in a way that it is not for an infant. Anna Stilz elaborates:

> We build our lives on the assumption that our goals, relationships, and pursuits will not be unexpectedly destroyed through forced displacement. If I structure my goals and choices against the background of continuing legal residence in a particular territory, and if I am there through no fault of my own, then respect for my autonomy tells in favor of allowing me to remain there, since it would be impossible for me to move without damage to nearly all my life plans.[39]

One might respond that young people are likely aware of their immigration status and the possibility of deportation, and so they should take that into account in making life plans. But what that uncertainty and anxiety are likely to do

[39] Anna Stilz, *Nations, States, and Territory*, 121(3) Ethics 572, 583–84 (2011).

is inhibit life planning altogether and produce mental health problems, which are also a threat to a youth's development as an autonomous person.

To address this worry, the conditional should be dropped when a youth satisfies some criteria of embeddedness. The rule should consider how much of childhood a person has spent in a particular country, or where the person has primarily lived during the final few years of minority, and should confer an entitlement on that basis irrespective of available alternatives. There are many examples of legal rules founded on an established connection, at the international and domestic levels. The 1961 statelessness convention, after providing that a state party may choose to grant its nationality only upon application and may choose to make the application period begin only at age eighteen, further provides, in Article 1(2)(b), that a state party may condition approval of the application on a showing "[t]hat the person concerned has habitually resided in the territory of the Contracting State for such period as may be fixed by that State, not exceeding five years immediately preceding the lodging of the application nor ten years in all." As noted in Chapter 4, the UNHRC has interpreted ICCPR Article 12's (right to enter) reference to "his own country" as including a country where a person's life has been centered even if the person is not a national there. International bodies have applied a test of "effective nationality" or "dominant nationality" in disputes between nations over who has power to tax or otherwise impose duties on individuals or represent them in international fora. The ICJ, in its *Nottebohm* decision, held that citizenship, if it is to command respect from other nations, must have "as its basis the social fact of attachment, a genuine connection of existence, interests and sentiments, together with the existence of reciprocal rights and duties." This makes experiential connection a necessary condition for acquiescence by other states, and the position advanced here is that it should also be a sufficient condition for a host nation to be under a duty to offer citizenship to young adults.

The Council of Europe has also endorsed a habitual-residence requirement, in its 1999 "Recommendation on the Avoidance and Reduction of Statelessness," and countries across the globe have a waiting period of some years of continuous residence as a condition for naturalization of immigrants. At the state level, the United Kingdom confers citizenship on anyone who was born in the United Kingdom but not to U.K. citizen parents if the child remains resident in the United Kingdom for the first ten years of life. In the mid-twentieth century, American law provided that a person must reside continuously within the United States for a five-year period sometime between ages fourteen and twenty-eight in order to retain citizenship conferred on them at birth.[40] Outside the citizenship

[40] *See* Rogers v. Bellei, 401 U.S. 815 (1971) (upholding the law as applied to a *jus sanguinis* citizen against constitutional challenge).

context, international rules regarding child abduction call for assessment of a child's primary "national attachment," and domestic law in many nations governing custody disputes between parents also makes relevant a child's ties to a community.

Thus, assessing the importance of continued residence for a given young person is a familiar exercise for government agencies. Entitling a child to citizenship in the nation where they have mostly grown up is consistent with the "emerging human rights norm . . . [of a] 'right to be considered for naturalization,' on the basis of a genuine connection with a state (*jus connectionis*),"[41] which has widespread scholarly support and has received serious discussion in international law bodies since at least the 1930s.[42] The primary indicia of connection is long-term residence, so the morally arbitrary "accident of birth" (being born in a certain place or to parents who later choose to migrate) would still play a role in persons' fate, but the basis for a privileged status relative to others is not that accident per se but rather that it has led to a life experience that itself does have moral significance and provides a legitimate basis for distinguishing one person from another. Other factors, though, including the decisions and actions youth make in adolescence, might also rationally count for or against finding the sort of attachment to place that should matter.[43] A nation might require demonstration of pro-social behavior such as volunteering, school attendance, care for family members, or employment. (Requiring a history clear of any misbehavior is more problematic, as delinquency is often a consequence of adverse early childhood experiences.)

One specific implication of a *jus connectionis* element of citizenship election for new adults is that "DREAMers" in the United States—that is, persons who during childhood were brought into the United States illegally by their parents and then remained, would have a right to citizenship upon reaching the age of selection—not just to deferred deportation action—and to continue their lives here as long as they wish. No moral blame for their presence could be targeted at them, so they stand in the same normative position as any youths who were born in the United States to American citizens and have spent the bulk of their childhood in the United States. A young adult is no more deserving of U.S. citizenship for having been born in El Paso rather than having been brought to El Paso at age two or four by parents. Likewise with persons who migrated legally with parents on a temporary visa and ended up staying for the remainder of their minority.

41 Molnar, *supra* note 23, at 229, 248–49 (positing long-term residence as the primary indicator).

42 *See id.*, 248–49; Shachar, *supra* note 28. *Cf.* LAURA FERRACIOLI, LIBERAL SELF-DETERMINATION IN A WORLD OF MIGRATION 4 (2022) (arguing for a *jus paternas* basis for child citizenship, meaning grounded in children's need for protection by the authority governing wherever they reside on an ongoing basis).

43 *See* Shachar, *supra* note 28.

The situation of the typical unaccompanied minor is somewhat different. These youths are mostly twelve or older when they arrive and acting independently, though usually with their parents' blessing. Most are choosing a course of action they know the destination nation does not permit. This is not true of all; some present themselves at an official border crossing and request asylum. Others cross at another point and present themselves to border patrols with a request for asylum, in which case their only illegality is crossing at an unofficial point of entry. Still others cross surreptitiously and proceed inland without turning themselves in, so theirs is the full illegality that many existing members of the national community decry.

Surely, though, even if desperate adults can be blamed for entering without permission, though they typically are trying to escape extreme danger and/or destitution, a thirteen-year-old is less culpable and more deserving of compassion. For any type of crime, someone of that age is generally deemed less blameworthy because less developed in regulatory functions, appreciation of the impact of actions, and moral understanding. And for a "crime" with no readily apparent impact on other persons, committed in a great portion of instances to avoid gang or military recruitment—that is, being killed for refusing to join or agreeing to join and then committing infinitely worse crimes—it is difficult to impose blame at all. A destination nation *might* be justified in sealing their borders to prevent unauthorized crossings, but that does not mean it would be justified in punishing persons who cross while the nation has failed to seal its border. Analogously, I might be justified in putting up a high fence at the waterfront edge of my seaside property, to prevent anyone from coming on my land from the sea regardless of their reason, but that does not mean that if I fail to construct such a fence and a twelve year-old survivor crawls up to my house, despite "no trespassing" signs, that I am justified in having him arrested for trespassing or in tossing him into the sea.

This discussion has not and cannot address every scenario. The basic point is that the rule most respectful of settled life plans, existing relationships, emotional well-being, culture, and autonomy is one in which new adults have a right to citizenship in the nation of their primary attachment, even if other nations invite them, but also a right to choose an available alternative instead. "Available" is not necessarily identical to "offered," though; international law might develop a system for listing nations as unavailable because they are menaces to humanity.

The process of election could be as simple as that for registering to vote or obtaining a driving license, requiring in-person submission of proof of age and residence. Or a given nation might choose to require more evidence of connection, completion of a civics test, or proof of community service. Objections to conditions for citizenship other than simply length of residence are typically founded on worries about disparate treatment based on location of birth, but that would not be true of the regime I am proposing, where even the native-born must apply. A nation might also choose to inject an element of ceremony to application approval, to convey how greatly it values the individual, what civic responsibilities it expects citizens to fulfill, and so forth—in other words, something like the naturalization ceremony that new citizens of the United States, the United Kingdom, and many other nations now attend and typically relish.

5.5.2.2 Timing of selection

The question of timing for citizenship selection is a bit complicated. There is a large literature on whether chronological age should be used as a proxy for anything, and if so, whether individualized exceptions should be made. Let us assume it appropriate for citizenship to have an exceptionless age threshold, as is generally true for voting (one of the few rights tied to citizenship), whether for reasons of administrability, avoiding bias, or something else. (Assume also that all individuals' ages can readily be determined, though this is not actually true today.)

My own view is that the voting age in liberal democracies should be lowered to fourteen, an age by which young people typically have sufficient mental capacity and independence to make their vote as meaningfully theirs and well-considered as is likely true for the average thirty- or sixty-year-old (a low threshold, to be sure). Full defense of that view is not needed here. Others might think sixteen or some other age more appropriate for voting. The difficulty with tying voting and citizenship selection together is that choosing to become a citizen of a nation and subject to its government is quite different from expressing an opinion on whom one thinks best to represent the people in the government at a given point in time. Some of the same information is relevant to both, but voting does not have the same direct personal consequences. And it seems necessary to put off a decision to incur those consequences until one has sufficient practical freedom to choose against it—that is, to migrate to and live independently in another nation—so that the decision is a meaningfully comparative one.

Youth typically do not have that before age eighteen, if then. In developed nations, they are likely to be still in school, and in any nation, minors have limited ability to discover and apply for employment or to set up a household in other nations, at least in part because destination nations legally exclude them from certain types of employment and from the legal power to contract. Some might express readiness to choose citizenship at age fourteen or even younger, but it is problematic to make that choice effective and binding, if it could amount to accepting burdens such as military service and life-limiting financial obligations. And they do not have much to gain by securing citizenship at fourteen rather than eighteen—principally, political rights (though nothing in international law prevents a nation or political subunit from allowing noncitizens to vote, and there are examples of that being done), and perhaps also insurance against the possibility that the government of your preferred nation will change its mind about inviting you.

5.6 Objections

Some citizenship scholars emphasize the socio-psychological impact of belongingness that citizenship entails, contributing to social solidarity and thereby generating benefits both internally—less conflict, more cooperation—and externally—strength or at least the appearance of it. To such scholars, having a substantial portion of a nation's population be not part of that solidarity, because lacking the sense of belonging and commitment, threatens these important values. However, by and large, it is adults whose behavior and expression of commitment matters now. Children are not the source of strife between groups marked by ethnicity, religion, language, and so forth. Their cooperation is generally not needed for the smooth functioning of an economy or political system. And they are not consulted regarding their support for foreign policy decisions. In any event, children can still identify with a nation even though not citizens, and the social practice of selection at eighteen would make them more thoughtful about their home nation and their relationship to it.

A more child-focused concern is that universal child statelessness would exacerbate the existing phenomenon of children being treated as second-class members of society. That is possible, but also possible is the converse, that it would make adults more conscious of children's distinct personhood and right ultimately to individual self-determination. Adults might take less for granted children's adherence to a path laid out for them and their later availability to support the economy, government, and intermediate institutions. Children's more uncertain future citizenship might even give them greater political influence. Politicians now are often dismissive of minors who present policy proposals to them, essentially saying "come back when you've grown up." If less certain that young people will remain when they have grown up, a government official might listen to find out what it will take to ensure they do remain. Moreover, consistent with the point about discrimination, eliminating citizenship for all children would prevent anyone from becoming a *third*-class member of society, a victim of the intersectionality of age and nationality discrimination. If childhood generally entails some denigration, being an alien child must now entail even greater denigration, but universal statelessness would eliminate that basis for incremental devaluation and, indeed, the very concept of an alien child.

Under current international law, the state of an individual's nationality has the unique ability to advocate for them in international fora. A stateless child, it would seem, could have no such advocate. This representative capacity is quite narrow currently, however, and rarely invoked, almost never on behalf of children. It is difficult to envision any possible claim that could not be brought because of a child's statelessness; it would have to be one cognizable only in the ICJ, where only states can be parties and only the state of nationality can advocate on behalf of individuals. In contrast, an advocate can represent an individual child before a human rights committee. Further, any nation can now apply diplomatic pressure against another perceived as mistreating any children, regardless of the children's citizenship. Nothing in international law precludes any form of advocacy outside the ICJ. What is to stop the United States now, for example, from ordering U.S. companies to boycott a nation because it expelled children who ended up stateless on U.S. soil? Or imposing sanctions on some other nation because it forces children who are its own nationals to become soldiers at age ten?

Moreover, while we are theoretically reinventing the child's status in international law, we can theoretically adopt any mechanism of advocacy for children that might be effective—for example, creating an ombuds office for children with ICJ and diplomatic standing, perhaps even a seat in the UN General Assembly. The office could, like ombudspersons for children in some nations and political subunits, be empowered to file lawsuits and lobby legislatures on behalf of any children harmed by state action, and even to introduce legislation. International protection of refugees again provides a model; in 1928, the Assembly of the League of Nations authorized the High Commissioner for Refugees to exercise consular functions on behalf of refugees, substituting for a state of nationality. Evan Criddle and Evan Fox-Decent write that "from the beginning, international refugee law conceived of itself as imbued with the mission of providing surrogate legal status and protection to individuals fleeing persecution."[44] As with refugees, with children it cannot be assumed that their home state is inclined and able to serve their needs. An international agency can operate as a fallback, ready to substitute for a derelict home nation's government.

To both previous two concerns, I would also respond that if children become less tied to a specific state in the popular view of them and more directly connected to international institutions, there might emerge a stronger sense of global responsibility for ensuring all children adequate resources for their healthy upbringing and development, including food, shelter, safety, education, and health care. Refugee law again constitutes an example of the idea being recognized.[45] This shift in locus of responsibility would incidentally reduce any

[44] Evan J. Criddle & Evan Fox-Decent, Fiduciaries of Humanity: How International Law Constitutes Authority 247 (2016).

[45] *See* Sonja C. Grover, Child Refugee Asylum as a Basic Human Right: Selected Case Law on State Resistance 8 (2018).

shame developing countries now feel, as discussed in Chapter 3, from the appearance of not being able to take care of "their own."

All this discussion of effects is largely speculation. What motivates the proposal is principally the observation that currently citizenship disserves a great number of children in serious ways. Many millions of today's children could have dramatically better lives if able to migrate internationally, but their nations of residence are blocking their migration, citing the children's citizenship as the source of their authority, with the support of international bodies and instruments. One solution to that considered in this chapter is to eliminate citizenship for all children, and there is reason to believe this would also improve the lives of all other children in the world, not just those in highly adverse circumstances. Another solution, analyzed in the next chapter, would be to redefine the meaning of citizenship for children, to have international law constrain in certain ways the package of rights, duties, and liabilities that citizenship may comprise.

A very different sort of objection some might have is that nations—at least those with meager resources—*ought* to be able to favor some children over others in provision of health care, schooling, and other publicly funded benefits—specifically, offspring of adult citizens, who have contributed in certain ways to the state and its economy. This presumably is the thought behind the ICESCR provision affording developing nations some leeway in extending benefits to non-national adults. The idea appears in some other positive-rights treaty provisions as well, such as that in the 1954 statelessness convention for public pension benefits.[46] Further, the objection might go, we identify children of citizens by conferring citizenship on them as well.

One problem with this reasoning is a moral one; it rests on an assumption that it is justifiable to impose costs on certain children, depriving them of something to which they are otherwise entitled, because of something about their parents over which they have no control. Another problem is the falsity of two implicit empirical premises: First, that noncitizen parents do not contribute to the economy and public fisc of the nation where they reside. More likely they are being exploited, working harder for less pay relative to citizens, to the benefit of employers and consumers. Second, that the only way to benefit differentially one group of children is by imposing a legal status on them, one that happens to have other, more concerning consequences. That is false because the state could simply issue vouchers to citizen parents, for use in accessing various social supports. I am not recommending this, just noting the falsity of the premise.

[46] Art. 24.1(b)(ii) ("National laws or regulations of the country of residence may prescribe special arrangements concerning benefits or portions of benefits which are payable wholly out of public funds, and concerning allowances paid to persons who do not fulfil the contribution conditions prescribed for the award of a normal pension.").

A view about children's citizenship consistent with the idea of children's status deriving from parents' is the suggestion of Peter Schuck and Rogers Smith that citizen parents give "imputed consent" to their children's citizenship.[47] On this view, states may and must confer citizenship on children of their adult citizens, because the parents hypothetically give their consent on behalf of the child and would demand the ability to do so as a condition for giving their own allegiance to the state. Schuck and Smith are driven by two aims: (1) fortifying a consensual view of citizenship in which the consent of both the individual and the nation are necessary for citizenship to arise, and (2) providing a basis for discriminating between native-born children whose parents are in the United States legally and those whose parents are not. Because neither aim reflects concern about children's own moral status and needs, the view is riddled with problems. One problem is that if implicit or presumed parental consent suffices on the individual side, then hundreds of millions, if not billions, of the world's children—both those living in countries other than the United States and those living in the United States with "illegal alien" parents—now have consented to the United States imposing its citizenship on them. Schuck and Smith think parents' own citizenship does some work on the other side of the equation—that is, the polity's consent—but they supply no reason for thinking it relevant on the individual side.

Another problem on the individual side is that there is no moral basis for giving parents unconstrained power to decide children's citizenship. Schuck and Smith have American citizenship in mind, so they implicitly suppose the power could not possibly disserve any child, but applying the argument globally defeats that supposition. Why would morality or international law sanction empowering parents to consent on behalf of a child to any citizenship of the world whatsoever without limitation, regardless of the value of the citizenship? And why would one impute to parents in, for example, Afghanistan, the most dangerous nation on earth according to some rankings, and terribly oppressive of females, an insistence to have this power as a condition for agreeing themselves to be citizens of that nation? Conversely, would Schuck and Smith deny U.S. citizenship to children of citizen parents who state explicitly that they do not demand that power as a condition for their own citizenship, or that they decline (for no good reason, let us suppose) to give consent to their children becoming U.S. citizens? What must really be underwriting any intuitive appeal to the Schuck-Smith argument is an assumption that the citizenship is very good for the child; the parents' citizenship and supposed demand for power do not do any analytical work on the individual consent side. And even in the United States, that assumption is unwarranted; as explained in Chapter 4, citizenship per se is of little or no positive value to children anywhere.

[47] SCHUCK & SMITH, *supra* note 1, at 116–18.

The polity side of the Schuck-Smith consensual citizenship arguments is also on shaky ground, morally and empirically. Morally, it suggests some children rightly receive a (supposedly) profound benefit because their parents happen to stand in a privileged place, which has all the injustice-baggage of inherited class and wealth.[48] Empirically, it presupposes certain adults, identified by current citizenship, have leverage enough to demand citizenship for their children, on threat of leaving the country. Why would the polity not respond, "good riddance" and welcome the hundreds of millions of adults who would happily become U.S. citizens even if they could not ensure their children would also be granted U.S. citizenship? Some adults might have greater leverage than others in this imaginary bargaining situation, but not because of existing citizenship. An illegal immigrant who is a genius and/or extremely hard working presumably would have greater leverage than a citizen who is unemployed and living on welfare payments. Other factors might influence bargaining power, but it is difficult to see how current citizenship could be among them.

5.7 Conclusion

Citizenship is a legal status with mixed consequences, potentially on the whole quite bad, imposition of which on children cannot be defended on grounds of actual, hypothetical, or proxy consent. For children as a group, a condition of universal statelessness seems pareto optimal; none would be made better off by receiving citizenship, insofar as the marginal benefits of citizenship are real only for adults, and some would be made worse off, insofar as citizenship entails certain liabilities especially for children—in particular, state power to inhibit or altogether prevent migration from horrible to adequate or better circumstances, and provides a basis for discrimination that is invidious but currently has a veneer of legitimacy. Like autonomous adults, children have a presumptive human right, founded upon their distinct personhood and moral claim to sovereignty, against any state forcing its citizenship on them so it can exert extraordinary power over them.

48 *Cf.* Ayelet Shachar, The Birthright Lottery: Citizenship and Global Inequality (2009).

6
Limits on Power over Non-Autonomous Persons

6.1 Introduction

Previous chapters highlighted and addressed harms that befall children because of home-state control over them. Chapters 2 and 3 focused specifically on home states' prevention of exit, arguing international law should ascribe to children an independent right to leave, typically exercised by a proxy, and should reject various potential justifications for forcing children to remain. Chapter 4 showed citizenship conferral more broadly operates to prevent betterment of children's lives, and so Chapter 5 argued international law should cease forcing children into this legal relationship with states that entails presumptive, and to some extent exclusive, power that states use to control children's lives in ways seriously detrimental to them.

This chapter considers an alternative way of addressing the broader problem of harmful government control over children. So long as international law authorizes and pressures states to claim children as citizens, it should clarify a state's proper role in fundamental aspects of children's lives so they no longer use their practical power over citizen children in ways harmful to them in order to serve other interests. In addition, this chapter shows legal actors at the international level also need to adjust their approach to wielding authority over children's lives. At international and domestic levels, there is currently lacking a well-developed theory of how government, at the most basic level, ought to approach whatever role it assumes in children's lives. This chapter presents such a theory.

Section 6.2 identifies all levels of government that exert power over children's lives. These include the international legal order as well as nations and political subunits. Section 6.3 considers which aspects of human life are, in general, properly subject to government control for statist purposes, and which not. It locates decisions as to family relationships and emigration within the latter category. Sections 6.4 and 6.5 analyze which aims government at any level may properly pursue when exerting control over such aspects of non-autonomous persons lives. The analysis yields the view that any government should view its role as purely fiduciary in nature, as exercising on behalf of the child a right equivalent

International Migration of Children for a Better Life. James G. Dwyer, Oxford University Press. © Oxford University Press 2025.
DOI: 10.1093/9780197752333.003.0006

to the right of self-determination that autonomous persons possess in those realms of life, which right is not qualified by interests and aims of other persons or of society. Section 6.6 explores implications of this view in the international law context.

6.2 Which Governments Currently Exert Power over Private Individuals?

If the government of State X blocks persons from exiting or entering, prevents persons from forming or continuing a family relationship, or blocks entities from outside the territory of State X from attempting to provide vital assistance to residents of that territory, then obviously State X's government is acting upon and exerting power over those private individuals. The prevailing view among international law officials and scholars, though, is that international laws and institutions are not acting on those persons in that instance and so have nothing to answer for. It is a situation of inaction on the part of the international legal order rather than action.

To see why that view is wrong, first recognize the fallacy inherent in the conventional description of international law more broadly. Under that description, "international law" is just a set of agreements between or among autonomous states. There is no world government, no effective global authority issuing laws. Each state has antecedent, presumptively absolute sovereignty within its territory, and each is presumptively also free to act as it wishes beyond its borders except insofar as restricted by other states' sovereignty over their own territories or by its voluntarily undertaken obligations to other states (e.g., treaties governing use of international waters). Because any other state's internal sovereignty is also near absolute, a strong principle of nonintervention—sometimes referred to as "external sovereignty"—historically has precluded even humanitarian intervention in other states without their consent. The voluntarily undertaken obligations are embodied in treaties, as to which there is an opt-in rule (no commitment unless expressly chosen by ratification), and/or in customary international law, as to which there is an opt-out rule (all states are bound by norms emanating from more or less uniform state practice when it reflects an "ought judgment" (*opinio juris*) rather than merely self-interest, unless a given state expressly and consistently objects).

The problem with the conventional view lies in failing to recognize that the fundamental background principles of internal and external sovereignty are products of collective action by the world's states and have law-like properties because that collective action has government-like attributes—that is, is regarded as effective to establish authoritative commands. The UN Charter acknowledged those principles, but states had collectively agreed on them long before. The global coming together (partly actual, as at Westphalia, partly metaphorical) to establish and then continually reaffirm these principles to govern international relations itself constitutes a form of collective governance, just as an assembly of enfranchised citizens in a pure democracy, collectively deciding on and then reaffirming or revising rules by which all will be governed, can be called government even if it produces no standing legislature or executive. Today, any given state receives respect from other states for its claim of exclusive control of a territory and its residents, however illiberal and oppressive its rule, and it refrains from interfering with other states' like claim, as a normative rather than merely prudential matter, because that is what "we states" have all agreed to, have established as a supranational rule governing interactions among states and between states and human individuals.[1] It is not just threat of war that states today invoke to back demands for noninterference with their treatment of their resident population; it is also a law-like transnational rule that every state has participated in creating.

That collective, government-like action to bestow on each nation's government presumptively unchecked, exclusive power over the humans on its territory has deep effects on individuals. It puts individuals at the presumptively complete mercy of one state, that in which they happen to reside, without a right to receive assistance from another. (Diplomatic advocacy for nationals is an agreed-upon exception to this, and it is not a matter of individual right.) Yet today moral theorists generally regard the human individual as the sole possessors of moral status; states per se have none. This collective action to radically subordinate individuals to states thus requires defense, or else should be deemed invalid.[2]

In that light, emergence of human rights pronouncements in the twentieth century can be viewed as grudging recognition by states that their power must be defensible to individuals and not absolute. But that development does not go nearly far enough, because the individual rights recognized are limited and each state continues to be deemed (with the narrow exception of peremptory norms) entitled not to embrace this development—that is, to refuse to allow "its people" to possess effective human rights. Further, it gets things backward; the starting point in establishing just rules of international order should not be absolute state

[1] *Cf.* Nicaragua v. United States, 1986 I.C.J. 14, ¶ 202 ("The principle of non-intervention . . . is part and parcel of customary international law."), ¶ 205 (referring to "matters in which each State is permitted, by the principle of State sovereignty, to decide freely. One of these is the choice of a political, economic, social and cultural system . . ."), ¶ 263 (rejecting argument by United States that existence of a dictatorial regime justified its intervention in Nicaragua in the form of arms supplies for the *contras*).

[2] *Cf.* Evan J. Criddle & Evan Fox-Decent, Fiduciaries of Humanity: How International Law Constitutes Authority (2016) (presenting an account of national authority founded upon respect for the dignity of the individual).

sovereignty but rather no authority of any entity over the human individual. A defense of world government, and of its subjecting individuals to international rules about allocation of power over them, if it begins at a no-authority position—that is, the same place defense of national government begins in liberal political theory, presumably will end up supporting only a world government that is servant of the world's people rather than of states or rulers.[3]

Thus, the conventional view of the individual's place in the international order—namely, no place—is also flawed. On the conventional view individuals were not subjects of international law at all and had no direct relationship with international bodies. This was reflected in the legal rule that if one state harmed nationals of another, those persons had no direct recourse in the international legal system; it was a wrong against the other state, not an infringement of any right of the individuals. Further, until the modern era individuals had no recourse under international law against *their own* state for harms it inflicted on them, both because only states held rights under international law and because of the principle of internal sovereignty. Many nations have long chosen to provide internal means for individuals to complain, in domestic tribunals, about harms by their own government officials, but international law was indifferent to whether that was the case. And many states never have. Still today, individual rights are largely seen as dependent on the will of states. If a given nation declines to ratify a particular human rights convention, ratifies it but only subject to various reservations, agrees only to substantive commitments and not to the authority of any tribunal to receive complaints from individuals, or ratifies a convention but later withdraws from it (subject to any constraints on withdrawal a state initially agreed to), there is no apparent basis in international law for criticizing, let alone overriding, that choice.

In addition, if an international body overseeing states' compliance with their voluntarily undertaken treaty obligations itself acts badly—for example, by distorting the content of the obligations to favor self-serving authoritarian regimes—individuals again have no recourse. There is no appellate tribunal standing above, for example, the UNHRC, and no independent legal action

[3] Prominent contemporary theorists of public-authority legitimacy have converged via somewhat different normative paths on a fiduciary conception of national government, while also establishing a deep historical pedigree for this view. *See, e.g.*, ANNA STILZ, TERRITORIAL SOVEREIGNTY: A PHILOSOPHICAL EXPLORATION (2019); Paul B. Miller, "Fiduciary Representation," *in* EVAN J. CRIDDLE ET AL. EDS., FIDUCIARY GOVERNMENT 21–48 (2018); GARY LAWSON & GUY SEIDMAN, "A GREAT POWER OF ATTORNEY": UNDERSTANDING THE FIDUCIARY CONSTITUTION (2017) (showing the American founders viewed the national government as a fiduciary possessing only those powers explicitly conferred); Evan J. Criddle, "A Sacred Trust of Civilization: Fiduciary Foundations of International Law," *in* ANDREW GOLD & PAUL MILLER EDS., PHILOSOPHICAL FOUNDATIONS OF FIDUCIARY LAW 404–22, 417 (2014) ("States exercise sovereign power over legal interests which international law vests exclusively in people under the principle of self-determination."); EVAN FOX-DECENT, SOVEREIGNTY'S PROMISE: THE STATE AS FIDUCIARY (2011).

that can be taken against such a body. Further, only states have seats and a right to speak in the quasi-legislative UN General Assembly and the quasi-executive Security Council, and there is no effective mandate that states speak there in furtherance of the will or welfare of their people. In a sense, then, individuals still have no rights directly against, and seem to have no direct relationship with, international authority. If they suffer from unredressed harms by any state, the posture of the international community and UN bodies is seen as one of inaction, of acquiescence, even incapacity to act, and therefore nonresponsibility. If harmed by an international organization (IO), they are dependent on the inclination of their state to complain.

This conventional view of the international community's relationship to individuals reflects the same action/inaction fallacy that commonly plagues analysis of domestic law—that is, perceiving government's empowerment of some other entity to control the lives of private individuals (e.g., under coverture, giving husbands legal power over wives, and today according parents plenary legal power over children) as government inaction, forbearance from interfering in a supposedly natural order, rather than government action placing individuals in a situation of disempowerment and danger. The international legal order's adoption and continual reaffirmation of the principles of internal and external sovereignty constitute profound action upon individuals, as does the operation of the institutional apparatus it created to enforce both principles—that is, international adjudicative and executive bodies charged with enforcing the norm of exclusive and plenary power of each state over persons and property within its territory. If Nation X tries to help residents of Nation Y in any manner deemed an infringement of the latter's territorial sovereignty, Y can lodge a complaint against X in an international tribunal and get a judgment ordering X to desist.

The international community's posture toward individual persons is therefore one of aggressive action affirmatively placing individuals—especially children—under the comprehensive domination of a state, carried out without regard to the justness or capacity of the state's rulers. Recall Chapter 4's account of the intense pressure international actors have created to force all humans into a nationality, regardless of actual or hypothetical choice, preferably at birth. Absent this imposition of a universal claiming scheme, and absent the accompanying international law rules of sovereignty, other states or any nonstate actors could, without violating any international law, intervene without the state's permission to protect individuals against government or other domestic threats to well-being (violence by private actors, natural disasters) regardless of where persons are located. Because of this fabricated rule of sovereignty, international bodies and other states stand ready to assist any state in repelling such uninvited intrusion into its internal affairs. If not for this norm, there is no telling what entities—formal UN bodies, nongovernmental organizations, and so forth—might now exist with an inclination and capacity—much like protective agencies at the local level—to act within nations whose government mistreats or fails to protect and provide for vulnerable persons on their territory.

Given the crucial role international law actually plays in their fate, individuals can validly point a finger of responsibility at the international legal order when their state affirmatively mistreats them with impunity—by violence, by imposing unjustifiable burdens, by denying important benefits, by blocking exit—or fails to provide needed protection or assistance. It is not the case that their only legitimate complaint is against their nation's government. Persons who suffer from unchecked harmful state action might rightly ask of the UN or of other nations: "How dare you presume to assign to this (corrupt, tyrannical, incompetent, etc.) government such power over my life, to put me under its foot?" And those who suffer in childhood, after being prevented from exiting for a better life, might add: "How dare you have presumed to tie me to this state in the first place, to give it authority to claim me exclusively as its subject, and on top of that to confer on it power to treat me as its resource, its property?" This international legal regime amounts to an only partially successful modus vivendi, not an institutional embodiment of defensible principles of justice.

The parallels with domestic laws that reify historically prevalent private power are clear. International law's implicit conferral on states of presumptive power to, for example, block emigration of women from places where they suffer oppression, a power that any state may but need not waive (e.g., by ratifying the ICCPR), is of a piece with coverture law's empowering of husbands to block wives' attempt to exit an abusive home (i.e., by authorizing physical chastisement by husbands, giving complete financial control to husbands, and entitling husbands to receive police assistance in securing return of wayward wives). We now recognize coverture law's empowerment of husbands to dominate wives as blameworthy state action rather than merely inaction. Similarly, international law's conferral on states of power to impose their nationality on children born within their territory and thereafter control children's relational lives, access to fundamental developmental goods, movement, and interaction with outsiders, which destroys many children's opportunity for a minimally decent life, amounts to direct action upon children by the global legal community. It resembles domestic laws conferring on biological parents entitlement for their own sake to insist on being invested with legal parenthood and thereafter to control children's relationships with other private parties (grandparents, teachers, peers, etc.), access to basic goods, movement, and residence, and to exclude potential outside sources of assistance and protection. Whether one approves of it or not, one must concede that it is government action, action with profound effect on children's lives.

Significantly, the presumptive power over an individual's life that internal and external sovereignty give states is comprehensive in scope—that is, extends to every aspect of life, public and private. It is not confined to realms liberal societies treat as properly subject to the "police power," to public regulation. Rather, it also encompasses matters we in liberal Western societies have decided should be (even though international law does not require that it be) outside the authority of government—that is, matters central to the private lives of autonomous persons. States are empowered to decide for themselves, with an international-law guarantee of noninterference by outsiders, whether they will adopt the liberal stance of forbearing from intrusion into private life or instead use their conferred power to its full extent and impose all-encompassing regulation, even over family life, intimacy, religious practice, education, medical care, and so forth. And to decide for themselves, without interference, whether and in what way they will assume control over central aspects of non-autonomous persons' lives.

Finally, note that the international community has also taken more overt actions regarding state power over individuals. This has laudably included efforts to shift power from states to persons. It has urged and facilitated states' voluntary waiver of some power; the General Assembly has promulgated and promoted human rights conventions that in part constitute state agreement to stay out of certain aspects of private lives and forbear from restrictions on personal freedom beyond what is necessary to prevent harm to others. So international law confers exclusive and plenary power over individuals, without justification, but then provides a means for states to waive some of it, if and for so long as they choose. There is also the jus cogens principle that has emerged in the past century, which subtracts some increment of lawful freedom from states regardless of their consent, authorizing (but not necessarily compelling) international actors or other nations to intervene to stop certain types of especially egregious domestic state action. Recent decades have also seen support develop for a legal duty of humanitarian intervention to prevent or stop such action.

Thus, "plenary" does not today mean absolute, and state power arguably is shrinking as respect for persons grows. However, the conceptual starting point remains plenary sovereignty, and current incursions on sovereignty rule out only what the international community regards as the most extreme abuses, not including the principal obstacles to children's migration out of horrible places and enjoyment of family life. Further, the international community has at the same time also urged, even coerced, states to exert *greater* power over private lives in certain ways. Sometimes that is clearly salutary (e.g., urging states to act more aggressively to prevent violence in intimate relationships). Other times it is not (e.g., UNICEF's coercing nations to stop allowing children to leave via adoption and the CRC's command to factor interests and wishes of parents, kin, and communities into state decisions about children's lives). When this push for states to exert greater control over private life is directed at children and not salutary, the reason is typically that the international legal community is aiming to protect interests of states (e.g., against loss of population or constraints on cultural practices), their leaders (e.g., against embarrassment), and/or certain private entities (cultural, ethnic, or religious minorities; parents; etc.), rather than aiming solely to do what is best for each child all things considered.

In sum, not only states but also the international community and international bodies are acting upon individuals in a blanket fashion, and we can make further headway toward a defensible normative framework for children's migration by going back to a proper square one, asking what justifies government at any level in exerting power over individuals and—of particular importance here—whether that justification extends only to some aspects of human life, not to all. Then we can ask further what the nature of a government's role should be when acting upon non-autonomous persons, including what aims it may properly pursue in different areas of their life where its involvement is appropriate. This likely includes some where it would not presume to tread if dealing with autonomous persons. Beliefs about government power over autonomous persons, and general moral principles those beliefs reflect, might provide the best starting point or normative background for thinking about government involvement in the lives of non-autonomous persons. Autonomous persons have been the focus of most philosophical work and political deliberation, and in practice they receive the fullest respect of lawmakers, who must consider political backlash and potential application of the law to themselves. Proper respect for non-autonomous persons as beings of equal moral worth presumptively requires treating them in equal or equivalent ways.[4]

6.3 Proper Bounds of Government Authority over the Individual

Internal sovereignty is a collection of powers and privileges. It is often characterized as control over a particular territory, but really it is control also (perhaps even primarily) over people, those who happen to be located at a given point in time on such portion of the earth's surface. The notion that any governing regime which exercises a particular state's internal sovereignty without any sense of obligation to the people, instead using the power for self-serving ends, should enjoy the deference that international law historically has dictated

[4] On the moral status of children and its implications, *see* James G. Dwyer, Moral Status and Human Life: The Case for Children's Superiority (2011).

for states is patently indefensible. It is like saying that if someone discovers a foundling on their property and decides to hold the child captive to exploit for labor and sex, that person should, simply because now possessing practical power over the child, have all the legal powers local law accords parents. It does not become more appropriate if that child, asked sometime later, says the captor is their "daddy." A legal regime that confers powers and rights on such holders of practical power is itself complicit in the crime. It shares responsibility for whatever happens to the child thereafter. So too with an international legal order that grants sovereignty to holders of practical control over a territory who have no sense of commitment to the welfare of the inhabitants. That legal order is an accomplice to any abuse the inhabitants suffer. To avoid such complicity in crimes against humanity, human rights abuses, destruction of lives, and avoidable suffering, the international legal community must hew to defensible principles for exertion of authority over persons. In turn, national governments must as well.

To that end, it is helpful first to identify different realms of life over which government at any level might wish to exert control and to ask whether it is proper for it to do so in all such realms. Then we can ask what norms should constrain government in any realm as to which its control is proper. Governments operate in many capacities, and different norms might be apt for different functions. The most familiar government function is the police power, and on the most defensible view of that power the government exercises it as servant of "The People" collectively, an agent for all members of society, reaching decisions based on consideration of everyone's interests, giving equal weight to like interests of all persons, fairly balancing interests that conflict.[5] Evan Criddle maintains that instantiation of a fiduciary conception of internal sovereignty is now a necessary condition for a nation's enjoying external sovereignty under international law:

> Just as a guardian or trustee may exercise discretionary powers on behalf of a beneficiary who possesses the legal right to wield these powers but lacks legal capacity to do so (due to age or other disability), international law permits states to exercise public powers for and on behalf of a people that is unable (both legally and practically) to engage in effective self-governance without institutional representation. And just as a guardian or trustee bears fiduciary duties to respect the beneficial interests of their appointed beneficiaries, international law requires states to use their entrusted discretionary powers for the equal benefit of their people or risk forfeiting sovereign authority through

[5] Fox-Decent, *supra* note 3, at 34–47. This is true even when government officials are adjudicating competing individual rights and allegations of individual harm, as in contract and property disputes or enforcement of criminal laws. Legislatures and courts consider broader societal effects of potential decisions (e.g., general deterrence with criminal law enforcement, public-policy limitations on enforcement of terms in contracts, wills, and trusts).

international intervention, partition, federative autonomy for an affected region, or other remedies.[6]

With respect to any inhabitants of its territory, then, a state's regime may not legitimately wield power over them for its own self-serving purposes, may not treat them as instruments for its use or disserve them simply to display its power. One implication of this for the rulers of any nation where dire circumstances prevail, because of civil war or famine or other disaster, is that they may not obstruct assistance to the nation's people from outside sources absent compelling reasons tied to the well-being of those people. Chapter 9 will explore this further.

Additional constraints on government appear when we differentiate the police power role of government at any level from other functions. Police power is presumptively apt for what might loosely be termed "the public realm," where persons interact with others in non-intimate ways. In the public realm, government rightly guards against injury to property or person and generally promotes overall societal welfare.[7] Paradigmatic exercises of police power by a national or local government are enactment and enforcement of statutes criminalizing violence and theft, protecting public goods such as the environment, and facilitating movement and interaction in public spaces (e.g., highway construction, traffic rules); resolving property or contract disputes; and promoting general health and welfare where collective action problems make private action inadequate (e.g., mandating vaccinations to stop spread of disease, funding the arts). Police power can also be apt in the private realm, however, if and to the extent risk of harm inheres in personal interactions there (e.g., domestic violence).

At the global level, the UN might be said to carry out a police power function with respect to human society as a whole—directly in areas of life best handled by a global authority and delegating to states decision-making best exercised at that level. It might serve police power functions similar to those which states now perform, or like those that a federal government such as that of the United States perform—for example, legislating against and prosecuting interstate crimes (e.g., wars of aggression) and crimes by private parties that cross state borders or that occur outside all states' borders (e.g., on the high seas); coordinating international cooperation (by states and by nonstate entities in different nations) to protect the environment; overseeing international movement of persons;

[6] Criddle, "A Sacred Trust of Civilization," *supra* note 3, at 417.

[7] *See* Maureen E. Brady, *Turning Neighbors into Nuisances*, 134 Harv. L. Rev. 1609, 1659 (2021) (stating that "police power" "demarcates the boundaries within which the government can affirmatively regulate for the health, safety, and welfare of its citizens, limiting some rights to protect the greater good"); Santiago Legarre, *The Historical Background of the Police Power*, 9 U. Pa. J. Const. L. 745, 774 (2007) ("'police power' normally refers to the authority of the states for the promotion of public health, public safety, public morals, and public welfare").

resolving interstate property and contract disputes; and generally promoting human well-being in any ways optimally done at that highest level.

At any level of government, the ideals of giving equal consideration to all and devotion to the good of the whole might not be realized much in practice, because in any society some members are more powerful or favored than others. The point here is that the inherent nature of police power is service to all of society equally, which at times must, given the inevitability of conflicting interests, entail sacrificing interests of some persons to some extent or denying some of their desires, to protect others or promote the greater good of the whole.

Importantly, the police power is not all-encompassing. Modern liberal societies, at least, treat many important aspects of life as out of bounds for government in its police power capacity, not subordinated to statist aims or aggregate welfare, instead the province of self-regarding private decision-making. These are matters as to which autonomous adults possess a right of self-determination. A precise description of that sphere is challenging, but roughly speaking matters within it satisfy two conditions: (1) they are central to and primarily about an individual's own life, and (2) decisions in that realm generally do not threaten others with harm. For ease of reference, let us label these Category A matters. Inherently public matters (not central to and primarily about one individual's life, or else involving interpersonal harms) we can refer to as Category B matters. For present purposes we need not establish where exactly the line lies between the two categories or precisely define the concepts of "central," "primarily about," or "harm." There are enough clear cases on each side.

Liberal legal systems generally repose authority as to Category A matters, insofar as they pertain to an *autonomous* individual's life, exclusively with that individual. These are considered matters of self-determining right even though exercise of the right might negatively affect others, in ways not considered harm in the sense of wrongful injury or violation of rights—for example, by merely offending or upsetting them.[8] They include such choices, within a range of available options, as: with whom a person agrees to form and continue close personal relationships; whether and how a person receives education or obtains medical treatment for illness or injury; and who will provide them with other forms of personal service—legal, financial, home maintenance, and so forth. Any of these choices might disappoint or anger other individuals or undermine the aims of some group or organization, yet the state does not presume therefore to seize control of those aspects of an autonomous person's life, to satisfy others' preferences, however intensely felt they might be. Nor does it presume to force an individual to take others' preferences or interests into account when making

[8] *See* Anna Folland, *The Harm Principle and the Nature of Harm*, 34 UTILITAS 139 (2022); Piers Norris Turner, *"Harm" and Mill's Harm Principle*, 124 ETHICS 299, 299–300 (2014).

such choices about their lives, standing ready to override a choice that causes offense or upset. Thus, for example, if I, an autonomous person, have diabetes, whether I take insulin is a Category A matter and entirely up to me. A liberal state would not presume to compel me to do so on the grounds that it would be best for other individuals, such as my family members, or for society generally, even if that is true.

Because we are analogizing the international legal order to a unitary state or a federation, we might wonder whether there is a similar division of decision types for states—that is, whether some areas of national life should be out of bounds for the international legal order. Article 2(7) of the UN Charter might be read to say so, in suggesting the UN lacks authority "to intervene in matters which are essentially within the domestic jurisdiction of any state." If some matters are inherently within a realm of self-determination for states, though, I believe it must be so for reasons different from those why most people think we should respect individual autonomy. Specifically, the prevailing view is that a right of individual self-determination rests on a foundation of moral respect for the individual, in both the personal sovereignty and non-alienation ways discussed in Chapter 5. States do not warrant such respect; they are not living, breathing, thinking, feeling organic beings with moral status. Treatment of them only as means rather than as ends in themselves is entirely appropriate. If deference is owed to states more in some realms than others, then it is more likely to be because that is assumed generally best for human welfare or protection of individual rights. Conversely, the international legal order, if it is also to rest on liberal political principles and embody moral respect for the individual, should not in the first place purport to bestow on states authority to act upon individuals in ways contrary to the moral respect they are owed. Ultimately, the international community must justify to human individuals any ascription of power it gives states over them, just as a state ought to be able to justify the power over individuals that it gives to local government or to private parties (e.g., guardians). In fact, the international legal order might delegate to or share with states some moral *duties* owed to individuals, to ensure they receive due respect from all government and private entities. Later chapters will focus on such duties.

Returning to the distinction between matters of self-determining right and matters of public concern in the case of autonomous persons, we should deem the international legal order also precluded from exerting power over Category A aspects of such persons' lives. This would mean it presumptively should not purport to bestow on states, or recognize states as inherently possessing, internal authority over Category A aspects of individuals' lives. A defensible principle of internal sovereignty would limit deference to states only in Category B aspects of social existence, and only to the extent the state is in the best position to regulate those aspects. Other states, individually or collectively, have no business ascribing to an illiberal regime internal sovereignty with respect to, for example, nonharmful intimate behavior between autonomous adults, individuals' personal attire, or any individual's choice of educational program, medical treatment, or religious adherence. States might be *permitted* to involve themselves is some personal affairs, at the invitation (actual or imputed) of private parties, but not entitled by virtue of sovereignty. If that is correct, treaties pronouncing individual human rights to noninterference in such realms of life merely articulate what was already true before the treaties existed.

As for rights of particular significance in a migration context, choice in family formation is among the aspects of personal life that modern liberal societies treat as within the realm of self-determining freedom. Choice of career and educational courses leading to it are additional examples. And especially pertinent here, a decision to leave the place where one is living to pursue a career, family life, or greater freedom elsewhere is generally a matter of self-determining right for autonomous adults, and the ICCPR treats it as such. (Chapter 8 will consider how to treat within this framework a decision to enter a new place.) The departure might greatly sadden other individuals—family and friends. It might send a message of negative judgment about one's current place of residence and its government. It might contribute to a weakening of the community one is leaving, if part of a larger attrition. Yet none of these concerns justifies constraining an autonomous person's decision; none transform it from a personal to a public matter. The international legal community therefore has no rightful authority to declare that decision subject to state control, directly or indirectly (e.g., by giving states exclusive power to issue identity and travel documents), for such reasons.

This casts the ICCPR right "to leave any country" in a new light, as merely rhetorical statement of a fact true before any states ratified the Covenant. Even an international-law positivist could concede this point when viewed from an absence-of-lawful-authority angle: Neither any international body nor any state could ever rightly have claimed power to deny freedom to leave, absent a legitimate police power rationale such as national security or enforcement of criminal or contract law. The international community never itself held that legal power, so it could not confer it on states. Likewise as to rights in connection with interpersonal association and family formation. The appearance of gratuitously bestowing them by ratifying treaties is misleading.

In fact, the ICCPR arguably is problematic insofar as it creates or reinforces the false impression that states *do* lawfully enjoy a presumption of power over every aspect of their subjects' lives, and that persons lack negative rights against government interference in their lives absent magnanimous choice by their state to ratify that treaty and forgo reservations.[9] Given that some major countries

[9] The Universal Declaration of Human Rights speaks throughout of "recognizing" rights that

have not ratified the ICCPR, this would mean billions of people in the world, under international law, are in a position of legal liability as to matters the treaty covers, or that their state would not exceed the proper bounds of its authority by completely dominating their lives.

On a liberal conception of the inherent role of the state, any state's nonratification of the ICCPR should be seen as irrelevant to the existence of limits on state authority and of negative human rights for residents of that state; they have had them already, as incidents of personal sovereignty, which no international body ever had authority to take away by presuming to gives states power over them. From this perspective, the international law regime committing states to respect the plenary power each exercises internally, under the banner of "sovereignty," was simply a power grab lacking in normative justification, or reification of a preexisting overextension by domestic governments. The UN Charter, though "reaffirm[ing]" in its preamble "faith in fundamental human rights," perpetuates this power grab, by reinforcing the notion of a domestic sphere where the state enjoys plenary power, which UN bodies have consistently interpreted to be all-encompassing rather than limited to inherently public (Category B) matters. In this respect the Charter itself arguably violates fundamental human rights and underwrites states' violations of fundamental human rights. These pacts might have been necessary when made to prevent greater harm to humanity, from war, but nevertheless we should recognize what international law does by accepting illiberal governments and promising them noninterference, as a matter of their supposed right, in their behavior toward their nationals inside their borders.

6.4 Government Role in Non-Autonomous Persons' Lives

The international legal order intrudes into the lives of non-autonomous persons even more deeply than it does into the lives of autonomous adults. In addition to establishing the basic background principles of internal and external sovereignty, which can worsen the plight of any person in dire circumstances, international law adds to the lives of non-autonomous persons special-rights conventions that sanction state control of many private and personal aspects of life for purposes other than those persons' welfare. The UN Children's Rights Convention and the UN Convention on the Rights of Persons with Disabilities are not supposed to detract from rights that non-autonomous persons enjoy under general human

"everyone has," suggesting observation of something already existing rather than creation or conferral. The ICCPR contains a few passages with similar language but more often speaks to what rights persons "shall have" or what they "shall be entitled" to do, in each case seeming to have "henceforth" implicitly embedded.

rights treaties, but in practice the CRC clearly does, as explained in Chapter 1, and the CRPD might as well.

That the CRC's divided loyalties gave me reason to reject it as a starting point for child-centered analysis does not mean it is normatively flawed. Perhaps all decisions as to children, including whether they may exit a nation or join a family, *should* reflect a balancing of interests of everyone affected by them in any way. This chapter provides an assessment of that proposition.

This analysis is necessary and pertinent because, even though the ICCPR and ICESCR trump the CRC as a matter of positive law, whenever the former gives children greater protection, in practice no domestic or international bodies are effectuating that principle. The UN condones the CRC's diminishment of children's rights by failing to enforce the priority of the general rights conventions. It might have done so by having one or more of the existing general rights implementation bodies (Human Rights Committee; Committee on Economic, Social and Cultural Rights; Human Rights Council) oversee the performance of the Children's Rights Committee or simply take on implementation of the CRC themselves. Instead, the UN delegated to an autonomous and highly politicized Children's Rights Committee independent authority over children worldwide. This is further action by the international legal order upon children, and it requires defense.

With respect to matters inherently public, police power decision-making seems just as appropriate with non-autonomous persons as it is with autonomous persons, so no different analysis is needed for non-autonomous persons in that realm. Other people have a right against harm by non-autonomous persons just as much as against harm by autonomous persons, and some matters impacting non-autonomous persons are not central to or primarily about their individual lives. Thus, state action preventing minors or mentally ill adults from acting violently toward others properly reflects consideration of all affected persons' interests and allows the interests of those who would be physically harmed to trump the liberty interests of the non-autonomous person to the extent necessary to prevent the harmful behavior. Interpersonal violence is a Category B matter. So is infrastructure spending; though it affects children (e.g., duration of school bus rides, safety on family trips, parent availability), it does not directly pertain to fundamental and private aspects of their lives, and it is not a matter each autonomous individual has a right to dictate insofar as it affects them.

But with Category A matters, things are more complicated. Governments permissibly, perhaps obligatorily, involve themselves in some way in such matters so that infants' fate is not left to private whim. It cannot leave matters such as family formation to children's own decisions, obviously. Some other entity must make such decisions for infants. Empowering private parties legally to do so might be possible, but note that that would itself be government action requiring defense;

it is not a way to avoid the question of *how* government may exert control over these matters. Governments in fact currently interject themselves into Category A aspects of non-autonomous persons' lives at international, national, and local levels.

At the international level, law currently dictates which state has control over and primary duties toward a child. Though autonomous persons have, at least in theory, a self-determining right to choose from among all nations offering them a right of residence, and perhaps also citizenship, international law does not try to accord newborn children an equivalent right to the best available nation but instead assigns children even to the worst. Presumably this reflects in part deference to each state's view of who its people are and each nation's interest in having members, which is a consideration other than, and potentially in conflict with, a child's well-being. Chapter 5 challenged that exertion of power. In this chapter, we take that aspect of international law as given and ask whether there are constraints on other types of government decisions made on behalf of children in Category A aspects of their lives. Some such further decisions by the international legal order are embodied in the CRC, which speaks to children's legal family relationships, treatment within those relationships, schooling, medical care, and so forth. Some provisions are too vague to provide clear answers to important questions—for example, who are a child's "parents" within the meaning of various provisions aiming to ensure a child remains with and under the control of such (birth parents, legal custodians, the persons raising them, etc.)? Some CRC provisions might be explicable entirely in terms of serving children's welfare, but many clearly serve the interests of others—for example, protecting parental prerogative to direct children's education—or of cultural and religious groups. Some seem straightforwardly designed to protect state interests, such as Article 29's mandate that a child's education "be directed to . . . development of respect for . . . the national values of the country in which the child is living," regardless of whether those values are repugnant.

Nations and political subunits within them have also long made choices in Category A matters of life for non-autonomous persons. They do so, generally with more clarity and specificity than the CRC, through domestic laws relating to, for example, legal family membership, school attendance, and medical care. Those laws make, or empower a state agency to make, some decisions directly (e.g., legislation saying children of a certain age must attend school and that all schools must conform to certain curricular requirements, court-ordered medical treatment for a cognitively impaired adult). As to some other matters, they legally empower certain private parties, typically guardians, to make decisions (e.g., among schools, religious exercise, residential location). Some domestic laws governing Category A aspects of non-autonomous persons' lives appear entirely aimed at serving what the state regards as their well-being (e.g., a metabolic-screening mandate for newborns). However, one can easily find examples of legislation and court doctrines relating to children's upbringing that aim at least in part to serve parents and/or ideological groups for their own sake. For example, one cannot plausibly explain in child welfare terms laws that: confer legal parenthood on birth parents with no regard for a past history of horrible child abuse; empower any and all legal parents to waive children's state-law right to attend school and substitute entirely unmonitored homeschooling; exempt religious objectors from child health care (e.g., metabolic screening and vaccinations) and medical neglect laws; grant parents and teachers an exception to general prohibitions on hitting other persons; or, as shown in Chapter 3, preclude international adoption. Legislators explicitly invoke parental entitlement as purported justification for many such laws.[10]

Though government at various levels routinely exerts its power into Category A aspects of non-autonomous persons' lives, in ways that profoundly impact their basic welfare and lived experience, there has been remarkably little concerted attention among jurists or political theorists to the nature of government's expanded role in the case of non-autonomous persons. Should government officials approach these Category A aspects of non-autonomous persons' lives the same way they approach Category B matters for everyone—namely, deploying a police power decision-making process that weighs and balances the interests of all affected persons, possibly ascribing rights to persons other than the non-autonomous persons or even to groups (community, church, nation)? Or is there another model of decision-making that is more appropriate for Category A aspects of non-autonomous persons' lives, one that aims to approximate autonomous persons' exercise of their right to self-determination? Different approaches to decision-making can have dramatically different impacts.

6.4.1 Introducing parens patriae

The concept Anglo-American legal systems have for centuries deployed domestically to explain and justify government control over central aspects of children's and incompetent adults' lives is parens patriae, which translates as parent of the country. Other Western legal systems use analogous concepts. The international

[10] The concept of parental rights makes sense only as an instrument for serving parents' own interests. Invoking children's welfare as basis for parental rights, as courts and scholars sometimes do, rests on confusion, a misplacement of the rights. A moral claim arising from a non-autonomous person's own interests would belong to that non-autonomous person, not anyone else. On the directionality of duties and the correlativity of duties with rights, *see* Gopal Sreenivasan, *Duties and Their Direction*, 120 ETHICS 465, 484 (2010); Matthew H. Kramer, *Refining the Interest Theory of Rights*, 55 AM. J. JURIS. 31, 32 (2010).

legal order could equally well adopt this concept for its decision-making about non-autonomous persons.

Parens patriae is a beneficent uberguardian role in which government attends in some fashion to the needs of vulnerable persons unable to protect or advance their own well-being. There is long and widespread acceptance that an enlightened society will assign to its government the function of protecting persons unable to safeguard their own interests[11] and that in doing so, government exercises a power or jurisdiction that is special, in the sense of being different in some way from government activity in contexts involving only autonomous persons.[12] How exactly it is different, though, has never been a subject of close study. Courts and scholars in the English-speaking world have failed to articulate the precise nature of this special role—in particular, which aims government may pursue in this role, and which considerations properly influence government action predicated on this special authority. Participants in the drafting of the CRC did explicitly discuss the ultimate question of whether *only* children's interests should factor into certain types of decisions about their lives, which could be viewed as a debate about the nature of parens patriae. They ultimately answered that question in the negative, in blanket fashion, settling on language for Article 3 that, in conjunction with other provisions protective of parents, kin, and culture, sound like a police power approach to every aspect of children's lives, implying children's interests are never all that matters ("In all actions concerning children ... the best interests of the child shall be a primary consideration"). But there was no effort to develop a theory of decision making for non-autonomous persons to support that choice, which is patently inconsistent with the prevailing approach to decision making for incompetent adults in Category A aspects of their lives.

I develop a theory in the remainder of this chapter. I begin by clarifying the range of possible coherent conceptions of parens patriae and then identify the conception most consistent with the normative underpinnings of modern liberal legal systems and general human rights law.

6.4.2 Competing conceptions of parens patriae

In judicial decisions and legal scholarship, one finds two seemingly disparate understandings of the parens patriae role that have much currency. First, some

[11] *See* Legarre, *supra* note 7, at 764 ("The doctrine of parens patriae is present in some form and under some name in every reasonable legal system, for no reasonable state would wish to violate the basic ethical imperative of looking after children deserted by their parents").

[12] Sallyanne Payton, *The Concept of the Person in the Parens Patriae Jurisdiction over Previously Competent Persons*, 17 J. MED. & PHIL. 605, 641 ("The parens patriae jurisdiction ... is fundamentally unlike other powers of the state.").

scholars and domestic courts appear to treat parens patriae decision-making as a matter of simply paying special heed to the interests of dependent persons in matters affecting them.[13] In light of such persons' inability to advance their own rights and interests, government actors bear responsibility to ensure those rights and interests receive consideration—perhaps heightened in some way, perhaps equal—along with other individual interests and even collective societal interests and aims that might be impacted by decisions, in some sort of balancing if those several interests do not all align. This conception (henceforth "the special-heed conception") seems implicitly to suppose that, given non-autonomous persons' inability to advocate for themselves, absent assertion of parens patriae authority, their interests would receive no consideration at all in law and policy decisions. Or in private decisions; government officials might cite their parens patriae responsibility to explain why they have gotten involved in some aspect of non-autonomous persons' lives at all, when no one asked them to do so—for example, intervening to block choices by guardians or parents it deems injurious.

This special-heed conception appears most often in cases involving children, rather than incompetent adults. For example, in a U.S. Supreme Court case concerning parental control over children's visitation with grandparents, *Troxel v. Granville*, Justice Stevens invoked in dissent "this Court's assumption that a parent's interests in a child must be balanced against the State's long-recognized interests as parens patriae . . . and, critically, the child's own complementary interest in preserving relationships that serve her welfare and protection."[14]

A different conception is more prevalent, however. Many domestic courts and commentators depict parens patriae as a fiduciary role in which the state acts as proxy decision maker or agent solely for the incompetent individual, appointing and overseeing immediate caregivers but also sometimes itself directly making decisions for or providing care to non-autonomous persons, with those persons' welfare as its only aim. A distinctive feature of a fiduciary role is a duty of undivided loyalty, of sole devotion to the interests of the "principal," as if standing in the shoes of the principal. The prevailing view of government in its police power

[13] *See, e.g.*, Matter of Sallmaier, 378 N.Y.S.2d 989, 991 (1976) ("The decision to exercise the power of parens patriae must reflect the welfare of society as a whole, but mainly it must balance the individual's right to be free from interference against the individual's need to be treated, if treatment would in fact be in his best interest."); John Seymour, *Parens Patriae and Wardship Powers: Their Nature and Origins*, 14 Oxford J.L. Stud. 159, 186 (1994) ("The fact that the need to treat the welfare of the child as the paramount consideration is a distinguishing feature of some types of proceedings does not mean that these proceedings can be conducted without regard to the interests of others who might be affected.").

[14] 530 U.S. 57, 88 (2000). *See also In re* Spence (1847) 2 Ph. 247, 252; 41 E.R. 937, 938 ("The jurisdiction of this Court . . . as representative of the Crown, with regard to the custody of infants rests upon this ground, that it is the interest of the State and of the Sovereign that children should be properly brought up and educated; and . . . the Sovereign, as parens patriae, is bound to look to the maintenance and education . . . of all his subjects.").

role is also as a fiduciary, but for society generally. In contrast, in its parens patriae role, on this view (henceforth "the fiduciary conception"), government is a fiduciary for an individual, like a private guardian but using state instrumentalities to advance the ward's welfare.

If this is the nature of a government's parens patriae role, then presumptively it must adopt a singular aim of serving the dependent person's interests or effectuating that person's actual or imputed wishes—in executive, legislative, or judicial decision-making. It should not allow other individuals' interests or collective societal aims to influence its decisions at all.[15] As with private fiduciaries such as attorneys and guardians, the government's duty of loyalty would proscribe both self-dealing and simultaneously serving another person, group, organization, or institution with potentially conflicting interests.[16] That a person or entity occupying a fiduciary role as to Person X is also serving separately as a fiduciary to Person Y (e.g., someone serving as conservator for two or more incompetent adults) or to collective entity Z (e.g., a lawyer who does work for a private organization or a local government as well as for individual clients) does not change this; they may serve only Person X in the course of directing Person X's affairs. One commentator writes regarding formerly competent adults:

> Under the law that has governed the *parens patriae* jurisdiction ever since it was created in the Middle Ages in England, a person whose powers of self-management have been taken from him by the state has a right that those who exercise the power to manage his affairs on his behalf do so in a fiduciary capacity.... The state takes jurisdiction only as a trustee: the jurisdiction has been designed to avoid vesting in the state any authority or incentive to act in a self-interested manner vis-à-vis the incompetent...[17]

[15] *See* Evan J. Criddle, *Liberty in Loyalty: A Republican Theory of Fiduciary Law*, 95 Tex. L. Rev. 993, 995 (2017) (opining that the duty of loyalty is best viewed as guarding against domination, "by ensuring that a fiduciary's actions are legally required to track the terms of her mandate and the interests of her beneficiaries"); Seth Davis, *The False Promise of Fiduciary Government*, 89 Notre Dame L. Rev. 1145, 1158 (2014) ("Fiduciary law is built around the axiom that '[t]he foremost duty which a fiduciary owes to its beneficiary is undivided loyalty.' ").

[16] One private fiduciary role, the trustee of an irrevocable trust, does typically entail serving multiple parties with competing interests, and the duty of loyalty there requires fairness among beneficiaries, along with proscription of self-dealing, conflicts of interests, and using the role to serve nonbeneficiaries. This is a special type of fiduciary, in any event, non-analogous insofar as used by a property owner to administer wealth gratuitously transferred to others, rather than representing a client's or ward's inherent rights.

[17] Payton, *supra* note 12, at 617. *See also id.*, 616 ("designed from the beginning to be wholly fiduciary duties ... the state's role has been exclusively that of trustee"); Cruzan by Cruzan v. Dir, Missouri Dep't Health, 497 U.S. 261, 315–16 (1990) (Brennan, Marshall, and Blackmun, JJ., dissenting) ("Missouri has a *parens patriae* interest in providing Nancy Cruzan, now incompetent, with as accurate as possible a determination of how she would exercise her rights under these circumstances."); *Re Eve*, 31 DLR (4th), ¶ 73 ("it is to be exercised in the 'best interest' of the protected person"), ¶ 75 ("The discretion is to be exercised for the benefit of that person, not for that of others.... This is

Outcomes in high-profile legal disputes concerning severely brain-damaged adults on life support have reflected this view.[18]

Nineteenth-century legal scholar John Norton Pomeroy wrote similarly, regarding state protection of children, that "exercise of the jurisdiction depends on the sound and enlightened discretion of the court, and has for its sole object the highest wellbeing of the infant."[19] Other scholars and numerous courts have likewise characterized parens patriae as calling for exclusive focus on the welfare of the child when agencies of government at any level must get involved, rejecting a police power approach to governing non-autonomous persons' lives—that is, an approach in which other interests would factor in.[20] Other authorities come close by describing the state's role as that of a "wise parent" or guardian.[21] The same view could readily be applied to international agencies.

particularly so in cases where a court might be tempted to act because failure to do so would risk imposing an obviously heavy burden on some other individual."), ¶ 82.

[18] *See In re* Guardianship of Schiavo, 851 So. 2d 182, 186–87 (Fla. Dist. Ct. App. 2003) ("this case is not about the aspirations that loving parents have for their children. It is about Theresa Schiavo's right to make her own decision, independent of her parents and independent of her husband. In circumstances such as these, . . . trial judges . . . serve as surrogates or proxies to make decisions about life-prolonging procedures. . . . [T]he trial judge must make a decision that the clear and convincing evidence shows the ward would have made for herself."); Cruzan v. Missouri Department of Health, 497 U.S. 261, 286 (1990) (rejecting parents' assertion of a right to decide about life-sustaining care of adult offspring, stating: "[W]e do not think the Due Process Clause requires the State to repose judgment on these matters with anyone but the patient herself"); *In re* Quinlan, 355 A.2d 647, 661–62 (N.J. 1976) (same, stating: "We do not recognize an independent parental right of religious freedom to support the relief requested"). *See also* O'Connor v. Donaldson, 422 U.S. 563, 573–75 (1975) (stating that preference of the public not to see mentally ill persons is not a permissible consideration in commitment decisions); *In re* Terwilliger, 450 A.2d 1376, 1382 (Pa. Super. Ct. 1982) ("[I]n making the decision whether to authorize sterilization, a court should consider only the best interest of the incompetent person, not the interests or convenience of the individual's parents, the guardian or society").

[19] III Pomeroy, *Equity Jurisprudence* (1883), § 1307, 330 n.1.

[20] *See also Re J* [1992] 4 All Eng. L. Rep. 614 (characterizing the court in medical treatment cases as "adopting the standpoint of reasonable parents who had the child's best interests at heart without regard to their own interests"); Wentzel v. Montgomery General Hospital, 447 A.2d 1244, 1253 (Md. 1982) ("It is a fundamental common law concept that the jurisdiction of courts of equity over such persons is plenary so as to afford whatever relief may be necessary to protect the individual's best interests."); J v. C [1970] AC 668, 697 (Guest LJ) ("the law administered by the Chancery Court as representing the Queen as *parens patriae* never required that the father's wishes should prevail over the welfare of the infant. The dominant consideration has always been the welfare of the infant."); Smith v. Smith, 26 Eng. Rep. 977, 977 (Ch. 1745) ("It is not a profitable jurisdiction of the crown, but for the benefit of infants themselves"); *Developments in the Law—The Constitution and the Family*, 93 Harv. L. Rev. 1156, 1199 (1980) ("when the state acts as *parens patriae*, it should advance only the best interests of the incompetent individual and not attempt to further other objectives, deriving from its police power, that may conflict with the individual's welfare"), 1200 ("it should exercise the *parens patriae* power solely to further the best interests of the child").

[21] *See Re* Jules [2008] NSWSC 1193, 16 ("In exercising this jurisdiction, the Court endeavours to act as would a wise parent. . . . [T]he Court may in place of the parents make those decisions which it considers appropriate in the best interests of the child."); *Re* J [1992] 4 All Eng. L. Rep. 614 (characterizing the court in medical treatment cases as "adopting the standpoint of reasonable parents who had the child's best interests at heart without regard to their own interests"); R v. Gyngall [1893] 2 QB 232, 239 (stating that parens patriae is "not a jurisdiction to determine rights as between

Outcomes in legislative deliberation or in adjudication of or administrative response to individual cases clearly can turn on whether government actors adopt the fiduciary conception, thus considering *only* the non-autonomous person's interests, or instead adopt the first conception identified, the special-heed conception, throwing those interests into a mix with other persons' interests and general societal aims and then trying to balance somehow those potentially competing considerations. For example, if doctors petition a court to order medical care for a child, the court might do so if only the child's welfare matters in that situation, but might refuse if it balances against the child's welfare all other affected interests, such as those of parents and their co-religionists who wish to have the child's life governed by their ideology, those of siblings in an overcrowded house, and those of the health insurance company, perhaps along with collective societal aims such as avoiding the costs of enforcing a court order, lowering the price of medical care by reducing demand, and so forth.

The CRC would look very different if the drafting committee and the UN General Assembly had adopted the fiduciary conception of *their* role in connection with Category A aspects of children's lives. The Convention might have had one substantive part dealing with public matters, insisting children have protections like those of adults in connection with the state's carrying out of its police power functions, such as criminal law enforcement. And another part dealing with inherently private matters, matters that autonomous adults are entitled to decide for themselves based solely on their own interests, as to which a state party must act purely as fiduciary for each child, standing in to exercise the child's rights for him or her, making the child's interests its sole consideration. Instead, the entire document reflects the special-heed conception; the drafters and UN representatives clearly approached the CRC as a balancing exercise throughout.

6.4.3 Contrasting parens patriae with other government functions

This inconsistency regarding the nature of parens patriae decision-making might stem in part from a tendency among some to think government always acts in the same way, regardless of its role in a particular situation—specifically, the police power mode of decision-making, which is the most familiar. In fact, however, governments act in many capacities, and different modes are recognized as appropriate for different capacities. A national government might act as: actor

a parent and a stranger, or as between a parent and a child. It was a paternal jurisdiction . . . in virtue of which the Chancery Court was put to act . . . in the place of a parent, and as if it were the parent of the child, thus superseding the natural guardianship of the parent.").

in international affairs, competitive business operator, employer, jailor, speaker in commercial advertising or the public square, service provider, funder of private service provision, party to purchase contracts, or educator. IOs and local governments might also serve in such a variety of roles. Each role has its own scope of authority and concerns, its own set of powers and duties, and its own governing norms and constraints. Recognition of this appears in international law, for example, with respect to sovereign immunity, which applies to states and their officials carrying out inherently governmental functions but might not apply when they act in ways private enterprises also do, such as entering into purchase and employment contracts.[22] In the United States, somewhat different lines of constitutional doctrine pertain to various state functions. Individual rights that constrain government when it acts in its police power role might do so to a lesser degree or not at all when it operates in one of the other roles, especially those that approximate that of a private actor. For instance, government employees have diminished free speech rights in relation to government qua their employer.[23] Likewise, UN bodies sometimes act in roles analogous to private parties—for example, as employers and as tenants or landlords—and operate under different rules in those capacities than when carrying out their core function.

How, then, to reason to a conclusion about the nature of the parens patriae role, the role of special protector of non-autonomous persons, within the range of government functions? We might begin by considering whether and how it differs conceptually from the police power function, with which it is most often conflated or conjoined. This function has always been the primary focus of political theorists, who typically presuppose the people on whom governments act are autonomous.

6.4.3.1 No distinction view

Relative to the police power, one possible view of the parens patriae role is that it is not distinct; it is simply what we call exercise of police power when non-autonomous persons are centrally involved. This would be consistent with the special-heed conception. Its invocation might simply counter a tendency to do police power decision-making badly when non-autonomous persons are impacted, leaving them out of a cost-benefit equation that should include everyone's interests and objectively weigh each. Invoking government's parens

[22] *See* UN Convention on Jurisdictional Immunities of States and Their Property, Part III.

[23] *See* Enquist v. Oregon Dep't Agr, 553 U.S. 591, 598 (2008) ("there is a crucial difference, with respect to constitutional analysis, between the government exercising 'the power to regulate or license, as lawmaker,' and the government acting 'as proprietor, to manage [its] internal operation.'"); Garcetti v. Ceballos, 547 U.S. 410, 421 (2006) ("when public employees make statements pursuant to their official duties, the employees are not speaking as citizens for First Amendment purposes, and the Constitution does not insulate their communications from employer discipline.").

patriae responsibility could be a reminder: "Don't forget mentally disabled persons' lives matter too!"

There are problems with this view. First, it makes parens patriae legally and analytically superfluous and its invocation therefore likely to confuse and mislead. Second, under the banner of parens patriae, governments have in practice extended their decision-making authority to Category A areas of non-autonomous persons' lives—that is, to matters generally deemed outside the proper ambit of state police power, such as with whom one forms close mutually chosen personal relationships, whether and how one receives medical treatment for illness or injury, or education, and who will provide other services relating to one's person or property. Though such choices might disappoint or anger other individuals or undermine the aims of some group, the state does not presume, as part of its police power function, to decide these things for private individuals nor to force individuals to balance interests of other persons or of any groups against their own when making choices about such matters, if they threaten no harm to others.

Thus, to treat parens patriae as simply police power applied to non-autonomous persons' lives, the legal system presumably should either (1) constrict parens patriae action to the established normal bounds of police power action, deeming government involvement in Category A matters improper even as to non-autonomous persons, or (2) provide normative justification for treating only non-autonomous persons' Category A matters as appropriate for police power action, such that everyone's interests weigh in government decisions. Doing choice 1 seems unsatisfactory, because it leaves non-autonomous persons vulnerable in important areas of their lives. Yet no theorists have even attempted to fulfill choice 2. To do so, it clearly would not suffice simply to point out that non-autonomous persons are unable to make certain decisions for themselves. For as described in Section 6.3.2, there is another available approach to making decisions for such persons—that is, as a fiduciary.

6.4.3.2 Complete distinction view

Now consider the opposite position: the parens patriae role is completely distinct from the police power role. There is no overlap; they never pertain to the same situation. Parens patriae takes over where the police power role must stop. Police power extends to government efforts to improve general welfare and to prevent one person—whether autonomous or not—from harming another. It is properly at work in civil commitment and juvenile delinquency proceedings, insofar as the state acts to protect others in the community from harm a mentally ill adult or youth might commit. But it does not extend to Category A matters for any persons, whether autonomous or not. Instead, parens patriae pertains to Category A matters for non-autonomous persons, and exclusively so.

Presumably, this differentiation would mean the practical operation of the governments' roles in the two realms differs. In the police power role, government, as agent for all of society, considers interests of all members of society. An operationally different parens patriae government function would therefore presumably entail the government's considering interests of less than all members of society in rendering decisions within the purview of that function. Given that, by all accounts, this is a role adopted at least in part to protect the welfare of non-autonomous persons, naturally those non-autonomous persons whose lives are the subject of government decision-making would be included among those whose interests receive consideration. If they are the only persons whose interests may properly influence decisions, governments should act on a fiduciary conception of parens patriae. The question then is whether, on a conception of parens patriae as distinct from police power, there are *any* other entities—individuals, groups, societies—with interests impacted by decisions concerning Category A aspects of non-autonomous persons' lives who ought also to be considered in parens patriae decision-making.

The answer cannot be *all* such other entities. That would return us to the position of no practical distinction between parens patriae and police power. The point of distinguishing the two roles must be to signal that with parens patriae decision-making some who have interests at stake are not to be included within the government actors' scope of concern; those interests of others are real but irrelevant. Now if it can be shown that some subset of all other entities stands in a privileged position, such that they rightly have their interests considered even though the actually impacted interests of some other persons are not, then we might settle on a third conception of parens patriae. Call it "the subgroup conception."

Note that the point of adding others' interests to those of the autonomous person whose life is centrally at issue must be that these might conflict with and to some degree override the welfare of the non-autonomous person. If they were presumed entirely consistent with the latter's well-being, it would be analytically superfluous to add them and to posit this third conception (except perhaps as a tiebreaker in the rare case when two alternatives are equally good for the non-autonomous person, a possibility considered in Section 6.3.3.4). Plausible candidates for this privileged position might include spouses, siblings, adult offspring of elderly persons with dementia, parents of minors, grandparents, and other extended family members, perhaps also neighbors, teachers, fellow town residents, and religious or ethnic communities to which caregivers belong. Among them, it is not immediately clear on what objective basis one would distinguish. Or between any of them and individuals or groups who take an interest yet do not intuitively seem plausible candidates (e.g., right-to-life activists, in connection with pregnancy-related decision-making for non-autonomous women; social media companies; gun manufacturers; dictators embarrassed by departure of children). In other words, on what rational basis could one say: "Well, *those* impacted persons/entities should not be considered *at all*, because this is parens patriae decision-making we are doing, but interests of these other impacted persons/entities *should* be considered, and should be treated as a basis for potentially sacrificing the welfare of the non-autonomous person to some degree, even though this matter falls within Category A and therefore for autonomous persons would be left for them to decide based solely on their own interests"? Further analysis might reveal a basis, but unless and until one materializes we should—if parens patriae is to be a function distinct from police power—exclude *all* others. That would leave us with the fiduciary conception of government in its parens patriae role, concerned solely for the welfare of the dependent individual.

An intuitive reaction for some will be that a limited class of other individuals have moral *rights* in connection with these matters that are central to the lives of non-autonomous persons, such as their medical care. That is very unlikely intuitively to include IOs, states, or other political entities. Rather, people's minds turn to family members. If some kin have rights, a government decision adverse to their wishes might in fact cause "harm to others," if the concept of harm includes any infringement of persons' supposed other-regarding moral rights. Government thus might properly aim, in its decisions about central aspects of non-autonomous persons' lives, to avoid conflict with those others' wishes.

With respect to autonomous persons, the law today in liberal societies does *not* recognize rights of anyone else in connection with such matters, even though often other individuals and groups take an intense interest (e.g., husbands regarding wives' use of contraception, Native American tribes regarding members' marital and residential choices, some churches regarding individuals' choice of intimate partners, and parents regarding adult offsprings' choice of spouse or career). But maybe something about being non-autonomous makes it appropriate to ascribe to others rights as to those aspects of one's life. For example, an elderly incompetent person's offspring might anguish over the type of long-term care facility the parent will enter, perhaps believing the parent's only chance at eternal salvation requires ending life in a facility run by the religious denomination the offspring recently joined. The fiduciary model of deciding for the parent would render the offspring's anguish of no direct relevance, because it does not constitute "harm" to them. Yet how can government be indifferent to family members' anguish? Have they no right in this situation?

Section 6.5 discusses normative obstacles to ascribing such rights to others in Category A aspects of non-autonomous persons' lives, but here note the conceptual implications of doing so: this response amounts, in effect, to denying that there are any aspects of non-autonomous persons' lives inherently in Category A (condition 2 would not pertain). Then, one must also say either:

a) all aspects of non-autonomous persons' lives fall into Category B, with government decision-making about them properly influenced by *any* other persons' desires, though especially those who have a moral right to the government's direct concern for their wishes, and also by collective societal aims, taking us back to the no-distinction position, or
b) there is some third category of personal matters, call it Category C, that is fundamentally "about" a central aspect of non-autonomous persons' lives yet as to which
   i) some others (but not all who take an interest) can and do have moral rights, of a sort (other-regarding) that no one has in relation to autonomous persons, such that they can be "harmed" by effects (e.g., anguish, embarrassment) not considered harms when occasioned by decisions autonomous persons make about their own lives, which "harms" can be a basis for sacrificing the non-autonomous person's well-being to some degree, whereas
   ii) interests of all persons lacking such rights are entirely irrelevant to government decision making even though it impacts them.

Theorists have not directly addressed the possibility of such a Category C realm of life, where the subgroup conception of parens patriae decision-making would pertain. There has been considerable effort among philosophers to mount a convincing theoretical defense for ascribing other-regarding moral rights to just one set of other persons in connection with the lives of just one set of non-autonomous persons—namely, parental rights regarding minor offspring. That exertion thus far has been unsuccessful.[24] But in addition, there has been *no* effort to explain why opening the door to *some* third parties (parents) does not let in *all* whose interests could be impacted. Or would let in a larger-though-limited subset of all who have strong feelings about how a non-autonomous person's life goes. Extended family members or even neighbors might care greatly about, for example, whether their state requires academic accountability of a child's evangelical Christian school.

[24] *See* James G. Dwyer, *Deflating Parental Rights*, 40 LAW & PHIL. 387 (2021). Significantly, though there is substantial positive law today pronouncing such rights, creators of such law—including the U.S. Supreme Court—generally do not posit that parental rights ever justify sacrificing children's interests to any degree.

In other words, attempts at making the positive case for ascribing to parents moral *rights* to control their children's lives (as opposed to possessing authority as a matter of the child's rights) have not attempted to show that any other persons impacted by government decisions as to central aspects of a child's life should be *excluded* from consideration. (Note: Showing the parent-child relationship is a unique type of relationship cannot suffice; every type of relationship is unique (that is what it means to be a type), and no normative implications follow from uniqueness per se.) Moreover, there has been no philosophical attention devoted to third-party rights regarding incompetent adults—that is, whether spouses, offspring, or guardians of such adults possess moral rights to legally effective power over their lives, power that could entail sacrificing what government officials deem in their best interests. (Existing law recognizes no such rights.[25]) Thus, much theoretical work would need to be done to support the subgroup conception of government's role and recognition of a Category C realm of life for non-autonomous persons.

6.4.3.3 Simultaneous view

A further possibility worth considering is that police power and parens patriae are distinct roles but a government can and should operate in both simultaneously with respect to some decisions concerning non-autonomous persons. Some scholars and courts have at times suggested this idea, but without defending or explaining it.[26] If it is a Category A matter for a child or incompetent adult, then again, defense is needed for injecting interests of other persons or of society into the equation. If it is a Category B matter, it is unclear what work reference to parens patriae does, given that the government legitimately takes a

[25] *See* Kicherer v. Kicherer, 400 A.2d 1097, 1100-01 (Md. 1979) ("a court of equity assumes jurisdiction in guardianship matters to protect those who, because of illness or other disability, are unable to care for themselves. In reality the court is the guardian; an individual who is given that title is merely an agent or arm of that tribunal in carrying out its sacred responsibility. . . . See generally 1 W. Blackstone, Commentaries 463. Whereas consanguinity is a factor that may well be given consideration by the chancellor in the appointment of a guardian because nearest of kin are more likely to treat a ward with kindness and affection . . . , appointment to that position rests solely in the discretion of the equity court . . .").

[26] *See, e.g.*, Prince v. Massachusetts, 321 U.S. 158, 166–69 (1944) (first pronouncing that the City of Brockton was acting in a parens patriae role by prohibiting guardians from enlisting children to distribute religious tracts on the streets, and suggesting that the City's authority in that role simply trumped guardians' wishes, such that no balancing was required, but then also explicitly invoking the state's police power role, pointing to general societal interests in positive child development, as justification for upholding the City's ordinance); *Ex parte* Wallace, 190 P. 1020, 1022 (N.M. 1920) ("in all cases the state is *parens patriae* to the child, and it has power to, by legislation, control the right of the child to inherit, to take it from its parents, and give it into custody of others, to determine what is for the best interests of the child, and that which will promote the welfare of the state."); Lois A. Weithorn & Dorit Rubinstein Reiss, *Providing Adolescents with Independent and Confidential Access to Childhood Vaccines: A Proposal to Lower the Age of Consent*, 52 Conn. L. Rev. 771, 799–800 (2020) ("Two of the best-known regulatory structures justified by both the *parens patriae* and police power authorities are compulsory education laws and prohibitions on child labor.").

police power approach, considering all affected interests. It seems unlikely that invoking parens patriae would serve to magnify a non-autonomous person's interests in Category B matters—that is, that the court would apply some multiplier to those interests, such that other individuals' interests or collective societal welfare would appropriately be sacrificed to a significant degree for the sake of serving lesser interests of non-autonomous persons ("sorry, you have to allow that child to steal vegetables from your garden"). That would itself require justification (as it seems to violate the equal-consideration requirement for police power action) and clarification (e.g., what is the number by which actual interests are multiplied?) that neither courts nor legal theorists have provided.

In fact, though, if the two roles do differ, occupying both simultaneously is a conceptual impossibility. If parens patriae is distinct from police power, it must be so because it requires excluding consideration of some persons' interests. Government actors cannot so exclude some persons' interests and still be doing police power decision-making, because the latter entails considering everyone's interests. If parens patriae is distinct, the two roles are logically incompatible.

6.4.3.4 Sequential view

A final possibility worth mentioning is that a government might carry out both roles in controlling Category A matters, but sequentially rather than simultaneously. An initial assessment from a strict fiduciary perspective could narrow choices to a set of those equally good for the non-autonomous person, and if the set contains more than one potential choice, then a police power analysis of those choices might be applied to choose from among them.[27] (Considering interests of just certain other persons, rather than all, is also possible, but again normative justification would be needed for including some and excluding others.) One way of interpreting "primary" in CRC's Article 3 could be in this temporal sense of considering children's interests first rather than giving them greater weight (though in either case there is the problem of the indefinite article preceding it). From a consequentialist perspective, this might appear morally innocuous or even optimal in theory, to break best-interest ties by reference to others' preferences or interests.

As a general matter, however, the law does not permit fiduciaries to make their own or third parties' interests even a tiebreaker. One reason for this is practical—namely, recognition of human powers of self-deception and rationalization. The law demands fiduciaries avoid all temptation to sacrifice interests of their principals in order to benefit themselves or third parties. Ira Samet explains:

[27] To narrow the range only to those "not very bad" for the non-autonomous person, rather than going further to identify the best option(s), would amount to adopting the no-distinction or subgroup conception; there can be no theoretical reason for broadening the range except to accommodate interests of others.

> The duty of loyalty . . . instructs fiduciaries to take the principal's goods as the sole end of their actions. The duty is further grounded in the no-conflict rules, which forbid the fiduciary from taking any (unauthorized) actions that may, even accidentally, serve her own interests. These strict rules are in place because, in situations of conflict, the risk that something other than the principal's best interests will influence the fiduciary is high. The working of the human mind is such that it is extremely difficult, if not impossible, to exercise judgment in a proper manner (ie, as required by the duty of loyalty) where the personal interests of the decision maker are involved.[28]

There is no reason to be more trusting of government actors than of private fiduciaries in this respect. Another reason for the positive-law rule against considering any other interests even as a tiebreaker is more normative—namely, discomfort with treating an individual's inability to choose for themselves as an occasion for using their lives to any degree to satisfy others' preferences.

We are left then with three contenders for a best conception of the parens patriae role. On one, it is not distinct from the police power role, it is simply what we call police power when its exertion especially impacts non-autonomous persons. Or more narrowly, when it is exerted in areas of non-autonomous persons' lives equivalent to aspects of autonomous persons' lives generally considered outside the proper ambit of police power authority (Category A)—that is, when application of police power is extraordinary. On this conception, we need justification for extending the police power function to those aspects of only some persons' lives, and arguably we should jettison the concept of parens patriae as misleading analytical surplusage. On the other conceptions, parens patriae is meaningfully different from police power and operates when police power authority is inapposite. This is when decisions to be made are of a type that autonomous persons are entitled to make for themselves on entirely self-regarding grounds. In one variation (the fiduciary conception), government officials acting in a parens patriae capacity should concern themselves *solely* with the welfare of the non-autonomous person, giving that person a right equivalent to that which autonomous persons possess. On another (subgroup) conception, officials may aim to satisfy wishes of some other interested persons but not all.

Choice among the three options (special-heed/no-distinction; fiduciary; subgroup) thus clearly raises the question whether there is normative justification for government's considering interests of any other persons when it makes decisions about central aspects of non-autonomous persons'

[28] Ira Samet, "Fiduciary Loyalty as Kantian Virtue," *in* GOLD & MILLER, *supra* note 3, at 125–40, 126.

lives under the parens patriae banner. If no, the fiduciary conception is best. If yes, choice between the special-heed/no-distinction and subgroup conceptions depends on whether government ought to distinguish among persons other than the non-autonomous person in choosing whose interests properly influence its decisions, treating interests of some as relevant but interests of others as irrelevant. Identifying a best conception of the parens patriae role seems therefore to require endorsing one or more normative premises, in addition to narrowing the options on conceptual grounds. The next section illustrates this and offers reasons for favoring the fiduciary conception.

6.5 Normative Underpinnings to Police Power and Parens Patriae Authority

Whether a government is justified in allowing other parties' interests to influence decision-making about Category A aspects of non-autonomous persons' lives might depend on why it ought to forbear from constraining, for the sake of other persons' interests or collective aims, autonomous persons' self-determining choices in those aspects of life. That reason might be inapplicable to non-autonomous persons, entirely or in some contexts. Justification might instead or also depend on what affirmative warrant government has for injecting itself into such aspects of life with non-autonomous persons.

6.5.1 Extending the moral basis for autonomous person's self-determination

There is a variety of philosophical accounts and political views as to where the limits of state power should be drawn in the standard case—that is, government interaction with autonomous persons. Choice among conceptions of parens patriae could depend on to which basic normative outlook one generally adheres, assuming one is principled and aims for rational consistency across contexts and persons. Space does not permit canvassing all. Reference to deontological and utilitarian views suffices to make this point.

A deontological outlook predominates in international human rights discourse, in domestic individual-rights jurisprudence in Western liberal societies, and in scholarship on state legitimacy. From this perspective, government owes every individual a presumptive negative duty of noninterference, especially in private life, because each has an inherent dignity that gives rise to rights of integrity of body and mind, sovereignty over one's own life and person, and freedom to live by one's own values.[29] For autonomous persons, government's negative duty is overridden when individual choices threaten incursion on the integrity, sovereignty, or liberty of others, otherwise not.[30] The inherent dignity is also incompatible with treating anyone as an object of other individuals' or any group's rights.

Declarations of rights emanating from this perspective rarely explicate the basis for ascribing dignity—that is, what it is about human individuals that commands respect. If presently existing autonomy were the sole source of moral worth and rights, the negative duty of noninterference might not be owed to non-autonomous persons at all, and they might be proper objects of others' rights. This would leave government free to insert itself into their lives however it wishes (unless it owes a duty of restraint regarding them to a third party), or to serve wishes of private parties who take a particular interest.

Such a view of moral worth, however, has little support among theorists today.[31] It is contrary to prevailing moral intuitions reflected in the international human rights regime and Anglo-American legal systems, which ascribe right-conferring dignity to both autonomous and non-autonomous humans. For all its flaws, the CRC at least does that for children, and the UN CRPD does so for adults with cognitive impairments.[32] Court decisions in many jurisdictions reflect this broader view of which persons have inherent dignity and a presumptive right of inviolability and non-instrumentalization, demanding (1) special justification for government exertion of power over intimate aspects of the lives of children or incompetent adults as well as of autonomous persons—specifically, justification tied to their welfare, and also (2) that the exertion not go beyond what that justification supports.[33] Political theorists also embrace this broad ascription of dignity and, based upon it, a fiduciary account of public authority over non-autonomous persons. For example, Evan Fox-Decent writes:

> The child has dignity by virtue of her moral personhood, and dignity proscribes regarding her as if she were a mere thing. By the same token, legal personality

[29] *See* Adam Etinson, *What's So Special About Human Dignity?*, 48 PHIL. & PUB. AFF. 353 (2020); Rachel Bayefsky, *Dignity, Honor, and Human Rights: Kant's Perspective*, 41 POL. THEORY 809 (2013); GEORGE KATEB, HUMAN DIGNITY (2011). *See also* ICCPR, Preamble ("these rights derive from the inherent dignity of the human person").

[30] *See* Folland, *supra* note 8; Lawrence v. Texas, 539 U.S. 558, 578 (2003) ("The present case . . . does not involve persons who might be injured").

[31] *See* DWYER, *supra* note 4, ch. 2.

[32] *See* UNCRC, Preamble (invoking "the inherent dignity and the equal and inalienable rights of all members of the human family"); United Nations Convention on the Rights of Persons with Disabilities, Preamble, (a) (similar).

[33] *See Re* Kara, [2020] NSWSC 1083 (2020), ¶ 63 ("the parens patriae jurisdiction . . . must be exercised with great caution"), ¶ 65 ("in exceptional cases where deprivation of liberty is a necessary consequence of the exercise of the parens patriae jurisdiction for the protection of the child and the promotion of his or her welfare, the making of orders by the Court as parens patriae that interfere with the personal integrity and liberty of a child will not contravene the child's human rights").

> and the idea of dignity intrinsic to it supply the moral basis of the beneficiary's right to the fiduciary obligation. A relationship in which the fiduciary has unilateral power over the beneficiary's interests can be understood as a relationship mediated by law only if the fiduciary (like the parent) is precluded from exploiting her position to set unilaterally the terms of their relationship with the beneficiary. The fiduciary principle renders the beneficiary's entrusted interests immune to the fiduciary's appropriation because those interests, in the context of fiduciary relations, are treated as inviolate embodiments of the beneficiary's dignity as a person. In short, the fiduciary principle authorizes the fiduciary to exercise power on the beneficiary's behalf, but subject to strict limitations arising from the beneficiary's worth as a person and vulnerability to fiduciary power.[34]

This implicitly rules out extension of police power into Category A aspects of non-autonomous persons' lives, thus suggesting parens patriae action in that realm is distinct, not police power by another name. And it suggests that when a government or other entity has authority to take some action qua proxy for a non-autonomous person, because appointed to exercise that person's rights in his or her behalf, it may not use that power to serve other purposes or persons. It therefore supports the fiduciary rather than subgroup conception of parens patriae.

From a utilitarian perspective, on the other hand, one might say government, at a meta-level of lawmaking, must always consider the interests of all members of society, à la the police power, even regarding intimate aspects of autonomous persons' lives. If it refrains in practice from substituting its own choices for those of autonomous persons in Category A matters, that is only because as to these areas of personal life maximum aggregate societal welfare is generally achieved by ascribing legal "rights" of self-determination to such individuals. Government control of those areas of life would not optimally promote societal welfare, because, inter alia, (1) the individual has the greatest interests at stake and is better positioned than government officials to determine what best serves those interests, and (2) even when autonomous persons make poor choices, they and others learn from this and become more capable of utility-maximizing decisions in the future.[35] From this outlook, at least part of government's rationale for withholding the police power from Category A matters (or appearing to) in practice might not apply, or might apply to a lesser degree, or might apply in some decision contexts but not others, with non-autonomous persons. Though they also typically have the greatest interests at stake in those aspects of their lives, they

[34] Fox-Decent, *supra* note 3, at 45–46.
[35] This is an abbreviated version of John Stuart Mill's argument in *On Liberty* (1859).

are assumed not in the best position to judge their own welfare, and the costs for them and others of bad decisions would too often outweigh the benefit of any learning they realize from mistakes.

On this view, the government's parens patriae role might not be distinct from the police power. Reference to it might serve simply to remind decision makers that non-autonomous persons' interests matter and are weighty. Or signal why paternalism is appropriate in those contexts for these persons, or why government supplants or supplements private guardians as advocates or caregivers in some contexts.[36] Or it might mark out a subcategory of decisions as to which government officials should in practice focus exclusively on non-autonomous persons' interest, but for pragmatic rather than normative reasons; even a utilitarian view could support the fiduciary model of decision-making at the operational level in some contexts, in light of human imperfections, while allowing for the subgroup or special-heed conception to govern in others.

A utilitarian approach to regulation of non-autonomous persons' private lives thus appears more indeterminate than the deontological view in terms of which decision-making model is best. Within it, any invocation of parens patriae would not reflect an inherent, normative constraint on normal police power decision-making. Taking into account all affected interests would be morally appropriate,[37] and if acting against a non-autonomous person's interests in some instances in some Category A aspects of their lives would promote aggregate welfare, the state should do that. For example, it might refuse to allow termination of a mentally disabled woman's life-threatening pregnancy, because the unborn child will be cognitively high-functioning and saving the child would satisfy preferences of family members and anti-abortion activists.

Such an example makes doubtful that widespread commitment to utilitarian thinking best explains liberal states' current practices regarding Category A matters. One would be accused of moral vacuity for presenting an argument grounded in utility-maximizing cost-benefit analysis regarding such moralized issues as abortion or gender-transition services. One might further test this sociological hypothesis by identifying aspects of private life as to which that

[36] *Cf.* Reno v. Flores, 507 U.S. 292, 316–17 (1993) (O'Connor J, concurring) ("this *parens patriae* purpose was seen simply as a plausible *justification* for state action implicating the child's protected liberty interest"); *Developments, supra* note 20, at 1199 ("The *parens patriae* power . . . is the state's limited paternalistic power to protect or promote the welfare of certain individuals, like young children and mental incompetents, who lack the capacity to act in their own best interests.").

[37] It is uncertain whether it would ever allow for ascription of legal "rights," as opposed to authority held as a matter of privilege, to some individuals other than the non-autonomous person whose life is centrally at issue. Making such a person an object of others' rights is socially denigrating and could cause public and private decision makers routinely to undercount that person's interests. Moreover, others' interests in controlling the non-autonomous person's life, however strongly subjectively felt, are not especially weighty from an objective perspective—certainly not "fundamental" (recall the example of pro-life activists determined to prevent abortions for mentally disabled women).

outlook's broad empirical assumptions regarding *autonomous* persons are most doubtful (perhaps marital choice), and then considering the likely popular reaction to a proposal that the state assume greater control of those. The point here is not to challenge any version of consequentialism by show of hands, but simply to identify for anyone drawn to that outlook its possible implications not only for parens patriae but also for treatment of autonomous persons. People might reasonably be pluralist in their ethical outlooks, applying consequentialist reasoning in some policy contexts and a deontological (or other) normative framework in other contexts, but it would be odd and require defense to switch normative frameworks—for example, from deontological to consequentialist—as to the same area of life simply because a different group of human beings is under discussion.

6.5.2 The positive justification for intervention

Moving to the affirmative case for government involvement in Category A matters for non-autonomous persons, we ask what moral basis any government has for exerting control over central aspects of their lives. The deontological view, at least, demands such justification, and modern social contract theories with deontological underpinnings make this burden of justification explicit.[38]

The justification seems straightforward. Non-autonomous persons have important needs they cannot satisfy themselves, and the state is best positioned to make certain decisions on their behalf.[39] They need to enter nurturing relationships with protected legal status, to be removed from relationships that prove damaging, and to be ensured daily care and treatment when ill or injured regardless of their legal caregivers' disposition. Children need education, and many adults with intellectual disabilities can have much more flourishing lives if provided habilitation services. Government therefore aims to ensure these things for non-autonomous persons. Its doing so is supported by, rather than an insult to, the foundational value of human dignity.

In other words, government respect for non-autonomous persons and their human potentiality actually requires, or at least permits, breaching the

[38] *See* T.M. SCANLON, WHAT WE OWE TO EACH OTHER (1998); JOHN RAWLS, POLITICAL LIBERALISM, at IX (1993).

[39] *See* Durham Children's Aid Society v. BP, O.J. No. 4183, ¶ 29 (2007) (Ontario); *Re* Eve, 31 DLR (4th), ¶ 73 ("The parens patriae jurisdiction is . . . founded on necessity, namely the need to act for the protection of those who cannot care for themselves."); Wellesley v. Beaufort, 38 Eng. Rep. 236 (Ch. 1827) ("this jurisdiction . . . is founded on the obvious necessity that the law should place somewhere the care of individuals who cannot take care of themselves, particularly in cases where it is clear that some care should be thrown round them").

metaphorical wall of integrity around them to address their needs and, when possible, facilitate their maintaining or developing toward autonomy.[40] This seems a complete justification and the best, perhaps sole, justification available from a deontological perspective. From a contractarian standpoint, we might characterize the warrant for this state action as resting on hypothetical consent of non-autonomous persons, along lines Chapter 5 discussed. If able to make a rational choice, they would agree to government involvement in their lives for this purpose.[41]

A final step in the analysis, enabling us to select between the fiduciary and subgroup conceptions of parens patriae, if operating from the deontological outlook, would be to recognize that, because of the background right against intrusion into private life, the power any government exerts in Category A aspects of non-autonomous persons lives must not outrun its justification.[42] A "least restrictive means" condition applies—intrude only so far as necessary to serve the aim that justifies your intruding at all. Thus, that a government has *some* warrant for assuming some control over non-autonomous persons' private life does not license government actors then to use that control for any and all purposes they might choose, including treating these persons instrumentally to serve interests of other persons or collective entities.[43] That would be contrary to respect. This point also supports the normative objection to the sequential approach to parens patriae decision-making—that is, to establishing a range of decisions supposedly equally good for a non-autonomous person and then choosing from among them based on others' interests; such would treat the person instrumentally and inject an aim unsupported by the threshold justification.

Imagining ourselves one day losing our self-governing faculties lends intuitive support to this conclusion. We would not now assent to the proposition that such an eventuality would create a legitimate opportunity for government, without prior authorization by us while competent, to use us in ways

[40] *See* Tamar Schapiro, *What Is a Child?*, 109 Ethics 715 (1999).

[41] *See* Peter Vallentyne, "Libertarian Perspectives on Paternalism," *in* Kalle Grill & Jason Hanna eds., The Routledge Handbook of the Philosophy of Paternalism 182–93 (2018). We might imagine representatives of future persons in Rawls' Original Position agreeing to such a regime.

[42] *See* Lionel Smith, *Parenthood Is a Fiduciary Relationship*, 70 U. Toronto L.J. 395, 428 (2020) ("When a person, the fiduciary, acquires powers not for her own benefit but, rather, to allow her to attend to the interests of her beneficiary, then the fiduciary must use those powers in what she perceives to be the best interests of the beneficiary. That is what the powers are for; that is the basis on which and the purpose for which they are acquired; and that is how they must be used. Any other use is a misuse."); *Re* Eve, 31 DLR (4th), ¶ 77 ("It must be exercised in accordance with its underlying principle. . . . The discretion is to be exercised for the benefit of that person, not for that of others."), ¶ 82 ("[I]t is easy to understand the natural feelings of a parent's heart. But the parens patriae jurisdiction cannot be used for her benefit.").

[43] *Cf.* Smith, *supra* note 42, at 442–43 ("In 1934, when the Dionne quintuplets were four months old, the Ontario government took them from their parents. . . . They were put into a kind of zoo, which millions of people paid to visit. . . . At the time, this might have seemed justifiable to some . . .").

currently (while we are competent) impermissible without our consent—for example, to subject us to medical experimentation or organ harvesting, or to empower a particular family member to dictate our treatment solely to placate that family member or enable them to act on a religious command they believe themselves under. We would not assent to that proposition even if we recognize that we would in that situation of mental incapacitation need government actors to assume some authority over our personal lives for the sake of our own basic welfare.

Nor would we assent even if the proposition were qualified with a side constraint, such as that the medical experimentation, organ harvesting, or guardian appointment must not cause us *grievous* harm, or that the benefit to others must clearly and substantially outweigh the cost to us, or even that others' interests control only when two or more options seem to the decision maker more or less equally good for us.[44] We might make such other-regarding choices for ourselves while autonomous, and we might while autonomous authorize a guardian to make other-regarding choices for us, but we would not now endorse the proposition that government may on its own choose to do that in governing our lives after we lose capacity, without our prior authorization. We might or might not believe we have a positive entitlement to government solicitude for us in our vulnerable situation, but we would expect that *if* the state chooses to breach the normative wall around us in reaction to our loss of autonomy, and to exert power over our person, that it will do so *only* in order to effectuate what it deems beneficial for us or to carry out wishes we expressed while competent. From another angle, we would say that losing our mental faculties does not amount to forfeiting our personhood, human dignity, or right against the state's treating us instrumentally in connection with central aspects of our lives. Rather, we would say, "Leave us alone except insofar as you are going to try to benefit us." The state must act solely for the purpose that is the raison d' etre of its power in these personal aspects of life.

The deontological view thus again, from this different angle, points to the fiduciary conception of parens patriae as best among the three identified. And it seems the view most of us would adopt in thinking about ourselves becoming non-autonomous. A utilitarian might say simply that we should not think so much about ourselves, that we are immorally self-centered. Again, though, this

[44] *See* Payton, *supra* note 12, at 617 ("Were it not for the fiduciary nature of this custody, which gives the ward rights against his custodians, the incompetent's disappearance as an empowered legal person would work a forfeiture exceeding any punishment imposed under the criminal law. . . . The fiduciary nature of the parens patriae jurisdiction over formerly competent incompetents therefore is critical to the legitimacy of the state's exercise of power over them, since the state . . . would otherwise in effect confiscate the body and property of an incompetent human being, on the sole ground of his incompetence."), 641 ("The powers of the state over the incompetent are tolerable only if fiduciary in nature and if administered in good faith out of fiduciary motive.").

assessment of connections between normative outlooks and parens patriae does not aim to establish a moral "truth of the matter," and certainly is not exhaustive. Its conclusion is simply that from one normative outlook—one that underwrites our convictions about permissible government treatment of us, while we are competent or after we lose competence—we would land on the fiduciary conception of parens patriae as best among the three conceptions identified as distinct and coherent.

From a utilitarian outlook, one might instead endorse extension of police power into some or all Category A matters and government control of even intimate aspects of individuals' lives in order to serve some greater good, but then one should be prepared to accept that there is no in-principle obstacle to doing that even with respect to our lives as autonomous persons, absent justification for treating only non-autonomous persons' lives instrumentally in this way. But a utilitarian analysis might be indeterminate; it could conceivably also recommend the fiduciary conception to government control over non-autonomous persons' lives in practice, at least as to some types of decisions. Still other normative perspectives might yield one or another definite conclusion or might also be indeterminate. Regardless of outlook, one should apply any perspective's fundamental principles consistently across persons, absent demonstration that they should not apply to some, and avoid the sort of ad hoc assertion and sui generis pseudo-reasoning that characterizes most attempts at normative writing on child law. The fiduciary conception of parens patriae appears most consistent with the regime of individual rights that autonomous adults in liberal Western societies have come to expect for themselves.

6.6 Implications of Adopting the Fiduciary Conception of Parens Patriae

Were all legal systems unambiguously to adopt the fiduciary conception of parens patriae, this would necessitate a substantially different way of viewing children and regulating children's lives. No legal system would ascribe to any person or entity other than the individual child *rights* in connection with Category A aspects of children's lives, nor even consider others' interests in making surrogate decisions for a child in that realm. This bolsters conclusions reached in Chapter 3 about permissible infringements of children's right to leave and in Chapter 5 regarding imposition of citizenship. International law, to the extent it assigns "custody" of children (via nationality) and direct decision-making to any governmental entity regarding Category A matters for children, would do so solely based on which entity is best positioned to serve children's well-being. The state where a child resides would have no entitlement to play that role; it should demonstrate inclination and capacity to serve in a fiduciary role faithfully itself, just as applicants for adoption of a child must demonstrate their fitness. If it is not best positioned, even though a child resides on its territory, which is certainly true of some national regimes today, then international law might require withholding citizenship and direct an international agency to make some decisions on behalf of children there, something similar to current UN efforts to serve internally displaced persons, only more robust. International law would emphasize that whatever entities exercise authority over children must do so in a manner designed to accord to children rights equivalent to those which adults enjoy. That means government acts solely as agent for the child and not in its usual police power capacity, so the best interests of the child should be the sole consideration. There should be no direct consideration of interests or rights of parents, extended family, community, or nation.

In addition to assigning responsibility for children at this macro level, it would be appropriate for international law to impose child-centered substantive constraints on international agencies and nations as to how they treat children within Category A aspects of their lives, without needing the consent of those agencies or nations to those constraints. Instead of the horse trading and deference to cultural variations that occurred in drafting the CRC, such regulation should be developed with no direct concern for a nation's culture, pride, or ambitions. Such things would, at most, be of indirect relevance to the extent they inevitably limit how children's welfare and developmental needs can in the real world be satisfied.

This will seem presumptuous and heavy-handed, but the basic idea is that if it would be illicit to force autonomous adults to compromise what they believe to be in *their* best interests for the sake of such national interests, then it is also illicit to force that compromise on children.[45] Being non-autonomous does not justify instrumental treatment that is unjustified as to autonomous persons. There are challenges in modeling fiduciary decision-making on behalf of persons who have never developed their own conception of the good (and for those who previously had one but now are of severely diminished mental capacity),[46] but no state or cultural community has a *right* to have the conception of the good prevailing among its competent adult members baked into the model. So, too, with interests of parents and other adults that wormed their way into CRC provisions; they should not corrupt fiduciary decision-making for children.

[45] *See* Criddle, *supra* note 15, at 995 (arguing the duty of loyalty guards against domination, "by ensuring that a fiduciary's actions are legally required to track the terms of her mandate and the interests of her beneficiaries").

[46] I address these in James G. Dwyer, The Relationship Rights of Children (2006), ch. 7.

Thus, for example, liberal theorists should be willing to say that no nation may deny education to girls as a matter of explicitly gendered policy. That nation's prevailing cultural view regarding gender difference, and parents' strong desires that their girls remain at home to serve the family, are of no direct relevance. Concern about the practical impact on girls of requiring an experience for them that conflicts with the view of them prevailing in their society or with their parents' wishes is a legitimate one, but the reality is that forcing a change of practices tends to change prevailing cultural views and family expectations. When all girls begin attending school in such a society, because of legal mandate, then no individual girls should suffer significantly from the clash with past practices and lingering attitudes and expectations. In other words, while the international community might for pragmatic reasons justifiably proceed cautiously in trying to transform illiberal cultures or get children out of them, lest it make matters worse for those it is trying to help (but based on objective assessment of risks, not frivolous or disingenuous worries), normative deference to national cultures per se is out of place in acting on behalf of children.

At the state level, no nation's laws should ascribe *rights*—constitutional or otherwise—to any other persons nor any collective entity in connection with Category A aspects of children's lives, and interests of other individuals or groups should play no direct role in formulation of the laws governing parentage, child protection, schooling, medical care, or migration for children. Rather, any government that presumes to exercise control over those matters must do so solely as an agent or surrogate for the child, not as agent for society as a whole nor for any other individuals. Of course, states may and should delegate much authority to immediate caregivers, typically parents, over children's daily life, but not as a matter of entitlement for them and only to the degree dictated by children's welfare—for example, empowering parents to make choices as to schools and health care, but within a range of options that education experts view as acceptable, and not empowering them to keep their children confined in institutions for years on the off chance they might be able and inclined to resume custody.

Regarding migration, choice of location among those practically available to a person is something as to which adults generally possess an unconstrained right. They may choose based solely on their own interests, without compulsion to sacrifice for the sake of other individuals or their native country. States are expected to make all regions of the territory they control open to all legal residents and to permit adults to exit the country at will. With respect to children, all nations should be encouraged to communicate their openness to welcoming children currently in inhospitable circumstances. An appropriate surrogate decision maker should be empowered to choose on behalf of any given child any alternative to his or her current location—within the current nation of residence or in one of those others—that on the whole appears best for that child, taking into account all relevant, evidence-based interests of the child but no interests of anyone else. This assessment would give prominent place to a child's interests relating to family life, existing or potential, but it would not factor in the interests of other persons in an existing or potential family, nor community or national interests. It would also consider quality of life in different places, without concern that this might reflect badly on some nations. A child's current state of residence should possess no power to block or inhibit in any way a child's exit for any reason other than necessity to prevent genuine and probable harm to that child. And international law should in no way obligate other states to acquiesce to a home state's breach of its fiduciary duty to children, or to refrain from attempting to facilitate a child's international migration for sake of a better life.

It is worth reiterating that prevailing practice as to incompetent adults, including never-competent adults, closely resembles the model of decision-making I advance here for children. In connection with appointing and overseeing guardians for incompetent adults, one does not see manifest any belief that certain family members have entitlements, to serve in the role or to be free in that role from constraints reflecting the state's judgment of the non-autonomous persons' well-being. There is general acceptance that only that ward has rights and that compromising the ward's interests for the sake of the desires or values of family members or others, no matter how intense their feelings about such things, would be immoral. Nor does one find in the UN Convention on the Rights of Persons with Disabilities any compromising of such persons' rights or welfare for the sake of national pride or supposed rights or interests of others. There is no reference to a right of guardians to direct incompetent adults' exercise of rights to education, habilitation, health care, expression, participation in political and public life, or anything else. Those adults' right to migrate is not conjoined with any other person's right nor conditioned on being accompanied by anyone else. No rights of those adults whatsoever are qualified with a phrase like the CRC's "taking into account the rights and duties of his or her parents, legal guardians, or other individuals legally responsible for him or her," or direction that states respect the "rights and duties of parents or, where applicable, the members of the extended family or community as provided for by local custom" and respect "the rights and reputation of others." There is no hint that incompetent adults must participate in an imposed culture, rather than being free to choose as able what cultural practices, if any, they will experience. There is no command that their education or habilitation "be directed to . . . development of respect . . . for the national values of the country in which [they are] living." Conversely, the CRC lacks a provision like the CRPD's Article 1, pronouncing a fundamental purpose "to promote, protect and ensure the full and equal enjoyment of all human rights and fundamental freedoms by all persons . . . and to promote respect for their inherent dignity."

6.7 Conclusion

This chapter's analysis has presupposed continuation of the existing allocation of power over children's lives across levels of government. Chapter 7 will carry further the suggestion in Chapter 5 that children would be better served by shifting some direct control over their lives from national to international bodies. This chapter has established that, regardless of whether an authoritative decision-making body is international, national, or subnational, if it presumes to exert control over children's lives, it should differentiate inherently public matters from those pertaining to areas of children's lives corresponding to areas of adults' lives in which adults possess rights of self-determination. It should aim to ensure children comparable rights in each realm. For the latter realm, including matters of migration and family life, that means viewing itself as acting as a fiduciary agent for a child, which precludes *obstructing* children's paths toward a better life for the sake of national interests or interests of other individuals. I have not yet considered, though, whether any government has an affirmative obligation to *facilitate* children's migration, enjoyment of a nurturing family life, or securing of other means to life improvement. Chapters 7 and 8 will do so.

7
The International Community's Duty to Assist

7.1 Introduction

Previous chapters primarily addressed children's negative rights against their home state or any international organization (IO) obstructing their escape from adverse situations. Chapters 7 and 8 now address what are generally viewed as positive rights of individuals against government—rights of affirmative assistance—and correspondingly, positive duties governments owe to individuals. This chapter asks whether the international community bears a collective positive obligation to facilitate children's escape from dire circumstances, and Chapter 8 whether any state other than that of a child's current residence has such an obligation.

7.2 Existing Legal Duty

There is language in some international instruments suggesting a duty on the part of the UN or other international body, owed to individuals, affirmatively to promote fulfillment of individual rights. A few mention children specifically.

The UN Charter itself does not clearly do either. It conceives of the UN as primarily a policing authority charged with preventing aggression by one state against another, and secondarily a platform for nations to cooperate in solving or preventing other problems, including human rights violations. Within Chapter I of the Charter, Article 1 explicitly denies that the Charter authorizes UN intervention in any state's domestic affairs. Chapter IX commits the UN to promoting better living conditions throughout the world, including observance of human rights, but for the purpose of creating peaceful relations among nations and with no explicit commitment to serve that purpose by any means other than helping to coordinate the work of other entities ("specialized agencies").[1] Chapter X creates

[1] *Cf.* Independent International Commission on Kosovo, The Kosovo Report 168 (2000) ("the Charter provisions relating to human rights were left deliberately vague, and were clearly not intended when written to provide a legal rational for any kind of enforcement . . . Human rights were given a subordinate and marginal role in the UN system in 1945, a role that was understood to be, at most, aspirational.").

International Migration of Children for a Better Life. James G. Dwyer, Oxford University Press. © Oxford University Press 2025.
DOI: 10.1093/9780197752333.003.0007

an Economic and Social Council and authorizes it to engage in various activities to improve knowledge of and facilitate interstate agreement about economic and social progress, but it does not impose on the Council duties to take affirmative steps toward realization of human rights, other than a vague statement that the Council "shall promote . . . observance of human rights and fundamental freedoms." Further, no "branch" of the UN (General Assembly, Security Council, International Court of Justice) stands in a direct relationship to individuals (i.e., elected by, charged with serving, accepting complaints from).

Human rights treaties (ICCPR, ICESCR, CRC, CEDAW, CRPD) impose duties on state parties, which will be important in Chapter 8, but not on the UN or other international bodies. Each creates a committee to receive, review, and provide feedback on states' compliance reports, but without suggesting that this reflects a duty owed by the committee or the UN to individuals. The committee is simply a means for states to achieve universal compliance with their agreement. Thus, although these treaties are often characterized as transforming international law, moving away from the classical view in which only states were subjects, they do so by instantiating in international law obligations of states—not of international institutions—toward individuals.

The Universal Declaration of Human Rights, which is not a treaty but has some lesser degree of normative force, differs from the human rights treaties insofar as it speaks simply of individuals possessing various rights, without specifying what entity owes corresponding duties. In a couple of passages, it refers obscurely to action at the international level. The Preamble announces that "every organ of society . . . shall strive by teaching and education to promote respect for these rights and freedoms by progressive measures, national and international, to secure their universal and effective recognition and observance." Article 28 declares: "Everyone is entitled to a social and international order in which the rights and freedoms set forth in this Declaration can be fully realized." These statements fall short of pronouncing an enforceable duty on the part of any international organ to do something for betterment of individuals' lives.

The real change in thinking about the international community's normative position relative to individuals inheres instead in the emergence, in the 1990s and early 2000s, of a principle of international obligation to prevent or stop the most extreme human rights violations. Reacting to genocides in Rwanda, Bosnia, and elsewhere, the international community decided that standing by out of deference to state sovereignty is morally unacceptable. A shift occurred in debates about intervention, from permissibility to obligatoriness. A series of conferences, studies, and proposals ultimately produced the UN World Summit Outcome Document of 2005 (WSOD), declaring that states and the international community have a "Responsibility to Protect" (R2P) persons from mass atrocities. WSOD places primary responsibility on each state to act within its own territory "to protect its populations from genocide, war crimes, ethnic cleansing and crimes against humanity." But it also sets forth a secondary responsibility of "the international community."

The articulated collective duty includes anticipation and prevention of atrocities as well as reaction to those that nevertheless occur. The international community should first "encourage and help States to exercise" their primary responsibility and, toward that end, establish under UN auspices "an early warning capability"—that is, ongoing monitoring of situations anywhere in the world that could develop into a mass atrocity. But when a state defaults as primary obligor, despite assistance or offer thereof when danger is detected, the global community has a duty to act itself. That action preferably would consist of "diplomatic, humanitarian and other peaceful means," including naming and shaming, threats of criminal prosecution, and sanctions. If such measures fail, however, it can include military intervention, upon approval by the Security Council.

This statement of R2P is practically modest but symbolically momentous. Its modesty in practice stems from: its limitation to the most extreme and deliberate state actions—namely, genocide, war crimes, ethnic cleansing, and crimes against humanity; its dependence on Security Council authorization for intervention by force; and its lack of concreteness regarding the duty to prevent.[2] Because of these limitations, it rarely results in humanitarian action.[3] The first two limitations might be defensible in principle. The potential for intervention to make matters worse might justify refraining unless the situation is so bad it could hardly get worse (which might be true only in the listed circumstances) or unless there is near-universal global consensus (reflected in agreement by all permanent members of the Security Council) that intervention is appropriate. The explanation for the limitations, though, clearly includes the lingering embrace of the norm of state sovereignty. The precursor 2001 report of the International Commission on Intervention and State Sovereignty (ICISS), entitled "Responsibility to Protect," had contemplated a broader scope of situations when a duty would arise—including state collapse and environmental disasters.

[2] The UN published a "Framework of Analysis for Atrocity Crimes" in 2014, articulating means of assessing risk of genocide, crimes against humanity, ethnic cleansing and war crimes. (UN Joint Office, 2014). It lists risk factors and identifies indicators for each. Some international agencies have also developed lists of precursor situations.

[3] The Global Centre for the Responsibility to Protect states on its website that "R2P has been invoked in more than 80 UN Security Council resolutions," but those resolutions uniformly emphasize the "first pillar" of R2P, each state's primary responsibility to prevent atrocities in its territory. Likewise with the "50 Human Rights Council resolutions and 13 General Assembly resolutions" that the Centre boasts. On the prevailing confusion over the early warning mandate, *see* Federica D'Alessandra & Shannon Raj Singh, *Operationalizing Obligations to Prevent Mass Atrocities: Proposing Atrocity Impact Assessments as Due Diligence Best Practice*, 14(3) J. Hum. Rts. Prac. 769–93 (Nov. 2022).

It also hinted at heightened responsibility to children, in provisions relating to child soldiers, land mines, and starvation. In part because of objections appealing to state sovereignty, the UN opted for a more parsimonious, generally applicable duty.

R2P is symbolically momentous, though, because it embodies a conception of states *and the international community* as what Evan Criddle and Evan Fox-Decent term "fiduciaries of humanity,"[4] and with positive duties of protection owed to peoples, not just negative duties to avoid inflicting harm. Even in antiquity, some theorists conceived of the state as fiduciary. Among the Greeks, Plato and Aristotle characterized public officials as guardians who had a duty to protect and promote general welfare. The great Roman philosopher and statesman Cicero also spoke of public officials as guardians and trustees. More recently, John Locke urged a view of public authority as an entrustment by the people for the sake of their safety and well-being. On this view, government can properly claim authority over a people only insofar as it faithfully serves that people. Positive duties flow in a sense from a negative duty not to exert dominion over people unless committed to fulfilling purposes for which the people created government and invested it with powers, just as private fiduciaries have positive duties to promote well-being because that is the only reason why they were appointed. Legislative power, Locke wrote, is "only a fiduciary power to act for certain ends." Likewise with the American founders; Criddle and Fox-Decent write: "American revolutionaries such as the authors of The Federalist Papers invoked the fiduciary conception of state authority in support of republican democracy, insisting that all public institutions and public officials must be subject to meaningful public accountability for their discharge of public powers."[5] Recent decades have seen this idea extended to the international realm. Government at every level is now generally viewed as existing to serve the people, to act affirmatively to protect and promote human welfare, and accountable for its performance. On this view, the UN, like a state, has no legitimate authority except insofar as it aims to serve the world's people, with equal regard for all.

That general idea leaves open, however, the question of how extensive a government's duty is to serve people's well-being. Any fiduciary's remit is defined, not unlimited. R2P itself remains quite limited in scope. There has been little consideration since 2005 of extending that statement of collective international responsibility to more circumstances, or of hardening the narrow obligation into treaty form. Secretary General Moon contended in 2009 that extension to nonconflict phenomena such as pandemics, natural disasters, and famine

[4] *See* Evan Criddle & Evan Fox-Decent, Fiduciaries of Humanity: How International Law Constitutes Authority 8–9 (2016).

[5] *Id.*, 14.

would be both impolitic and impractical; it "would undermine the 2005 consensus and stretch the concept beyond recognition or operational utility."[6] The concern about losing consensus is plausible, the concern about implementation not much. Domestic laws extend police authority far beyond mass murders, to lesser violence, severe neglect of dependent persons, and local disaster (flooding, house fire, etc.). In any event, Moon recognized that the UN and other IOs, as well as regional bodies, can and may address other threats to human welfare, if they so choose, in ways short of "intervention," such as fact-finding missions to detect signs of developing dangers, attempting to persuade national leaders, denying states positions in international and regional governance bodies, and imposing embargoes and sanctions.

Another pertinent development worth noting, consistent with the R2P outlook, was an institutionalizing of international criminal prosecution of state officials who commit heinous crimes, roughly the same atrocities listed in the WSOD, with creation of the International Criminal Court (ICC) in 1999. Its governing treaty, the Rome Statute, suggests a heightened duty owed to the most vulnerable persons; Article 54 directs the prosecutor "to give particular consideration to sexual violence, gender violence and violence against children in its investigations and prosecutions" of international crimes.

In addition to international governing bodies, specific agencies the General Assembly has created and (itself or by treaty) charged with positive duties to serve particular populations also exert influence over individual persons. UNICEF is a prominent example, focused on children and exerting substantial influence on how developing countries treat children. The UN High Commissioner for Refugees is another, and several scholars have called for recognizing childhood as a basis or cause of persecution,[7] which would prod the Commission to devote special attention to children and make receiving nations more inclined to grant asylum to children. The legal obligation of receiving states not to return someone to a state of nationality or previous residence currently rests upon a person's being more likely than the average person to experience serious harm in that state, to be singled out by a ruling regime for oppression. Children are specially targeted for violence and exploitation, by state actors as well as private ones, because of their relative incapacity to resist, and in addition they have greater difficulty documenting the already recognized forms of persecution against them (e.g., based on ethnicity).

[6] Ban Ki-moon, Implementing the Responsibility to Protect, Report of the Secretary-General, U.N. Doc. A/63/677, Jan. 12, 2009. Others have echoed these concerns, but with no more plausibility regarding practicality. Ultimately, the real reason for narrowness of vision is fear of losing political consensus, which is valid as a practical matter, if not a theoretical one.

[7] *See, e.g.*, Samantha Arnold, Children's Rights and Refugee Law: Conceptualizing Children Within the Refugee Convention (2018); Jason Pobjoy, The Child in International Refugee Law (2017).

7.3 Moral Obligations

Regardless of what international law now provides, does the international community have a collective *moral* duty to protect vulnerable persons and to help ensure fulfillment of human rights? If so, is such duty different in content or magnitude as between children and adults? And might it be fulfilled by facilitating migration?

The WSOD text does not offer a normative basis for a positive obligation. It implies only that default by a nation's own government weakens its claim to external sovereignty sufficiently to *permit* the international community to intervene. There would need to be an independent moral basis for IOs to have a duty to step into the breach when a state's regime defaults, or to act regardless of a home state's behavior, such that we could point a blaming finger at them if they remain inactive in the face of state maleficence, indifference, or incapacity. Instruments creating institutions whose purpose is to promote and protect human rights or to respond to crises likewise lack a statement of reasons why the international community has a duty to create those institutions for those purposes. Perhaps their functions are morally gratuitous, and beneficiaries of their work should simply be grateful that any IOs happen to try to improve their situation.

7.3.1 Good Samaritan obligation

One possible normative basis for a positive obligation is the moral duty any purposive entity might have to respond to vulnerability and suffering when uniquely positioned to do so. It seems plausible to suppose the international community is at least sometimes best positioned to intervene in dire circumstances that threaten persons' fundamental well-being, and that in such instances it is morally wrong for it to sit by and watch the suffering, death, and destruction of lives. The prevailing sentiment that drove development of R2P was of this sort: frustration and shame that the world stood by watching while atrocities occurred, when surely it could have done something to inhibit genocidal state regimes.

Moral philosophers have constructed Good Samaritan theories upon such sentiments, though focused on individuals' "duty to distant others." Most trace this line of reasoning to Peter Singer's 1972 article, "Famine, Affluence, and Morality,"[8] so I will term it the Singer Theory. He suggested such duty of individuals might be fulfilled by contributing financially to international aid organizations, which in turn would have an obligation to use the contributions they receive to carry out aid operations. The moral duty to persons in dire need in that

[8] 1 Phil. & Pub. Aff. 229 (1972).

case, though, resides elsewhere than in the IOs, in individuals, with IOs merely conduits and owing a duty to contributors, to follow through on representations made to donors, and not necessarily to the recipients.

Perhaps, though, there is an analogue to the Singer Theory for IOs as moral agents. The basic approach is to start by provoking intuitions about our personal moral obligations to others who are nearby and in life-threatening circumstances. A child drowning in a pool or lake you stand beside is a common example. No one else is around to help, and at little cost to yourself you can save the child (e.g., throw a life preserver). The theorist then asks, "Don't you think you *ought* to do that?" Most of us have the intuition that we should, that we do have such a positive moral obligation (even though Western legal systems generally impose no legal obligation), and that we would do something seriously immoral if we just stood nearby watching passively as the child drowned, or walked off indifferently.[9] We would likely think the same if we modify the hypothetical to add another character to the drama, another bystander, perhaps even the owner of the property where the pool or lake lies, but stipulate that that person is unwilling or unable to throw the life preserver, or could do so only with more difficulty and less effectiveness.

Having established an intuition about the hypothetical nearby scenario, the theory posits that helping to save lives on the other side of the planet is not morally different—that is, a child starving in Darfur is not in a morally different position than a child drowning nearby. Singer is a utilitarian, and the aggregate utility gain in either case seems great and obvious. But a Kantian might also conclude that a moral agent has a presumptive duty of beneficence when confronted with grave threat to the life of another person, another repository of ultimate value. Singer must address a reader's objection that he or she is not uniquely positioned to send money to the distant needy, but for present purposes we need not examine how he does so, because our concern is with IOs, which generally are not just another of millions of potential sources of equally effective intervention.

So, supposing we do have this intuition about the nearby drowning child, we might think agents for IOs should have the same reaction, because they typically become aware of threats to humanity around the world far more readily than the rest of us; might actually be nearby to persons in places wracked by violence, destruction, or destitution (so we do not even need the premise that distance from the moral agent is an arbitrary fact); and likely have greater recognized authority and resources than other entities that could act. They should see themselves, qua officials for the IO, as having a moral obligation to do something in their official

[9] *Cf.* Barbara Herman, *The Scope of Moral Requirement*, 30 PHIL. & PUB. AFF. 227, 227 (2002) ("It is generally agreed that there is a duty of easy rescue; we are required to provide aid when that will prevent or relieve dire conditions for someone, when the cost to us is slight or moderate.").

capacity to address those threats, using the means they have at their disposal. The government of the nation where the tragedy is occurring, or of a province or city where horrible circumstances exist, might have a primary duty, because presumptively best positioned to care for people resident in the territory it governs. If that government is unwilling or unable, like the other bystander in the local example, however, the UN or any subsidiary IOs becomes the agent best situated to rescue. So the moral duty to act arises, to ameliorate the tragedy in light of the victims' humanity. In many situations, we might add, the most effective way to save people in danger, possibly the only way, is to help them relocate. Then the positive obligation becomes one specifically to facilitate migration.

How demanding is the duty? Singer's initial hypothetical entailed trivial self-sacrifice, but by a succession of modifications to the hypothetical he arrived at a conclusion that the duty is to do as much as one can without sacrificing something of comparable importance, which in a life-saving situation would be quite substantial. Other theorists derive a less burdensome duty—for example, for Caspar Hare, "moderate sacrifice."[10] For IOs, military deployment is a big deal, entailing not only a financial cost but also risk to service members and to the organization's reputation and viability. However, spending hundreds of millions of dollars on food and medical aid, even billions, each year is no great hardship for the international community (putting aside the real-world failure to adequately fund some IOs), and arranging transport of people to a more hospitable environment might be even less costly than trying to care for them amid chaos and violence. The real obstacles to relocation are likely to be not transportation cost but rather that other places will not accept them (a topic of Chapter 8) and that the ruling regime in the inhospitable environment might obstruct rescue of any kind (a topic of Chapter 9).

Rather than explore further diverse theories of cosmopolitan altruism, I will simply consider whether any Good Samaritan moral obligation might differ as between children and adults. Any ethical tradition could support a duty to both autonomous and non-autonomous persons, if it makes both objects of moral concern. Among the main traditions, utilitarianism might most straightforwardly put duty to children first, such that if all cannot be helped then children should have priority, for reasons previously noted—that is, they have more years of potential life at stake, and adverse experiences during childhood, when fundamental psycho-emotional development occurs, typically have lasting consequences of a kind that comparable experiences during adulthood do not.

[10] Caspar Hare, The Limits of Kindness (2013), ch. 12. There are also those who defend the intuition that it is morally permissible, even required, to favor nearby needy persons over those distant. *E.g.*, John A. Weymark, *Must One Be an Ogre to Rationally Prefer Aiding the Nearby to the Distant Needy?*, 42 Phil. & Pub. Aff. 231 (2014). But that counterargument would be inapplicable in the case of IOs.

All else being equal, then, sparing a child from hellish experiences is more utility-enhancing than sparing an adult. A virtue ethics is likely to commend compassion for all, but perhaps also wisdom to channel one's altruism toward those in greatest need of help, at least among those with whom one has no special relationship, and one might plausibly regard children as generally less able to fend for themselves or endure severe deprivation.

A Kantian presumably would put duty to autonomous adults first and might even say young children and incompetent adults are owed no duties, because only rational moral agents command our respect. As discussed in Chapter 6, Kantians generally focus on respect for existing autonomy and have not given much thought to non-autonomous individuals. Some have argued for positive as well as negative duties owed to persons, including positive duties not only to protect against insults on a person's autonomy but also to promote development of autonomy. The latter move, though, appears ad hoc rather than a result of sound reasoning grounded in Kantian premises. Kantian philosophy, however, does not exhaust deontological theory, and it offers no persuasive argument for treating autonomy as the only predicate for moral regard.[11] There is an element to the broader deontology tradition since Kant of simply respecting humanness, of viewing everyone's life as infused with moral significance and dignity. But that might generate only a negative duty against incursion in a person's life; it is difficult to see how it would generate a positive duty to make an individual's life go better rather than worse, as it seems an all-or-nothing sort of attribute, or even to protect an individual from extinction by wrongful acts of others.

Still other deontologists, though, have argued for a still broader scope of moral subjects, defined by sentience, and a moral obligation to respond solicitously to suffering in, or threat of loss to, any sentient creatures, or at least those with some sense of self, because capacity for those experiences commands respect.[12] Presumably, the greater the suffering or threatened loss an individual is experiencing the more compelling or demanding the obligation arising from that respect. Thus, we can find an element of, or partial convergence with, consequentialist thinking in both virtue ethics and deontology. Some versions of each might therefore lead in this context to the same conclusion as a utilitarian one—namely, that threats to children's welfare warrant greater concern than comparable threats to adults' well-being, because more is at stake for children. Popular

[11] *See* James G. Dwyer, Moral Status and Human Life: The Case for Children's Superiority (2011), ch. 2. Kant's starting premise that we accord moral worth to ourselves because of our rational and moral capacities, which he uses to ground ascription of moral worth to others with those capacities, by appealing to the principle of universalizability, itself is not well defended; our moral valuation of ourselves and our ends might be unwarranted.

[12] *Id.*

moral precepts are consistent with this conclusion; communities and parents should put children first.

I have gone through these theories of altruistic obligation rather breezily, because all are largely stipulative and appeal more to intuition than to well-established basic moral principles. Also because a stronger foundation for IO duty is available—namely, the principle of accepting responsibility for the consequences of one's actions, including by ameliorating any adverse consequences. This transforms the duty from what might be viewed as an imperfect one of beneficence to a perfect one of justice.

7.3.2 Duty arising from past actions

Ascribing to the international community a duty to rescue predicated on responsibility for its own actions requires identifying actions that played a causal role in atrocities or disasters. Yet the prevailing view of such crises is that any culpability on the part of the international legal order lies in its failure to act, its standing idly by, its being too passive because of indifference or deference to state sovereignty. This is a misperception, however, and one common at every level of society; government action is often hiding in the background unseen until someone points it out. Illustrating this well is a U.S. Supreme Court decision very familiar to American constitutional scholars, in which the Court rejected a claim that a local government breached a constitutional duty to a child by (as the Court saw it) failing to protect him from harm by his father.[13] Child Protection Services (CPS) caseworkers had repeatedly returned Joshua Deshaney to his father's custody after removing the boy from the home following brutal beatings, without adequately ensuring he was safe, and Joshua ended up severely and permanently brain damaged. His mother sued the agency on his behalf. The Court opined that as a general matter the U.S. federal Constitution contains a charter of only negative rights against government, and so does not impose on the state at any level a duty to protect individuals from private harm. The Fourteenth Amendment Due Process Clause "is phrased as a limitation on the State's power to act [and] its language cannot fairly be extended to impose an affirmative obligation on the State to ensure that those interests do not come to harm through other means." There is "no affirmative right to governmental aid." One might view the international legal order's foundational documents the same way.

The Court suggested, though, that an exception to this principle of no state obligations to protect arises when the state creates the danger to the individual or deprives a person of "freedom to act on his own behalf"—for example, by

[13] Deshaney v. Winnebago County Dept. Soc. Serv., 489 U.S. 189 (1989).

taking the person into its custody. But it concluded in that case that "the State played no part in creating" the danger to Joshua, and when he was abused he was not in state custody, so was not being restrained from self-help by the state. CPS was an innocent bystander, at worst failing to act as a Good Samaritan ("the most that can be said of the state functionaries in this case is that they stood by and did nothing . . ."). A state might choose to impose a duty to protect on itself, but the federal Constitution does not impose such a duty on it. Further, as if to provide moral justification for the agency's inaction in this case, the Court noted that the agency might have been charged with violating the father's rights if it had "moved too soon to take custody of the son away from the father."

The many reasons why the Court's reasoning was wrong are transferable to the international context and help to establish a positive duty (or what on the surface seems a positive rather than negative duty) on the part of the international community to help individuals in dire circumstances. The basic problem with the Court's analysis lies in the failure to acknowledge that the state played a crucial but-for causal role in the devastating harm to Joshua, in many ways. First, Wisconsin made Randy Deshaney the legal father of Joshua, seemingly with no regard for his capacity to nurture. Parentage laws constitute an important part of the unseen background of government involvement in family life. Further, Wisconsin conferred on Randy presumptive legal entitlements of custody and freedom of conduct, including a right to hit for disciplinary purposes and a right to exclude other persons from Joshua's home and life more generally. In addition, as the dissent noted, Wisconsin had created a system of child protection with exclusive authority to intervene in homes to protect children. The rest of society presupposes and relies on the state system and channels all maltreatment reports to that agency. Absent Randy's state-conferred legal status and legal entitlements, or absent the state's claim of exclusive authority to intervene in family life, anyone else—for example, neighbors that heard his cries—could have assumed custody of or intervened to defend Joshua. So, although the state did not deprive Joshua of the ability to protect himself, because as a child he never had that ability, it deprived him of potential private agents willing to act to protect him. In addition, what even the dissent failed to emphasize, CPS—the state's agent—repeatedly held physical possession of Joshua, which was a situation of safety for him, but then transported him to and physically deposited him in his father's home, a situation of grave danger. This is equivalent to depositing an infant in the middle of a highway. If CPS did that, it would be irrelevant to its culpability that it did not have custody and was not blocking people from trying to save the infant.

Further, investigation into the causes of child abuse reveals that often it stems ultimately from social and economic conditions the state has played a role in creating. Maltreatment is highly correlated with concentrated poverty and with the dysfunctions, such as substance abuse, that poverty often produces. State policies (economic, zoning, infrastructure, etc.) play a significant role in existence of poverty and its concentration in particular residential areas, particularly in inner cities. Bigotry on the part of privileged and dominant groups also plays a role, and that often does its work through state apparatuses. In addition, child abuse tends to be intergenerational, so an abuser today was likely once a victim of abuse that would not have happened if the state had not been so reckless in placing children into legal family relationships a generation ago.

A similar story can be told about the role of the international community in creation of horrendous circumstances for individuals, and the story is especially apt in the case of children in danger. As discussed in Chapters 4 to 6, the international community assigns persons to states, forces nationality and its liabilities upon them, and it does so with no regard for the capacity of a particular nation to provide for and protect people. Children have far less ability than adults to unassign themselves, or to protect themselves, and for both children and adults the international legal order has prescribed presumptive return of them to their fatherland should they happen to wander off into other people's homelands seeking help.

Further, the international community confers on nations tremendous and exclusive power over persons living on their respective turfs. Brad Roth observes: "What is clear beyond cavil is that state sovereignty, far from being a status that conceptually precedes international legal order, is itself a creature of that order. The international system does not merely acknowledge sovereignty, but operates to preserve it . . . and even to create it . . ."[14] Having done so, the international legal order only obliquely suggests that other nations may make some effort to protect persons from abuse of that state power; the prevailing sentiment in the humanitarian community is that intervention should be only through or under authorization by international institutions, not undertaken unilaterally. The dominant message to persons suffering terribly because of their state's brutality, indifference, or incapacity, and to any outside parties that might wish to help them, is that the only proper avenue of external assistance is through the international legal order's agencies—that is, the human rights committees and ICC prosecutors. Yet at the same time the international order does not perceive itself to be under a general duty to act, and so its agencies assigned the task of assistance are largely ineffectual when they do act and often stand by and do nothing.

Significantly, the Court in *Deshaney* conceded that if a state does "voluntarily" undertake to help children in dire circumstances, then it might be held liable for doing so negligently; the Court simply maintained that the liability would have to be under state law (i.e., if a state happened to choose to let people sue it for damages in its own courts) rather than federal constitutional law. The

[14] Brad Roth, Sovereign Equality and Moral Disagreement 55 (2011).

international legal order might well be said to operate negligently in fulfilling the promise that human rights treaties and declarations have effectively made to individuals—especially with respect to children. It has effectively shunted them into a treaty regime (the CRC) that shrinks their rights and treats them as captives and possessions. Yet there is no recourse in any forum for holding the international legal order accountable for this.

In addition, various IOs impact conditions for people in one nation or another by the policies they adopt.[15] The World Trade Organization has been accused of exacerbating economic inequality between the developed and developing worlds. For example, it constrains poor countries' ability to export their goods and services and to import generic drugs. Instead of creating a free market in which the industrious can rise and all benefit from lower prices for essential goods replicated and mass produced in advanced economies, it suppresses progress in developing countries. It handicaps producers in those countries with higher tariffs than are imposed on rich countries, and it protects the monopolies that intellectual property rights create.[16] Poor countries accept rules skewed against them because they are powerless to refuse or because their leaders are duped, corrupt, or both.[17] The International Monetary Fund also has a great impact on poor nations. It puts pressures on their rulers that could make them more authoritarian. International pressure to limit certain activities for the sake of climate preservation is also viewed by developing countries as placing a disproportionate burden on them.

Because of these various actions of the international legal order, it bears responsibility for the plight of any person in dire circumstances whose predicament is explainable in terms of conduct by a state exercising power the international legal order has given it by ascription of sovereignty, in circumstances the international legal order has created that foster oppressive regimes. This could be viewed as a positive obligation arising from past failure to fulfill negative obligations—namely, duties not to: push people into a legal relationship with a state regime that is abusive, indifferent, or dysfunctional; accord to such a regime excessive power and control; and impose policies likely to drive some regimes in an authoritarian, oppressive, even murderous direction. If I threw the child in the lake, my obligation to rescue is even clearer, and the international legal order might be seen to have effectively thrown nationals of the worst states "in the lake," knowingly subjecting them to state abuse of power or incapacity and

[15] Responsibility and causation certainly become more complex in relation to substantive policies and actions of IOs. *See generally* ANDRE NOLLKAEMPER & DOV JACOBS, DISTRIBUTION OF RESPONSIBILITIES IN INTERNATIONAL LAW (2015).

[16] THOMAS POGGE, WORLD POVERTY AND HUMAN RIGHTS: COSMOPOLITAN RESPONSIBILITIES AND REFORMS 20–21 (2d ed. 2008).

[17] *Id.*, 29.

continuing to impose economic and other policies that create conditions conducive to such abuse. Moreover, the harm done in the case of lakes is generally greater when done to children than when done to adults, because of the former's lesser capacity for self-help and exit, so the duty is stronger. Analogously, the international legal order's responsibility is stronger in the case of children. Its subjugation of them to state dominance is more complete than in the case of adults, and their subjugation is more clearly not a result of their exercise of agency. The obligation this gives rise to is to change local conditions, including by inserting life-saving measures and by retracting some of the power and attendant ability to harm that it has conferred on the territory's ruler—when that is likely to be effective quickly.[18] Otherwise, to get the child out.

Importantly, this account leads to a conclusion that the international legal order's moral responsibility exists independently of whether any state acts to protect, including the ruling regime where a crisis is occurring. It is not secondary to or merely derivative from state responsibility. This attribution of responsibility is nevertheless compatible with some version of subsidiarity *in practice*, one in which for *pragmatic* reasons local government is typically expected to respond first to human needs, and other levels of government merely monitor and assist unless and until the more local authorities fail. But when the pragmatic reasons are absent, as when a state has repeatedly shown indifference or incapacity, the international moral obligation counsels in favor of earlier intervention. The earliest "intervention" might be to stop intruding in a particular way into the relationship between individual and state—namely, pushing people into a nationality status and residential situation vis-à-vis such a state. As suggested in Chapter 5, suspending a state's nationality-conferring power is one potential response to a state's maltreatment of a people. Analogously, when a birth parent has a sustained record of serious child maltreatment, the state should stop placing newborns into a legal relationship with, and legal custody of, that birth parent.[19]

There is some support for this account of IO responsibility to prevent state abuse (including endangerment as well as direct harm) or neglect (including both inability and unwillingness to protect and provide) in theorizing about state legitimacy. Evan Fox-Decent appeals to nondomination as a limitation on government and argues that some higher authority—such as the international legal order that imbues national government with sovereignty—is needed—not

[18] *Cf.* Criddle & Fox-Decent, *supra* note 4, at 3 ("a state's claim to exercise sovereign authority is derived from, and wholly dependent upon, the satisfaction of its relationship duties to the people subject to its legal powers.").

[19] *See* James G. Dwyer, *A Constitutional Birthright: The State, Parentage, and Newborn Persons*, 56 UCLA L. Rev. 755 (2009).

just in cases of mass atrocity, but on a standing basis—to guard persons against state domination:

> [S]tate power without the rule of law places public officials in a relationship of domination vis-à-vis their people, since those officials could abuse their powers with impunity. For republicans, domination is an evil independently of whether the power holder actually mistreats the people subject to her power. Domination denotes dependence, which is living at the whim or mercy of another. . . . [T]he rule of law supplies a republican antidote to domination by ensuring that individuals are subject to general laws rather than the arbitrary power of their rulers.[20]

That rule of law would be supranational—that is, an international legal order imposing and enforcing norms of nondomination.

Young children seem inherently and inevitably dependent and subject to domination, but Fox-Decent can be read as saying that it is an offence to the dignity of any person, whether autonomous or not, that another entity should wield power over their life free of principled and enforced constraints tied to their rights as human beings. Even a child should not have to depend on favorable whims of state authorities. Government at every level should be constrained to act upon any people solely for the purpose of guarding or promoting their interests, either in the aggregate (police power) or to fulfill a particular individual's human rights.[21] There is no justification for conferring power over persons on a state for any other purpose. An antidote to state domination of persons is an international legal order that adopts and enforces uniform (given the equal dignity of persons) norms for state treatment of individuals, and it is made obligatory by that order's empowerment of states.

Still, we might ask what is the extent of the international community's responsibility? Existing international law concerning humanitarian intervention allows uninvited intervention by the international community only in cases of mass atrocities. But the moral argument leads to a responsibility of much broader scope—in theory, encompassing every state failing, every state abuse of power, and every seriously adverse consequence of state domination in which the international legal order has played a causal role. Fiduciary law generally holds fiduciaries liable for significant harm they cause a principle or ward by breaching their duties; what ultimately determines liability is not the type or

[20] Evan Fox-Decent, Sovereignty's Promise: The State as Fiduciary 26 (2011).

[21] *See also* Criddle & Fox-Decent, *supra* note 4, at 3 ("states must treat their people always as ends rather than mere means (the Kantian principle of non-instrumentalization), and they must refrain from assuming arbitrary power over the legal and practical interests of their people (the republican principle of non-domination)").

degree of harm but the standard of care and types of care expected. A typical rule adopts a standard of reasonable diligence in selection, direction, and oversight of agents.[22] When misconduct is feared or detected, the superordinate fiduciary must act to prevent or stop it, including by retracting conferred powers. As with subsidiarity, practical considerations must inform fulfillment of the duty, and they will sometimes counsel in favor of restraint and incrementalism. But the moral responsibility to stop apparent harm is potentially limitless.

7.4 Conclusion

The humanitarian community needs to change the conversation about R2P, so that it is no longer characterized in Good Samaritan terms, a matter of compassion and aspiring for a better world. It needs to emphasize consistently the international community's role in enabling and fostering bad behavior by states. And child advocates need to comprehend and counter the ways international law and IO practices are especially causing harm and endangerment to children.

[22] *See, e.g.*, Uniform Trust Code Sec. 807 ("The trustee shall exercise reasonable care, skill, and caution in: (1) selecting an agent; (2) establishing the scope and terms of the delegation, consistent with the purposes and terms of the trust; and (3) periodically reviewing the agent's actions in order to monitor the agent's performance and compliance with the terms of the delegation.").

8
Other States' Duty to Assist

8.1 Introduction

This chapter turns focus to nations other than a child's home country, to analyze their normative position in relation to children in dire circumstances elsewhere in the world. It considers whether moral duties of assistance arise from the same bases as the duties ascribed to the international community in Chapter 7—that is, capacity and/or having participated in creating the circumstances—or other bases. Whereas the international community's duties were singular, the content of other nations' duties is variable, in part because there are more than one and some possible foundations for a duty vary across them, but also because other nations, unlike the international legal order, constitute potential alternative places to live—that is, could assist by facilitating immigration.

Readers might think attention to immigration long overdue in this book, but an important point of fact relevant to children's migration is that receiving countries are generally far more welcoming of young children than they are of adults, with attitudes toward adolescents somewhere in between. Because of this fact, obstacles to exiting bad circumstances are more salient for much of the world's youth—particularly those who are unparented—than are obstacles to entering a good situation. Two phenomena reflective of this reality are the very high interest in developed countries for international adoption and past instances of those countries accepting large numbers of young children evacuated from dangerous places. Consider that, if in 2024 the international community had rallied behind the idea of evacuating children from Gaza, given that nations were not receptive to mass migration of an undifferentiated refugee population, most likely Western countries would collectively have welcomed all whose parents consented to their departure, for temporary fostering and possibly permanent care (for any later unable to reunify with family). Or they might have pitched in to fund temporary shelter of children at sea, awaiting return when hostilities cease.

With that factual assumption in the background, this chapter begins by examining existing international law governing foreign states' individual obligation to come to the aid of people living in terrible conditions, as always watchful for any special treatment of children. It then, as in other chapters, shifts to normative analysis and delves into theoretical writing on state obligations to rescue. The final section considers various possible means by which a nation might discharge any such duties. That includes liberalizing immigration, so I will peer

International Migration of Children for a Better Life. James G. Dwyer, Oxford University Press. © Oxford University Press 2025.
DOI: 10.1093/9780197752333.003.0008

into the philosophical literature on immigration. I will not attempt to rehearse all arguments for and against open borders and assess the merits of each; an entire book would be needed to do just that adequately. Rather, I will simply ask whether arguments are weaker or stronger as applied to children rather than adults.

8.2 Existing Legal Duty

As with the responsibility of international organizations affirmatively to protect persons, a legal duty of states arises most clearly in connection with a small set of heinous acts. The Genocide Convention, in its first article, commits each state party to "undertake to prevent and to punish" that specific atrocity. Though generally regarded as a commitment only to nonmilitary efforts, the ICJ has interpreted it to mean each state party has an obligation as to the whole world, not just its own territory, calibrated to its relative capacity to influence conduct of particular other nations.[1] This positive legal duty is sufficiently strong and concrete as to be enforceable via adjudication; any state party to the Convention can bring a claim against any other state party that was aware of the risk or ongoing commission of a mass atrocity and had the capacity (including the requisite knowledge for effective action) to prevent or limit it, but failed to act.[2]

Similarly, the Geneva Conventions impose on state parties an obligation to prevent war crimes, and the prevailing view today is that this includes a positive duty to ensure other states—even nonparties—also refrain from war crimes.[3] The Obama administration in 2012 accordingly created an "Atrocities Prevention Board, with the primary purpose of coordinating a whole-of-government approach to prevent mass atrocities and genocide" and a global remit. In 2016, Barack Obama reaffirmed and further elaborated the Board's responsibility,

[1] Application of the Convention on the Prevention and Punishment of the Crime of Genocide (*Bosnia and Herzegovina v. Serbia and Montenegro*), Judgment of Feb. 27, 2007, ¶¶ 183, 430, 432 (holding that state parties are "under positive obligations, to do their best to ensure that such acts do not occur," in light of their "capacity . . . to influence effectively the action of persons likely to commit, or already committing, genocide," taking into account geographical distance, strength of political ties between the states, and "its particular legal position vis-à-vis the situations and persons facing the danger, or the reality, of genocide"). Scholars have interpreted the last passage to call for consideration of: what kinds of legal recourse a state has available to it for preventing an atrocity; what jurisdiction various courts—international, regional, or domestic—have over potential state actions, and how that jurisdiction might be used to dissuade perpetrators; whether a state shares any treaty commitments with potential perpetrators that might provide legal avenues for preventive action; and whether a state could support any legal proceedings initiated by those at risk.

[2] *See* Federica D'Alessandra & Shannon Raj Singh, *Operationalizing Obligations to Prevent Mass Atrocities: Proposing Atrocity Impact Assessments as Due Diligence Best Practice*, 14 J. Hum. Rts. Prac. 769 (2022).

[3] *Id.*

which included developing an early warning system, leading cooperative efforts among friendly nations, and identifying strategies for discouraging or holding accountable persons in power with an inclination to commit atrocities.[4]

Significantly, the four Geneva Conventions and two additional protocols of 1977 call for extra protection of children. Article 77 of Additional Protocol I, for example, says "children shall be the object of special respect and shall be protected against any form of indecent assault. The Parties to the conflict shall provide them with the care and aid they require, whether because of their age or for any other reason." In 2000, the UN Security Council issued Resolution 1314 likewise calling for special protection of children in armed conflict, including demobilization and reintegration of child soldiers.

In the main human rights treaties, party states take on duties to all persons. As noted in Chapter 4, the treaties mostly do not speak of individuals having rights against their state of nationality or residence specifically, but rather simply of individuals having particular rights. (A notable exception is the right to enter "one's own nation.") In the case of ICCPR negative rights, this is naturally *erga omnes*; a state's duty not to torture or suppress religious exercise is equally great as to any person in the world and not dependent on citizenship. The ICESCR speaks broadly throughout of individual rights to positive benefits of various kinds without tying them to persons' own country. (The CRC, in contrast, appears to ascribe obligations owed to children only to their nation of current residence; Article 2(1) provides: "States Parties shall respect and ensure the rights set forth in the present Convention to each child within their jurisdiction . . .").

Some specialized treaties also pronounce a duty undifferentiated by nationality or location. Article 98 of the UN Convention on the Law of the Sea ascribes a duty to rescue to any ship that is able, without regard to flag, formalizing a longstanding rule of customary international law. The Search and Rescue Services Treaty of 1979 creates zones of duty, but these are not coextensive with territorial zones and have nothing to do with sovereignty; they are simply regions where a nation is in the best position to assist and therefore has a duty to do so, consistent with the Singer Theory of moral responsibility discussed in Chapter 7.

Not yet hardened into treaty form at the global level, the Responsibility to Protect doctrine (R2P), embodied in the 2005 World Summit Outcome Document (WSOD), might be read as a limitation on the treaty obligations. It implies that individual states have neither duty nor permission ever to intervene by actions on the territory of another state uninvited, even with respect to

[4] Executive Order 13729—A Comprehensive Approach to Atrocity Prevention and Response (May 18, 2016).

atrocities happening next door. Primary responsibility for peace, safety, and satisfaction of basic human needs lies with each state as to its own territory and the people on it (Para. 138). Should a state fail in this, international organizations (IOs) are the only identified backup, with the UN Security Council having presumptive control over peacekeeping and security measures (Paras. 80, 139). This stance reflects inability of nations to agree on principles regarding unilateral action, rather than universal opposition.[5] Some nations do oppose any unilateral humanitarian intervention by any state, because that constitutes incursion on a state's sovereignty by an outside force that the target state has never accorded any authority regarding its affairs and as to which the target state does not participate in deliberations and decision making. In other words, they adhere to an outdated view of sovereignty as compromised only by a state's own agreement.

The current international-law rule therefore appears to be that nations have no obligation to undertake humanitarian intervention unilaterally but have a duty to support UN humanitarian efforts. In contrast, at least one regional treaty body, the African Union, pronounces in its Constitutive Act an affirmative obligation of each state party to respond to certain "grave circumstances," which are essentially those addressed by R2P—war crimes, genocide, crimes against humanity, including by intervening in other states if necessary. Secretary General Ban Ki-moon characterized this as emphasizing non-indifference rather than non-intervention.[6]

8.3 Moral Obligations

As with IOs, we can go beyond existing legal obligations to ask which moral duties, if any, a nation individually bears with respect to humanitarian crises in other nations. One potential basis for a nation's duty to improve conditions elsewhere, not shared with IOs, is its responsibility to protect and serve the welfare of its own people, which a nation might fulfill by acting abroad in a way that incidentally improves life for residents of another country. For example, if European countries perceive that masses of refugees are straining their infrastructure and resources, to the detriment of their nationals, they might take steps to make life more livable in refugees' home states, so that fewer migrate. The U.S. government might protect its people from the scourge of fentanyl and other drugs by acting against producers and traffickers in Mexico, Columbia,

[5] *See* Jeremy A. Haugh, "Beyond R2P: A Proposed Test for Legalizing Unilateral Armed Humanitarian Intervention" (2014), https://libraetd.lib.virginia.edu/public_view/tt44pn37g (last visited Sept. 29, 2024).

[6] Ban Ki-moon, Implementing the Responsibility to Protect, Report of the Secretary-General, U.N. Doc. A/63/677, Jan. 12, 2009.

and other countries where the ruling regime is unable or unwilling to take such action. This might incidentally make life safer for inhabitants of those countries and keep people, especially children, from being drawn into illegal activity. We are principally concerned here, though, with duties owed to persons in other countries, rather to one's own citizens or residents. There are several possible bases for such duties.

In the immigration context, some theorists posit as a starting point a negative duty rather than a positive one—namely, a negative duty not to inhibit movement or liberty of the person. They believe this presumptive universal right puts the burden on a receiving state to justify having less than fully open borders.[7] This might be plausible if the end condition contemplated is simply presence on a territory, which could be valuable as simply an escape from threats outside the territory. (There is still need to explain why exclusion of any person from any place in the universe—including other people's homes, hospital operating rooms, the international space station, and North Korea—constitutes an infringement of a basic right and so requires defense.) But really what is at stake in the immigration context is integration into the society of the receiving state and enjoyment of various state-provided benefits. And for that, the appeal must be, it seems, to a positive duty. If someone enters and is treated as if they don't exist, that is not a tenable long-term situation. They need the government and society of the receiving nation to recognize and respond to their existence and to do things (issue documents, give benefits, integrate them into a community) to support their well-being and bring them into social membership in some form. So a moral basis for a duty to perform affirmative acts seems necessary.

One straightforward moral basis, also not shared with IOs, arises from explicit agreement, in the treaties noted in Section 8.2. A nation might be thought to have, like any other purposive agent, a moral obligation to fulfill its promises. In theory, persons all over the world have a reliance interest in their doing so; they might justifiably formulate and carry out a life plan on the assumption that all nations of the world owe them certain duties should they happen to fall into desperate circumstances. The agreed-upon duties, though, might only be ones of assistance outside the territory of needy persons' country or internally with consent of that country's rulers, so not including uninvited intervention nor welcome into the obligated state's society.

For more basic moral duties, not dependent on choosing to obligate oneself legally, we can apply to nations the same theories applied to IOs in Chapter 7—that is, Good Samaritan and responsibility for past actions. In addition, many theorists predicate an obligation to open borders on the fact of great inequality

[7] *E.g.*, Alex Sager, Against Borders: Why the World Needs Free Movement of People 24, 28–29 (2020).

of wealth and well-being across nations, coupled with some conception of global distributive justice. Let us assume for the moment that any duty would be fulfilled only by means other than uninvited action on another state's territory, so permissibility is not an issue.

8.3.1 Good Samaritan obligation

The bystander duty arises from unique ability to rescue. Ability can consist of proximity and/or resources. Chapter 7 posited that UN agencies are often best positioned to intervene. They are in a sense always proximate to every crisis; the UN has developed an institutional framework for action within states; and the UN appears less threatening as an intervenor than an individual state, because it would not be suspected of trying to seize territory or exploit a target nation. Yet the UN is often paralyzed in the face of crisis, and member states have been stingy in contributing to its humanitarian aid resources. In Singer's drowning child hypothetical, our intuitions would likely be that if the bystander who appears more able to rescue fails to act for any reason, the next best-positioned person should take over; they may not sit idly by blaming the child's death on the closer bystander. They become best positioned because of the closer person's incapacity or indifference. This might be true of individual states when the UN fails to act. Thus, NATO bombing to stop the atrocities in Kosovo occurred after Russia and China blocked Security Council action. Likewise, following Russia's invasion of Ukraine in 2022, given Russia's ability to block a UN response, Western Europe perceived itself to have not only self-protecting motivation but also moral obligation to give military and other support to Ukraine, including provision of weapons that would strike targets on Russian soil. Ukraine is a neighbor and Western Europe has relatively great resources, more than those of Ukraine's neighbors to the east who support its cause. The United States also has great resources and showed solidarity with Ukraine, at least initially, but sentiment grew among Americans that Europe rather than the United States should take the lead. Were there any moral (rather than self-serving) basis to that sentiment, it could be that the greater distance of the United States makes it not as well positioned, because aid delivery is more difficult.

In other circumstances, though, an individual state might be better positioned than the UN even if the UN were prepared to act, because better equipped and prepared. If I am holding a life preserver, I might be better positioned to save the drowning child than someone initially standing closer who does not have one to throw, so I would have a primary obligation to act in some way, and it might reduce the chances of rescue to pass the life preserver to the closer person instead of undertaking the rescue myself. Analogously, if Mexico asked for help in combatting an internal crisis of violence (e.g., drug cartels attempting a coup) or natural disaster, the United States might be better positioned than the UN to provide it. Trying to channel our assistance through a UN agency might only make it less effective. To watch disaster unfold and do nothing, explaining that the UN has primary moral obligation, would appear callous and immoral.

A primary means of rescue in many cases, discussed in Section 8.4.2, is accepting refugees. Proximity is an aspect of being best positioned in that regard, but so too is having the capacity to absorb and provide opportunities for a decent life to immigrants. Nations with advanced economies will generally have greater capacity of that kind, though language difference might lessen the capacity in some places. With respect to immigrant minors specifically, the capacity to absorb and provide for includes having resources and institutions for welcoming them into families, schools, medical offices, and so forth. This depends on culture as well as resources. In many of the wealthiest nations adoption of children is familiar and valued, robust adoption programs exist, and interest in adopting is high among the population, and they have substantial ethnic and cultural diversity as well. In some other wealthy nations, particularly non-Western nations, this is less the case. Thus, the United States quite plausibly has a moral obligation to welcome more child immigrants than it currently does, including by pressuring Central American states to facilitate international adoption of the children they are warehousing in orphanages or neglecting on the streets. Travel between the United States and Central America is easy because of the proximity, and the United States has the greatest capacity of any nation on earth to welcome such children. And for the same reasons why IOs might generally have a greater duty to children than to adults, individual states might have as well. If so, foreign aid should perhaps be targeted primarily at programs for children, and immigration rules should be more liberal with minors, as they arguably now are in some receiving nations. Section 8.4 gives further reason for that conclusion.

8.3.2 Duty arising from past actions

As to responsibility for past actions as well, the account for individual states is substantially different from that for international organizations and varies across nations. No individual state conferred sovereignty or its attendant powers on another, nor assigned persons to other nations, nor presumed to establish a singular and ineffective system of protection of persons against abuse or neglect by their home state.

State responsibility might arise indirectly from participation in IOs, though. Some nations have played a greater role in shaping political or economic policies of IOs that have adversely impacted developing nations. Thomas Pogge explains:

> When groups competitively pursue their interests within a framework of rules, these rules themselves and their adjudication typically become objects of the competition and may then be deformed by stronger parties to the point where the framework becomes manifestly unfair. . . . Inflicting seriously unjust rules upon others is harming them.[8]

Pogge characterizes as "institutional cosmopolitism" the view, developed in the realm of personal morality, that "one ought not to participate in an unjust institutional scheme (one that violates human rights) without making reasonable efforts to aid its victims and to promote institutional reform." Pogge extends this idea to international law, on the grounds that "all human beings are now participants in a single, global institutional scheme."[9] The same precept can apply to national morality; states, as representatives of particular communities of persons, if they are members of and have the capacity to influence the norms enforced by the UN, World Trade Organization, International Monetary Fund, UNICEF, and so forth—as is certainly true of the wealthiest nations—have an obligation to make reasonable efforts to ensure those organizations do not commit, condone, or tolerate violations of human rights. When they fail to make such efforts, they owe reparations.

Pogge portrays this as a negative duty, not to contribute to injustice, which can be fulfilled only by nonmembership or use of membership to try to effect justice. Thus, objections to the Singer Theory based on lack of special relationship to the distant suffering are irrelevant; we owe all human beings, regardless of relationship, a negative duty not to harm them. This is as true of participating in an international economic system that plays a substantial causal role in the abject suffering of the world's poorest inhabitants as of murdering people with one's gun.[10] Pogge writes:

> The move from an interactional to an institutional approach thus blocks one way in which the rich and mighty in today's developed countries like to see themselves as morally disconnected from the fate of the less fortunate denizens of the Third World. . . . It overcomes the claim that one need only refrain from violating human rights directly. . . . We are asked to be concerned about human rights violations not simply insofar as they exist at all, but only insofar as they are produced by social institutions in which we are significant participants. Our negative duty not to cooperate in the imposition of unjust practices, together with our continuing participation in an unjust institutional scheme, triggers

[8] Thomas Pogge, World Poverty and Human Rights: Cosmopolitan Responsibilities and Reforms 15–16 (2d ed. 2008).

[9] Thomas Pogge, *Cosmopolitanism and Sovereignty*, 103 Ethics 48–75, 50–51 (1992).

[10] *Id.*, 56.

> obligations to promote feasible reforms of this scheme that would enhance the fulfillment of human rights.[11]

And, one might add, a duty, unless and until those reforms occur, to rescue persons anywhere in the world in horrendous circumstances in which the international legal order has played a causal role.

Individual nations also owe duties of compensatory or remedial assistance because of past unilateral actions upon other nations, and possibly because of actions of their nationals as well, such as corporations operating abroad. Conventional wisdom has it that wealthy nations and their businesses with foreign operations (especially agriculture and mining) have so distorted the trajectory of poor nations as to share much of the blame for the poverty, disorder, insecurity, and vulnerability to natural disaster, along with corrupt, oppressive, genocidal, or incompetent local regimes that the wealthy nations have propped up.

Colonialism is a common target of blame. Though it would be difficult to establish what a former colony would be like if never colonized, the prevailing assumption is that any such nation would be healthier politically and economically. Accordingly, though it is not a written rule, "there is the general sentiment in international practice that as former colonial powers, certain countries have continuing special responsibilities to take action to ensure stability and peace in their former colonies (Britain in Sierra Leone, France in the Ivory Coast, and Portugal in East Timor, for example)."[12] Some responsibility might also arise from the cultural connection the colonizer has with the colonized, if it makes the former better positioned than other affluent nations to offer certain forms of assistance (services in country, accepting immigrants). But the stronger basis is owing amends.

A powerful nation need not have colonized a weaker one, however, to have inflicted harms on it. Harm might have resulted from military action, support for an unjust national regime, unfair trade practices, or something else. Wealthy and powerful nations have acted directly in some ways that helped bad actors create and sustain conditions and regimes in poor and weak countries that stifle the ability of their peoples to improve their circumstances. They do so by supplying weapons for oppressive autocrats to violently take over and hold on to governments, by fostering a culture of corruption with bribes to get leaders' support for wealthy nations' objectives and by enabling self-serving rulers to steal a nation's resources and put its people under crushing debt for personal gain.[13]

[11] *Id.*, 52.

[12] Kok-Chor Tan, "The Duty to Protect," *in* TERRY NARDIN & MELISSA S. WILLIAMS, NOMOS XLVII: HUMANITARIAN INTERVENTION 84–116, 97 (2006).

[13] POGGE, *supra* note 8, at 29.

This account yields a conclusion that a wealthy nation, such as France, likely owes individual duties to the people of other nations—specifically, its former colonies and nations whose despots France has materially supported in the past, and it shares with other wealthy nations responsibility to address crises in any nations crippled by policies of IOs in which they held substantial sway. What is left out of this account is any basis for attributing an obligation to nations that have never been colonizers, have not given significant aid to bad actors abroad, and have not played a large role in IOs. Arguably some relatively wealthy nations match that description—for example, Canada. (Though it might well owe reparations to people within its territory.) The moral duty of such nations seems just that of a bystander, fully satisfied by contributing proportionately to UN humanitarian efforts, and perhaps by taking in a proportionate share of refugees, where proportionate is defined as an allotment based on population or GDP among nations who do not bear a special responsibility because of past harms, after those who do have a special responsibility have taken on their disproportionate share.

8.3.3 Distributive justice

Finally, some philosophers have derived a national obligation of foreign assistance, including a duty to permit immigration, from the bare fact of gross inequality of life prospects and life quality across nations.[14] Much of the literature considers whether theories of distributive justice developed in a domestic context, such as that of John Rawls, can be transposed to the international realm, treating membership in a particular society as another morally arbitrary fact for which people should not suffer, and assuming institutions exist that are capable of evening out to a substantial degree guarantees of basic liberties, economic and other opportunities, and wealth holdings. Some deny justice is required across societies, however, because different peoples do not stand in relationships of reciprocity with each other. I will not delve into these debates, which also warrant book-length treatment on their own. I will instead just note that, as in the domestic justice context,[15] none have much to say about what is owed to children as a matter of justice, even though childhood generally puts persons in the category of least advantaged and most vulnerable (consider, for example, unparented street children in India, many very young, who sleep in cardboard boxes at

[14] *E.g.*, Loren E. Lomasky & Fernando R. Reson, Justice at a Distance: Extending Freedom Globally (2015); Joseph H. Carens, *Aliens and Citizens: The Case for Open Borders*, 49 Rev. Pol. 251, 258 (1987).

[15] *See* James G. Dwyer, Religious Schools v. Children's Rights (2001), ch. 6.

garbage dumps and spend their days begging and scrounging to survive rather than attending school, easy targets of violence and enslavement).

8.4 Ways of Fulfilling the Obligation

Assuming some basis exists for ascribing to some nations a moral duty to alleviate human suffering elsewhere in the world, there are, just as with IOs, numerous alternative means by which a nation might discharge the duty. A given basis for ascribing a duty might connect only or best with certain means, or it might be entirely indeterminate as to choice of means.

8.4.1 Range of options

Available options include various ways of inducing improved conduct by the other nation's government (e.g., offering assistance, diplomatic pressure, trade boycott, asset seizure); various ways of directly improving conditions for individuals within another nation's territorial boundaries (e.g., airdropping food and medical supplies, sending in aid agencies or peacekeeping forces with state permission, or possibly without (see Chapter 9)); and offering aid outside the boundaries of a nation where people are in dire need, including by facilitating their migration. As with IOs, when home state cooperation is lacking, this last option is more likely to be optimal. Nations that owe a duty of redress should be thinking of immigration permission as a primary means of discharging that duty.[16]

When alternative means of fulfilling a duty are available to a given nation, its choice might be determined by its own people's preferences. Christopher Wellman supposes the people of some nations would make immigration the last option rather than give it priority. He argues that even a liberal state has a right to adopt a quite restrictive and self-serving immigration policy; it can fulfill by other means any obligation it has to suffering people elsewhere—in particular, by trying to improve conditions in the territory where would-be immigrants now live, even by military intervention if necessary.[17] The last suggestion seems to reflect an assumption of profound irrationality on the part of a debtor nation's people, that they would prefer risking their citizens' lives, and condemnation by the international community, rather than letting in more people.

[16] *Cf.* Ryan Pevnick, Immigration and the Constraints of Justice: Between Open Borders and Absolute Sovereignty (2011) (arguing immigration policy should be more open for nationals of states on which the receiving country has inflicted harm).

[17] Christopher Heath Wellman, *Immigration and Freedom of Association*, 119 Ethics 109–41, 129 (2008). Helping them migrate to some third nation is another possibility.

And realistically, situations in which a nation is seriously contemplating military intervention in another country are unlikely to be ones in which bombing would be seen as a substitute for immigration visas. But the idea of improving conditions internally has more sense behind it. For example, the United States might address the problems of gang recruitment and trafficking facing children in Central America's Northern Triangle by funding creation of children's villages with boarding schools in remote areas of those countries, a place for young people to stay safely until adulthood, instead of migrating to the United States. If the American people prefer that, regardless of whether it is better for the United States economically—considering the possibility that local government or cartels will seize the property and the investment will be lost—than bringing the youths here, then so be it. However, to be clear, whether there is a duty to discharge (as opposed to how it is discharged) cannot itself depend on a people's willingness to help others; that would be incompatible with the concept of a national moral duty.

8.4.2 Immigration policy

Allowing persons in other countries to migrate into one's own might actually be less costly than many forms of intervention in their home state, especially if one accepts as an empirical premise that under certain circumstances (which now appear to prevail in the main destination countries) new entrants to a society are a net economic benefit.[18] In any event, if a nation has not done what it ought by other means, then when people who arguably are owed reparations show up at the border, allowing them in and providing them care is surely morally requisite. The nation's failure to redress past harms by improving conditions in the sending country has itself now caused these people the additional suffering of separation from loved ones and an arduous and perilous journey. It is not implausible to think, for example, that the United States has never taken adequate corrective or compensatory measures to atone for its self-serving support of dictators in various Central and South American countries during the past century. The steady stream of people leaving those countries today just to survive, and then showing up at the southern U.S. border in hope of finding refuge, partly reflects the consequences of those U.S. interventions. The United States' moral failing is thus not merely declining to be a Good Samaritan but refusing

[18] *See* David J. Bier, "Unlocking America's Potential: How Immigration Fuels Economic Growth and Our Competitive Advantage," CATO INSTITUTE (Sept., 13, 2024), https://www.cato.org/testimony/unlocking-americas-potential-how-immigration-fuels-economic-growth-our-competitive# (last visited Sept. 30, 2024).

to accept responsibility for consequences of its past actions when an opportunity to do so arrives at its doorstep. It compounds its wrongful actions rather than remediating them.

The open-borders literature largely operates without an assumption of responsibility for past action, however, and it is important to see how the debate might be improved by greater consideration of subgroups within migrant populations—in particular, children—and whether some groups stand in a different moral posture than others. As with the literature on sovereignty, there is a lot of simplifying regarding borders. One kind of simplifying is assuming an undifferentiated mass of would-be immigrants on one side and on the other side an existing citizenry who all have the same views on immigration policy, cultural change, and the desirability of sharing space with new members. Another present in some theorizing is positing a false binary—completely open borders or completely closed borders (or perhaps severely constrained and solely self-serving conferral of permission to enter). What is realistically at stake is where on the spectrum between these two poles a potential receiving nation will situate its immigration policy. From that perspective, the main point I will make regarding immigration is just that any affluent nation should have a more liberal policy regarding children than regarding adults.

8.4.2.1 Preference of receiving society

One reason for this is the preference of the people of the receiving nation. In paying debts to outsiders, the state still acts as fiduciary for its people, fulfilling the people's collective obligation as their agent, and therefore should do so in whatever manner best serves them. Analogously, a conservator for an adult with diminished capacities must pay the ward's medical and other bills, but in doing so the conservator should exercise any discretion in how they do that—for example, in terms of timing or source of payment—in a manner that best serves the ward's interests or expressed preferences. Additionally, some theorists argue for immigration restrictions on freedom of association grounds, contending that addition of members to a society should depend on mutual consent, which most significantly means consent by existing members to add new members.[19] If it makes sense to speak of "a societal preference," giving priority in immigration to those whom existing members collectively prefer would be consistent with that view.

There is some concrete evidence that populations within receiving countries are far more sympathetic toward children who migrate on their own than toward adults alone or whole families who cross borders without

[19] *E.g.*, Wellman, *supra* note 17.

permission.[20] One reason is greater sympathy, consistent with greater compassion for children in other contexts. From an American perspective, we routinely see reports from war zones that emphasize the number of children killed, innumerable journalistic accounts of the suffering of and danger to children migrating north to the U.S.-Mexico border, the child-centered outcry against the Trump administration's decision to separate children from parents as a deterrent, and the greater public support for international adoption than for the foreign bride phenomenon. Immigration proceedings are generally expedited for unaccompanied minors,[21] and while cases are pending, there is a push to house the children in home-like settings. The United States has at times declined to expel minors in situations where it would expel adults, presumably with popular support. For example, in 2021 the Biden administration announced it would not expel children arriving in the United States despite an unprecedented migrant surge along the southern border. Homeland Security Secretary Alejandro Mayorkas explained simply: "[T]hat's not who we are." The United States was expelling families and adults, but it would not turn back "young, vulnerable children."[22] In the same spirit, the Obama administration created a Central American Minors Program, providing children in El Salvador, Guatemala, and Honduras who have a parent legally resident in the United States the opportunity to apply in their home country for admission to the United States as refugees.[23] In addition, one does not see Americans decrying the presence of international adoptees per se (societal racism does not differentiate between adoptees and others, and the hostility behind charges that international adoption constitutes neocolonial exploitation, discussed in Chapter 3, is directed at adoptive parents rather than children).

Attitudes toward children accompanied by parents also seem more favorable than attitudes toward adults, at least adults who come without children. Based on my family's experience housing a refugee family and having a daughter who teaches in a public school with a large immigrant population, there tends to be an outpouring of community support for the children and extraordinary efforts

[20] *See, e.g.*, Hannan Adely, "Biden's Border Action Could Affect Kids; Asylum Ban Might Lead to Splitting More Families," Indianapolis Star, June 11, 2024 (citing states that have passed legislation providing benefits specifically for unaccompanied minors); Cristian Farias, "A Change for 'Dreamers,'" Int'l N.Y. Times, June 7, 2019 (noting most U.S. voters are supportive of young noncitizens who were brought to the country many years ago by their parents).

[21] Fast-tracking can have the downside of preventing effective legal representation; cases move so fast lawyers have little time to prepare a defense. *See* Lorelei Laird, "Minding the Kids," ABA Journal, Dec. 2014, at 51–57. The United States has changed policies on fast-tracking minors several times.

[22] *See* Zachary Warmbrodt, "Biden DHS Chief Says 'Border Is Closed' But U.S. Won't Expel Children," Politico, Mar. 21, 2021.

[23] The Trump administration closed the program, but President Biden reopened it within two months of taking office. *See* USCIS, "Central American Minors (CAM) Program," https://www.uscis.gov/CAM (last visited Oct. 7, 2024).

to give them as near as possible a normal childhood experience. There is joy in seeing their progress in forming friendships, learning the local language, and losing the fear and sadness that accompany a hasty escape from a life-threatening situation. Much of this goodwill carries over to the parents; having children dispels suspicion and creates a vehicle for developing friendships and being offered help. Childless adult émigrés generally receive a colder reception.

Breaking down the supposed opposition to immigration in receiving nations just in this minimal way, pointing out variation in attitudes toward different potential immigrants (along with variation regarding immigration generally), suggests it is problematic to transpose to a huge collective entity such as a nation or "a people" an idea (freedom of association) that has developed at the interpersonal level in domestic jurisprudence. What might make more sense is to think about individuals' right to freedom regarding one-to-one relationships in the immigration context. The right typically encompasses not only preservation of existing relationships (so it can underwrite family-based visas) but also formation of new ones (so can underwrite, e.g., fiancée visas). Consider, then, all the citizens of the major receiving nations of the world who would gladly welcome into their homes one or more of the minors who travels to their country's border. Imagine a child welfare agency identifying such citizens, perhaps by polling persons already certified as foster parents. And suppose that agency also went to the border and created a registry of the minors at the border who would like to join such a household, at least temporarily. And it then matched minors and caregivers, facilitated video conversations so they could get to know each other, and informed immigration authorities of the reciprocal wish to live together. This would constitute a much more plausible right-of-association situation, and in it the right supports immigration rather than opposing it. In the United States, something like this happens now after minors arrive and apply for asylum; those referred to the Office of Refugee Resettlement are matched with sponsors for a home placement while their legal cases are pending, and many of the minors no doubt subsequently form or deepen personal ties that they and the sponsors wish to continue indefinitely. One might suppose they have a right of association that should be respected by allowing them to remain.

8.4.2.2 Preference for those who pose less threat to posited values

A second reason for giving unaccompanied children priority in immigration is that they inherently give rise to less concern about societal change. The basic thrust of arguments against open borders is that unconstrained immigration would eventually undermine national identity, cultural cohesion and practices, and political systems and values.[24] As noted in Chapter 2, many of the same

[24] For a survey of the arguments, *see* SAGER, *supra* note 7, chs. 5, 6.

concerns could arise from mass emigration, yet no theorists argue they justify blocking the exit door. But let us assume for sake of analysis that they might justify blocking the entrance door.

One common response to these asserted justifications for more closed borders is that they rest on an exaggerated prediction of the transformation greater immigration would cause.[25] This is especially so if we dispense with binary thinking and contemplate substantially liberalized but not completely jettisoned immigration rules, and especially if we recognize that societal change is almost always a very gradual process. Wellman might counter that existing members of a society are entitled to decide effectively (presumably by majority vote; he should not assume unanimity on such matters) that they do not want to risk dramatic and sudden transformation or to accept even gradual change.[26] David Miller, in that vein, places much weight on the fact that citizens have an interest in controlling "the way that their nation develops, including the values that are contained in the public culture."[27]

Another, more compelling response, though, is that they rest on an exaggerated normative valuation of such an interest in ensuring sameness over time and avoiding upset. Even if such values register on the positive side of zero, they would be trivial in comparison to the fundamental needs and even survival of people who happen to have been born in an inhospitable place. If I contemplate the possibility that in a century the U.S. population will be mostly not of European origin, English might no longer be the official or dominant language, and many aspects of American culture will be dramatically different (e.g., our British colonial past might no longer be of interest), I feel a little disconcerted. So what? Wellman suggests other people care more than I do, stipulating opaquely that "citizens will often care deeply . . ."[28] But again, so what? Refugees from the Northern Triangle and Venezuela are escaping severe oppression, destitution, and threats to their lives. In what other context of life-determining importance do we allow some people's feelings of disconcertedness or "often car[ing] deeply" to dictate how others are treated? In the abortion context, for example, no one suggests the practice should be stopped because it upsets right-to-lifers, even though their feelings seem far more intense than are mine about the future of America. The same is true, incidentally, of internal domestic migration; places changes as a result, and this disappoints long-time or former residents, but no one thinks that sufficient reason to prohibit or even control the migration.

[25] *E.g.*, *id.*, 17, 66–68.

[26] *Cf.* Christopher Heath Wellman, "Freedom of Movement and the Rights to Enter and Exit," *in* SARAH FINE & LEA YPI, MIGRATION IN POLITICAL THEORY: THE ETHICS OF MOVEMENT AND MEMBERSHIP 80–101, 83 (2019).

[27] David Miller, "Immigration: The Case for Limits," *in* ANDREW I. COHEN & CHRISTOPHER HEATH WELLMAN EDS., CONTEMPORARY DEBATES IN APPLIED ETHICS 200 (2005).

[28] Wellman, *supra* note 26, at 83.

All aspects of life are subject to change because of people coming and going—workplace, clubs, favorite recreational places. Yet somehow only when change results from arrival of the neediest humans on the planet from outside one's borders does one believe one's rights infringed.

Further, the normative assessment ought also to consider whether the receiving state has played a role in creating the dangers inhering in the native environment of immigrants, while exploiting their nation of origin, in ways that helped sustain the receiving state's cultural life. That increases the burden of justification for excluding. Moreover, the value of desire-satisfaction or culturally related interests on the receiving state side are not so singular; in any nation there are likely many citizens who "often care deeply" about helping persons in dire need and/or increasing the cultural diversity of their nation. And probably a supermajority who "often care" not at all either way.

Miller suggests, though, there is more to anxiety about cultural transformation than mere wistfulness. It could threaten social cohesion and peaceful civic life, and that provides stronger justification. He portrays "convergence . . . in language use, in political values, and in norms of socially acceptable behavior" as valuable because "it allows people to interact with less friction, it helps to generate trust, which in turn supports active democracy."[29] He also notes that a nation's economic planning typically rests in part on population predictions and that a government might identify a particular population size as optimal. One might suppose having such a target justifies imposing limits on procreation before turning away already existing people whose survival is at stake, given the relative importance of the two interests at stake, but Miller supposes a nation choosing to do both.

Other theorists have challenged Miller's view and similar views of others on various grounds. The response to immigration anxiety as a general matter that I will add is to say the features of current national life that immigration restrictions are said to preserve, if they truly exist and truly would be threatened by substantially liberalized immigration rules, would be less threatened by some immigrants than by others. One characteristic some have mentioned as a possible legitimate basis upon which a receiving nation might choose to discriminate for this reason is native language, another similarity of culture.[30] I will not opine on those.

Another potential characteristic, which theorists have not considered, is age, or life stage. Children simply are likely to have less impact on the things

[29] David Miller, "Is There a Human Right to Immigrate?," *in* FINE & YPI, *supra* note 26, at 11–31, 28. *See also* Sarah Song, "Why Does the State Have the Right to Control Immigration?," *in* JACK KNIGHT, NOMOS LVII: IMMIGRATION, EMIGRATION, AND MIGRATION 39 (2017) (invoking the importance of "a common view of the rights of individuals" and of "trust and solidarity").

[30] *E.g.*, *id.*, 200–01.

people worry about. Some worry about change in political culture. Children do not vote. Some worry about loss of current common culture. Children carry their native culture with them to a lesser degree than adults do, and they more readily assimilate and internalize a receiving nation's cultural outlook and practices. Some worry about societal coherence if we no longer have a common language. Children acquire a new language with remarkable facility and quickly prefer the language of their peers at school and in the neighborhood to that of their parents. Some worry about integration of immigrants into the economy, if huge numbers arrive with little education and only menial skills. Children can receive an education after arrival and be trained in skills needed in the receiving nation's economy. The time gap between their arrival and their entry into the workforce gives government time to factor their numbers into economic and social planning. In many such respects, infants are "the perfect immigrants," but all are true to some degree of older children as well.

If this response is correct, that children pose lesser threat, and perhaps no threat, to values upon which closed border policy is defended, and if children need to migrate because of miserable circumstances to which a receiving nation has contributed, by its participation in the international legal order and perhaps also by unilateral action, and has failed to mitigate, then it seems there is no justification for denying any child entry. If so, the logical alternative to the current border situation, with children crossing by dangerous means because destination nations do not authorize their entry, would be to revise human rights instruments to give all children a right to enter every nation. This is consistent with the conclusion of Chapter 5 that children should not be treated as belonging to their native country; for children, no country is "their own," unless and until they choose one in adulthood. International relocation for children would then be like interstate relocation within the United States or transnational relocation within the European Union. And potential receiving nations that bear an unfulfilled moral duty of redress to the peoples of sending countries should also be actively facilitating migration of children who need to get out of an untenable situation. That would include pressuring governments of sending nations to allow exit of children, by releasing unparented children currently in institutions who can be welcomed into families in receiving nations, facilitating adoption of street children as well, and not obstructing the exit of older children.

Such a rule of "open borders for children," however, would likely generate a great increase in border crossings by unaccompanied minors. That raises further concerns based on numerosity rather than difference. Open borders for children would erase whatever deterrent the hazards of illegal entry now add to those presented by the dangers inherent in the journey to the border. Parents need only get their children to an official point of entry and have them walk across, possibly into the arms of a relative or friend of the parents. Border officials would have to admit them. This would likely cost families far less than current payments to chaperones ("coyotes" in the Latin American context) who facilitate an illegal entry, and eliminate one source of danger (e.g., swimming across the Rio Grande and then crossing a vigilante-patrolled desert), thus changing families' calculus for deciding whether migration makes sense for the children, leading to affirmative choices in less pressing circumstances and/or enabling some to send their children to the border in a safer fashion (e.g., with a ticket to sit inside the train instead of riding on top of it, or by plane). In some poor nations, families might not have any money for travel, so a perilous journey (e.g., crossing the Mediterranean in an overcrowded raft) might still be unavoidable and would remain as a substantial deterrent, but refusal of entry no longer would be, and receiving nations might even choose to fulfill their duty in part by themselves providing safe transportation for minors. One can imagine at least a short-term surge of child migration.

From a child-centered perspective, a legitimate concern is that this might mean many more family separations, so the children would lose something in terms of nurturing and comfort. But we should assume parents and other family members are in a better position than we are to determine whether it is the best choice for a child and that no parents who love their children would send them off alone to the United States or Italy or Singapore unless they perceived a very large welfare gain for the children all things considered. Among the things they likely consider is that there is a great deal of anxiety interfering with family life in the hometown.

From a self-centered perspective, current members of the receiving nation would worry about system capacity. Would the stream of children entering be so great as to overwhelm the ability of the nation to absorb them, or more concretely the capacity of schools, health care facilities, family-hosting agencies, and so forth? The answer would vary by nation and depend on both available resources and political will to commit additional resources. Nations that have experienced a drop-off in birthrate recently might have excess capacity, and those worried about having a robust working population in the future to support the elderly population should welcome the arrival of a substantial number of young persons whom they can readily train and acculturate, committing whatever resources they must. Many developed nations are experiencing a steady decline in birth rates, and it might be quite sensible for them to aim to maximize child immigration, with children cared for by relatives, unrelated host families, or adult citizens willing to adopt. There would likely be far less political opposition to these immigrants, compared to a surge of adult immigrants. Indeed, receiving nations might view themselves as in competition for child immigrants with other nations also facing depopulation. Where they are highly valued, though, children should not even need a *right* of entry; a nation acting rationally (which does not always happen) would grant them permission regardless.

In addition to entry permission, there is the question of deporting persons who have entered illegally. In the legal regime I propose, that could no longer be the case with children. There would no longer be such a thing as an alien child. But in the current real world it is very common. Even so, children are in a better normative position. The strong sentiment among many people in receiving nations that illegality should not be condoned or rewarded, that instead it should be punished, with criminal prosecution and/or deportation of "illegals," is clearly misplaced with respect to young children. They typically are brought into a country by adults, passive participants in the entry. The sentiment also has less purchase as to older children who enter of their own accord, because (1) many are sent off by adult family members and told where to go and what to do, so their actions are likely not entirely self-driven; (2) they are less able than adults to protect themselves in the threatening environment of their home state; and (3) they are less able than adults to navigate the official immigration process.

Conversely, some believe the case for being allowed to stay increases with time spent in the country, and one might suppose that favors older persons. A great number of people across the globe gain entry to a nation before receiving permission, and the immigration policy question arises later. If soon after entry, the practical situation is little different for anyone from that just before entry, and the reasons given for ascribing to children an unqualified right to enter in an ideal world give them a stronger claim to stay in the real world.

If instead government review of someone's case occurs after they have spent considerable time in a new nation, the situation is different; the longer the time, the stronger the claim to stay, or so some theorists maintain. And, as Michael Blake notes, less reason for a nation to expel them.[31] There is still an age component to popular intuitions about that situation, however, and that is reflected in some different legal treatment. Resentment about the immorality of illegal entry by adults lingers, and so receiving states might still expel those who arrived as adults even several years after the fact. In contrast, there is more sympathy for persons who arrived as young children and now have grown up as, in effect if not in law, members of the receiving nation's society—in part because they are blameless, and in part because their self-conception, life plans, and development toward mature political membership are likely bound up with their current nation and locality of residence, and understandably so, in a way less true of those who arrived in adulthood.[32] Attitudes toward those who

[31] Michael Blake, *Equality without Documents: Political Justice and the Right to Amnesty*, 40 Canadian J. Phil. 99 (2010).

[32] Carens makes this case elegantly. *See* Joseph H. Carens, The Ethics of Immigration 24–31, 50 (2013).

arrive as tweens or teens are likely to lie somewhere between these poles. In the United States, the Department of Homeland Security adopted a rule (DACA) in 2012 allowing persons who arrived illegally while under age sixteen to defer deportation proceedings, whenever they are initiated, for a two-year renewable period.[33]

From a moral theoretical standpoint, all such persons have some claim, arising from the value of respecting a life plan and the social and economic ties it entails. Though rule utilitarians might conclude the best border policy for long-term aggregate well-being is one that tolerates no illegal entries, they might also conclude the best rule for situations when a nation fails to adopt and enforce such a policy, and instead tolerates a great number of unlawful entries, is one disabling the nation from expelling any such persons after a certain amount of time has passed. A Kantian might deem illegal entry by autonomous adults immoral, violative of the Categorical Imperative (though proper analysis would likely reveal much complexity), but also regard expulsion after many years of residence too great a threat to a person's autonomy. The latter concern would likely be dominant for a Kantian thinking about persons who entered a country as children. Anna Stilz, for example, writes:

> Occupancy of territory is connected to autonomy because it plays an important role in almost all of our plans. We build our lives on the assumption that our goals, relationships, and pursuits will not be unexpectedly destroyed through forced displacement. If I structure my life goals and choices against the background of continuing legal residence in a particular territory, and if I am there through no fault of my own, then respect for my autonomy tells in favor of allowing me to remain there, since it would be impossible to move me without damage to nearly all my life plans.[34]

As explained in Chapter 5, it is, in fact, quite difficult to draw a moral distinction between a person brought into a country illegally as an infant from a person born in the country's territory. But I have made a case here for treating older children as also blameless, even entitled to enter, at least vis-à-vis any nation with a moral obligation to address their plight. And for viewing them as a blessing rather than a burden.

[33] Challenges to the rule under the Administrative Procedure Act suspended the rule for some time, but ultimately were rejected by the Supreme Court. *See* United States v. Texas, 599 U.S. 670 (2023).

[34] Anna Stilz, *Nations, States, and Territory*, 121 ETHICS 572, 583–84 (2011). *See also* CARENS, *supra* note 32, at 150.

8.5 Conclusion

Individual nations owe a moral duty to rescue when best positioned to do so and/or when they owe a duty of redress for past wrongful actions that played a causal role in current human misery. When they fail to fulfill this duty by improving local conditions in other countries, they can do so by facilitating relocation of those who are suffering, including immigration into the duty-bearing nation's territory. In that regard, many of the wealthiest nations, including the United States, have a moral duty to leave the door wide open for children and to pressure home states to let the children go through that door to a better life.

9
Permissible Intervention

9.1 Introduction

Our final inquiry is into the permissibility of supererogatory humanitarian intervention even against the will of a nation's governing authority, by an international organization (IO), another nation, or private actors. We can take for granted that truly humanitarian aid *requested* by a state is permissible, but what if the state where terrible circumstances exist objects, is unresponsive to offers of assistance, or has no operative government capable of consenting?

This returns focus to the normative position of a child's home state, raising questions now about state power to block external actors from access to people and, conversely, state obligation to allow humanitarian aid from outsiders. In many instances, states have blocked efforts to save people in crisis on their territories, including children. In recent years: Sudan expelled humanitarian organizations from Darfur. Ethiopia's military blocked aid to Tigray. Bangladesh denied UNICEF access to Rohingya people in refugee camps. Burma obstructed international relief after Cyclone Nargis. Sri Lanka denied UN aid agencies and humanitarian workers access to displaced persons during its civil war. Venezuela intercepted an American aid convoy and seized AIDS medicines. And so on.

Sometimes the obstruction comes from nongovernmental actors, such as paramilitary groups like al-Shabaab in Somalia and various militias in Sudan, and the government is unwilling or unable to stop them. Is all this excusable as the prerogative of the sovereign state? Or have these states breached a duty to their people, of active efforts to facilitate external aid? If so, may outside agents use force to get around local resistance? Do the answers to any of these questions differ when considering children in need versus adults?

In the course of answering these questions, this chapter will consider perhaps the most dramatic manner of rescuing children from unlivable conditions—mass evacuation. Domestic child protection agencies in the United States have on occasion removed children en masse from reclusive communities thought to be systematically abusing minors. Perhaps there should be a comparable response to "national child maltreatment." In thinking about this, one should bear in mind the point Chapters 6 and 7 pressed, that the international community is already deeply implicated in the predicament of children suffering because of their home state's iniquity or ineptitude, having empowered that state to claim

International Migration of Children for a Better Life. James G. Dwyer, Oxford University Press. © Oxford University Press 2025.
DOI: 10.1093/9780197752333.003.0009

those children as members and exert plenary power over them. As in the domestic child protection realm, it is not a question of *whether* the state will insert itself into children's lives, but rather of *how*—by stepping in to protect children or by continuing to empower and embolden those lording over them.

Whether or not an official international child protection agency with such power exists, perhaps individual nations are sometimes justified in taking matters in other parts of the world into their own hands, just as private individuals and organizations in the United States did regarding parental maltreatment before state and local governments created child protection agencies? And if nations, too, fail to act, should not private individuals and organizations be able to take matters into *their* own hands, attempting to save children however possible from a dire fate, as American missionaries did in Haiti after the 2010 earthquake? Do children have a right against interference with any entity's efforts to preserve their basic welfare and even lives?

The traditional response simply cites sovereignty as a conversation stopper. That will no longer do. A child-centered perspective, in particular, requires being more open-minded about these possibilities, once we free ourselves from the notions that children belong to a nation (Chapter 5) and that national leaders are entitled to deference for their own sake (Chapter 6). It might lead us to think about *regulating* such outsider actions to ensure they do good overall instead of prohibiting them. Section 9.2 addresses nonmilitary means of assistance, some more coercive than others, and Section 9.3 addresses humanitarian use of force. Then Section 9.4 considers arguments against the permissibility of uninvited intervention.

9.2 Intervention Without Use of Force

If we think of force as militarized action against a state, we can easily conceive of numerous ways that do not involve force to try to help a population in need, on a sliding scale of coerciveness.

9.2.1 Offers of assistance

Some responses to crisis are certainly permissible. Any outsider may offer aid of various kinds to the governing regime, or directly to the people in need with the hope the government will not obstruct. Governments that are simply incapable of addressing the crisis might respond positively. Thomas Pogge opines that "[m]ost of those living in life-threatening poverty could easily be protected through the funding of locally providable vaccination programs, basic schooling, school lunches, safe water and sewage systems, housing, power plants and networks, banks and micro lending programs, and road, rail, and other communication links."[1]

Many IOs, nations, and private entities are devoted to this. What reaches people in crisis is patently insufficient, however. This is in part because funding for such efforts is inadequate to meet all need. In some instances, though, needed resources are available but targeted recipient states refuse, and it is somewhat unclear under international law to what extent they have a duty to accept outside assistance. Some treaties commit parties to cooperating with IOs for the sake of persons in grave need, but principally by sharing information, perhaps also permitting monitors to enter.[2] As for allowing outsiders to enter one's territory to change local circumstances, the conventional view is that a state has a right of refusal as a matter of sovereignty.[3] However, even four decades ago, before the emergence of the Responsibility to Protect (R2P), the ICJ appeared to narrow the proscription so that it ruled out only use of force on another state's territory. It construed the UN Charter's prohibition of "threat or use of force" on another, unwilling state's territory as inapplicable to efforts by one nation simply to transport basic goods (food, medical supplies) to persons—including members of rebel groups—in another nation even without permission. In *Nicaragua v. U.S.*, the Court opined that, although mining ports and supplying arms to rebel groups violated the Charter, "strictly humanitarian aid to persons or forces in another country . . . cannot be regarded as unlawful intervention, or in any other way contrary to international law."[4]

Since the *Nicaragua* decision there has been substantial movement toward an international law norm of expecting nations to permit assistance to civilians in dire need. The R2P that emerged and gained widespread endorsement in the 1990s entails not only the permissibility but an obligation on the part of the international community to act when a nation's rulers—for whatever reason—fail to address mass disasters. It would be incongruous to posit that external entities have a duty to act in the face of target-nation default yet may not act absent invitation. R2P embodies the contemporary view that state sovereignty

[1] Thomas Pogge, "Moralizing Humanitarian Intervention," *in* Terry Nardin & Melissa S. Williams, NOMOS XLVII: Humanitarian Intervention 158–87, 167–68 (2005).

[2] *See, e.g.*, Protocol relating to the Status of Refugees (1966), art. 2 ("The States Parties to the present Protocol undertake to co-operate with the Office of the United Nations High Commissioner for Refugees . . . in the exercise of its functions, and shall in particular facilitate its duty of supervising the application of the provisions of the present Protocol. . . . State Parties . . . undertake to provide [OHCR] information and statistical data requested . . .").

[3] *See* Report of the International Law Commission on the Work of its Sixty-First Sessions, U.N. GAOR, 64th Sess., Supp. No. 10, U.N. Doc. A/64/10 (2009), at 178.

[4] Nicaragua v. U.S., 1986 I.C.J. 14, at 242. *See also* Hum. Rts. Watch, "Sudan: Expelling Aid Agencies Harms Victims," Mar. 5, 2009, https://www.hrw.org/news/2009/03/05/sudan-expelling-aid-agencies-harms-victims.

is subordinate to certain rights of a society's members that operate against both the home state—including negative rights against obstruction of their access to means of survival—and the international legal order (positive rights to protection and assistance). And that sovereignty, far from being absolute and immune to forfeiture, is constrained and conditioned on minimal respect for and service to the welfare of the people. In fact, when a ruling regime operates systematically against the rights and welfare of a substantial portion of the population, including by refusing aid vitally needed by many people, the idea of invitation or consent becomes problematic. A great number of individuals, perhaps even a majority of the population, are not merely consenting but begging outside entities for aid. International law's traditional fixation on whoever holds the reins of governmental power as the only source of effective consent is difficult to maintain. The pertinent question today, then, is not whether outsiders may ever proceed coercively but rather when and how. For over a decade, the UN General Assembly has been deliberating about an international convention on the topic of "Protection of persons in the event of disasters," informed by draft articles on this topic that the International Law Commission (ILC) promulgated in 2016, which clearly state an obligation to seek and accept aid.

Further, even if no outsiders were legally permitted to coerce a nation into allowing aid, that would not mean the state has no international law duty to accept it; it would simply preclude a particular manner of enforcing the duty. R2P commits states to prevent certain atrocities within their territories (the first pillar), and when it fails to do so they owe a duty to their peoples to allow external actors to intervene (the second pillar). And given that one justification sometimes posited for the current limitations on R2P to intentional atrocities—that is, that in other circumstances the potential for making matters worse outweighs the benefit—is not especially plausible (coercion to enable food and medical care to reach famine-struck or earthquake-devastated regions, for example, seems unlikely to make matters worse for the people on the brink of death from starvation, even if it conceivably might do so in particular circumstances), expansion of its scope beyond the listed atrocities seems inevitable (at least if not first misused in many instances).[5] The ILC 2016 draft articles in fact extend the R2P duties to situations of disaster, which they define as "a calamitous event or series of events resulting in widespread loss of life, great human suffering and distress, mass displacement, or large-scale material or environmental damage, thereby seriously disrupting the functioning of society."[6]

[5] Humanitarian intervention in Libya in 2011 ultimately came to look like "regime change" and therefore triggered much criticism. Additionally, sometimes it just does not go well, as in Somalia in 1993 (pre-R2P, but authorized by the Security Council). But there have also been interventions widely viewed as successful.

[6] International Law Commission, Resolution 71/141, art. 3. *See also id.*, art. 11 ("To the extent that a disaster manifestly exceeds its national response capacity, the affected State has the duty to

Even before the 2005 World Summit Outcome Document (WSOD), foundational treaties suggested a state duty to accept assistance, and in a far broader range of circumstances. The UN Charter proclaims a duty of all nations to "take joint and separate action in cooperation" with the UN to promote realization of all human rights. The ICESCR echoes this commitment in Article 2, imposing on state parties a duty "to take steps, individually and through international assistance and co-operation" to address human needs "by all appropriate means." The ICESCR implementing Committee has interpreted this to mean that any state party "claiming that it is unable to carry out its obligation for reasons beyond its control . . . has the burden of proving . . . that it has unsuccessfully sought to obtain international support."[7] When aid is offered and brought to the nation's doorstep, it would make no sense for it to say, "We are not allowing entry because we are not ready for full realization of our people's rights."

The ICCPR obligates states more vaguely to adopt whatever "measures as may be necessary to give effect to the rights recognized," and welcoming external assistance is a measure sometimes necessary to effectuate even some negative rights, insofar as they operate against not only persons' own government but also against nongovernmental forces within a territory—for example, the Article 6 right to life. Moreover, the government's deliberately blocking assistance that persons need to avoid great suffering or death should be viewed as itself a violation of a negative duty, even of peremptory norms against torture or genocide, if the government's aim is to inflict suffering or to exterminate a people, in which case even criminal prosecution is possible.[8] Many view state refusal of help as equivalent to not seeking help, as inaction, but in fact it is an affirmative act of obstruction causing harm and preventing realization of human rights. An outside entity offers medical care, food, or other essentials to individuals who desperately need and want it, but the ruling regime intrudes into that mutually desired transaction, stopping the IO's workers at the border, attacking them, or confiscating their supplies. The regime thereby violates a negative right of those

seek assistance from, as appropriate, other States, the United Nations, and other potential assisting actors.").

[7] Comm. on Economic, Social, and Cultural Rights (CESCR), General Comment No. 12: The Right to Adequate Food, U.N. Doc. E/C.12/1999/5 (1999), at 17. *See also* CESCR, General Comment No. 3: The Nature of State Parties Obligations, U.N. Doc. E/1991/23 (1990), at 13.

[8] *Cf.* Convention Against Torture and Other Cruel, Inhuman or Degrading Treatment or Punishment, 1465 U.N.T.S. 85, 23 I.L.M. 1027 (1984) (defining torture as "any act by which severe pain or suffering, whether physical or mental, is intentionally inflicted on a person for such purposes as . . . punishing him for an act he or a third person has committed or is suspected of having committed, or intimidating or coercing him or a third person, or for any reason based on discrimination of any kind. . . ."); Rebecca Barber, *Facilitating Humanitarian Assistance in International Humanitarian and Human Rights Law*, 91 Int'l Rev. of the Red Cross, 371, 385 (2009) (contending that failure to accept humanitarian assistance constitutes "violence to life" within the meaning of Common Article 3 of the Geneva Conventions).

suffering individuals just as much as it would by confiscating goods they ordered from a foreign company that are being delivered by cross-border transit, or by taking those goods away from those who already have it in their grasp. Further, the obstruction need not be so concrete and dramatic as interdiction at the border; simply issuing a refusal, with implicit threat of physical repulsion, amounts to the same.

More specialized human rights and humanitarian instruments more explicitly articulate a duty to accept help, including: the 2003 Brugges Resolution on disaster relief, stating that nations "are under the obligation not arbitrarily and unjustifiably to reject" proffered assistance; the 2016 ILC "Draft articles on the protection of persons in the event of disasters," announcing, in Articles 11 and 13, duties to seek assistance from other states or IOs when a state is unable to address a disaster on its own and to not refuse offers of assistance arbitrarily; and the Guiding Principles on Internal Displacement, admonishing that permission to provide care "shall not be arbitrarily withheld." The CRC, in Article 4, hints at such a duty as well: "With regard to economic, social and cultural rights, States Parties shall undertake such measures to the maximum extent of their available resources and, where needed, within the framework of international co-operation."

The moral consensus in the international community is thus clear,[9] and any insistence that a state must be a party to some instrument to be under a duty is a legal rather than moral argument. Moreover, it is a dubious legal argument dependent on an increasingly disfavored view of sovereignty (and perhaps also on a failure to recognize the customary international law status of some human rights). The proper moral view of the state is that it is a fiduciary. A condition of serving in such a role is accepting both negative obligations not to inflict harm and positive obligations to secure needed goods and services. A state unable to provide for residents itself must seek and accept outside help, just as a parent who is himself incapable of providing medical care to a sick or injured child must solicit professional help and certainly not block access to the child if an ambulance arrives to provide emergency services. Such abuse of the guardian position is grounds not only for overriding the guardian's choices and actions but also for terminating the position.

Another way to support a presumption of permissibility morally as to IOs is to point to the primary basis for ascribing a duty to them discussed in Chapter 7—namely, the benefit IL gives states by creating a norm of external sovereignty vis-à-vis other states and affording them a share of global power in the form of seats

[9] *Cf.* David Fisher, Law and Legal Issues in International Disaster Response: A Desk Study (2007) (listing international law sources manifesting global consensus on the duty of affected states to accept assistance if needed).

in UN bodies. This deference and empowerment are properly conditioned upon satisfying conditions of effective legitimacy, on "living up to the moral demands of sovereignty."[10] Absent fulfillment of this expectation, what justification does the international legal order have for imputing sovereignty to a state?[11] Looked at another way, the international legal order is free to condition state recognition and participation in global governance on state acceptance of IO authority within its borders, including authority to pass judgment and to set aside sovereignty when its conditions go unfulfilled, just as a local government properly conditions parental powers on acceptance of expectations regarding treatment of children and of government authority to judge fulfillment of those expectations, under threat of withdrawing the powers.

A state's duty to accept offers of assistance cannot be unlimited, of course. The ILC's draft articles state that a nation should not withhold consent "arbitrarily." J. Benton Heath identifies potentially legitimate reasons a state might have for refusing outsider assistance: "The offer of assistance may be redundant; the state may already have the situation under control; or the aid might be culturally or logistically inappropriate. The actor making the offer might be disreputable, or motivated by military or economic goals."[12] Some of these, such as concerns about cultural fit and provider motivation, might suffice only for preferring one source of help over another, not for refusing all help when people are in crisis conditions. To Heath's list we might add that a particular problem might simply be not sufficiently extensive or systemic to warrant obligating a society to allow foreign agencies into its midst—for example, minor natural calamities or isolated incidents of public or private violence. As with intervention in a family, the costs of intrusion are more likely to exceed the benefits when problems are minor or isolated. But states often have patently illicit motivations for refusing external assistance, such as fear that their ill treatment of a persecuted minority will be exposed or a desire that such group continue to suffer (e.g., what is sometimes termed "famine crime," deliberate indifference to the starvation of a despised minority).

As between children and adults, there are reasons to ascribe to home states a stronger obligation to children to allow aid. There are the usual utilitarian grounds for a stronger claim on the part of children—that is, that early development is foundational to one's entire life, more potential years of life ahead, lesser

[10] EVAN FOX-DECENT, SOVEREIGNTY'S PROMISE: THE STATE AS FIDUCIARY 55 (2011).

[11] *Cf.* Pratap Bhanu Mehta, "From State Sovereignty to Human Security (via Institutions?)," *in* NARDIN & WILLIAMS, *supra* note 1, at 259–85, 264 ("It is international recognition that partly constitutes the state and confers upon it the characteristic rights and immunities of a state. And, therefore, the international community would be well within its rights to insist on certain rules for recognition, which could include things such as the observance of human rights.").

[12] J. Benton Heath, *Disasters, Relief, and Neglect: The Duty to Accept Humanitarian Assistance and the Work of the International Law Commission*, 43 N.Y.U. J. INT'L L. & POL. 419, 450 (2011).

capacity for self-help. In this context, there is also less plausibility with children to one justification a home state might give for blocking aid—namely, worry that the recipients will use it to support rebellion or otherwise undermine the regime. The state might also say that in practice it cannot block aid only to adults and let it go through to children, because the two groups are living together, but in theory at least we can say children's right to receive is greater, if this kind of objection has any moral purchase.

9.2.2 Carrots and sticks

In addition to offering material assistance, IOs or states surely may proffer a failing state inducements to improve its service to its people, such as promising favorable treatment in trade or representation in international bodies as a reward for changing policies or practices, without infringing its sovereignty. Conversely, other nations also are clearly free legally and morally to signal disapproval and to withhold benefits in an attempt to influence—for example, withdrawing favorable trade status or ending diplomatic relations. As an exercise of their own sovereignty, other nations may tax or prohibit imports from a country whose government is violating its basic obligations. Other nations are also legally free to regulate their own nationals, including by prohibiting them from doing business with that country. A group of nations might do this cooperatively to effectuate a multilateral embargo. None of those things constitutes intervention that infringes the country's sovereignty as conventionally understood, despite the internal effects.[13] Similarly, refusing to form or continue a relationship with another individual unless they change their behavior does not infringe their right of self-determination; neither individuals nor nations have a right that their choices be costless, that others not dissociate or disfavor in response. Some such measures could cause further harm to the population of the country, though, so might be practically unavailable to conscientious outsiders.

Somewhat murkier is the legal status of more intense financial measures, especially when undertaken without UN approval. One is seizing assets of a nation or its oligarchs.[14] Western nations have struggled with this issue in connection with the Russian war of aggression against Ukraine. Another is orchestrating a multilateral boycott, particularly if it entails pressuring third nations into joining.[15] Delving into the nuances would not aid the analysis here.

[13] *See Nicaragua*, *supra* note 4, at ¶ 245.

[14] For the complexities of the law governing this practice, *see* Evan J. Criddle, *Humanitarian Financial Intervention*, 24 Eur. J. Int'l L. 583 (2013).

[15] *See* Brad R. Roth, Sovereign Equality and Moral Disagreement: Premises of a Pluralist International Legal Order 78–79 (2009).

9.2.3 Facilitating exit

The preceding discussion considered only direct action on a nation's territories or direct interaction with the nation's government. Legal and policy scholarship on humanitarian intervention generally supposes entry into a dysfunctional state's territory is necessary to ameliorate the crisis there.[16] Get food and medical care to the people in the place they now inhabit, repel attacks on an oppressed people by government forces or by nonstate armed groups. It is also possible, though, to aid people in crisis outside their home state. Of course, international aid organizations direct much attention to people who have evacuated themselves or who have been forcibly pushed by government forces or armed groups—that is, internally displaced persons and refugees. But there is rarely consideration in the international legal community of drawing people out from horrible circumstances to a safe space—that is, mass evacuation, even as a first resort, even though that would appear far less interventionist—at least within a contemporary moral outlook, in which persons are not property of their nations—than sending in aid workers with military guard. State sovereignty pertains only to domestic affairs; it poses no obstacle to efforts by IOs or other states to provide assistance outside a state's borders, including by permitting and facilitating immigration. As discussed in Chapter 2, state sovereignty clearly does not entail power to block exit, absent extraordinary police-power justification unlikely to apply to people in dire need.

Exit to safety is not always readily available, of course. The safety would typically be in another state's territory, and often a neighboring state is unable or unwilling to take in a great number of people, and it might not be under a duty to do so (see Chapter 8). Sometimes neighbors largely close their points of entry. In 2024, there was attention to the possibility of large-scale migration from to Gaza to Egypt, for people already displaced and repeatedly told to move to avoid bombing. But Egypt would not allow a mass migration, so multitudes were trapped in life-threatening circumstances. Not considered in that circumstance, or in many others when huge numbers are in danger, was the possibility of limiting the exodus to a nonrandom subset of those seeking escape. In particular, there was no call for getting children out first and foremost. Nondiscrimination

[16] *Cf.* INDEPENDENT INTERNATIONAL COMMISSION ON KOSOVO, THE KOSOVO REPORT 194 (2000) ("The method of intervention must be reasonably calculated to end the humanitarian catastrophe as rapidly as possible, and must specific ally take measures to protect all civilians, to avoid collateral damage to civilian society . . . There must be a serious attempt to find a peaceful solution to the conflict. This solution must ensure that the pattern of abuse is terminated in a reliable and sustainable fashion, or that a process of restoring adequate governance is undertaken."); HUGO SLIM, HUMANITARIAN ETHICS: A GUIDE TO THE MORALITY OF AID IN WAR AND DISASTER 17 (2015) ("Some form of territorial presence and continuing tolerance by authorities has always been essential to humanitarian action.").

is a core principle of humanitarian organizations, but the primary concern is for "invidious discrimination" based on morally arbitrary yet prejudice-inducing characteristics such as religion, race, ethnicity, political party, and social class.[17] Discrimination based on age, especially when in special solicitude for children, is not typically cited as suspect. In fact, language in human rights treaties, including the Geneva Conventions, encourages prioritizing child well-being.[18] The situation is equivalent to a sinking ship with too few lifeboats. First come, first served is one approach, but another is to favor children and their primary caretaker. When available spots fall drastically short of demand, it might become children-only.

Prioritizing children for exit would be justified in part for reasons previously posited for a stronger duty to children. This includes the utilitarian ones noted earlier, but also children's clearer lack of responsibility for any manmade crises; their having less to lose by relocation, in terms of cultural embeddedness, employment, other economic relationships, and property ownership; and their lesser ability to appeal to the outside world for intervention onto the home state's territory. It is thus consistent with the humanitarian principle of calibrating action to need or threatened loss. And it is presumably what parents would instinctively choose—that is, that their children have priority over themselves. This is one way to view the *Kindertransport* in the early days of World War II; allied nations would not accept all Jews wishing to leave, and Great Britain offered homes just for children. So parents put their children on trains and watched them leave, recognizing that survival was more important for the children even than remaining with their families, and experiencing some solace when contemplating their own fate in knowing their children were safe. Other nations were at fault for not accepting larger numbers, and the same might be said of the Gaza situation in 2024, but the international community sometimes must respond to the world as it is and adopt a triage approach to rescue.

So, what if in late 2023 and in 2024 one or more European nations had sent ships to the coast of Gaza (Israel claimed authority over the territorial waters, but would be expected to consent to this operation, or failing that, then to just outside the territorial waters) and communicated to Gazans that children, but only children, would be welcomed on board and taken to safety—perhaps to foster homes, but perhaps simply to remain at sea on passenger ships—until safe conditions prevailed in Gaza. Older children would serve as caretakers for the younger ones, so the only adults needed on board would be those necessary to operate the ship and maintain order, maximizing the space available for

[17] *Id.*, 56.

[18] Geneva Convention Relative to the Protection of Civilian Person in Time of War, 1949, 75 U.N.T.S. 287, art. 23 (requiring free passage of "essential foodstuffs, clothing and tonics intended for children under 15, expected mothers and maternity cases").

children. Parents or other adults responsible for children who wished to safeguard them in this way, by consenting to their departure, could attach to each child identifying and contact information for the child and family members. IOs might take written and biometric information from participating families to facilitate reunion. Then the children would be transported to the ships. Instead of depending on aid agencies being able to enter despite ongoing bombing and other obstacles, children would go to a place where there are no obstacles at all to caring for them.

Gaza is not a state, but even if it were, would this evacuation have infringed its sovereignty if it objected? It is difficult to see how. Or what other normative objection there could be, even if children were evacuated regardless of parental consent. The trauma of separation for children and adults, even if temporary, should not be overlooked, but lifeboat situations are non-ideal, and death is worse. Such separations happen routinely in far less drastic circumstances, when a child's home is unsafe because a parent is unable to protect the child. Evacuation from a nation is a child-protective intervention writ large, and a fiduciary governing authority should deem the removal, even without parents, to be in the children's best interests all things considered. (This is even clearer for the many whose parents were killed.) Because nearly all children stayed, many thousands were killed by Israeli bombing. A few cruise ships, paid for by IOs and/or nations in fulfillment of duties established in prior chapters, could have accommodated those children, housed them safely at sea for as long as necessary, then returned them to their families. Why did that not happen?

We can imagine other child-evacuation scenarios in the many crisis areas of the world today—such as Darfur, Libya, Nigeria, and Haiti. Where there is a government ostensibly in control, the message to them is that they are not fulfilling their duties to children (or to parents, communities, etc.), and like a neglectful or abusive parent, they must facilitate the protective removal or at least step aside. And in addition to IOs and states, private entities might also participate in the evacuations (e.g., commercial cruise lines). The obstacles to doing so seem attitudinal rather than normative. Nations or private parties with capacity to transport and accommodate large numbers of children lack interest in far-away crises and/or wrongly suppose it would violate some right of the home state, or of parents and other adults in that state, to remove children and only children. Unable or unwilling to save all, they save none.

9.3 Use of Force

If a state fails in its duties to its people, despite any nonmilitary forms of coercion attempted, is military action permissible? There is no clear prohibition on

UN use of force to aid persons in dire circumstances when their government is causing and/or failing to ameliorate their plight. As previously noted, though Article 2(7) of the UN Charter is often said to prohibit intervention in domestic affairs, it actually says only that the Charter itself does not authorize UN intervention in domestic affairs, and non-authorization is not equivalent to prohibition. A justificatory basis for intervention might lie elsewhere—for example, in the UDHR, the Geneva Conventions, human rights treaties, or peremptory norms.

In cases of mass atrocity, there is clearer authorization for uninvited military intervention, with Security Council approval. If state behavior can plausibly be said to threaten international peace and security, then the Charter authorizes such intervention. And the WSOD, which is not law but evidence of an emerging norm, endorses use of force in a nation with Security Council approval to prevent or stop such atrocities even absent a threat to outsiders, as a last resort when both the nation's own efforts and the UN's provision of assistance have failed to do so. The Security Council has authorized armed intervention many times to address humanitarian crises, with general acceptance of the permissibility.[19] These efforts have had mixed success, but one should expect a steep learning curve with this still-nascent practice of global policing.

Less accepted is military action by states, independently of IOs, against another for humanitarian purposes. The UN Charter's Article 2 prohibition on "threat or use of force" by states is limited to actions that operate "against the territorial integrity or political independence of any state." A narrow reading of that would allow for military protection of aid efforts on a state's territory, so long as this does not amount to seizing control of territory or threatening regime change. The international community appears to have adopted a broader reading of the prohibition under which any uninvited use of force on another nation's territory violates its territorial integrity, yet at the same time the community tolerates such violations when it appears all for the good. For example, many silently applauded NATO bombing in Kosovo to avert genocide and U.S. bombing in Syria to deter further atrocities by its government, even though these were widely regarded as unlawful. So instead of infusing some meaning into the limitation such that use of force for strictly humanitarian purposes is officially permissible, the community chooses to render that language meaningless and superfluous and to engage in informal and unexplained unofficial grant of permission.

[19] *See* Thomas W. Simon, Genocide, Torture, and Terrorism: Ranking International Crimes and Justifying Humanitarian Intervention 162 (2016) ("Forceful, military humanitarian intervention to halt the crime of genocide has overwhelming international support."); Roth, *supra* note 15, at 141 (citing Somalia, Haiti, Rwanda, and Albania as instances of pre-authorization and Liberia and Sierra Leone as instances of "post hoc endorsements," as well as acquiescence in some cases, such as exaggerated U.S. interpretation of authorization for humanitarian action in Iraq).

Morally, individuals in humanitarian disasters have a right *erga omnes* to receive help, as shown in previous chapters, and the prioritizing of the duty in international instruments—that is, home state first, then outsiders—might receive support from practical considerations more so than normative ones. With adults, one might contend that the rest of the community with which the individual shares a social contract bears primary responsibility. But it is questionable whether the social contract is any more real with respect to a nation than with respect to the world. And, in any event, children more clearly cannot be viewed as voluntary participants in a social contract at any level, so it is difficult to discern any plausible moral reason why their first recourse must be to the government of their state of current residence.

9.4 Against Permissibility

Critics pose both practical and normative objections to liberalizing of intervention norms.

9.4.1 Practical objections

Common pragmatic concerns are reflected in preconditions for intervention that the International Commission on Intervention and State Sovereignty (precursor to the WSOD) would have imposed, framed as "precautionary principles" or "criteria of legitimacy."[20] In particular, nations' motivations are typically more self-serving than altruistic, and the consequences are radically unpredictable so might amount to a worsening of the situation.

9.4.1.1 Exploitation disguised as altruism

History supports a supposition that humanitarian intervention is rarely truly altruistic. Indeed, one might think the fiduciary conception of the state rules out altruism; the duty of loyalty would preclude using a nation's resources to help people in other nations unless that somehow furthers the interests of one's own people. National leaders should and typically do view their primary loyalty as owed to their own people and the interests of their own nation, which inevitably influences their approach to offering foreign aid or intervening without consent,

[20] The full list is "right authority, just cause, right intention, last resort, proportional means and reasonable prospects." ICISS Report at Sec. 4.16. *See also* Global Centre for the Responsibility to Protect, "What Is R2P?," https://www.globalr2p.org/publications/the-responsibility-to-protect-a-background-briefing/ (last visited Oct. 1, 2024) (listing seriousness of harm threatened, proper purpose, last resort, proportional means, and balance of consequences).

whether unilaterally or in conjunction with other states or by supporting IOs. And this creates the danger of exploitation disguised as altruism. Paternalistic humanitarian aims were often cited in support of colonial occupation and oppression. Pratap Bhanu Mehta observes that "those powers likely to intervene are enormously complicit in producing some of the conditions that occasion humanitarian intervention in the first place, [so] claims to carry out duties based on solidarity with the victims cannot be taken at face value."[21] Brad Roth more bluntly cautions against "risk of objectively harmful interference by self-interested, arrogant, or sophomoric intermeddlers."[22]

In part because of this concern, some contend intervention is appropriate only when carried out by institutions created and designed to do this faithfully, and that this is at the IO level. Roth writes: "International legal processes militate against powerful states' penchant for invoking universal principles to rationalize unilateral (and typically self-serving) impositions upon weak states."[23] Locating responsibility at the higher, international level does not, however, entirely dispel the concern. Thomas Pogge writes: "International relations are characterized by great inequalities of power, great moral corruption of those in power (in the poor countries no less than in the rich), high stakes, and the absence of effective mechanisms of binding adjudication." The more powerful nations tend to dominate IOs, and they can serve themselves in aid operations, purchasing the local regime's cooperation as necessary.

We should therefore not be entirely sanguine about authorizing IOs or individual states to charge forward with any interventions they characterize as rescue missions. "In such a context especially," Pogge contends, "the optimal public rules are not ones that instruct agents to do what they believe is optimal or ones under which a military operation becomes legitimate merely because it is approved by some group of governments." Pogge prescribes as a potential solution "on the international level an effective judicial organ for the authoritative interpretation and adjudication of international law—in real time if needed." This is analogous to court approval of a local police or child protection agency intervention in a home. But Pogge also notes that powerful nations might be able to distort judicial decision-making as well, by threatening to withdraw from the agreement giving such an adjudicative body authority.[24]

Some scholars push back against this concern, contending that predictions of pretextual invocation of R2P are overblown.[25] Brian Barry has observed that

[21] Mehta, *supra* note 11, at 259–85, 264.
[22] Roth, *supra* note 15, at 5.
[23] *Id.*, 57.
[24] Pogge, *supra* note 1, at 174–76.
[25] *See, e.g.*, Ryan Goodman, *Humanitarian Intervention and Pretexts for War*, 100 Am. J. Int'l L. 107 (2006).

some nations (e.g., Scandinavian countries) are less self-serving in their approach to foreign aid than others (e.g., the United States), and that the former have actually been proportionately more generous.[26] Mark Stein opines that it might be to the good if nations use a humanitarian pretext when determined to intervene for self-serving reasons, because that gives them a face-saving reason to make some effort to actually make the population of the target country better off.[27] Another counterargument is that nations with capacity to help are unlikely to do so unless they have some self-serving reason, so insisting on purely altruistic intentions would result in inaction almost every time.

9.4.1.2 Unintended consequences

Experience has shown humanitarian intervention faces many obstacles, some of which are difficult to anticipate. Worth noting, though, is that intervention might sometimes be more successful the earlier it occurs; some past failures have resulted partly from waiting too long out of deference to sovereignty.

Internally, the reactions of government and nongovernment entities matter a great deal, and those can be unpredictable. Coercion of a bad actor might provoke them to act even worse or badly in another way. Or aid might diminish outcry against those causing the crisis and give them normative space to become more aggressive. The aforementioned proposal to get children out first, for example, might cause a state to become even more brutal toward the adults who remain, because then violent acts appear less condemnable. ("We let the children go, so be thankful for that.")

Moreover, the individuals carrying out humanitarian operations might not be angels, and oversight of them might be inadequate. There have been instances of individuals behaving quite badly while working for international relief agencies or peacekeeping forces. There could also be adverse effects on international relations broadly, if an intervention is controversial. Roth argues that uninvited interventions stoke global divisions and harden authoritarian resolve in the target state and in other states. If instead powerful Western nations reassured weaker countries whose people are now suffering that they will continue to enjoy autonomy, and if intervenors take a constructive and cooperative approach rather than heavy-handed coercion and moral condemnation, a target country might be more likely to respond positively. It and other potential target nations will perceive less threat externally, so less need to oppress domestically to

[26] Brian Barry, "Do Countries Have Moral Obligations? The Case of World Poverty," TANNER LECTURES ON HUMAN VALUES (1980) ("as a sheer matter of practical politics, moral appeals may be more effective than appeals to self-interest").

[27] Mark S. Stein, *Unauthorized Humanitarian Intervention*, 21 SOC. PHIL. & POL. 14, 34–35 (2004). However, it might also delay or blunt legitimate criticism of the intervention, if given any credence, and the intervenor's idea of humanitarianism might not match anyone else's (e.g., Russia's "saving" of Ukrainian children by kidnapping them).

remain in control.[28] One sees the same sorts of arguments against intervention in households to protect victims of interpartner violence or parental abuse; a soft touch, some think, might be more effective in the long run.

Some of the practical concerns arguably are less in connection with saving children, if that aim could be isolated. Outsiders are less likely to see gains for themselves in helping non-autonomous persons, so their motives might typically be more purely altruistic. There might be less local knowledge about the interests at stake that outsiders lack if child well-being is more generic than adult preferences and perceptions. Relatedly, there is less reason for concern about cultural appropriateness with individuals who are less embedded in a culture.

9.4.2 Normative objections

I will leave to other disciplines assessment of the foregoing empirical speculations. The pertinent question here is not about feasibility but whether overriding a state's will is permissible in theory, or instead an illicit violation of sovereignty. If we stipulate that coercive intervention would save many people from horrible suffering and death without significant practical downside, then the preceding discussion supports a presumption in favor of the moral appropriateness of doing it. A presumption in favor of intervention might also be justified when the cost-benefit situation is a closer call, if it would clearly serve children well. Whether the context is IO intervention in a national crisis or a child protection agency's intervention in an abusive home, children's suffering presumptively results from a failing on the part of the powers in control of their lives, whereas adults' suffering often results from their own bad choices. And because of the reasons given above for prioritizing children's rescue, children's rights more often outweigh potential adverse consequences—in particular, when the consequences are for adults.

In addition to practical concerns, though, there is normative resistance to coercive intervention. Few scholars today would invoke the trope of state sovereignty that prevailed at the founding of the UN—that is, an inherent or natural right of states or their rulers. Most accept something like UN Secretary-General Deng's idea of "sovereignty as responsibility" and the idea that a state can forfeit its sovereignty by failing in its fiduciary duties, either globally or as to a segment of the population that it fails to serve. Instead they appeal to values that state autonomy serves for a nation's people—in particular, collective self-determination and cultural preservation.[29] Related to self-determination, some urge acceptance

[28] *See* Roth, *supra* note 15, at 15–17.

[29] *Cf.* Anna Stilz, *Nations, States, and Territory*, 121 Ethics 572, 574 (2011) (noting "the currently dominant account of territorial jurisdiction, the nationalist theory . . . holds that the state derives its

of reasonable pluralism in the way nations govern themselves; powerful liberal Western democracies should not assume their approach is the only acceptable one and attempt to impose it on others, and "discrete political communities" have a collective moral right to decide their own fate and even "to be wrong about justice."[30]

A weakness common to these arguments is oversimplification. First, they tend to treat sovereignty as an all-or-nothing thing, rather than asking *how much* insulation from outsider interference is necessary to serve any important values. Second, they treat cultural preservation as an all-or-nothing thing, as if any intervention into a territory will destroy a culture completely, as if a people post-intervention will have forgotten its language, religion, and traditions. Third, many write as if culture in the abstract is an unqualified good, as if all cultures are worthy of preservation, and in their entireties. But history provides examples of cultures, or aspects of cultures, best left on the dung heap. If one believes it presumptuous to judge any existing cultures as unworthy, in whole or in part, then one should equally mourn the death of all past cultures, including that of, for example, Nazi Germany, apartheid South Africa, and colonial blends of imperial culture and local servility culture.

Further, anti-interventionists often appear to assume a nation's people constitute unified wholes politically and culturally, and that every such whole is capable of self-determination of a sort worthy of respect. Hugo Slim contends helping people respectfully, with "cooperation rather than control," "enables a person or a community to remain the subject of their lives, not objects in the lives and purposes of others." To provide humanitarian assistance and protection properly, an agency must "increase people's autonomy and agency as human beings."[31] This seems to presuppose a people and its governing regime aligned in their aims, just struggling a bit to realize those shared aims; outsiders should support and empower "the nation" in the abstract and not impose their own aims on it. Even if we think only of autonomous adults, however, any site of mass human rights violations must be one where much of the people and its governing regime are at odds and where self-determination so conceived is absent and not on the

territorial rights from the prior collective right of a nation to that territory" and advancing her own view that "a state has rights to a territory if and only if . . . its system of law 'rules in the name of the people,' by protecting basic rights and providing for political participation"), 578 ("the legitimate state theory agrees with the nationalist view that 'states can claim territorial rights . . . as representative of the people that they govern' . . . [and] enacts legislation in the public interest"), 579 (stating that in the legitimate-state view "the state is like a guardian who represents a group of individuals"), 587–89 (elaborating on the idea of the state as guardian constrained to act in the interests of and with respect for the rights of the ward—that is, the people); Akhil Amar, *Of Sovereignty and Federalism*, 96 YALE L.J. 1425 (1987).

30 *See, e.g.*, ROTH, *supra* note 15, at 5.
31 SLIM, *supra* note 16, at 2.

horizon. Many nations are riven with factionalism and governed by regimes that use internal sovereignty to deny some groups within the society ability to participate in national self-determination or to preserve their particular cultures. Allen Buchanan notes that "an extremely authoritarian political order is, under realistic circumstances, likely to be incompatible with the group (the people) being self-determining."[32]

For such nations, coercive intervention might serve the posited values better than nonintervention. Indeed, it is difficult to think of instances when humanitarian intervention was contemplated in which the people who were suffering participated equally in political decision making and were suffering because of their own cultural perspective and practices. Except perhaps in cases of natural disaster, massive suffering likely reflects authoritarian rule that is oppressive and indifferent to the interests and values of much or all of "the people."[33] Supporting and empowering people, bolstering capacity for self-determination, if that is even possible, then seems to require overcoming the governing regime's resistance. Intervention by IOs or other states would not infringe the sovereignty of the people but rather serve it. Buchanan reaches that conclusion, contending that outsiders are permitted to intervene forcibly to establish conditions for a people to exercise self-determination, independently of aiming to prevent human rights abuses.[34]

In a vein like that of Slim, Jeffrey Whitman opposed military intervention to guard human rights, on the grounds that each people must develop on its own an endogenous collective preference for justice and human rights. Leaving them to their own devices has the instrumental value of facilitating national character development, and this must trump immediate protection of human rights. Coercive imposition of order and protection of individuals displaces that process and so makes it less likely that a society will develop that desire and expectation; it will remain vulnerable to tyrants.[35]

This argument, like Slim's, rests crucially on certain questionable empirical assumptions. One is that forcibly protecting oppressed people inherently

[32] Allen Buchanan, *Self-Determination, Revolution, and Intervention*, 126 ETHICS 447, 454 (2016). *See also* Anna Stilz, "The Value of Self-Determination," *in* DAVID SOBEL ET AL. EDS., OXFORD STUDIES IN POLITICAL PHILOSOPHY VOL. 2, at 98–127, 110 (2016) ("Where citizens' joint activity is carried on solely out of fear, it carries no moral weight. It is possible to freely cooperate with others only where one is not unduly vulnerable with respect to one's essential needs and interests.... There must also be some institutional channel by which governing officials are required to take notice of public opinion, and respond to it.").

[33] *See* SLIM, *supra* note 16, at 15 ("Frequent cries of agency outrage about the lack of 'humanitarian access' are usually the result of governments or armed groups dictating what they want humanitarian agencies to do and not to do. Sometimes their choices are wise and humane. Often they are cynical and inhumane.").

[34] Buchanan, *supra* note 32, at 471.

[35] Jeffrey P. Whitman, *An End to Sovereignty?*, 27 J. SOC. PHIL. 146–57 (1996).

undermines a society's development toward genuine respect for human rights. Whitman offers by way of support just his own characterizations of a few historical instances of humanitarian intervention not going especially well. One might suppose, however, that giving a long-oppressed people a taste of freedom and security they have never enjoyed will motivate them to make it a permanent condition, and correspondingly, that a long-oppressed people who never experience any other condition will perpetually accept it as inevitable and even proper. People who live in liberal democracies are typically shocked by how widespread is support for autocratic rulers in illiberal nations, despite the relatively miserable conditions in which most people in them live. Conversely, the history of peoples overthrowing an oppressive, authoritarian regime without outside assistance seems not especially rosy; that usually fails, and when it succeeds, does not usually lead to stability, security, and freedom.

Again, though, I will leave the empirical questions to others. I will instead challenge an unacknowledged and undefended normative premise that seems implicit in Whitman's argument—namely, that the value of a nation developing a certain character in the long run simply trumps whatever benefit intervention might give to individuals now, like saving a great number of people from death, as the NATO bombing in Kosovo is widely thought to have done. A utilitarian might endorse Whitman's position when reasonably anticipated long-term welfare benefits outweigh short-term welfare costs, but one cannot simply stipulate that that will be true always or even usually. And from a deontological perspective, the argument is troubling insofar as it treats current members of society instrumentally in service of a speculated future society in which they might not participate.

Further, Whitman offered no reason for limiting the proposition to nations, so ultimately it seems to counsel in favor of eliminating criminal law and protective intervention at every level of governance. Perhaps unconstrained collective self-determination should prevail over external forces of law and order at the level of family, community, city, and province, as well as nation, for an ethos of genuine respect for human rights and other virtues of collective life to develop. Violence done to vulnerable people in the meantime is simply less morally important than making space for that development. This line of reasoning requires much more support than Whitman presented.

Contrariwise, some argue that a more robust global regulatory authority would enhance the sovereignty of individual states and facilitate self-determination of peoples, by discouraging arbitrary and self-serving unilateral interventions by powerful nations. UN Secretary-General Moon contended that implementation of R2P would strengthen rather than undermine sovereignty, because its aim is to help states fulfill their fiduciary duties to their people, to get them to succeed rather than descend into failure too deep for recovery.[36] John Tomasi draws a parallel to America's growing pains in the eighteenth century. He notes Americans' eventual realization, after experience with the Articles of Confederation, which created a government roughly resembling the current international legal order, that "the strongest guarantor of individual liberty would be a strong central state, so long as the foundation of that state was drawn up wisely."[37] He goes on to show that the factual situation across the colonies and later states in early America was much like that across nations today. Miriam Ronzoni writes: "[G]lobal background justice may require states to give up their *formal* sovereignty to some extent in order to protect their *effective* one."[38] Her focus is the world economic order, but the same might be said of the human rights sphere, that stronger international institutions would enable more disciplined and even-handed responses to human rights crises.

The most obvious route to permissibility, the preceding discussion suggests, is state forfeiture of sovereignty by failing in its fiduciary duty. Many political theorists have endorsed this idea in the abstract.[39] Few speak openly in favor "regime change" per se, but clearly sometimes that is a necessary remedy. Review of other fiduciary relationships (guardians, trustees, attorneys) reveals that replacement is uniformly a potential consequence of serious breach of duty, whether by intentional abuse of authority, willful neglect, or simply incapacity. International peacekeeping forces and aid agencies act as partial and temporary substitutes for a failed regime, supplying the security and social provisions that the regime did not, pending a more permanent substitute arising from within.

Who should issue a judgment of state failure is an important practical question. Roth worries that powerful nations will, if allowed to do so unilaterally, make such judgments in a self-serving rather than objective fashion. But the response to that worry cannot be categorical prohibition of intervention. Roth himself sees in the current international regime a more or less workable set of procedures that provides some check on unprincipled unilateralism while also enabling action (albeit only in a limited range of cases, those on the R2P list) when there is broad consensus on such a judgment—namely, Security Council authorization with the backup "Uniting for Peace" procedure in the General

[36] Ban Ki-moon, Implementing the Responsibility to Protect, Report of the Secretary-General, U.N. Doc., A/63/677, Jan. 12, 2009.

[37] John Tomasi, *Sovereignty, Commerce, and Cosmopolitanism: Lessons From Early America for the Future of the World*, 20 Soc. Phil. & Policy 223–46, 226 (2003). This view that strong central authority can best safeguard individual liberty was urged long before, by Hobbes and others.

[38] *See* Miriam Ronzoni, *The Global Order: A Case of Background Injustice? A Practice-Dependent Account*, 37 Phil. & Pub. Aff. 229, 249 (2009).

[39] *See, e.g.*, Allen Buchanan, *Toward a Theory of Secession*, 101 Ethics 322, 331 (1991) ("the state's exercise of power is legitimate only if it refrains from exploiting one group for the benefit of others. An implicit premise of the argument is that failure to satisfy this fundamental condition in effect voids the state's claim to the territory").

Assembly.[40] As explained earlier, the current limited scope of R2P to mass atrocities does not reflect a principled normative judgment so much as political realities and incrementalist thinking. It could be just as workable in other circumstances.

Perhaps, though, the defenses of sovereignty noted earlier, in addition to failing to consider the possibility of forfeiture, begin in the wrong place. They assume a world of sovereign states, with all humans subject to at least one of them, each state independent of the others and cloaked with a moral right to autonomy, and put the burden of persuasion on those who would breach or compromise sovereignty. Roth writes that "a State's freedom of action and exclusivity of territorial control remain the default positions that a claim of international legal obligation must, by some authoritative justification, overcome."[41] But a nation is not like an individual person, a single unit of moral worth, with that sort of basic claim to presumptive inviolability; it is a collection of persons and contains the potential for some to violate the moral rights of others. An assumption of dominion by some people (rulers) over other people within a supposedly "discrete political community" arguably is not the right starting point.

The starting point should be, as these theorists themselves generally suppose, service to all based on equal consideration. As to autonomous persons, there is no empirical basis for ascribing to them choice of a regime of insularity at the national level, any more so than at subnational levels. Roth contends that humans "have a morally important interest ... in being part of a territorial political community that maintains the last word on its internal public order,"[42] but even supposing that to be true, he provides no argument for making the nation the level at which the last word must reside to satisfy such interest. A people's collective self-determining choice might just as well be for a strong transnational governing authority, to ensure national governments act as fiduciaries should. It might even be for legal authorization at the highest level (international law) of unilateral action by another entity at the same level (i.e., another state) if necessary to protect the people's interests, including survival, basic rights, and internal justice for all. Analogously, a local community might collectively choose to authorize private individuals to intervene in a household (and so not be charged with trespass) where abuse or tragedy (e.g., fire) is occurring if its government cannot act in time. All the theorizing about self-determination takes place, curiously, in the complete absence of evidence of what people around the world

[40] ROTH, *supra* note 15, at 162.
[41] *Id.*, 8.
[42] *Id.*, 104. *See also id.*, 114 ("the collective capacity to make fundamental decisions—and to have outside actors acknowledge their status as governing law—has a moral value independent of the justice or injustice of the decisions themselves.").

actually want in terms of authority over them and of permissions for other entities of whatever sort to help them.

9.4.3 Permissibility to rescue children in particular

With respect to children, a conditional caretaker conception of the state has even more purchase, and state sovereignty has less. It is more problematic to take for granted the international regime established in 1945 as a starting point for theorizing when addressing the plight of persons who can in no way be viewed as having sanctioned its creation or continuation. Even if one ascribes to current adults post hoc assent to that regime and posits that they are free to live by illiberal norms under autocratic rule if they so choose, that line of reasoning makes no sense as to children. Nor can one say children were represented by proxy in 1945 or are today; there is no evidentiary basis for that. One should perhaps say a state altogether lacks authority—never earned, rather than lost—regarding children on its territory, if it has disregarded their well-being and rights. Analogously, a property owner who finds babies in the back yard and decides to raise them for servitude, rather than to ensure them whatever care they need for healthy development, can have no legitimate claim to the children nor objection to police entry to supplant the property owner's control of them.

The trope of sovereignty has less purchase with respect to children also because they are less capable than adults of protecting themselves against abuse of power, by use of personal physical or financial capacity or by communication with other potential sources of protection. In the domestic child protection sphere, potential maltreatment of children gives the state a reason for observation and, if necessary, intrusion that it otherwise would not have. Lack of autonomy counsels in favor of a diffusion of authority, we might say. Thus, on a proper view, parentage is a legal status the state confers subject to the condition of shared responsibility with the state. A public agency constitutes an external authority with capacity to counterbalance the custodians' unique ability to harm the child. A nation's authority over children should be regarded in the same way, as conditioned upon willingness to be subject to monitoring and intervention as necessary to guard the child against abuse of custodial power. Further, the permissible scope of intervention should be greater for children. For some of the same reasons that IOs and other nations owe a heightened positive duty to children in dire circumstances, as shown in prior chapters, so too does the children's home state. Failure to fulfill the duty is therefore more readily to be found.

In this light, the CRComm's review of country self-reporting every five years falls dramatically short of what the international legal order could be doing to improve child safety and well-being. It is ineffectual by design, and in practice it looks away from some failures on the part of states, because of undue deference to local authority. Sara Dillon relates that currently "[t]here is no established doctrine of international expert access to children living out of family care," that in fact no public international agency is charged with monitoring the treatment of these children, and that any researchers or investigators who attempt to locate and document living conditions for unparented children are met with arrogant effrontery and obstruction by state officials and employees of child-housing institutions, emboldened by the CRC's approval of child warehousing.[43] This inexcusable behavior creates high risk of abuse. It puts children in state custody in a worse position even than adult prisoners and detainees, who have a well-established right to contact with human rights monitors. Dillon documents the severe developmental harm of long-term institutional care and the pronounced vulnerability that hiding those children creates. She argues that the situation of these children is no more a matter of purely domestic concern than is that of prisoners of war being housed within an enemy state's territory. International law has long granted IOs power of access to, and denied states the privilege of remaining entirely unsupervised in handling of, prisoners of war.[44] Yet young institutionalized children are even more vulnerable—unable to speak out, unable to defend themselves against physical abuse, less likely to remember and report what is done to them, with no one outside attentive to their welfare. Many of the same concerns apply with unaccompanied minor immigrants, or children separated from their caregivers at the border, who are placed in detention facilities, so agencies with a mission to ensure their welfare should have access to those children also.

Daniel Esty has suggested that regulatory bodies with a focused mission can thrive even in the absence of a robust government-like structure at the global level and can operate in a more disciplined way than the more visible "branches" of the UN. Such an agency is at least somewhat less likely to trigger knee-jerk anti-internationalist objections than do proposals to swell the power of the General Assembly and the ICJ or to eliminate the veto power of permanent Security Council members.[45] So a robust international child protection agency with license and duty to intervene in a targeted way to protect and assist children specifically, like a domestic child protection agency, might be more effective (at least after initial experience helps to refine its approach) and less controversial than ad hoc unilateral or even Security Council–authorized measures.

[43] Sara Dillon, *Time for a Truth-Based Policy: Humanitarian Access to Children Living Without Family Care*, 27 FLA. J. INT'L L. 23, 53–59 (2015).

[44] *Id.*, 39–41.

[45] Daniel C. Esty, *Good Governance at the Supranational Scale: Globalizing Administrative Law*, 115 YALE L.J. 1490 (2006). When its Appellate Body was functional, the WTO might have been an example supporting Esty's hypothesis (though some complained of its tendency to exacerbate global inequality).

Further, the normative objections noted earlier are less applicable to children. They do not participate in the home state's internal process for realizing a people's self-determination. They do not act in consort with fellow citizens but rather are acted upon and treated like nonmembers. The noble notion of deference to a people's autonomy therefore can do no work against children's human rights.

Buchanan posits that "a group is self-determining only if either all members have the opportunity to exert some influence by participation in the processes of group agency or those who do not participate authentically identify with those processes or their outcomes or the principles they exemplify."[46] Other theorists of sovereignty also speak of self-determination as if all members must participate in or at least assent intelligently to the outcome of collective decision-making; the volition of each member of a society plays an essential role.[47] Children generally do not participate in political decision-making. Children are already, before intervention by external actors, more "the objects of others' intentions" and less the "drivers of their own fates" than are adults.

As for the alternative to direct participation, Buchanan explains: "The idea is that if an individual is not able to participate with some effect in the processes of collective decision making and action, she must be able, on reflection, to regard those processes or the outcomes they produce or the principles the processes are based on as something she can endorse or at least accept, if she is to be included in the group that is said to be self-determining."[48] This suggests a fairly robust intellectual capacity as a precondition for being part of the group around which a shield of sovereignty arises. Any children who do not have that capacity would be outside that group. That would seem to mean that, in fact, no nation can be regarded as self-determining, or else that non-autonomous persons should be regarded as not even part of any "people" that engages in self-determination and enjoys sovereignty. If so, arguments against intervention founded upon a people's self-determination simply do not apply to children. It therefore makes no sense to speak of refraining from aiding them out of respect for national self-determination.

A nation vis-à-vis young children is, rather, engaging in *other*-determination, like a colonizer, and so rightfully subject to oversight by a higher authority.

[46] Buchanan, *supra* note 32, at 455.

[47] *E.g.*, Stilz, *supra* note 32, at 98 ("We have a duty not to interfere with a foreign political order because that order reflects the will of the people subject to it."), 102 ("a people is born only when members engage in institutionalized political cooperation, and come to value that cooperation . . . To be self-determining, members . . . must appropriately see themselves as joint authors of those institutions, though participation in a cooperative enterprise they value. . . . [I]t is especially significant for individuals to be ruled by an authority that reflects, in some way, their own priorities . . . Because a self-determining state reflects its people's shared will, it has a special claim not to be interfered with or removed.").

[48] Buchanan, *supra* note 32, at 455.

Similarly, talk of "family autonomy" is inapt, insofar as it is meant to imply all members of a family share in, as equals, collective decision-making; either it does not exist, or its meaning is confined to adult family members, who vis-à-vis children engage in other-determining practices. In either case, it makes no sense to assert it as a basis for opposing child-protective intervention. In fact, extending the aforementioned conclusion about intervening to promote national self-determination, we might endorse not only efforts to create institutions conducive to democratic decision-making but also efforts that foster individuals' personal ability to participate in collective agency in the future if they lack it now. This could mean intervening on behalf of any children whose healthy cognitive development is now substantially threatened—for example, by malnutrition, disease, emotional deprivation, or psychological trauma.

One might think children and non-autonomous adults, though not participating, are *represented* in collective decision-making, by their guardians. There are several problems with this move. First, democracies generally do not give extra votes to guardians for any non-autonomous persons. Second, even if they did, guardians are not entirely reliable proxies in political decision-making, and in fact might routinely advocate against wards' interests—for example, with respect to decision-making on child protection policy, state regulation of religious schools, and corporal punishment. Were some external authority to judge in each instance whether representation of children in the political process is worthy of respect, because it does in that instance serve their interests, it might as well simply decide directly whether outcomes are good for children and, if not, impute to children a choice in favor of outsider intervention to protect them. Third, proxy voting, even when faithful to a ward's interests or perspective, does not necessarily fulfill the purposes that give direct participation its value, such as seeing oneself as a joint author of the laws that govern one's lives. Finally, many nations are not democratic, and even most adults cannot participate in national policy formation, so only "authentic identification" could underwrite self-determination in those nations, and as to that, it is even more difficult to treat anyone as representing children.

9.5 Conclusion

The international community is clearly permitted to intervene to a far greater degree than it now does in local circumstances to spare children from state violence, confinement, or incapacity to ensure their basic well-being in the face of disaster. State sovereignty is no more an obstacle to this than parental right or homeowner dominion should be. The institutional framework for child protection at the international level need not remain so weak. Substantively, R2P may be extended to more circumstances even for adults, and it can be broader still for children. While international response remains anemic, any individual nation has special license to act on behalf of children suffering national maltreatment in another, like a neighbor who hears children screaming next door in a community with no police. Rather than prohibit this, international law should create an incentive structure that rewards nations for undertaking child welfare interventions in good faith and punishes them for doing it in bad faith.

Conclusion

The gap is wide between the moral rights of children currently trapped in life-crushing circumstances and the international legal order's treatment of them. Children have a moral right to legal protections equivalent to those which adults demand for themselves, not the cramped rights of the CRC. Children, in fact, have stronger moral rights than adults in connection with getting out of horrible circumstances such as war, famine, abject poverty, and arbitrary confinement in institutions. Yet international law treats them as chattel by forcing nationality and its liabilities upon them, a badge of ownership insulating states from criticism for confining and abusing children. International law assigns to nations plenary power over all aspects of children's lives, subjecting even the most fundamental aspects of their private lives to police-power interest balancing, failing to appreciate that government at every level—international, national, and local—may properly act only as a fiduciary for the child when presuming to control core realms of his or her life, such as family life and place of residence.

Both the international community and individual nations bear duties to bridge this gap between law and morality and to redress harms already inflicted. A means of redress and rescue for children that has received insufficient attention is international migration. This is not a universal panacea, but it clearly is the best intervention for a great portion of the world's children now living in misery and pronounced danger. The places where they now live are not going to be transformed in time to spare them lifetime damage and loss. They need to get out.

Due regard must always be paid to children's existing psychological, emotional, and social relationships, particularly with parents if they are actually caring for a child. Ideally, children relocate with such parents. But when children are not being parented, when parents are unwilling or physically incapable of relocating, or when the outside world will not accept their parents, survival and minimally adequate conditions for healthy development must take priority. That is the hierarchy of human needs. Children need to get out of the hellish places, and they need to be let in to good places. Actors at national and international levels have a moral duty to make that happen, in part simply because they can, but even more compellingly because many of them have played a causal role in creating the terrible circumstances that threaten children's fundamental well-being.

The implications for specific legal contexts are straightforward. A nonpoliticized human rights organization needs to take over the role of assessing nations' respect for children's human rights, and it needs to treat long-term stays in orphanages as a human rights violation. There is no tenable justification for this widespread practice depriving children of good lives in more hospitable environments via international adoption.

Handling of international custody disputes between parents should consider any great disparity in life prospects between the parents' respective nations of residence, with no deference to a culture that entails denigrating the child (e.g., gender subordination, oppression of sexual minorities) or that simply cannot plausibly be called the child's own (e.g., because he or she is an infant).

There should be no barrier to entry of children into any nation. Further, IOs and nations have an affirmative obligation, in countries where they bear some responsibility for the spread of destitution, destruction, and dysfunction, to help minors migrate, so they can evade predation or escape abject suffering, with no per se prioritizing of domestic destinations.

When massive life-threatening crises arise, especially armed conflict, the first thought the outside world should have is how to get the children out of harm's way. There should be an international agency charged with only this, always prepared for a mass evacuation of children. All nations should contribute to funding this emergency response, but nations with greater responsibility for the conflicts or turmoil should pay disproportionately. The killing and maiming and orphaning of tens of thousands of children happen with such frequency, and often with high predictability, that it is condemnable for the rest of the world to sit by watching on their television screens, or not watching at all.

In all these contexts, self-doubt is healthy, caution is wise, but those should guide determined efforts to fulfill our collective duty to spare children from the worst of adults' failings. They do not excuse our failure to make the commitment or to think hard and creatively about how to fulfill it effectively, unhindered by misguided notions of national sovereignty or ownership of children.

Index

For the benefit of digital users, indexed terms that span two pages (e.g., 52–53) may, on occasion, appear on only one of those pages.